Essentials of
Planning, Selecting, and Tailoring
Interventions for Unique Learners

Essentials of Psychological Assessment Series

Series Editors, Alan S. Kaufman and Nadeen L. Kaufman

Essentials

of Planning, Selecting, and

Tailoring Interventions for

Unique Learners

Edited by

Jennifer T. Mascolo
Vincent C. Alfonso
Dawn P. Flanagan

WILEY

Library of Congress Cataloging-in-Publication Data:
Essentials of planning, selecting, and tailoring interventions for unique learners / edited by Jennifer T. Mascolo, Dawn P. Flanagan, and Vincent C. Alfonso.
  pages cm – (Essentials of psychological assessment)
  Includes index.
  ISBN: 978-1-118-36821-3 (pbk.); ISBN: 978-1-118-41735-5 (ebk); ISBN: 978-1-118-42065-2 (ebk)
  1. Linguistic minorities–Education. Children of minorities–Education.Multicultural education./
LC4065Children with social disabilities–Education. 2. Special education. 3. Remedial teaching. 4. Students with disabilities–Education. I. Mascolo, Jennifer T., editor of compilation. II. Alfonso, Vincent C., editor of compilation. III. Flanagan, Dawn P., editor of compilation.
  LC3969.E77 2014
                                                                     371.9–dc23

To my most precious blessings:

My children, Michael, Matthew, and Mia:

Your smiles light up my day,
Your kindness warms my heart,
Your voices are music to my ears,
Your love touches my soul,
You make my life complete

I love you with all of my heart ("to infinity and beyond")
—Mommy

My husband, Michael:
For your love, for your unwavering support and encouragement, and for always
believing in me

All my love forever
—Jennifer

To my colleagues, students, and friends at Fordham University, especially in the
Graduate School of Education where I spent 19 years preparing for my current position.
I hope to make you proud!

Thanks for everything!
—Vinny

In loving memory of my mother, for a life time of listening, guiding, supporting,
believing, encouraging, and loving

Forever in my heart
—Dawn

CONTENTS

SERIES PREFACE

I n the *Essentials of Psychological Assessment* series, we have attempted to provide the reader with books that will deliver key practical information in the most efficient and accessible style. The series features instruments in a variety of domains, such as cognition, personality, education, and neuropsychology. For the experienced clinician, books in the series offer a concise yet thorough way to master utilization of the continuously evolving supply of new and revised instruments, as well as a convenient method for keeping up to date on the tried-and-true measures. The novice will find here a prioritized assembly of all the information and techniques that must be at one's fingertips to begin the complicated process of individual psychological diagnosis.

Wherever feasible, visual shortcuts to highlight key points are utilized alongside systematic, step-by-step guidelines. Chapters are focused and succinct. Topics are targeted for an easy understanding of the essentials of administration, scoring, interpretation, and clinical application. Theory and research are continually woven into the fabric of each book, but always to enhance clinical inference, never to sidetrack or overwhelm. We have long been advocates of "intelligent" testing—the notion that a profile of test scores is meaningless unless it is brought to life by the clinical observations and astute detective work of knowledgeable examiners. Test profiles must be used to make a difference in the child's or adult's life, or why bother to test? We want this series to help our readers become the best intelligent testers they can be.

Essentials of Planning, Selecting, and Tailoring Interventions for Unique Learners is an exciting addition to the *Essentials* series. This innovative edited book contains dynamic chapters contributed by esteemed practitioners and researchers in the field of psychology, all of which assist practitioners in working with students who have learning difficulties. Each chapter provides concrete, step-by-step procedures for assessing and interpreting cognitive and academic performance and other relevant factors (e.g., teaching style, curricular materials) for the purpose of intervention planning—with a unique focus on demonstrating how to *individualize interventions* for students using actual case examples.

Part I of this book ("Intervention Planning") teaches practitioners how to gather and interpret data in a manner that will assist them in identifying and defining specific targets for intervention.

Part II ("Selecting and Tailoring Interventions") provides rich discussion and information relating to the specific academic, cognitive, and behavioral manifestations of students with learning difficulties in reading, math, writing, and oral language. Each chapter describes how the difficulties interfere with specific classroom tasks and explains how to select, modify, or otherwise *tailor* an intervention (or strategy, accommodation, etc.) based on that information.

Part III ("Interventions for Underserved and Mis-served Populations") teaches practitioners how to recognize, and intervene with, students from underserved and mis-served populations who are at risk for learning failure. These often-ignored populations include students with executive functioning difficulties or inefficient memory strategies as well as English-language learners and students from impoverished environments.

Overall, *Essentials of Planning, Selecting, and Tailoring Interventions for Unique Learners* is a comprehensive practical resource that explains how to conduct assessments for intervention and how to individualize interventions to meet the unique needs of struggling learners. This book will give practitioners the skills they need to be key members of any team or committee that is involved in intervention planning in the schools.

Alan S. Kaufman, PhD, and Nadeen L. Kaufman, EdD, Series Editors
Yale Child Study Center, Yale University School of Medicine

ACKNOWLEDGMENTS

We wish to thank Sherry Wasserman, editorial program coordinator at John Wiley & Sons Inc., for her support throughout this project. We are further grateful for advice and encouragement from Marquita Flemming throughout the production process as well as the early assistance and feedback from Suzanne Ingrao and additional, invaluable assistance from Rose Sullivan during the final stages of production. We also extend our heartfelt gratitude and appreciation to the contributing authors for their research and scholarship, professionalism, and diligent efforts in producing such meaningful chapters. Finally, we wish to thank Alan and Nadeen Kaufman for their continued support of the *Essentials of Psychological Assessment* series, which aims to bridge theory and practice in such a way that sound judgments can be made when working with children and their families.

Part I

INTERVENTION PLANNING: DIAGNOSTIC ASSESSMENT, RESPONSE TO INTERVENTION, AND CONSULTATION

One

A SYSTEMATIC METHOD OF ANALYZING ASSESSMENT RESULTS FOR TAILORING INTERVENTIONS (SMAARTI)

Jennifer T. Mascolo
Dawn P. Flanagan
Vincent C. Alfonso

The term *intervention* is one that is familiar to anyone working in a school system. Adjectives such as *research-based* and *evidence-based* when placed in front of this term elevate it to an indubitable status. This is primarily because these descriptors suggest that the intervention was subjected to a rigorous evaluation and was found to be effective, meaning that when implemented with fidelity, it leads to positive outcomes (e.g., Cooney, Huser, Small, & O'Connor, 2007; Flanagan & Alfonso, 2011).

Not surprisingly, then, evidence-based interventions are often the ones that are used first in either general or specialized instructional settings as compared to those interventions and techniques without such support. In general, it is incumbent upon practitioners to use evidence-based interventions with students who struggle academically. It is also prudent to use comprehensive interventions that can meet students' multiple manifest academic difficulties (e.g., remedial reading programs that contain the five essential components of reading; Feifer, 2011). However, it is clear from the literature that despite their overt relevancy, not all comprehensive, evidence-based interventions address the academic needs of every student effectively (e.g., Della Tofallo, 2010; Hale, Wycoff, & Fiorello, 2011).

In a tiered service delivery model, interventions are planned for and selected based on universal screening data. For example, students who are at risk for reading difficulties may receive *Wilson* if their reading difficulties are related primarily to decoding difficulties or *Read 180* if their reading difficulties are related primarily to comprehension difficulties (e.g., Feifer, 2011, and Chapter 5, this volume). When a student does not respond as expected to evidence-based interventions, a comprehensive evaluation is often recommended to gain a better understanding of the nature of and basis for the student's learning difficulties. It is through a comprehensive and focused evaluation that the intervention process moves from *planning and selecting interventions* to *tailoring interventions*. Planning and selecting interventions is typical of a *standard treatment protocol* Response to Intervention (RTI) service delivery model, whereas tailoring interventions is more consistent with a *problem-solving* RTI model.

PLANNING AND SELECTING INTERVENTIONS VERSUS TAILORING INTERVENTIONS

Planning and selecting interventions is conceptualized here as the process of identifying evidence-based interventions that are most often used in standard service delivery models to address manifest academic difficulties that are revealed via progress monitoring (e.g., a particular reading program is selected by a district as a Tier II intervention for students with reading fluency difficulties). On the other hand, a primary focus of *tailoring* interventions involves understanding the student's pattern of cognitive and academic strengths and weaknesses and how this pattern interacts with the instructional materials used by the student as well as classroom instructional factors, environmental factors, and other individual/ situational factors that may facilitate or inhibit learning. The goals, therefore, are (a) to use information about a variety of intrinsic and extrinsic factors to tailor specific interventions; and (b) to ensure that a student has appropriate access to the curriculum by minimizing or bypassing the adverse affects that cognitive and other weaknesses have on the student's learning. Tailoring interventions may include *M*odification (e.g., instructional, curricular), *A*ccommodation, *R*emediation, and *C*ompensation. The acronym, *MARC*, can be used to assist in remembering these methods of tailoring interventions, which are defined in Rapid Reference 1.1.

A METHOD FOR TAILORING INTERVENTIONS

This chapter provides a *S*ystematic *M*ethod of *A*nalyzing *A*ssessment *R*esults for *T*ailoring *I*nterventions (SMAARTI). This method, as initially conceptualized by Mascolo (2008), involves the organization, analysis, and synthesis of assessment data to aid in understanding the cognitive basis of students' learning difficulties. Based on multiple data sources, the steps of SMAARTI assist in identifying various

≡ Rapid Reference 1.1 Methods of Tailoring Interventions

Tailoring Method	Brief Description	Examples
Modification	Changes content of material to be taught or measured; typically involves changing or reducing learning or measurement expectations; may change the depth, breadth, and complexity of learning and measurement goals.	Reducing the amount of material that a student is required to learn Simplifying material to be learned Requiring only literal (as opposed to critical/inferential) questions from an end-of-chapter comprehension check Simplifying test instructions and content
Accommodation	Changes conditions under which learning occurs or is measured, but does not change or reduce learning or assessment expectations. Accommodations may include timing, flexible scheduling, presentation, setting, and response accommodations.	Extending time on exams Assigning a project in advance or allowing more time to complete a project Aligning math problems vertically, as opposed to horizontally Providing a separate room to work Having a student dictate responses to a scribe
Remediation	Techniques or programs used to ameliorate cognitive and academic deficits. Academic interventions typically focus on developing a skill, increasing automaticity of skills, or improving the application of skills. Cognitive interventions typically focus on improving cognitive processes such as working memory capacity and phonological processing. There are many techniques, published programs, and software designed for the purpose of remediation.	Evidence-based programs listed at What Works Clearing House: http://ies.ed.gov/ncee/wwc Reading programs appearing on the Florida Center for Reading Research website: www.fcrr.ord Techniques and materials from the Reading Rockets website: www.readingrockets.org CogMed (Pearson) Spotlight on Listening Comprehension (LinguiSystems, 2006)
Compensation	Procedures, techniques, and strategies that are intended to bypass or minimize the impact of a cognitive or academic deficit.	Teaching the use of mnemonic devices Organizational aids or techniques Teaching a student to outline or use graphic organizers

methods of tailoring intervention (i.e., MARC) that make instruction more accessible to the student, thereby improving learning. SMAARTI is used when a student fails to respond as expected to evidence-based interventions (typically those used at Tier II) and, therefore, undergoes a comprehensive evaluation that includes an assessment of cognitive functioning.

STEPS OF SMAARTI

SMAARTI consists of five steps (see Rapid Reference 1.2). While this method assumes that several forms of data have already been collected for a particular student and, therefore, will be viewed *post-hoc*, the steps of SMAARTI can also serve as a roadmap to the types of data that ought to be gathered in an initial evaluation to aid in tailoring interventions for students with unique learning needs.

DON'T FORGET
....

A comprehensive evaluation should include data from the following areas of functioning: (a) educational history and current academic performance; (b) familial factors and medical history; (c) cognitive performance (including Cattell-Horn-Carroll [CHC] ability domains and neuropsychological processes); (d) behavioral and social-emotional functioning; and (e) classroom/instructional/environmental observations. Other information that must be garnered during the course of an evaluation to ensure that interventions are practical include parent/home resources (e.g., time available to spend with student, parent interest/motivation, parents' level of language proficiency, computer in the home), student's schedule and routine, current and past interventions used, and current strategies used by the student. When necessary, a comprehensive evaluation may include assessment of cultural and linguistic factors as well as any other factors that will assist in differential diagnosis.

≡ *Rapid Reference 1.2 The Five Steps of SMAARTI*
....

1. Organize primary data using the CHC-based *Data Organization and Targets for Intervention* form (or DOTI form; see Table 1.1 and CD). *Primary data* include information from norm-referenced, standardized tests of cognitive and academic ability and neuropsychological processes and provide information about characteristics that reside mainly within the child (i.e., that are intrinsic). Examine all primary data to gain an understanding of the student's unique pattern of ability and processing strengths and weaknesses.

2. Determine whether academic weaknesses are empirically related to the cognitive weaknesses by reviewing the research on the relations among specific cognitive

abilities, neuropsychological processes, and academic skills (see Rapid Reference 1.4). An empirically established relationship between cognitive abilities or processes and academic skills allows practitioners to gain a better understanding of the potential reasons for the academic deficit. Knowledge of the underlying reasons for academic skill deficiency is necessary for both diagnosis and intervention.

3. Review manifestations of cognitive weaknesses, organize secondary data, identify initial targets for intervention, and identify types of academic skill deficits for remediation using the DOTI form. Determine whether identified cognitive weaknesses manifest in real-world performances in predictable ways. Refer to the CHC-based manifestations tables (see Rapid References 1.5 to 1.13) to gain an understanding of the various ways in which a weakness in a specific cognitive domain likely manifests generally, as well as more specifically in reading, math, and writing. Based on this information, integrate secondary data into the DOTI form. *Secondary data* include information from rating scales, classroom observations, and interviews with parents, teachers, and the student him- or herself. Like primary data, secondary data typically provide information about characteristics that are intrinsic to the child. When practitioners are able to observe the manifestations of specific cognitive deficits in classroom performance, for example, cognitive test results are ecologically valid. Be sure to note whether manifestations of cognitive deficits are pervasive (i.e., occur across settings) or setting-specific (e.g., occur only in school during mathematics instruction). When recording data in the DOTI form, hypothesize whether the cognitive areas of weakness should be targeted for modification, accommodation, remediation, compensation, or some combination thereof, and whether the areas of academic weakness are related to basic skill acquisition, fluency, or higher level skill (i.e., application).

4. Consider *tertiary data*, which are comprised of information about classroom instruction, instructional materials, environment, and strategies—that is, information about factors that affect learning and that are largely external to the student (i.e., extrinsic). Use the information in Rapid References 1.14 to 1.20 to tailor interventions for the purpose of minimizing the effects of cognitive weaknesses on learning and achievement.

5. Integrate data from all previous steps, design and implement an intervention, and monitor its effectiveness.

Step 1: Organize Primary Data Using the CHC-Based *Data Organization and Targets for Intervention* (DOTI) Form

In this step, practitioners may use the CHC-based DOTI form in Table 1.1 (also downloadable from CD) to organize primary data. Primary data include standardized test scores from cognitive and academic measures, special-purpose batteries (e.g., memory, language), district-wide testing programs (e.g., English Language Arts scores), and progress monitoring. As may be seen in Table 1.1, the DOTI form is organized into 10 CHC domains. It also contains an "other" category, which is reserved for use with measures not

Table 1.1 CHC-Based Data Organization and Targets for Intervention (DOTI) Form

CHC Cognitive/Academic Ability or Processing Domain	Normative Weakness and Information About Intervention	Within Normal Limits	Normative Strength and Information About Intervention
Fluid Reasoning (Gf) **Target for Intervention?**			
Crystallized Intelligence (Gc) **Target for Intervention?**			
Long-Term Storage and Retrieval (Glr) **Target for Intervention?**			
Short-Term Memory (Gsm) **Target for Intervention?**			
Visual Processing (Gv) **Target for Intervention?**			
Auditory Processing (Ga) **Target for Intervention?**			
Processing Speed (Gs) **Target for Intervention?**			
Reading (Grw-R) **Type of Skill Targeted**			
Writing (Grw-W) **Type of Skill Targeted**			
Mathematics (Gq) **Type of Skill Targeted**			
Other **Target for Intervention?**			

Note: Use the following guidelines for identifying strengths and weaknesses: Normative Weakness is defined by standard scores that are about one standard deviation or more below the mean; Normative Strength is defined by standard scores that are about one standard deviation or more above the mean; within normal limits is defined by standard scores that fall between ± 1 SD of the normative mean (i.e., standard scores between 85 and 115). If a cognitive domain is targeted for intervention, note whether it is targeted for Modification to Instruction/Curriculum (**M**), Accommodation (**A**), Remediation (**R**), or Compensation (**C**). When there is a need to target an academic area for intervention, note the type of skill targeted as either a Basic (or foundational) skill (**B**), Fluency (**F**), or a Higher-level (or applied) skill (**H**).

readily classified into one of the 10 CHC domains (e.g., measures of visual motor ability, attention, executive functions, social-emotional). The DOTI form has three columns for organizing data, allowing for normative strengths and weaknesses to be recorded in separate columns. As the note to Table 1.1

indicates, in general, standard scores that are about 1 standard deviation (SD) below the mean or lower are considered normative weaknesses and standard scores that are about 1 SD above the mean or higher are considered normative strengths.

To illustrate various aspects of SMAARTI, this chapter includes excerpts from a case study, a boy, Ayden Murphy, who has difficulties with learning (see Rapid Reference 1.3). A DOTI form for Ayden is included in Table 1.2. This table contains primary data only. For example, a quick review of the data included in this table shows that Ayden has cognitive weaknesses in Glr, Ga, and Gs as well as deficits in reading, math, and writing skills. He also has relative strengths, particularly in the area of Gv.

≡ Rapid Reference 1.3 Selected Information From a Psychoeducational Evaluation of Ayden Murphy

Name:	Ayden Murphy
Age:	10
Gender:	Male
Grade Level:	Fifth Grade

Reason for Referral:
Ayden was referred to the Spotswood Center for Psychological Services for an evaluation by his mother, Ms. Murphy. Ms. Murphy reported that she was concerned about Ayden's difficulties in reading, reading comprehension, and writing. More specifically, Ms. Murphy indicated that Ayden continues to have difficulty decoding words and is not able to write in complete sentences most of the time or form paragraphs. In general, Ayden's academic performance has declined markedly in the fifth grade and he has recently demonstrated much less interest in school, homework, and reading.

Selected Measures Administered/Evaluation Procedures:
Beery-Buktenica Developmental Test of Visual-Motor Integration, Sixth Edition (BEERY VMI)

(continued)

(continued)

Child Intake Interview

Parent Intake Interview (Source: Mother)

Test of Orthographic Competence (TOC)

Woodcock-Johnson III Normative Update Tests of Achievement (WJ III NU ACH); Form A, Age Norms

Woodcock-Johnson III Normative Update Tests of Cognitive Abilities (WJ III NU COG); Form A, Age Norms

Background Information:
Ayden is a 10-year-old Caucasian male who is currently in fifth grade at Jefferson Elementary. He resides with his mother, stepfather, maternal grandmother, and younger sister. Ms. Murphy reported that Ayden typically gets along with all members of the household. Ayden has no reported medical conditions and is seemingly in good health. Ayden's last vision exam was approximately a year ago. He wears glasses for nearsightedness. Although he has never had a hearing exam outside of school, his hearing has never been a concern and he has passed all screening exams conducted at school.

Ayden attended Washington Heights Day Care between the ages of 3 and 5 years. He has attended Jefferson Elementary School since kindergarten and is currently in the fifth grade. During kindergarten (age 5), Ayden's teacher reported that he behaved well, but had difficulty reading and making sound-symbol connections. During first grade (age 6), Ayden had a strict teacher whom Ms. Murphy believed was beneficial for him. Specifically, Ayden's first-grade teacher kept him on-task and worked with him often on an individual basis. Nevertheless, during second grade (age 7), Ayden continued having difficulty reading and also began misbehaving in the classroom. For example, he would often play with things in his desk during reading instruction and frequently left his seat during reading groups. In third grade (age 8), Ayden was described as having problems with reading and writing and, in fourth grade (age 9), he received additional help from a reading teacher. Although he continued to struggle in reading and writing in the fourth grade, his teacher reported that he made some improvement over the course of the academic year.

Ayden is currently in fifth grade (age 10). According to his mother, Ayden is currently receiving pull-out services, which include meeting with the remedial reading teacher for one period three times per week for 30 minutes.

In terms of social-emotional development, Ms. Murphy described Ayden as generally cooperative, even-tempered, friendly, happy, and affectionate. He reportedly gets along well with others. Ayden enjoys playing football, soccer, and X-Box. According to Ayden, his least favorite activities are reading independently and completing social studies homework, although Ms. Murphy reported that Ayden enjoys reading with his family. Ayden also likes going to the park, movies, and out to eat. Ayden attends Operation Exodus, which is an after-school program designed to help him complete his homework and explore various educational activities.

Table 1.2 DOTI Form for Ayden Murphy With Primary Data Only

CHC Cognitive/Academic Ability or Processing Domain	Normative Weakness and Information About Intervention	Within Normal Limits	Normative Strength and Information About Intervention
Fluid Reasoning (Gf)			Fluid Reasoning Factor $= 88 \pm 4$
Target for Intervention?			
Crystallized Intelligence (Gc)			Comprehension-Knowledge Factor $= 95 \pm 4$
Target for Intervention?			
Long-Term Storage and Retrieval (Glr)	Long-Term Storage and Retrieval Factor $= 77 \pm 5$		
Target for Intervention?			
Short-Term Memory (Gsm)			Short-Term Memory Factor $= 96 \pm 6$
Target for Intervention?			
Visual Processing (Gv)		Visual Processing Factor $= 107 \pm 4$	
Target for Intervention?			
Auditory Processing (Ga)	Auditory Processing Factor $= 72 \pm 5$		
Target for Intervention?			
Processing Speed (Gs)	Processing Speed Factor $= 84 \pm 4$		
Target for Intervention?			
Reading (Grw-R)	Passage Comprehension $= 70 \pm 5$ Reading Fluency $= 83 \pm$		Letter-Word Identification $= 90 \pm 4$
Type of Skill Targeted			
Writing (Grw-W)	Writing Samples $= 74 \pm 6$		Spelling $= 87 \pm 5$ Writing Fluency $= 95 \pm 5$
Type of Skill Targeted			
Mathematics (Gq)	Applied Problems $= 81 \pm 4$ Fluency $= 80 \pm 4$		Calculation $= 107 \pm 4$
Type of Skill Targeted			

(continued)

Table 1.2 (Continued)

CHC Cognitive/Academic Ability or Processing Domain	Normative Weakness and Information About Intervention	Within Normal Limits	Normative Strength and Information About Intervention
Other Target for Intervention?			

Note: Cognitive and Academic standard scores are from the WJ III NU COG and ACH batteries (Woodcock, McGrew, & Mather, 2001, 2007), unless otherwise noted. Use the following guidelines for identifying strengths and weaknesses: Normative Weakness is defined by standard scores that are about one standard deviation or more below the mean; Normative Strength is defined by standard scores that are about one standard deviation or more above the mean; within normal limits is defined by standard scores that fall between ± 1 SD of the normative mean (i.e., standard scores between 85 and 115). If a cognitive domain is targeted for intervention, note whether it is targeted for Modification to Instruction/Curriculum (**M**), Accommodation (**A**), Remediation (**R**), or Compensation (**C**). When there is a need to target an academic area for intervention, note the type of skill targeted as either a Basic (or foundational) skill (**B**), Fluency (**F**), or a Higher-level (or applied) skill (**H**).

Step 2: Determine Whether Academic Weaknesses Are Empirically Related to the Cognitive Weaknesses by Reviewing the Research on the Relations among Specific Cognitive Abilities, Neuropsychological Processes, and Academic Skills

In the initial step of SMAARTI, data were organized by CHC domain and normative strengths and weaknesses were identified. Prior to making classifications or diagnostic decisions and tailoring interventions, however, it is important to examine the relations among cognitive abilities, neuropsychological processes, and specific academic skills for the following reasons. First, information on cognitive-achievement relationships assists in interpreting the data entered on the DOTI form. Second, because specific learning disabilities are caused by underlying cognitive processing weaknesses, knowing the cognitive correlates of manifest academic difficulties assists in diagnosis (e.g., Flanagan, Alfonso, & Ortiz, 2012; Flanagan et al., 2013). Third, when empirical data are available to support a relationship between identified areas of cognitive and academic weaknesses, interventions designed to remediate academic skill deficits can be tailored in an attempt to minimize the effects of cognitive weaknesses on learning. Thus, in this step, practitioners should examine the information in Rapid Reference 1.4 to determine if identified cognitive and academic weaknesses are related empirically.

≡ Rapid Reference 1.4 Summary of Relations Between CHC Broad and Narrow Cognitive Abilities and Reading, Math, and Writing Achievement

	Reading Achievement	Math Achievement	Writing Achievement
Gf	Inductive (I) and general sequential reasoning (RG) abilities play a moderate role in **reading comprehension**.	**Inductive (I) and general sequential (RG) reasoning abilities are consistently very important for math problem solving at all ages.**	Inductive (I) and general sequential reasoning abilities (RG) are consistently related to **written expression** at all ages.
Gc	Language development (LD), lexical knowledge (VL), and listening ability (LS) are important at all ages. These abilities become increasingly important with age.	Language development (LD), lexical knowledge (VL), and listening abilities (LS) are important at all ages. These abilities become increasingly important with age.	Language development (LD), lexical knowledge (VL), and general information (K0) are important primarily after about the second grade. These abilities become increasingly important with age.
Gsm	**Memory span (MS) and working memory (WM) capacity.**	**Memory span (MS) and working memory (WM) capacity.**	**Memory span (MS) is important to writing, especially spelling skills, whereas working memory (WM) has shown relations with advanced writing skills (e.g., written expression).**
Gv	Orthographic Processing— **reading fluency**	May be important primarily for higher level or **advanced mathematics** (e.g., geometry, calculus).	Orthographic Processing—spelling

(continued)

(continued)

Ga	Phonetic coding (PC) or "phonological awareness/ processing" is very important during the elementary school years.		Phonetic coding (PC) or "phonological awareness/processing" is very important during the elementary school years for both basic writing skills and written expression (primarily before about grade 5).
Glr	Naming facility (NA) or "rapid automatic naming" is very important during the elementary school years. Associative memory (MA) is also important.	Naming facility (NA); associative memory (MA)	Phonetic coding (PC) or "phonological awareness/processing" is very important during the elementary school years for both basic writing skills and written expression (primarily before about grade 5).
Gs	Perceptual speed (P) abilities are important during all school years, particularly the elementary school years.	Perceptual speed (P) abilities are important during all school years, particularly the elementary school years.	Perceptual speed (P) abilities are important during all school years for basic writing and related to all ages for written expression.

Research on the relations among cognitive abilities, neuropsychological processes, and specific academic skills has mounted over the years (see Flanagan, Ortiz, Alfonso, & Mascolo, 2006; Flanagan, Alfonso, & Mascolo, 2011; Fletcher, Lyon, Fuchs, & Barnes, 2007; and McGrew & Wendling, 2010, for summaries). Much of the recent research on cognitive-academic relationships has been interpreted within the context of CHC theory (e.g., Flanagan et al., 2011) and with specific instruments developed from CHC theory (e.g., McGrew & Wendling, 2010). In addition, statistical analyses, such as structural equation modeling, have been used to understand the extent to which specific cognitive abilities explain variance in academic skills above and beyond the variance accounted for by g (e.g., Floyd et al., 2008; McGrew, Flanagan, Keith, & Vanderwood, 1997; Juarez, 2012; Vanderwood, McGrew, Keith, & Flanagan, 2001). Finally, many valuable resources summarize the research on cognitive and neurobiological processes associated with specific academic skill deficits (e.g., Feifer & Della Toffalo, 2007; Flanagan

& Alfonso, 2011; Fletcher-Janzen & Reynolds, 2008; Fletcher et al., 2007; Hale & Fiorello, 2004; Miller, 2010, 2013).

The research summarized in Rapid Reference 1.4 includes primarily studies on the relations among the various CHC broad and narrow cognitive abilities and specific neuropsychological processes and the major areas of achievement—namely, reading, math, and writing. Rapid Reference 1.4 shows that narrow abilities subsumed by Gc (lexical knowledge, language development, listening ability, general information), Gsm (memory span, working memory capacity), Ga (phonetic coding), Glr (associative memory, meaningful memory, naming facility), and Gs (perceptual speed) were found to be significantly and most consistently related to reading achievement. Similarly, narrow abilities within these same broad abilities were found to be related to writing achievement. Narrow abilities within the areas of Gf, Gc, Gsm, Glr, and Gs were found to relate significantly to math achievement, with Gf (induction and general sequential reasoning) showing a stronger relation to this academic area than either reading or writing.

A review of Ayden's DOTI form (Table 1.2) shows three areas of cognitive deficit and areas of academic skill deficiency in reading, math, and writing. Based on the information summarized in Rapid Reference 1.4, it appears that there is an empirically supported relationship between Ayden's cognitive weakness in Gs and his academic fluency in reading and math. There also seems to be an empirically supported relationship between his weakness in Ga (viz., the narrow Phonetic Coding ability) and his spelling ability and reading fluency (i.e., inefficient phonetic strategies slows down reading, thereby interfering with comprehension). Finally, Ayden has weaknesses in both the learning efficiency and retrieval fluency aspects of Glr, both of which are empirically related to higher level application of basic academic skills. Ayden's deficit in Glr and relative weakness in Gf together affect reading comprehension, math problem solving, and written expression adversely.

Step 3: Review Manifestations of Cognitive Weaknesses and Organize Secondary Data, Identify Initial Targets for Intervention, and Identify Types of Academic Skill Deficits for Remediation Using the DOTI Form

Once empirically established relations between cognitive and academic areas are identified, practitioners should consult Rapid References 1.5 to 1.13 to determine whether the identified cognitive-academic relationships are ecologically valid. These rapid references will prove particularly useful when organizing secondary data in the DOTI form. Secondary data include any information that can relate potentially to a specific aspect of the student's cognitive functioning that was not already included as primary data. Such information might include data obtained

CHC Broad Cognitive Abilities/ Neuropsychological Functions	Brief Definition	General Manifestations of Cognitive/ Neuropsychological Weakness	Specific Manifestations of Cognitive/ Neuropsychological Weakness
Fluid Reasoning (Gf)	Novel reasoning and problem solving; ability to solve problems that are unfamiliar. Processes are minimally dependent on prior learning. Involves manipulating rules, abstracting, generalizing, and identifying logical relationships. Fluid reasoning is evident in inferential reasoning, concept formation, classification of unfamiliar stimuli, categorization, and extrapolation of reasonable estimates in ambiguous situations (Schneider & McGrew, 2012). Narrow Gf abilities include Induction, General Sequential Reasoning (Deduction), and Quantitative Reasoning.	*Difficulties with:* Higher-level thinking and reasoning Transferring or generalizing learning Deriving solutions for novel problems Extending knowledge through critical thinking Perceiving and applying underlying rules or process(es) to solve problems	*Reading Difficulties:* Drawing inferences from text Abstracting main idea(s) *Math Difficulties:* Reasoning with quantitative information (word problems) Internalizing procedures and processes used to solve problems Apprehending relationships between numbers *Writing Difficulties:* Essay writing and generalizing concepts Developing a theme Comparing and contrasting ideas

Rapid Reference 1.6 General and Specific Manifestations of Crystallized Intelligence (Gc) Weaknesses

CHC Broad Cognitive Abilities/ Neuropsychological Functions	Brief Definition	General Manifestations of Cognitive/ Neuropsychological Weakness	Specific Manifestations of Cognitive/ Neuropsychological Weakness
Crystallized Intelligence (Gc)	Breadth and depth of knowledge and skills that are valued by one's culture. Developed through formal education as well as general learning experiences. Stores of information and declarative and procedural knowledge. Reflects the degree to which a person has learned practically useful knowledge and mastered valued skills (Schneider & McGrew, 2012). Narrow Gc abilities include General Verbal Information, Language Development, Lexical Knowledge, Listening Ability, Information about Culture, Communication Ability, and Grammatical Sensitivity.	**Difficulties with:** Vocabulary acquisition Knowledge acquisition Comprehending language or understanding what others are saying Fact-based/informational questions Using prior knowledge to support learning Finding the right words to use/say	***Reading Difficulties:*** Decoding (e.g., word student is attempting to decode is not in his/her vocabulary) Comprehending (e.g., poor background knowledge about information contained in text) ***Math Difficulties:*** Understanding math concepts and the "vocabulary of math" ***Writing Difficulties:*** Grammar (syntax) Bland writing with limited descriptors Verbose writing with limited descriptors Inappropriate word usage ***Language Difficulties:*** Understanding class lessons Expressive language—"poverty of thought"

17

Rapid Reference 1.7 General and Specific Manifestations of Auditory Processing (Ga) Weaknesses

CHC Broad Cognitive Abilities/ Neuropsychological Functions	Brief Definition	General Manifestations of Cognitive/ Neuropsychological Weakness	Specific Manifestations of Cognitive/ Neuropsychological Weakness
Auditory Processing (Ga)	Ability to analyze and synthesize auditory information. One narrow aspect of Ga is a precursor to oral language comprehension (i.e., parsing speech sounds or Phonetic Coding). In addition to Phonetic Coding, other narrow Ga abilities include Speech Sound Discrimination, Resistance to Auditory Stimulus Distortion, Memory for Sound Patterns (and others related to music).	**Difficulties with:** Hearing information presented orally, initially processing oral information Paying attention especially in the presence of background noise Discerning the direction from which auditory information is coming Discriminating between simple sounds Foreign-language acquisition	**Reading Difficulties:** Acquiring phonics skills Sounding out words Using phonetic strategies **Math Difficulties:** Reading word problems **Writing Difficulties:** Spelling Note-taking Poor quality of writing

CHC Broad Cognitive Abilities/Neuropsychological Functions	Brief Definition	General Manifestations of Cognitive/Neuropsychological Weakness	Specific Manifestations of Cognitive/Neuropsychological Weakness
Long-Term Storage and Retrieval (Glr)	Ability to store information (e.g., concepts, words, facts), consolidate it, and fluently retrieve it at a later time (e.g., minutes, hours, days, and years) through association. In Glr tasks, information leaves immediate awareness long enough for the contents of primary memory to be displaced completely. In other words, Glr tasks (unlike Gsm tasks) do not allow for information to be maintained continuously in primary memory (Schneider & McGrew, 2012). Glr abilities may be categorized as either "learning efficiency" or "fluency." Learning efficiency narrow abilities include Associative Memory, Meaningful Memory, and Free Recall Memory; fluency narrow abilities involve either the production of ideas (e.g., Ideational Fluency, Associational Fluency), the recall of words (e.g., Naming Facility, Word Fluency), or the generation of figures (e.g., Figural Fluency, Figural Flexibility) (Schneider & McGrew, 2012).	**Difficulties with:** Learning new concepts Retrieving or recalling information by using association Performing consistently across different task formats (e.g., recognition versus recall formats) Rapid retrieval of information Learning information quickly Paired learning (visual-auditory) Recalling specific information (words, facts) Generating ideas rapidly	**Reading Difficulties:** Accessing background knowledge to support new learning while reading Slow to access phonological representations during decoding Retelling or paraphrasing what one has read **Math Difficulties:** Memorizing math facts Recalling math facts and procedures **Writing Difficulties:** Accessing words to use during essay writing Specific writing tasks (compare and contrast persuasive writing) Note-taking Idea generation/production **Language Difficulties:** Expressive—circumlocutions, speech fillers, "interrupted" thought, pauses Receptive—making connections throughout oral presentations (e.g., class lecture)

Rapid Reference 1.9 General and Specific Manifestations of Processing Speed (Gs) Weaknesses

CHC Broad Cognitive Abilities/ Neuropsychological Functions	Brief Definition	General Manifestations of Cognitive/ Neuropsychological Weakness	Specific Manifestations of Cognitive/ Neuropsychological Weakness
Processing Speed (Gs)	Speed of processing, particularly when required to focus attention for 1–3 minutes. Usually measured by tasks that require the ability to perform simple repetitive cognitive tasks quickly and accurately. Narrow Gs abilities include Perceptual Speed, Rate-of-Test-Taking, Number Facility, Reading Speed, and Writing Speed (note that the latter two abilities are also listed under other broad CHC domains, including Grw).	**Difficulties with:** Efficient processing of information Quickly perceiving relationships (similarities and differences between stimuli or information) Working within time parameters Completing simple, rote tasks quickly	**Reading Difficulties:** Slow reading speed, which interferes with comprehension Need to reread for understanding **Math Difficulties:** Automatic computations Computational speed is slow despite accuracy Slow speed can result in reduced accuracy due to memory decay **Writing Difficulties:** Limited output due to time factors Labored process results in reduced motivation to produce **Language Difficulties:** Cannot retrieve information quickly—slow, disrupted speech; cannot get out thoughts quickly enough Is slow to process incoming information, puts demands on memory store that can result in information overload and loss of meaning

CHC Broad Cognitive Abilities/ Neuropsychological Functions	Brief Definition	General Manifestations of Cognitive/ Neuropsychological Weakness	Specific Manifestations of Cognitive/ Neuropsychological Weakness
Visual Processing (Gv)	Ability to analyze and synthesize visual information. The ability to make use of simulated mental imagery (often in conjunction with currently perceived images) to solve problems (Schneider & McGrew, 2012). There are many narrow Gv abilities, some of which include Visualization, Speeded Rotation, Closure Speed, Flexibility of Closure, Visual Memory, and Spatial Scanning.	**Difficulties with:** Recognizing patterns Reading maps, graphs, charts Attending to fine visual detail Recalling visual information Appreciation of spatial characteristics of objects (e.g., size, length) Recognition of spatial orientation of objects	***Reading Difficulties:*** Orthographic coding (using visual features of letters to decode) Sight-word acquisition Using charts and graphs within a text in conjunction with reading Comprehension of text involving spatial concepts (e.g., social studies text describing physical boundaries, movement of troops along a specified route) ***Math Difficulties:*** Number alignment during computations Reading and interpreting graphs, tables, and charts ***Writing Difficulties:*** Spelling sight words Spatial planning during writing tasks (e.g., no attention to margins, words that overhang a line) Inconsistent size, spacing, position, and slant of letters

Rapid Reference 1.11 General and Specific Manifestations of Short-Term Memory (Gsm) Weaknesses

CHC Broad Cognitive Abilities/ Neuropsychological Functions	Brief Definition	General Manifestations of Cognitive/ Neuropsychological Weakness	Specific Manifestations of Cognitive/ Neuropsychological Weakness
Short-Term Memory (Gsm)	Ability to hold information in immediate awareness and use or transform it within a few seconds.	**Difficulties with:** Following multistep oral and written instructions Remembering information long enough to apply it Remembering the sequence of information Rote memorization Maintaining one's place in a math problem or train of thought while writing	**Reading Difficulties:** Reading comprehension (i.e., understanding what is read) Decoding multisyllabic words Orally retelling or paraphrasing what one has read **Math Difficulties:** Rote memorization of facts Remembering mathematical procedures Multistep problems and regrouping Extracting information to be used in word problems **Writing Difficulties:** Spelling multisyllabic words Redundancy in writing (word and conceptual levels) Identifying main idea of a story Note-taking

Rapid Reference 1.12 General and Specific Manifestations of Attention Weaknesses and Examples of Recommendations and Interventions

CHC Broad Cognitive Abilities/Neuropsychological Functions	Brief Definition	General Manifestations of Cognitive/ Neuropsychological Weakness	Specific Manifestations of Cognitive/ Neuropsychological Weakness
Attention	Attention is a complex and multifaceted construct used when an individual must focus on certain stimuli for information processing. In order to regulate thinking and to complete tasks of daily living such as schoolwork, it is necessary to be able to attend to both auditory and visual stimuli in the environment. Attention can be viewed as the foundation of all other higher-order processing. Attention can be divided into five subareas: selective/focused attention, shifting attention, divided attention, sustained attention, and attentional capacity (Miller, 2013). It is important to identify the exact nature of the attentional problem(s) prior to selecting an intervention, teaching strategies, modifying the curriculum, or making accommodations,	Easily distracted Lacks attention to detail; makes careless mistakes Difficulty discerning demands of a task (e.g., where to begin or how to get started) May only be able to attend to task in short intervals Difficulty changing activities Difficulty applying a different strategy when task demands change Difficulty attending to more than one thing or task at a time Cannot perform well when faced with multiple stimuli or an abundance of detail	***Reading Difficulties:*** Loses his or her place easily Easily distracted while reading Does not pick up important details in text ***Math Difficulties:*** Does not consistently attend to math signs Frequent mistakes on word problems ***Writing Difficulties:*** Has difficulty completing long assignments; difficulty following timelines

23

Rapid Reference 1.13 General and Specific Manifestations of Executive Functioning Weaknesses and Examples of Recommendations and Interventions

CHC Broad Cognitive Abilities/ Neuropsychological Functions	Brief Definition	General Manifestations of Cognitive/ Neuropsychological Weakness	Specific Manifestations of Cognitive/ Neuropsychological Weakness
Executive Functioning	Executive functioning is often understood as two broadly conceptualized areas that are related to the brain's frontal lobes: cognitive control and behavioral/emotional control. The cognitive aspects of executive functioning include concept generation (Gc/Glr); problem solving (Gf); attentional shifting (attention; Gs); planning; organizing; working memory (Gsm); and retrieval fluency (Glr). The behavioral/ emotional aspects of executive functioning relate to the inhibitory controls of behavior (e.g., impulsivity, regulation of emotional tone, etc.) (see Miller, 2010).	**Difficulty with:** Learning new activities, generating concepts, and solving problems Identifying goals and setting goals Planning (e.g., begins project without necessary materials; does not allocate sufficient time to complete task) Sequencing (e.g., may skip steps in multistep problems) Prioritizing (e.g., not sure what's important when taking notes) Organization (e.g., loses important papers; fails to turn in completed work; creates unrealistic schedule) Initiation (e.g., has difficulty getting started on tasks, assignments, etc.) Pace (e.g., often runs out of time on seatwork and exams; has difficulty completing homework due to unrealistic timeline) Shifting between activities flexibly; coping with unforeseen events Self-monitoring (e.g., doesn't check to insure that each step was completed; doesn't check work before submitting it) Emotional control (e.g., may exhibit inappropriate or over-reactive response to situations)	***Reading Difficulties:*** Sequencing; telling a story chronologically Prioritizing; extracting main idea and other important information Problem solving; drawing inferences from text ***Math Difficulties:*** Sequencing; remembering order of operations Prioritizing; figuring out what is important when solving word problems Shifting; attending to math signs on a page ***Writing Difficulties:*** Generating ideas to write about Sequencing a story Prioritizing main events in a story

Source: Adapted from Leslie E. Packer (Schoolbehavior.com); see also Packer and Pruitt's book, *Challenging Kids, Challenged Teachers* (Woodbine Press, 2010),

via observation, rating scales, record reviews, work sample analysis, and/or interviews. For example, if a mother reports, in a parent intake interview, that her son has *difficulty remembering* to take necessary items to a recurring event (e.g., soccer practice), this information can be considered secondary data and recorded in the Gsm section, given its potential relationship to memory. Similarly, if a mother reports that her daughter is highly anxious during essay exams, this information may be recorded in the Glr section, given that anxiety may interfere with retrieval of learned information.

To help build a knowledge base about the general and specific ways in which cognitive weaknesses manifest in real-world performance, particularly academic performances, Flanagan and colleagues (2013) developed Rapid References 1.5 to 1.13. These rapid references describe ways in which deficits in broad CHC abilities manifest in real-world performance (e.g., classroom activities). Rapid References 1.12 and 1.13 describe manifestations of deficits in attention and executive functions, respectively. It is important to note that these rapid references do not represent an exhaustive list of manifestations. Rather, they assist practitioners in extending their thinking beyond standardized test scores by considering how cognitive deficits impact learning in multiple settings (e.g., classroom and home).

Rapid References 1.5 to 1.13 are organized into four columns. For example, Rapid Reference 1.5 shows that the first column, "CHC Broad Cognitive Abilities/Neuropsychological Functions," identifies a CHC broad cognitive ability or neuropsychological process, in this case, Fluid Reasoning (Gf). The second column, "Brief Definition," provides a brief definition of the broad ability or process along with a list of narrow abilities subsumed by the broad ability. The third column, "General Manifestations of Cognitive/Neuropsychological Weakness," lists the types of difficulties that can be expected to manifest generally when there is a weakness in the cognitive domain. For example, difficulties with higher level thinking, problems with generalizing learning, and difficulty with rule application during problem solving may be evident when an individual has a weakness in Gf. "Specific Manifestations of Cognitive/Neuropsychological Weaknesses" are listed in the fourth column and typically center on the types of difficulties that may be seen in specific academic domains (e.g., reading, writing, math). Rapid Reference 1.5 shows that individuals with a weakness in Gf may have difficulties drawing inferences from text (reading comprehension), apprehending relationships between numbers (math application), and developing a theme when writing (written expression), to name a few.

When secondary data sources reveal that cognitive deficits manifest in specific academic areas as expected based on the information in Rapid References 1.5 to 1.13, the empirically supported cognitive-academic relationships have ecological validity, which is critical for tailoring interventions effectively. *Ecological validity* refers to "the relation between real-world phenomena and the investigation of these phenomena in experimental contexts" (Shmuckler, 2001, p. 420). In SMAARTI, this relationship is akin to an empirically supported below-average cognitive-achievement consistency, where the relationship is supported by real-world manifestations—an important marker for specific learning disability identification (see Flanagan et al., 2013).

It is important to keep in mind that secondary data need not be consistent with standardized test results (i.e., primary data) to be included in the DOTI form. That is, while convergence among data sources provides ecological validity for standardized test findings, a lack of convergence calls into question the validity of the primary data, which is equally important and suggests a need to evaluate the primary data more carefully (e.g., approach to tasks, sufficiency of evaluation, malingering). It is also important to realize that even when secondary data converge as expected with primary data, such as in the example of the boy who repeatedly forgot his soccer gear, alternative hypotheses may also be tested. For example, rather than a Gsm deficit, this student may have difficulties with attention or organization—characteristics that may warrant a different approach to intervention as compared to a Gsm deficit.

Additional secondary data may include information obtained via a work sample analysis, parent–teacher interviews, observations, error analysis, or records review (e.g., report cards, classroom tests, teacher notes/comments). For example, if a practitioner reviewed several math tests with low scores, the scores may be entered in the Quantitative Knowledge (Gq) domain in the normative weakness column (e.g., "math quiz 3/10/13—score 63; math quiz 4/2/13—score 59"). Similarly, practitioner comments from work sample analysis may be included (e.g., "10 spelling errors out of a 25-word writing sample" may be entered for the Writing domain [Grw-W] in the normative weakness column).

Table 1.3 shows that secondary data in the form of parent and teacher reports about Ayden's academic performance converge with standardized test data in the areas of Glr, Ga, and Gs. For example, Ayden's teacher reported that he has difficulty working within time limits and his mother reported that he is slow to complete his homework. Both of these reports are consistent with his observed weakness in the cognitive area of Gs, thus providing ecological validity evidence for the observed Gs deficit. Table 1.3 also shows that Ayden's teacher indicated that he does better on multiple-choice tests as compared to essay tests. Such an observation is consistent with an individual with Glr difficulties, as essay tests require recall of information, whereas multiple choice tests require recognition, thereby minimizing the demands on Glr.

As shown in Table 1.3, the DOTI form also provides space for practitioners to hypothesize about the cognitive and academic areas that may need to be targeted for intervention. For example, when it is hypothesized that a cognitive domain should be targeted for intervention, then the practitioner should make a note of whether he or she believes the intervention should focus on *Modification* (instructional or curricular), *Accommodation*, *Remediation*, *Compensation*, or some combination thereof, using the letters *M*, *A*, *R*, and *C*, respectively. For young children in particular, when academic weaknesses are found, intervention is primarily of the remedial type. While cognitive weaknesses should also be targeted for remediation in young children given brain plasticity (e.g., Fletcher-Janzen & Reynolds, 2008), depending on the area of weakness, young children may also need modifications to instruction, for example, to minimize the effect of the cognitive weakness, thereby allowing greater access to the curriculum. Worthy of note is that identification of strengths assists in determining what interventions may circumvent or limit the impact of a weakness.

Table 1.3 shows that Ayden's Gs deficit was a target for intervention. Specifically, the evaluator hypothesized that it may be necessary to make accommodations for Ayden's Gs deficit as well as make modifications to instruction or the curriculum in an attempt to minimize the effects of this deficit.

When it is determined that an academic weakness should be targeted for intervention, then the practitioner should make a note of the type of skill that is targeted for remediation. For example, the practitioner can use the letters *B*, *F*, and *H* to designate the skill as either a *B*asic (or foundational) skill, a *F*luency skill, or a *H*igher level (applied) skill, respectively. A deficit in a foundational skill suggests a need for basic skill building via explicit teaching designed to remediate the weakness (e.g., teaching a student how to subtract double-digit numbers). A fluency deficit suggests that basic skills, while present, are not automatic. Therefore, fluency deficits suggest the need for practice. When fluency deficits exist, it is important to examine whether the use of inefficient strategies may be interfering with the development of fluency (e.g., finger counting). Difficulties with higher level application of skills (e.g., reading comprehension, math problem solving, written expression) can be directly related to lower level deficits or they can reflect a breakdown in the student's ability to analyze or synthesize skills within an academic domain to problem solve or otherwise demonstrate higher

CAUTION

Cognitive deficit may not manifest in a specific academic area.

Table 1.3 DOTI Form for Ayden Murphy with Primary and Secondary Data

CHC Cognitive/Academic Ability or Processing Domain	Normative Weakness and Information About Intervention	Within Normal Limits	Normative Strength and Information About Intervention
Fluid Reasoning (Gf)		Fluid Reasoning Factor = 88 ± 4 **Teacher Report:** sometimes has difficulty generalizing what he has learned **C** (Compensation)	
Target for Intervention? Crystallized Intelligence (Gc)		Comprehension-Knowledge = 95 ± 4	
Target for Intervention? Long-Term Storage and Retrieval (Glr)	Long-Term Storage and Retrieval = 77 ± 5 **Teacher Report:** seems to do better on multiple-choice tests as compared to essays; difficulty remembering previously taught information **Parent Report:** spends hours studying—more than his friends; often has difficulty getting out what he wants to say		
Target for Intervention?	**M** (Modification) **A** (Accommodation) **C** (Compensation)		
Short-Term Memory (Gsm) **Target for Intervention?** Visual Processing (Gv)		Short-Term Memory = 96 ± 6 Visual Processing = 107 ± 4 TOC Orthographic Ability = 103 ± 3	

Target for Intervention?		**Teacher Report:** seems to do better with visual information (e.g., charts and graphs in math and science) **Ayden:** "I love to draw." Emphasize in program planning to the extent possible
Auditory Processing (Ga)	Auditory Processing = 72 ± 5 **Reading Specialist:** does not use phonetic strategies consistently; relies more on visual features and contextual cues to decode **Teacher Report:** mishears words frequently **R** (Remediation)	
Target for Intervention? **Processing Speed (Gs)**	Processing Speed = 84 ± 4 **Teacher Report:** has difficulty working within time limits **Parent Report:** takes a long time to complete homework **A** (Accommodation) **M** (Modification)	
Target for Intervention?		
Reading (Grw-R)	Passage Comprehension = 70 ± 5 **Teacher Report:** has difficulty retelling what he has read for monthly book reports Reading Fluency = 83 ± 5 **Reading Specialist and School Psychologist Observation:** oral reading is slow and laborious **Ayden:** "I can't read fast." **H** (Higher Level Application) **F** (Fluency)	Letter-Word Identification = 90 ± 4
Type of Skill Targeted		
Writing (Grw-W)	Writing Samples = 74 ± 6 **Teacher Report:** does not use vocabulary words in writing assignments; note-taking is difficult for him—verbatim note-taking as opposed to paraphrasing	Spelling = 87 ± 5 Writing Fluency = 95 ± 5

(continued)

Table 1.3 (Continued)

CHC Cognitive/Academic Ability or Processing Domain	Normative Weakness and Information About Intervention	Within Normal Limits	Normative Strength and Information About Intervention
Type of Skill Targeted Mathematics (Gq)	**H** (Higher Level Application) Applied Problems = 81 ± 4 **Parent and Teacher Reports:** difficulty with word problems Fluency = 80 ± 4 **Teacher Report:** slow but accurate **Classroom Tests:** Grade of "D" on all Mad Math Minutes	**B** (Basic Skill) - spelling Calculation = 107 ± 4	
Type of Skill Targeted	**H** (Higher Level Application) **F** (Fluency)		
Other	Ayden has recently begun to avoid reading for pleasure and seems to be developing anxiety related to reading aloud in school		Ayden is highly motivated to learn and puts forth considerable effort in all educational activities; does well with hands-on activities
Target for Intervention?			Capitalize on his motivation and incorporate interests into remedial activities

level thinking. Students who have difficulty with higher level skills often respond well to instructional aids and techniques such as graphic organizers, modeling, and procedural mnemonics.

Step 4: Consider Tertiary Data, Which Are Comprised of Information About Factors That Affect Learning and Achievement and That Are Largely External to the Student (i.e., Extrinsic)

At this step of SMAARTI, practitioners already have a good understanding of the nature of the student's learning difficulties based on primary and secondary data sources. However, additional data most likely need to be considered for tailoring interventions to meet a student's unique learning needs. Four categories of tertiary data, meaning data that are largely external to the student, should be considered prior to tailoring interventions, namely classroom instruction, instructional materials, environment, and strategies. A brief description of each category follows.

With regard to *classroom instruction*, practitioners should consider how factors such as pacing of instruction, timing and nature of feedback, responsiveness to students' questions, and quality of student–teacher interaction, for example, affect learning and achievement for the student in question. *Instructional materials* include the tools of teaching with which the student directly interacts and includes such things as textbooks, workbooks, electronic media (software programs, applications), and consumables (e.g., worksheets). Attention to instructional materials may assist in identifying factors that can inhibit learning (e.g., small font embedded in most graphics for a student with a visual perceptual difficulty, a large amount of text, visuals, and callouts on a page for a student with attention difficulties) or facilitate learning (e.g., use of an audio glossary on a published textbook's website to assist a student with weaknesses in vocabulary, phonemic awareness, and basic decoding skills). Factors in the home or school environment may also exacerbate or minimize the impact of a student's cognitive weaknesses and, therefore, should be considered carefully. Relevant *environmental* factors refer to the student's classroom or home physical space, including desk arrangements (student's and teacher's), room acoustics, environmental noise, lighting, temperature, use of resources (e.g., classroom learning aids such as posters, word walls), and classroom/home displays (e.g., homework board, bulletin boards of student work). Finally, *strategies* include any method or plan that is explicitly taught to or used by the student in an effort to compensate for cognitive weaknesses or deficits, thereby facilitating learning and achievement. Data relevant to each of these categories are gathered typically via classroom observations and teacher/parent/student interviews.

It is important to realize that most classroom observations and interviews are conducted prior to a comprehensive evaluation. Therefore, during an initial classroom observation or interview, the practitioner is not necessarily primed to gather tertiary data in an effort to determine what factors might facilitate learning or exacerbate learning difficulties because the specific nature and presumptive cause of the learning problem are not yet known or understood well. As such, it may be necessary to conduct additional classroom observations or interviews after the practitioner has a more complete understanding of the various and specific presumed causes of the student's learning difficulties. Moreover, it is likely that most practitioners are not very familiar with the instructional materials used by the teacher and student (e.g., textbooks, electronic media, worksheets) and, therefore, they are not in a position to give guidance on how certain features of instructional material may facilitate learning for a student. Therefore, practitioners should make an effort to familiarize themselves with relevant instructional materials.

Rapid References 1.14 to 1.20 include information, organized according to the four categories described earlier, that will assist practitioners in gathering tertiary data and considering these data for the purpose of tailoring interventions for students with specific cognitive weaknesses or deficits. There is one rapid reference for each of seven broad CHC cognitive abilities. For example, Rapid Reference 1.17 includes recommendations for a student like Ayden, whose learning difficulties are affected adversely by a deficit in Long-term Storage and Retrieval. To ensure that the adverse effects that a Glr weakness has on learning are minimized, the practitioner should consult this rapid reference to gain knowledge about how to intervene and tailor instruction for Ayden. Furthermore, when reviewing the information in this rapid reference, the practitioner should consider factors and strategies that capitalize on a student's area of relative strength. For example, Ayden has a relative strength in Visual Processing (Gv). Therefore, relevant recommendations include pairing verbal information with visuals, organizing materials to be learned using visual aids, and providing visual reminders (Post-its, color-coded systems). It is important to note that the information contained in Rapid References 1.14 to 1.20 is not meant to be exhaustive. For more information about recommendations for students with cognitive ability and processing weaknesses or deficits, see the other chapters in this book or other relevant resources (e.g., Mather & Jaffe, 2002). Copies of Rapid References 1.14 to 1.20 may be downloaded from the CD that accompanies this book.

Rapid Reference 1.14 Recommendations That May Facilitate Learning and Aid in Bypassing or Minimizing the Effects of a Fluid Reasoning (Gf) Deficit

Classroom Instruction	Instructional Materials	Environmental	Strategies
Use demonstrations to externalize the reasoning process (think-alouds)	Expanded answer keys containing the "reason" for correct/incorrect choices	Problem-solving charts (hanging or taped to desk)	Use metacognitive strategies (mnemonics that are memorable and that *accurately* represent the learning task)
Gradually offer guided practice (e.g., guided questions list) to promote internalization of procedures or process(es)	Guided lists for implementing procedures, formulas	Procedural charts/lists (hanging or taped to desk)	Use tools that help them categorizes objects and concepts to assist in drawing conclusions (e.g, graphic organizers, concept maps)
Offer targeted, explicit feedback	Models/examples	Preferred seating arrangements that provide easy access to a peer model with strong reasoning skills (e.g., for cooperative learning activities)	Listen to and separate the steps in completing a problem from the actual content used in a problem
Offer opportunities for learning formats that allow for reasoning to be modeled for the student (e. g, cooperative learning, reciprocal teaching)	Text features (boldface, italics)		
Compare new concepts to previously learned concepts (same vs. different)	Graphic organizers that allow for a visual depiction of relationships between and among concepts		
Use analogies, similes, metaphors, paired with concrete explanations, to support understanding when presenting tasks (e.g., "We are going to learn our math facts with *lightning speed*, that means we are going to learn them *fast*")	Manipulatives to demonstrate relationships (e.g., part to whole relationships)		

Rapid Reference 1.15 Factors That May Facilitate Learning and Aid in Bypassing or Minimizing the Effects of a Crystallized Intelligence (Gc) Deficit

Classroom Instructional Factors	Instructional Materials	Environmental Factors	Strategies
Provides an environment rich in language and experiences	Contains chapter Glossaries	Word-of-the-day calendar	Use KWL strategy to increase background knowledge
Incorporates frequent practice with and exposure to words	E-Glossaries available	Word walls	Use context when reading to ascertain meaning
Reads aloud to children	Provides vocabulary building activities (print or online)		Capitalize on opportunities to practice new words (listening for their use in television shows and other media, purposely using them in conversation)
Varies reading purpose (leisure, information)	Contains tools for priming background knowledge (e.g., Harcourt)	Distraction-free seating	Engage in activities such as word searches containing related terms (e.g., travel terms) and crosswords (note: puzzlemaker.com can create customized puzzles)
Works on vocabulary building	Includes story starters	Closed doors	Write a new word and its definition along with a drawing
Teaches morphology	Includes text features (boldface, italics)	Closed windows	
Capitalizes on opportunities to define words within instruction (e.g., "the composition of igneous rock, that is, what it is made of, is...")	Availability of video clips		

34

Includes supportive modalities (e.g., visuals, gestures) to increase understanding of language used	Audio glossaries
Embeds instruction within a meaningful context (e.g., relating words to learner experiences, increasing listening ability through game-like format)	Dictionaries
Develops vocabulary through naturalistic extension of language (e.g., if a student asks, "Can I start my work," the teacher might respond, "Yes, you can begin your work," naturally building synonym knowledge)	Thesaurus
Uses extension and expansion strategies (Mather, Lynch, & Richards, 2001)	Encyclopedias
	Use vocabulary cartoons (Burchers, 2000)
	Use text talks

Rapid Reference 1.16 Factors That May Facilitate Learning and Aid in Bypassing or Minimizing the Effects of an Auditory Processing (Ga) Deficit

Classroom Instructional Factors	Instructional Materials	Environmental Factors	Strategies
Enunciates sounds in words in an emphatic manner when teaching new words for reading or spelling	Video clips	Rules for talking and listening	Use comprehension monitoring (e.g., Does the word I heard/read make sense in context?)
Uses instructional techniques (e.g., work preview/ text preview) to clarify unknown words	Read aloud texts/features	Spelling lists	Engage in self-advocacy (e.g., asking for information to be repeated and/or clarified in regard to the misheard part)
Provides instructional supports (e.g., guided notes) during note-taking activities	Audio glossaries	Closed doors	Physically positioning oneself toward/ close to the speaker
Builds in time for clarification questions related to "missed" or "misheard" items during lecture	Supplement oral instructions with written instructions	Closed windows	Attending to speaker's mouth and/or gestures, facial expressions, during the delivery of information
Shortens instructions	Phonemic awareness activities	Distraction-free seating	Recording notes via audio methods to allow a mechanism for being able to fill in notes for completeness
Makes an effort to minimize background noise via the use of instructional commands (e.g., work quietly, refrain from talking with your neighbor)	Electronic textbooks	Noise minimizers (carpet, noise-reducing headphones)	Following along with written directions/text during the provision of oral instruction
Repeats or rephrases questions asked by other students to ensure that all students "hear" the question that is associated with the teacher's given response	Guided notes, graphic organizers	Preferential seating (close to teacher, away from heaters, fans)	Practicing spelling lists with visually based techniques
Emphasizes sight-word reading		Localize sound source for student by standing closer when delivering instructions	Use visualization strategies to remember things
Pauses when delivering oral instruction to allow time for student to process auditory information			Use written mediums (e.g., email, text) to preserve content/integrity of information communicated

Rapid Reference 1.17 Factors That May Facilitate Learning and Aid in Bypassing or Minimizing the Effects of a Long-Term Storage and Retrieval (Glr) Deficit

Classroom Instructional Factors	Instructional Materials	Environmental Factors	Strategies
Uses close-ended questions, yes/ no, true/false	Guided lists for implementing procedures, formulas	Procedural charts	Organizes material to be learned using visual aids (e. g., diagrams, flowcharts), auditory aids (e.g., chunking), or other tangibles (e.g., flash cards)
Uses consistent instructional routines	Practice guides	Word walls	Makes connections by relating material to be learned to oneself
Offers repeated practice with and review of newly presented information	Online review	Desk organizers	Relates concepts to be learned to one another via tools such as a concept map
Teaches memory strategies and encourages their use (verbal rehearsal to support encoding, use of mnemonic devices; Dehn, 2010)	Glossaries (electronic, audio, printed)	External memory aids (lists, audible timers)	Creates a schedule for distributed practice of material to be learned
Uses multiple modalities when teaching new concepts (pair written or visual with verbal information) to support dual recoding (Dehn, 2010)	Study guides	Calendars with visual references to due dates	Plans for regular review of material
Limits the amount of new material to be learned; introduces new concepts gradually and with a lot of context	Review sheets	Visual reminders (Post-its, color-coded systems)	Rehearses material to be learned via recitation, repetition

(continued)

(continued)

Is mindful of when new concepts are presented	Dictionaries (to support word retrieval)	Quiet environment or noise-reduction aids (headphones, cubicles, study carrels)	Studies and completes homework in a designated location with necessary materials
Makes associations between newly learned and prior information explicit	Thesaurus (to build vocabulary and minimize impact of retrieval weaknesses)	Preferential seating to minimize distractions when encoding	Uses active learning strategies (note-taking, flash cards, concept maps, chunking) in review sessions
Uses lists to facilitate recall (prompts)			Studies and reviews learning material immediately prior to sleeping
Expands vocabulary to minimize impact of word retrieval deficits			Uses organizational strategies such as semantic clustering (Dehn, 2010)
Builds in wait-time for student when fluency of retrieval is an issue			Uses verbal association strategies (eg, elaboration; Dehn, 2010)
Uses text previews to "prime" knowledge			Implements dual coding strategies (visual to verbal and vice versa)
Provides background knowledge first before asking a question to "prime" student for retrieval			Engages in self-testing
			Uses specific strategies for academic tasks (eg, PQRST, for reading comprehension; Dehn 2010)

Rapid Reference 1.18 Factors That May Facilitate Learning and Aid in Bypassing or Minimizing the Effects of a Processing Speed (Gs) Deficit

Classroom Instructional Factors	Instructional Materials	Environmental Factors	Strategies
Focuses on features of work products that are unrelated to time parameters (e.g., quality or accuracy of a response)	Practice guides	Clocks	Plan for long-term projects by using a realistic schedule that allows for consistent movement toward completion
Repeated practice	Online review	Written schedules	Preview important parts of text (end-of-chapter questions, title, subtitles, glossary of terms) to facilitate reading speed
Offers speed drills	Use computer activities that require quick, simple decisions	Desk organizers	Apply planning and time management strategies
	Books on tape		Use techniques such as skimming and scanning for reading activities
Extended time	Online activities/games (e.g., http://www .arcademicskillbuilders.com/ games/)		Use an outlining strategy for note-taking
Reduces the quantity of work required (including homework)			
Increases wait-times both after questions are asked and after responses are given			
Choral repeated reading			

Rapid Reference 1.19 Factors That May Facilitate Learning and Aid in Bypassing or Minimizing the Effects of a Visual Processing (Gv) Deficit

Classroom Instructional Factors	Instructional Materials	Environmental Factors	Strategies
Provide oral explanation for visual concepts	Video clips	Color-coded Information	Uses orthographic strategies for decoding (e.g., word length, shape of word); Uses "cover-copy-compare" technique—go to: http://www amblesideprimary.com/ambleweb/lookcover/lookcover.html
Reviews spatial concept and supports comprehension through use of hands-on activities and manipulatives (e.g., using models to demonstrate the moon's orbital path).	Enlarged text (via online zoom feature or alternative print copy of textbook, worksheet)	Preferential seating aimed at allowing the student to access visual material (e.g., smart board) manipulatives, visual aids, and other materials to support learning	Capitalizes on intact or strong auditory skills during learning/studying (e.g., uses phonemic skills for decoding tasks)
Provides verbal label for visual representations (e.g., "The shaded red bars represent women's votes, the green bars represent men's votes")	Highlights margins during writing tasks	Assigned note-taking buddy	Pairs visual information with verbal (mnemonics)
Provides written copies of oral instructions, lectures	Provides direct handwriting practice	Readers or scribes, where needed	Labels visual charts/graphs with verbal labels
Auditory cueing to supplement visual information/cues (e.g., "Look at the bar graph for weekly sales")	Provides visual supports (graphic organizers, graph paper)	Reduce visual distraction	Highlights or color codes important information

Provides graph-paper to assist with number alignment

Books on tape

Text-to-speech technology (screen and text readers)

Reading/scanning pens

Alternative lighting (natural light, non-fluorescent lighting)

Uses aids to support visual tracking (finger, index card, ruler)

Spaces items on a page

Uses applications or supports that allow for enlargement of fonts

Uses note-taking strategies (e.g., Cornell, outlining)

Rapid Reference 1.20 Factors That May Facilitate Learning and Aid in Bypassing or Minimizing the Effects of a Short-Term Memory (Gsm) Deficit

Classroom Instructional Factors	Instructional Materials	Environmental Factors	Strategies
Offers repetition of information	Practice guides	Color-coded information	Apply rote strategies (e.g., basic rehearsal, simple repetition) for information to be learned in the short-term
Reviews information and newly presented concepts often	Guided study	Math-facts tables (e.g., multiplication)	Encourage use of relational strategies (e.g., mnemonics)
Delivers information in manageable parts	Online review	Written schedules	Use elaborative rehearsal (associating new information with prior knowledge)
Evidences use of consistent instructional routines	Flash cards	Visual schedules (e.g., pictures)	Semantic rehearsal (creating a sentence using things to be remembered)
Uses meaningful stimuli to assist with encoding and allow for experiential learning (i.e., learning while doing)	Multisensory materials to facilitate encoding	Written reminders (homework)	Chunking
Provides opportunities for repeated practice and review			Paraphrasing
Provides supports (e.g., lecture notes, guided notes, study guides, written directions) to supplement oral instruction			Visual mnemonics (imagery, pegwords, loci, keyword method; Dehn, 2008)

Breaks down instructional steps for student	Chaining
Provides visual support (e.g., times table) to support acquisition of basic math facts	First-letter mnemonics
Outlines math procedures for student and provides procedural guides or flashcards for the student to use when approaching problems	Use tangible reminders (alarms, to-do lists, calendar schedules)
Highlights important information within a word problem	Apply specific academic strategies (e.g. write out all math computations, use a calculator, spellchecker)
Has students write all steps and show all work for math computations	
Uses writing programs or techniques that emphasize drafting first (e.g., Draft Builder 6)	
Teaches chunking strategies	

Step 5: Integrate Data From All Previous Steps, Design and Implement an Intervention, and Monitor Its Effectiveness

In this final step, practitioners integrate all data from Steps 1 through 4 to design and document an intervention. As seen in Rapid Reference 1.21, the SMAARTI Planning Form is organized into five columns. Practitioners should use information from the DOTI form to assist in planning and selecting educational strategies and tailoring interventions.

Ayden has several academic areas targeted for intervention. Ayden's difficulties in reading, math, and writing are related partly to associated cognitive weaknesses. The manifestations of these weaknesses and specific interventions and recommendations for addressing them appear in Rapid Reference 1.21.

Ayden's difficulties in reading decoding appear to be related partly to his Ga weakness in phonetic coding. These difficulties appear to be maintained partly by the fact that Ayden does not apply phonetic coding strategies and, instead, relies on the visual features of words in an attempt to decode them. While he has been fairly successful with this strategy and has acquired sight-word decoding skills (e.g., Letter Word Identification, SS = 90, Average), he is struggling in content areas, such as social studies and science, where new technical terms are introduced (e.g., *symbiotic, injustice*) that do not lend themselves easily to visual analysis. To support his decoding, and subsequent comprehension, it is suggested that Ayden use *audio glossaries* that accompany his science and social studies texts so that he can hear the words and definitions read aloud to him before he begins a new lesson. Beyond audio glossaries, an environmental accommodation, namely *preferential seating*, is suggested for Ayden. This is primarily due to Ayden's reported concerns with reading aloud in front of his classmates. Given his concern of social repercussions of his reading weaknesses (e.g., feeling embarrassed in front of his peers), Ayden is less likely to access teacher support to assist him in decoding unknown words. Preferential seating, close to the teacher's desk, can allow Ayden to access help more inconspicuously and can allow his teacher to monitor his need for help (e.g., she can have a bird's-eye view of his reading behaviors, such as pausing, that might suggest a difficulty with decoding). Finally, the *Great Leaps* program, which is presently used by Ayden's reading specialist, is recommended for continued use given its applicability to his age, his familiarity with and motivation in the program, and its focus on building fluency. Notwithstanding, because the phonemic awareness component of the program is primarily presented in the earlier grades, a *supplemental phonemic awareness activity* is being suggested for Ayden to be used at each reading session. This activity can be obtained via the use of the Month-by-Month Phonics and Vocabulary workbook.

Rapid Reference 1.21 / Review of Ayden's Cognitive Weakness–Academic Weakness Relationships

Academic Targets for Intervention (Step 1)	Suggested Remedial Program	Related Cognitive Weakness(es) (Step 2)	Manifestations of Cognitive Weakness(es) (Step 3)	Suggested MARC Interventions and Recommendations (Step 4)
Reading Decoding	Great Leaps Month-by-Month Phonics and Vocabulary, Grade 5 (Cunningham, Loman, & Arens, 2007)	Ga—Phonetic Coding	Does not use phonetic strategies consistently	Audio glossaries Preferential seating
Reading Fluency	Great Leaps	Gs, Glr	Reading is slow and laborious	Shortened passages Text preview
Reading Comprehension	Great Leaps	Glr, Gf	Has difficulty retelling what he has read in monthly book reports	Think-alouds Cooperative reading Cause/effect graphic organizers
Math Fluency	Arcademics	Gs	Is accurate but slow	Abbreviated math minutes with charting

(continued)

(continued)

Math Problem Solving		Glr, Gf	Difficulty with word problems	Math mnemonics Math concept card Procedural chart
Spelling	Folding-in technique; cover-copy-compare	Ga—Phonetic Coding	Mishears words frequently	Word wall Spellchecker Spelling dictionary with graph Preferential seating
Written Expression	Inspiration	Glr, Gf	Does not use newly learned vocabulary in writing assignments; note-taking is verbatim	Sentence strips Word bank Word wall Thesaurus Feedback Guided notes

While Great Leaps can also be used to address Ayden's difficulties with reading fluency, two additional recommendations, namely *shortened passages* and *text preview*, are recommended. The modification of shortened passages during class-wide independent reading is recommended primarily because Ayden's reading is described consistently as slow and laborious. Further, given his concerns about reading more slowly than his peers, Ayden has attempted to compensate by rushing through the reading, which has always resulted in difficulty with comprehension questions. When he reads at a more measured pace, he typically does not finish the passage and, as a result, often needs to answer the reading questions at home, which then necessitates a full rereading of the passage, thereby lengthening the amount of time spent in homework. Shortened passages can build his confidence by allowing him to finish his work at a similar rate as his peers, can facilitate his comprehension of the passages as it reduces the perceived need to rush, and, finally, can make a more efficient use of homework time as he will only need to read new material (if the remaining part of the assignment is still required of him). To further support his reading fluency, it is suggested that Ayden engage in a text preview whereby he reviews the chapter or passage title, headings, and new vocabulary prior to being tasked with reading a passage during class. While shortened passages can accommodate partly Ayden's weakness in Gs, the text previews can serve as a primer that can circumvent the impact of his Glr weakness (e.g., speed of lexical access).

In terms of reading comprehension, in addition to the Great Leaps program, it is recommended that Ayden's teacher continue to use *cooperative reading groups*, but pair him with a student with strong reasoning skills who can serve as a model during guided *think-alouds* (e.g., activities that help externalize the reasoning process by explicitly pointing out connections during reading, such as characters' feelings and their behaviors). To facilitate Ayden's comprehension and encoding of what he has read, and circumvent the full impact of his reasoning difficulties, it is also recommended that he use *graphic organizers* during reading tasks, specifically those that allow for relationships (e.g., cause and effect) to be readily seen.

Based on the evaluation data, Ayden has a specific weakness in processing speed (Gs) that impacts not only reading fluency, but also the automaticity with which he completes math problems. As described by his teacher, when Ayden completes "mad math minutes" with the class, he is always the last one working and rarely, if ever, completes a full sheet. As a result, Ayden has become averse to this daily math practice and has begun to show signs of escape/avoidance (e.g., asks to use the bathroom, repeatedly drops his pencil on the floor during the timed minute). To build Ayden's confidence and facilitate his engagement with this task, it is suggested that the *math minutes be abbreviated* (20 problems instead of 30). Additionally, it is recommended that Ayden *graph his progress* in terms of total numbers of items completed in a minute and total number of items accurate. Given that Ayden's accuracy is already high, it is expected that this latter number will be consistently high, thereby providing an immediate opportunity for positive feedback and reinforcement. The abbreviated sheet is expected to positively impact the total number of items completed, thereby building Ayden's confidence. The daily graphing will allow Ayden to focus on his individual progress rather than use his peers as a benchmark for judging himself. Finally, this format (graphing) capitalizes on Ayden's reported interest in working with visuals and is expected to be motivating in and of itself.

To further strengthen Ayden's automaticity with math facts, repeated practice in the home is recommended. Rather than focus on drill and practice via traditional methods (flashcards), a fun, web-based program, called *Arcademics*, is recommended. This website has several math games, presented in an arcade-like format. The Arcademics games are particularly attractive as a home-based intervention as they are also available as apps on the iPad, which increases the mobility of this intervention, an important consideration for Ayden, who spends two days a week at his grandmother's home after school. The games, such as Jet-Ski addition, provide visual feedback as well as audio feedback to Ayden relating to the accuracy and speed of his response (e.g., his jet-ski is propelled forward, at a fast pace, with accurate and quick responding).

Beyond fluency, Ayden's deficits within the areas of reasoning (Gf) and retrieval (Glr) limit his ability to apprehend patterns or underlying rules within problems as well as to retrieve procedures necessary to complete problems. To circumvent the impact of these weaknesses, it is recommended that Ayden be taught specific *mnemonics* to assist him with retrieving steps or sequences necessary to compute problems (e.g., PDMAS) and that he use a *math concept card* that is organized into four quadrants with each of four operations represented (i.e., addition, subtraction, multiplication, and division) along with associated words that denote each operation (e.g., "in all," "sum," "in total," "altogether" would appear under the addition symbol). Together, these supports are intended to facilitate Ayden's ability to identify the computations and/or procedures required to complete math word problems.

In writing, several interventions are recommended for Ayden. An initial recommendation is to allow Ayden to use *Inspiration software* during independent writing tasks. This visually based writing software program allows Ayden to capitalize on his relative Gv strength and can help circumvent the impact of his Gf weakness as it allows him to see relationships between concepts/ideas given the graphic organizer type format. Additional recommendations such as providing Ayden with *word banks* during the completion of specific tasks (e.g., answering end-of-chapter questions and/or short-answer test questions in content areas such as science or social studies) are offered. To facilitate his self-advocacy skills, it is suggested that Ayden be reminded of, and encouraged to reference, his classroom *word wall*, which contains a cumulative listing of weekly vocabulary words. It is hoped that this classroom resource will encourage Ayden to use newly learned vocabulary in his weekly writing assignments. Given that increasing one's vocabulary can minimize the full impact of a retrieval deficit, building Ayden's vocabulary is important. One way to achieve this is through implementing an instructional recommendation that involves having Ayden's teacher provide *feedback* on his writing by circling specific words and offering another term that is similar in meaning as well as circling one or two terms for which Ayden can offer an alternative. To accomplish this, Ayden can use a *thesaurus* to locate the circled terms and then select, from the listed choices, another word that would be equally effective in communicating his thoughts. Beyond a physical thesaurus, Ayden can be taught to use the thesaurus function in Microsoft Word.

Presently, Ayden takes notes verbatim as his retrieval difficulties impact his ability to quickly paraphrase what the teacher is saying and it also impacts the sequencing/organization of his thoughts. To address the latter issue, *sentence strips* are recommended during writing tasks. Use of such strips allows Ayden to write discrete thoughts or facts, as they come to mind, and then physically manipulate the strips into an organized, cohesive sequence, after he has generated discrete thoughts. To address his difficulty with paraphrasing or summarizing, *guided notes* are recommended. Such a support can help circumvent the impact of Ayden's Glr weakness. Further, guided notes can minimize memory demands during note-taking, thereby allowing Ayden to more fully attend to the lesson. Finally, the earlier recommendation for preferential seating is relevant to addressing Ayden's note-taking difficulties in that it can minimize any auditory distractions that might otherwise increase the frequency with which he mishears words. Further, it allows him and the teacher to have easy access to one another. As such, Ayden can more privately secure assistance with writing tasks and the teacher can discreetly check in with him during such tasks.

To address Ayden's spelling weaknesses and maximize the utility of the classroom word wall, Ayden can be reminded to reference this wall to assist him with spelling recently learned words. It is also suggested that Ayden be encouraged to use the *spellchecker function* on computer-based writing assign-ments. Based on his mastery of words, Ayden will be asked to build a *spelling dictionary*, generating an entry for each newly mastered word. Finally, it is suggested that his reading teacher use the *folding-in technique* with Ayden to build his sight-word reading/spelling skills. This technique aims to increase spelling/reading skills via a flashcard method that involves presenting 10 words, seven of which are known and three of which are "unknown." This 70/30 ratio of known to unknown results in consistently high rates of success during the task, with the aim of improving Ayden's confidence and motivation. To reinforce the words presented by his reading teacher, a recommendation to allow Ayden repeated practice via a *cover-copy-compare* web-based program is offered. With this program, Ayden's mother can build a word list containing the 10 words used in the folding-in technique. The computer program will show each word in isolation, then after Ayden right clicks the "cover" button, a hand will swipe in from the left side of the screen to cover the word, at which point Ayden will type the word and select the "compare" button. The hand will retract and the correctly spelled word will be revealed for comparison.

Practitioners should develop a plan for monitoring interventions and evaluating their benefit. Depending on their use and benefit, practitioners will summarize an outcome of the recommendations and suggest next steps. The next steps can involve one of three actions, Retain (RT), Refine (RF), or Reduce/Eliminate (RD/E). If the recommendation is being used and is working, the recommendation can be retained. If an element of the recommendation is not particularly effective or if there is an identified factor that can maximize its effectiveness, it can be refined. Finally, if the intended benefit is achieved (e.g., spelling accuracy increases substantially and consistently) or if the intensity of the recommendation can be adjusted, the support can be eliminated and/or reduced. It is important to distinguish between refining and reducing. A reduction of a support does not involve changing the support; rather, it involves modifying the frequency or intensity with which the support is delivered. A refinement involves changing an aspect of the recommendation.

SUMMARY

School psychologists and other practitioners involved in the assessment of students with learning difficulties routinely collect data related to students' social, emotional, behavioral, academic, and cognitive functioning. Parent intakes, classroom observations, teacher and student interviews, administration of standardized tests, and record reviews represent routine assessment activities. Despite the time and effort necessary to collect these data, they are rarely integrated in a systematic manner for use in tailoring interventions. Rather, data from comprehensive evaluations are used typically to determine a student's eligibility for special education services. While eligibility decisions are important and often drive the delivery of intervention resources, it is difficult to make sound choices regarding the nature and type of intervention needed for any given student without a detailed review of multiple data sources, including data gathered from cognitive assessment.

This chapter described a *Systematic Method of Analyzing Assessment Results for Tailoring Interventions* (SMAARTI) for students with learning difficulties. This method allows practitioners to define targets for intervention via a careful, research-based analysis of a student's quantitative and qualitative cognitive and academic strengths and weaknesses. The steps of SMAARTI assist the practitioner in understanding evidence-based connections between below-average cognitive and academic deficits and determining qualitative manifestations of observed cognitive weaknesses or deficits in real-world (e.g., classroom) performances. Once a student's unique below-average cognitive-academic consistencies are determined, SMAARTI assists the practitioner in tailoring interventions for the student. Ultimately, SMAARTI encourages practitioners to collect multiple data sources using multiple data gathering methods to ensure that any intervention that is recommended for a student is targeted specifically to his or her unique learning needs.

REFERENCES

Burchers (2000). *Vocabulary cartoons.*

Cooney, S. M., Huser, M., Small, S., & O'Connor, C. (2007). Evidence-based programs: An overview. *What Works, Wisconsin–Research to Practice Series, 6.* Madison, WI: University of Wisconsin–Madison/Extension.

Cunningham, P. M., Loman, K. L., & Arens, A. B. (2007). *Month-by-month phonics and vocabulary, grade 5.* Greensboro, NC: Carson-Dellosa.

Dehn, M. J. (2008). *Working memory and academic learning: Assessment and intervention.* Hoboken, NJ: John Wiley & Sons.

Dehn, M. J. (2010). *Long-term memory problems in children and adolescents: Assessment, intervention, and effective instruction.* Hoboken, NJ: John Wiley & Sons.

Della Toffalo, D. (2010). Linking school neuropsychology with response-to-intervention models. In D.C. Miller (Ed.) *Best practices in school neuropsychology: Guidelines for effective practice, assessment, and evidence-based interventions* (pp. 159–184). New York, NY: Guilford.

Della Toffalo, & Douglas, A. (2010). Best practices in school neuropsychology: Guidelines for effective practice, assessment, and evidence-based intervention. In D.C. Miller (Ed.), *Best practices in school neuropsychology* (pp. 159–183). Hoboken, NJ: John Wiley & Sons.

Elliott, S. N., Witt, J. C., Kratochwill, T. R., & Callan Stoiber, K. (2002). Selecting and evaluating classroom interventions. In M. R. Shinn, H. M. Walker, & G. Stoner (Eds.), *Interventions for academic and behavior problems II: Preventive and remedial approaches* (pp. 243–294). Bethesda, MD: National Association of School Psychologists.

Feifer, S. G. (2011). How SLD manifests in reading. In D. P. Flanagan & V. C. Alfonso (Eds.), *Essentials of specific learning disability identification* (pp. 21–42). Hoboken, NJ: Wiley.

Feifer, S. G., & DeFina, P. D. (2002a). *The neuropsychology of written language disorders: Diagnosis and intervention.* Middletown, MD: School Neuropsych Press.

Feifer, S. G., & DeFina, P. D. (2002b). *The neuropsychology of mathematics: Diagnosis and intervention.* Middletown, MD: School Neuropsych Press.

Feifer, S. G., & Della Toffalo, D. A. (2007). *Integrating RTI with cognitive neuropsychology: A scientific approach to reading.* Middletown, MD: School Neuropsych Press.

Flanagan, D. P., & Alfonso, V. C. (2011). *Essentials of specific learning disability identification.* Hoboken, NJ: John Wiley & Sons.

Flanagan, D. P., Alfonso, V. C., & Mascolo, J. T. (2011). A CHC-based operational definition of SLD: Integrating multiple data sources and multiple data gathering methods. In D. P. Flanagan & V. C. Alfonso (Eds.), *Essentials of specific learning disability identification* (pp. 233–298). Hoboken, NJ: Wiley.

Flanagan, D. P., & Alfonso, V. C., & Ortiz, S. O. (2012). The cross-battery assessment approach: An overview, historical perspective, and current directions. In D. P. Flanagan and P. L. Harrison (Eds.), *Contemporary intellectual assessment: Theories, tests and issues* (3rd ed., pp. 459–483). New York, NY: Guilford Press.

Flanagan, D. P., Ortiz, S. O., & Alfonso, V. C. (2013). *Essentials of cross-battery assessment* (3rd ed.). Hoboken, NJ: John Wiley & Sons.

Flanagan, D. P., Ortiz, S. O., Alfonso, V. C., & Mascolo, J. T. (2006). *The achievement test desk reference (ATDR): A guide to learning disability identification.* Boston, MA: Allyn & Bacon.

Fletcher, J. M., Lyon, G. R., Fuchs, L. S., & Barnes, M. A. (2007). *Learning disabilities: From identification to intervention.* New York, NY: Guilford Press.

Fletcher-Janzen, E., & Reynolds, C. R. (Eds.). (2008). *Neuropsychological perspectives on learning disabilities in the era of RTI: Recommendations for diagnosis and intervention.* Hoboken, NJ: Wiley.

Floyd, R. G., Clark, M. H., & Shadish, W. R. (2008, Aug.). The exchangeability of IQs: Implications for professional psychology. *Professional Psychology: Research and Practice, 39,* 414–423.

Hale, J. B., & Fiorello, C. A. (2004). *School neuropsychology: A practitioner's handbook.* New York, NY: Guilford Press.

Hale, J. B., Wycoff, K. L., & Fiorello, C. A. (2011). RTI and cognitive hypothesis testing for identification and intervention of specific learning disabilities: The best of both worlds. In D. P. Flanagan & V. C. Alfonso (Eds.), *Essentials of specific learning disability identification* (pp. 173–201). Hoboken, NJ: John Wiley & Sons.

Juarez, B. M. (2012). *Effects of general and specific cognitive abilities on reading achievement in a referred sample.* New York, NY: St. John's University.

Mascolo, J. T. (2008). *Linking assessment to intervention: The SMART approach* (Invited presentation). New York, NY: Fordham University-Lincoln Center.

Mather, N., & Jaffe, L. E. (2002). *Woodcock-Johnson III: Reports, recommendations, and strategies.* New York, NY: John Wiley & Sons.

Mather, N., Lynch, K., & Richards, A. M. (2001). The thinking blocks: Language, images and strategies. In S. Goldstein & N. Mather (Eds.) *Learning disabilities and challenging behaviors: A guide to intervention and classroom management.* Baltimore, MD: Brookes.

McGrew, K. S., Flanagan, D. P., Keith, T. Z., & Vanderwood, M. (1997). Beyond g: The impact of Gf-Gc specific cognitive abilities research on the future use and interpretation of intelligence tests in the schools. *School Psychology Review, 26,* 189–210.

McGrew, K. S., & Wendling, B. J. (2010, Aug.). Cattell-Horn-Carroll cognitive-achievement relations: What have we learned from the past 20 years of research? *Psychology in the Schools*, *47*(7) (Special Issue: Current research in Cattell-Horn-Carroll-based Assessment), 651–675.

Miller, D. C. (Ed.). (2010). *Best practices in school neuropsychology*. Hoboken, NJ: Wiley.

Miller, D. C. (2013). *Essentials of school neuropsychological assessment* (2nd ed.). Hoboken, NJ: Wiley.

Packer, L. E., & Pruitt, S. K. (2010). *Challenging kids, challenged teachers*. Bethesda, MD: Woodbine House.

Schmuckler, M. A. (2001). What is ecological validity? A dimensional analysis. *Infancy*, *2*(4), 419–436.

Schneider, W. J., & McGrew, K. (2012). The Cattell-Horn-Carroll model of intelligence. In D. Flanagan & P. Harrison (Eds.), *Contemporary Intellectual Assessment: Theories, Tests, and Issues* (3rd ed.) (pp. 99–144). New York: Guilford.

Vanderwood, M. L., McGrew, K. S., Flanagan, D. P., & Keith, T. Z. (2001). The contribution of general and specific cognitive abilities to reading achievement. *Learning and Individual Differences*, *13*(2) (Special Issue: Is *g* a viable construct for school psychology?), 159–188.

Woodcock, R. W., McGrew, K. S., & Mather, N. (2001, 2007) *Woodcock-Johnson III Tests of Achievement Normative Update*. Rolling Meadows, IL: Riverside.

🐾 TEST YOURSELF 🐾

1. **The evidence-based programs listed on sites such as What Works Clearinghouse (WWC) and the Florida Center for Reading Research (FCRR), and implemented with a student, serve as an example of:**

   a. A modification

   b. An accommodation

   c. Remediation

   d. Compensation

2. **When do you engage in SMAARTI?**

   a. As a pre-referral step

   b. During an initial evaluation

   c. After a student fails to respond to evidence-based interventions

   d. All of the above

3. **A comprehensive evaluation includes, but is not limited to, which of the following:**

   a. Educational history and current academic performance

   b. Familial factors and medical history

   c. Cognitive performance

   d. Behavioral and social-emotional functioning

   e. All of the above are part of a comprehensive evaluation

(continued)

(*continued*)

4. **All of the following are examples of primary evaluation data *except:***
   a. Standardized cognitive and academic scores
   b. Progress monitoring data
   c. Scores from district-wide testing programs
   d. Data from work sample analysis

5. ***True or False?*: Information relating to instructional materials used with a student is an example of tertiary data.**

6. **Secondary data typically provides information about characteristics that are**
   a. Related to the child's instructional materials
   b. Related to the child's instructional environment
   c. Related to intrinsic characteristics of the child him- or herself
   d. Operating in the child's home environment

7. **Step 3 of SMAARTI involves which of the following?**
   a. Reviewing manifestations of cognitive weaknesses
   b. Organizing secondary data
   c. Identifying types of academic skill deficits
   d. Identifying initial targets for intervention
   e. All of the above

8. **Aligning math problems vertically as opposed to horizontally, having a student dictate responses to a scribe, or providing a student with a separate room to complete work all serve as an example of:**
   a. A modification
   b. An accommodation
   c. Remediation
   d. Compensation

9. **Reducing the amount of material that a student is required to learn, simplifying material to be learned, or requiring a student to answer only a subset of a specific type of question on a mixed facts sheet all serve as an example of:**
   a. A modification
   b. An accommodation
   c. Remediation
   d. Compensation

10. **Teaching a student to use mnemonic devices or to outline and use graphic organizers is an example of:**
    a. A modification
    b. An accommodation
    c. Remediation
    d. Compensation

11. *True or False?*: **Understanding cognitive weaknesses and their relation to academic weaknesses is necessary for program planning in the SMAARTI approach.**

Answers: 1. c; 2. d; 3. e; 4. d; 5. T; 6. c; 7. e; 8. b; 9. a; 10. d; 11. T

Two

ESSENTIALS OF A TIERED INTERVENTION SYSTEM TO SUPPORT UNIQUE LEARNERS: RECOMMENDATIONS FROM RESEARCH AND PRACTICE

Devin M. Kearns
Christopher J. Lemons
Douglas Fuchs
Lynn S. Fuchs

Responsiveness-to-intervention (RTI) is a common way to think about preventing academic difficulties in children at-risk for specific learning disabilities (SLD). The idea of RTI is to prevent academic difficulties by providing evidence-based instruction at a level of intensity necessary for each student. Different students require different amounts of teacher support to be successful. Under RTI, schools provide all students with the specific level of support they require (Vaughn, Linan-Thompson, & Hickman, 2003). This means that students receive different levels—or tiers—of support based on their level of need. Figure 2.1 illustrates the idea that we want to find a level of intensity that is—just like Goldilocks looking for a chair—"just right" for the student we are teaching. We want the level of intensity to reflect the level of student need.

In this chapter, we provide details to help school teams design, implement, and determine the effectiveness of a multitier RTI system of support. We include guidelines for each step of this process, with emphasis on Tier 2 and Tier 3 support. We also address issues related to RTI implementation in middle and high school (Fuchs & Deshler, 2007; King, Lemons, & Hill, 2012), which is important

Tier 3

Tier 2

Tier 1

Least intense
- Large groups
  - Student self-managed instruction
  - Peer-mediated instruction
- Less explicit instruction
- Higher-level skills
  - Critical thinking
  - Grade-level content
- Instructors with knowledge of ways to push students' thinking and make them good self-motivated and self-regulated learners

More intense
- Small groups
- Explicit instruction
- Some basic and some higher-level skills
  - Math: Basic facts, computation, number sense, some problem solving
  - Reading: Decoding and fluency, some comprehension
- Strong instructors or highly-scripted program with adequate instructors who have received PD

Most intense
- Smallest groups
  - Tutoring
  - Pairs with teacher
- Highly explicit, simplified instruction
  - Very simple, clear language
  - Slow release of responsibility
- Basic skills
  - Math: Basic facts, computation, number sense
  - Reading: Decoding and fluency
- Instructors with knowledge of many ways to adapt programs to meet individual needs

Figure 2.1. Differences in Intensity Among Three Tiers of Instruction

In *Goldilocks*, she was looking for a chair that was "just right." For students, we are looking for an intensity of instruction that is also just right.

because RTI was initially conceptualized around the idea of preventing and remediating reading difficulties in early elementary school.

PRELIMINARY INFORMATION ABOUT RTI

Problem Solving Versus Standard Protocol

Although the term *RTI* is familiar to many, we review its structure because there are multiple models and various terms to describe the process. There are two prominent models of RTI, one called "problem solving" and the other "standard protocol." Problem solving involves a process of making decisions about interventions to meet individual students' needs, evaluating the effectiveness of these interventions, and then making new decisions about how to help the student based on the evidence collected. Whether the problem-solving model provides good evidence has been difficult to establish because it is difficult for researchers to test (Fuchs, Mock,

Morgan, & Young, 2003), but the idea of individualizing instruction is a good one. It has also been an important feature of special education for many years.

The standard protocol—which is our focus here—is different in that it involves a more rigid set of procedures for the first two tiers of intervention. The first tier, called *Tier 1* or *primary prevention*, involves the use of evidence-based academic curricula for reading and mathematics, implemented well by general education teachers. The second tier, *Tier 2* or *secondary prevention*, requires general education teachers to implement a structured, evidence-based program that provides targeted instruction in foundational basic skills for children who do not respond to Tier 1. The third tier, *Tier 3* or *tertiary prevention*, is used when students demonstrate poor response to Tier 2 instruction. In some versions of the standard protocol, Tier 3 is special education. We focus on the standard protocol approach to RTI for two important reasons. First, the value of a standard protocol system of tiered intervention has been demonstrated in a variety of studies examining beginning reading (Compton, Fuchs, Fuchs, & Bryant, 2006; McMaster, Fuchs, Fuchs, & Compton, 2005; Vadasy, Jenkins, & Pool, 2000), beginning math (Fuchs et al., 2008a), and middle school reading (Vaughn et al., 2010). Second, RTI systems are complicated systems that involve many moving parts—students, teachers, interventionists, curricula, and assessments are all parts of an RTI system, and it only works if they all fit together. We believe that a standard protocol approach to RTI increases the chances that school systems will be able to implement RTI efficiently and effectively because it decreases the number of moving parts in Tier 2: Only certain students are selected, teachers or interventionists receive specific training, and the curricula and assessments are determined a priori. In other words, Tier 2 is standardized and most individualization and problem solving occur primarily at Tier 3—this means that individualization will be required for fewer students and that higher-qualified interventionists will be responsible for designing and implementing instruction here. (See Fuchs et al., 2003, and Marston, 2005, for further description of the differences between standard protocol and problem-solving models.)

Progress Monitoring

Under RTI, schools monitor student progress frequently. Most often, schools use curriculum-based measurement (CBM; Deno, 1985; Fuchs & Fuchs, 2002). We will emphasize two uses of CBM, first for *universal screening* to identify at-risk students who may need Tier 2 or Tier 3 support and second for ongoing *progress monitoring* to track the improvement of at-risk students (Vaughn et al., 2003). CBM has been designed to allow teachers to measure efficiently progress toward long-term academic goals. The measures are technically adequate (e.g., have established reliability and validity) and are based upon over two decades of research (Stecker, Fuchs, & Fuchs, 2005).

CBM allows a teacher to estimate quickly whether a student is performing adequately in critical areas of instruction and to check regularly to see if the Tier 2 or Tier 3 instruction is producing academic improvement. A good way to think about CBM is to consider it an "academic thermometer" by which the teacher can quickly figure out which students are "okay" and which "have a temperature" and thus need additional attention to determine what is going on. And, once a teacher makes a plan to remediate the problem, teachers can check back often to see if the temperature is going down—signaling a positive response to intervention. An in-depth description of CBM is not the focus of this chapter. For a practical overview, see Hosp, Hosp, and Howell (2007). Additional resources include the IRIS Center (iris.peabody.vanderbilt.edu) and the National Center on Intensive Intervention (www.intensiveintervention.org).

TIER I PREVENTION

We begin with a description of the features of Tier 1 because Tier 2 and Tier 3 interventions occur in the context of Tier 1 intervention. In other words, students who are receiving higher-tier instruction almost always continue to participate in Tier 1 instruction, at least for some of the time. In addition, understanding the structure of Tier 1 will show how Tiers 2 and 3 differ in intensity.

Overview of Tier I: Evidence-Based Instruction

Tier 1 refers to the general education instruction all students are receiving from general education teachers. It includes the use of a "core program" (Baker, Fien, & Baker, 2010; Denton, 2012) that is *evidence-based* (Fuchs, Fuchs, & Stecker, 2010). By evidence-based programs, we, and others, mean programs that include instructional activities that have been studied and validated by researchers but that may not have been tested by researchers in their entirety (Fuchs, Fuchs, & Compton, 2012). For example, a Tier 1 mathematics program might include mnemonic devices to remember place value knowledge and algorithmic computation procedures (Scruggs & Mastropieri, 1990), include basic facts instruction (National Mathematics Advisory Panel, 2008), and teach children problem-solving "schemas" (Fuchs et al., 2008a; Jitendra, DiPipi, & Perron-Jones, 2002; Xin, Jitendra, & Deatline-Buchman, 2005), but this program may not have been tested by researchers as a unit. It is, therefore, evidence-based but not researched. Sometimes, schools add a particular *research-validated* program to the core program. A research-validated program is one that has been tested by researchers in its entirety and has been shown to provide positive student outcomes. Examples include:

- Class-Wide Peer Tutoring (CWPT; Greenwood, Delquadri, & Hall, 1989).
- Direct Instruction (DI; Adams & Carnine, 2003).
- Peer-Assisted Learning Strategies (PALS; Fuchs, Fuchs, & Karns, 2000; Fuchs, Fuchs, Mathes, & Simmons, 1997).
- Self-Regulated Strategy Development (SRSD; Harris, Graham, & Mason, 2003).

Tier 1 instruction should be systematic and explicit (Baker et al., 2010); generally effective, that is, effective for most students (Speece & Case, 2001); of high quality (Gersten et al., 2009a, 2009b); focused on grade-level skills and content; and implemented with fidelity (Hill, King, Lemons, & Partanen, 2012; Peng et al., 2011).

Instructional Tools: Qualities of Good Tier 1 Programs

Here, we emphasize ways to determine how well the Tier 1 program is working for students. There are two ways to do this:

1. Work to improve the quality of implementation. A core program is only as good as its implementation, and we—in our experience as educators and researchers—have observed that great differences in the quality of implementation of Tier 1 programs strongly affect student results. We found, for example, that teachers' fidelity of implementation with particular components of PALS has a direct impact on students' reading improvement (Peng et al., 2011). Many evidence-based programs are comprehensive, complex, and written by many authors, so the components may vary in quality. For example, an elementary Tier 1 reading curriculum may have excellent reading comprehension instruction but show weakness in phonics. However, determining whether there are weaknesses depends first on high-quality initial implementation with fidelity.

2. If implementation quality is consistently high, it is appropriate to evaluate whether the Tier 1 program provides all students with adequate instructional support in all elements of the academic domain. In some cases, a supplemental research-validated Tier 1 program would provide

additional benefits for all students. For example, supplemental SRSD may help improve reading programs with weak writing components; CWPT or PALS would help programs that include too little reading practice.

Implementation

We offer suggestions for developing strong Tier 1 implementation. First, implementing teachers must have an in-depth understanding of the core program (Baker et al., 2010). Achieving this knowledge may require program-specific professional development, although this can be done without outside consultants. Teachers can use planning or in-service time to review and discuss previously provided professional development materials and within the core program, with a focus on problematic parts of the program. This can improve implementation, even if time is limited (Van Keer & Verhaeghe, 2005).

Second, we often find that conducting observations with feedback can greatly increase quality of implementation. Teams of teachers could schedule time to conduct observations of one another and then use planning time to discuss them. These conversations may be tricky if they raise concerns about implementation quality, but critical conversation is important (Frykholm, 1998). Another way to observe and exchange feedback is by video-recording and then discussing Tier 1 lessons. Video-based feedback often improves classroom practices (Borko, Jacobs, Eiteljorg, & Pittman, 2008; Seidel et al., 2009).

Progress Monitoring

At Tier 1, schools conduct universal screening three times per year—at the beginning, middle, and end—to see which students appear to be on track and identify students who may need additional support. Student performance is often compared to a set of benchmarks, scores that are considered typical for same-grade students at that time of year. The benchmarks may be provided by the publisher of the CBM assessment used or based upon local district-established norms.

Generally in early elementary school, students below the benchmark at one of the screening points receive weekly progress monitoring for an additional four to six weeks to confirm the low level of performance (i.e., ensure that the low score was not a product of the student having a bad day) and see whether the student responds to Tier 1 instruction (e.g., even though the student's score was low, she is making rapid gains and thus is likely to meet the next important benchmark without additional intervention). Schools use this four-to-six-week confirmation period because researchers have found that some students who appeared weak very early in the academic year were "false positives" who were incorrectly identified as needing additional intervention. That is, they appeared to have academic difficulty but after a few weeks of quality Tier 1 instruction (and no additional intervention), they were doing fine. Eliminating false positives helps schools maximize their resources; this way, they do not need to create additional Tier 2 groups to accommodate students who do not really have academic difficulty.

After this four-to-six-week period, students who are not demonstrating adequate response to Tier 1 are referred to Tier 2. In some cases, particularly with older students, Tier 2 instruction is provided as quickly as possible (i.e., no four-to-six-week confirmation period). Additionally, many models of RTI include teacher evaluations of students as part of the referral system. In other words, a teacher may have concerns about a child's likely response to instruction even though the child achieved above the benchmark on CBM. If resources are available, this child would often receive supplemental Tier 2 instruction as well.

Making Adjustments

We are hesitant to recommend adjustments to evidence-based programs. All of the co-authors have observed schools hurrying to replace or supplement a core program for hypothesized weaknesses when the schools have not fully implemented the core program. However, we also realize that even evidence-based programs are not designed with every school in mind. In Tier 1, teachers often have students work independently on academic tasks and accrete knowledge in their own way (Connor, Morrison, Fishman, Schatschneider, & Underwood, 2007). For many children, this is precisely the right idea; Connor, Morrison, and Petrella (2004) found, for example, that third-grade students with higher reading skills had the greatest academic gains when teachers allowed children space to learn on their own. The implication is that if the students at a school tend to be particularly high performing, they may profit from more self-directed or peer-mediated instruction than the Tier 1 program involves. So, some adjustments would be appropriate.

CAUTION

When considering adjustments to Tier 1, implement with fidelity first. After that, choose adjustments carefully. Make sure core elements stay intact.

We recommend adjustments be undertaken cautiously. After a period of high-quality implementation, initial and midyear universal screening data can be reviewed. If they reveal students making insufficient progress (e.g., too many students below benchmark or high-achieving students not far enough above), some adjustments to the program would be appropriate. Providing teachers with latitude to make some changes to their instruction after a period of implementation with fidelity may lead to better outcomes for their students (Fuchs et al., 2009). It is important, however, that changes to curricula leave core elements in place (Brown & Campione, 1996; Davis & Krajcik, 2005) and that these core elements continue to be implemented with fidelity. These core elements are those parts of the program that have the strongest evidence base, and they should remain as is. For example, if a first-grade Tier 1 reading program has an evidence-based phonics component, it makes little sense to replace this with something else.

Considerations for Secondary Schools

In middle and high schools, Tier 1 differs in at least two ways as compared to Tier 1 in elementary schools. First, secondary teachers most often do not have an evidence-based core reading or math program. Instead, each content area teacher (i.e., English/language arts, foreign language, math, social studies, science) is responsible for teaching specific academic content outlined by academic achievement standards. For Tier 1 reading, schools should make literacy instruction a priority of every core content teacher (CCAAL, 2010). Biancarosa and Snow (2006) suggested that typical middle and high school students should receive "approximately two to four hours of [daily] literacy instruction and practice that takes place in language arts and content-area classes" (p. 4). Accomplishing such a task within the typical school day will require content educators to integrate some literacy instruction into their curriculum. All content area classes should include direct, systematic, and explicit instruction in vocabulary and comprehension (Biancarosa & Snow, 2006; Kamil et al., 2008). For example, a school may identify key academic terms (e.g., *clarify*, *logical*) that can be taught in and integrated into each content area class. Teachers can all use the same procedures for introducing vocabulary words (Baumann & Kameenui, 1991; Elleman, Lindo, Morphy, & Compton, 2009). Similarly, content area teachers can directly teach and practice effective reading comprehension strategies (e.g., "Get the gist," Klingner, Vaughn, Arguelles, Hughes, & Leftwich, 2004) with content-specific texts.

Another way that Tier 1 differs in secondary schools is in universal screening. For secondary-age students, the notion of prevention is generally irrelevant—schools are keenly aware of which students need more. Current research on RTI in secondary schools (Vaughn & Fletcher, 2012) suggests that performance on the previous year's high-stakes assessment, particularly for the lowest-performing students, may be all that is needed to place students directly into either Tier 2 or Tier 3 at the beginning of the academic year.

Summary

In Tier 1 prevention, schools implement evidence-based curricula for reading and math. They choose Tier 1 programs that are systematic and explicit, effective for most students, of high quality, focused on grade-level skills and content, and implemented with fidelity. Sometimes, schools supplement the core programs with research-validated curricula that provide more practice or good instruction in an area that is weak for the Tier 1 program. To make implementation strong, teachers need in-depth knowledge of the program content and should work with their peers to exchange observations and feedback. If schools make adjustments, they should be considered after Tier 1 has been implemented with fidelity, and those adjustments should leave core elements of the curricula in place. In secondary schools, RTI for Tier 1 literacy will likely involve infusing literacy instruction—particularly to develop vocabulary and comprehension strategies—across the subject areas rather than using a single program. Secondary schools may be able to use prior-year test results or other extant assessment data rather than screening to determine Tier 2 need for additional intervention.

TIER 2 PREVENTION

For some students, Tier 1 will not be sufficiently intensive to help them succeed. They require additional support to reach academic goals. This does not necessarily mean that Tier 1 was implemented poorly. There will always be students who require greater instructional intensity to be successful. In Tier 2, like Tier 1, the goal is to achieve effective implementation of a high-quality academic program with a track record of success based on good research. The difference is that the Tier 2 program will be more intensive.

Overview of Tier 2: Intensive Instruction

The basic idea of Tier 2 instruction is to provide instruction in an intensive way, namely one that is teacher-centered, explicit, more frequent and longer in duration than Tier 1, and conducted in small groups. We will talk about each of these features.

Teacher-Centered Instruction

As we pointed out in our description of how to make adjustments to Tier 1, many children will benefit from self-directed instruction. However, children with weaker skills tend to benefit most from teacher-managed instruction (Connor et al., 2004). Students who require Tier 2 should participate in activities where they work independently and collaborate with peers as well as participate in Tier 1 instruction. However, as Connor et al. suggested, students who need Tier 2 are likely to make the greatest improvements when teachers take charge of the learning.

Explicit Instruction

Teachers often ask students to infer the goal of instruction. A common way to teach new spelling patterns, for example, is to present students with slips of paper containing words they are to categorize on their own without teacher support (Bear, Invernizzi, Templeton, & Johnston, 2007). The teacher would present *pan, pane, them, theme, bit, bite, rod, rode, tub*, and *tube* and ask students to sort the words in a way that makes sense to them. Students would conclude that half the words end with *e* and infer the silent-e rule that the words without the *e* contain short vowels and those with it are pronounced with long sounds.

For children who have failed to make adequate progress in Tier 1, inferential teaching has two drawbacks. First, it is often inefficient. Sometimes, teachers justifiably accept this on the basis that students may retain new learning better if it fits into their existing knowledge network (Anderson, Spiro, & Anderson, 1978; Brewer & Nakamura, 1984). Students who reach Tier 2, however, did not profit from this approach, so teachers should be more direct. Directly and explicitly teaching the spelling pattern in Tier 2 is likely to be more effective and efficient. Second, less explicitness can produce confusion if students draw the wrong conclusions. By providing students with clarity from the beginning, we avoid the possibility that they will misunderstand the content by constructing knowledge incorrectly (Archer & Hughes, 2011; Denton, 2012).

There are several critical features to explicit instruction. Among the most critical is that we use clear, concise statements of lesson content (Fuchs et al., 2010). The following excerpt is from a reading program developed by some of us (Kearns, Fuchs, Fuchs, Compton, & Bouton, 2012) from a lesson to teach the final-*E* rule:

TEACHER: Today, we are going learn a secret letter team. Remember, a letter team is when two letters work together and say one sound. Here's our secret letter team. (Show student O_E.) In this secret letter team, the letters *O* and *E* work together. They say /ō/. What does the letter team say?

STUDENT: /ō/.

TEACHER: That's right! This letter team says/ō/. But, there is also this blank space. (Point to blank.) In a word, a letter goes here and separates the O and E. O and E work as a team to say/ō/but it's a secret letter team because they are separated! This secret letter team is *O-BLANK-E*. What is it?

STUDENT: *O-BLANK-E*.

TEACHER: Good! Now, let's look at some words. (Show student *O-BLANK-E* words, and point to *role*.) This word has *O-BLANK-E*. The O and E work together and make the sound/ō/. In between, the letter L goes in the blank.

Notice the difference between this and the description of the Tier 1 final-*E* rule instruction. Here, the teacher explains in clear language what the sound is, what the letter is, and how the pattern works. Students are not asked to infer anything.

A second critical feature is the gradual release of responsibility, that is, the development of self-regulation (Lienemann & Reid, 2005; Zimmerman, 2000). Archer and Hughes (2011), described this as the "I do, we do, you do" sequence. This clarifies the idea that teachers are in control of the learning at the beginning of instruction ("I do") and gradually increase the amount of student responsibility ("we do") until students can do the skill themselves ("you do"). In our final-*E* example, the instruction we described is at the "I do" level. In the remainder of that lesson, the teacher models sounding out final-*E* words and then does it with the student, moving to "we do."

A third principle is to provide students with lots of feedback, positive and corrective (Gersten et al., 2009a; Slavin, 2006). Corrective feedback has a positive impact on word reading and reading comprehension (Pany & McCoy, 1988), and it can work even better than positive feedback alone for improving fluency (Eckert, Dunn, & Ardoin, 2006). Many studies examining positive reinforcement indicate that it improves academic behavior (Akin-Little, Eckert, Lovett, & Little, 2004; Darch & Gersten, 1985; Maag, 2001; Sutherland, Wehby, & Yoder, 2002), even when the reinforcement includes tangible rewards. Cameron and Pierce (1994) found that tangible rewards do not decrease intrinsic motivation, except when they are given just for completing tasks rather than meeting accuracy criteria. Overall, both positive and corrective feedback helps children with Tier 2 needs.

Frequency and Duration of Instruction
It is important that Tier 2 intervention occur with sufficient frequency and duration to produce actual improvement in students' outcomes. Researchers recommend various amounts of time, but most recommend at least 10 weeks,

4 days a week, and 30 minutes per day in the case of elementary-level Tier 2 instruction (Denton, 2012; Fuchs, Compton, Fuchs, Bryant, & Davis, 2008; Fuchs et al., 2012; Scammacca, Vaughn, Roberts, Wanzek, & Torgesen, 2007; Vaughn & Linan-Thompson, 2003; Vellutino et al., 1996). There is little guidance for secondary schools, but because their school days are organized into periods, Tier 2 is easiest to execute and also appropriate, given students' needs, as its own class.

There has been some debate about whether to recommend students for Tier 3 after just 10 weeks of Tier 2 instruction or whether teachers should try a second round of 10 weeks of Tier 2 instruction. Vaughn, Linan-Thompson, and Hickman

CAUTION

If students appear to respond to a Tier 2 intervention but have not quite met the benchmark, provide a second round of intervention. If students make little or no progress, begin Tier 3 instruction.

(2003) and Vellutino et al. (1996) suggested the value of two 10-week cycles, although Vaughn and Linan-Thompson (2003) also suggested that "movement between levels [including Tier 3] is fluid and based on progress monitoring and mastery of benchmarks" (p. 145). In other words, students might move from Tier 2 to Tier 3 and back, depending on the level of intensity the student requires. Similarly, if the student is making progress in Tier 2 and is just below the benchmark, a second round of Tier 2 is probably best. We recommend moving students to Tier 3 if they demonstrate serious and continued nonresponse after a 10-week round of Tier 2. Providing a second round of Tier 2 under these circumstances would prolong an unpleasant experience and defer instruction that would meet seriously struggling students' academic needs (Fuchs et al., 2010).

Small Groups

Teachers need a smaller group than at Tier 1 because this is the best way to assure that all of the students are attending to the explicit instruction provided and to allow the teacher sufficient time to deliver immediate, corrective feedback to these students. One-to-one tutoring by an adult would probably produce even greater gains, but small-group instruction represents the most efficient use of schools' limited human and financial resources.

The optimal group size is not clear, although Vaughn and Linan-Thompson (2003) recommended one adult with four students, and Fuchs et al. (2010) simply "small and homogeneous groups" (p. 303). We view a 4:1 student–teacher ratio as appropriate, although we also believe that the size of the groups will necessarily depend on the resources the school has available to provide instruction.

≡ Rapid Reference 2.1 What Intensive Instruction Means

- Teacher-centered
- Explicit
- Frequent (10 weeks, 4 days a week, 30 minutes a day in elementary schools; 1 class period in secondary schools)
- In small groups (4:1 student–teacher ratio is good)

Instructional Tools: Selecting a Program

Under the standard protocol, Tier 2 instruction is not designed by school personnel. That is, schools do not create their own programs or ask teachers to build lessons independently. Rather, a team at the school or the district selects a program that teachers will implement for all students who require Tier 2 support. Selecting a program can be exciting, but possibly overwhelming given the many available options. We suggest the following guidelines for selecting a program: (1) choose one that meets our definition of intensive (see Rapid Reference 2.1), (2) make sure the program addresses critical skills in the academic content area of interest, and (3) do some relatively easy homework to determine the value of different programs.

Choosing an Intensive Program

Evaluate samples of instructional materials (these can generally be acquired for free from the publisher) with an eye on whether the instruction is teacher-centered and explicit. If there are many activities with independent work, students engaging in extended group discussions, or a lack of very clear language to describe the academic content, it is probably not a good fit for Tier 2. Look for a script or a very careful guide to instruction (Fuchs et al., 2010). Also, make sure the program provides all the necessary materials. Teachers should not be required to come up with their own texts or math problems or generate worksheets and posters themselves. A good Tier 2 program will provide all of the instructional language (explicitness) and day-by-day instructional plans (a scope and sequence with all the required materials) necessary. This standardization of Tier 2 is the hallmark of the standard protocol.

Addressing Critical Skills

Intensive instruction in Tier 2 must be targeted at critical skills. It is impossible for students to learn all of the state academic standards in a 35-minute session, and that is not the intent at Tier 2. Instruction needs to focus on the skills that will lead to greatest academic success. Several of the other chapters in this book provide detailed information about the kinds of skills to emphasize in intervention, so we do not review them here. When examining programs, be aware of the critical skills for the subject and analyze programs closely to make sure they limit their focus to those that most improve academic success. In literacy, some Common Core standards for language are examples of skills we think Tier 2 instruction should exclude (e.g., Grade 3: "Explain the function of nouns, pronouns, verbs, adjectives, and adverbs"). Learning Standard English conventions is no doubt good for students, but, to put it simply, struggling readers have bigger fish to fry.

Do Some Homework to Determine the Value of Programs

When schools are in the enviable position of selecting a Tier 2 program rather than inheriting one, many good Tier 2 options are available. Less good is that the sheer number may make it hard to choose one. After eliminating programs that are not intensive and address too many noncritical skills, as we just described, there will still be many choices. At this point, select a program that has been *validated* by researchers (Fuchs et al., 2012). Although there are many programs available, many fewer have been tested by researchers in the field. The best results will likely be obtained by using a program researchers have tested and retested to determine that it works for struggling students (Fuchs, Fuchs, & Burish, 2000). Fortunately, school teams do not need to read all of the research themselves. There are several websites that provide information about programs that are likely to work well. Rapid Reference 2.2 provides some options. Schools can use these resources to make a good decision about what Tier 2 programs make sense for them.

≡ Rapid Reference 2.2 Sources for Tier 2 Interventions

- The "Instructional Interventions" tools chart created by the National Center on Response to Intervention (http://www.rti4success.org)
- The What Works Clearinghouse, created by the U.S. Department of Education's Institute of Education Sciences (http://ies.ed.gov/ncee/wwc/)
- The Best Evidence Encyclopedia (http://www.bestevidence.org/), published by researchers at Johns Hopkins University
- FCRR Reports from the Florida Center for Reading Research

Implementation

Tier 2 Interventionists

A frequently raised question is "Who is qualified to be a Tier 2 interventionist?" We use the term *interventionist* instead of *teacher* to highlight the fact that this person is providing more intensive and specialized instruction than that provided in general education. Some researchers have suggested that Tier 2 interventionists should be adults with *special training* (Fuchs et al., 2012), but they need not be the most highly qualified teachers in the building. The special training is essential to allow them to implement the Tier 2 program effectively. So, we believe that paraprofessional teachers, student teachers, or even committed parent volunteers might be able to implement Tier 2 effectively if a highly qualified instructional expert provides them good training that involves lots of practice and checks their fidelity of implementation frequently. The people chosen to implement Tier 2 must meet three simple criteria: that they (1) work well with children, (2) have patience with children who may not get concepts quickly, and (3) have good common sense to make minor instructional decisions (e.g., realize that it makes sense to ignore minor off-task behavior). If potential interventionists do not meet these simple criteria, they should not teach Tier 2.

Some may question the recommendation of using less qualified personnel (e.g., paraprofessionals) as Tier 2 interventionists. Due to the standardization of Tier 2, personnel with fewer qualifications than a certified teacher can often be highly successful provided they meet the criteria outlined above and that they receive sufficient training, support, and supervision. In addition, we understand the realities schools face: Many will be unable to provide Tier 2 support without ways to contain the cost, and using less expensive personnel is one way to limit it.

Monitoring Fidelity

Regardless of who implements Tier 2, the interventionists must implement the intervention as intended. Tier 2 programs are chosen for the design of their instruction, so it is important they are taught as designed. Most often a checklist is developed that includes essential features of the intervention (e.g., following the intervention procedures, using scripted language, providing intervention for predetermined number of minutes) and indicators of instructional quality (e.g., providing positive reinforcement, use of corrective feedback). Some Tier 2 interventions even come with a fidelity checklist.

At least several times per year, a knowledgeable observer should complete the fidelity checklist while attending a Tier 2 session. This should be done more frequently for new or inexperienced interventionists, newly adopted interventions, and during the initial stages of RTI implementation. The data collected will help determine if additional training or support is necessary to ensure that students in

Tier 2 are receiving the intended instruction (i.e., what is in the program). In many schools, an instructional coach conducts the fidelity observations. We have found that when Tier 2 interventionists and observers understand that the primary goal of fidelity is to improve instruction rather than evaluate the instructor, the process works more effectively.

Before starting Tier 2, schools will need to determine the amount of Tier 2 flexibility allowed. As we said earlier, Tier 2 interventionists should follow the program closely, but perhaps slight changes are acceptable. Schools will need to decide what adjustments are allowable. During development of the fidelity system, the RTI implementation team will need to answer questions like these: Should the observer provide credit for following the script if the interventionist uses different words? What feedback should an observer provide if an interventionist only completed one of three parts of a program lesson during an observation because he believed the students needed additional practice? We describe making adjustments in a subsequent section; that section may provide some guidance.

Progress Monitoring

Just as intensity of instruction increases at Tier 2, so does intensity of monitoring progress. Most models of RTI suggest that students who are receiving Tier 2 instruction should be assessed at least every two weeks. Most often, this assessment is done on the students' instructional level. In other words, if a fourth-grade student is reading on a second-grade level (as determined by oral reading fluency measures), the Tier 2 interventionist would most likely assess progress on a second-grade level oral reading fluency probe. This measure would be more sensitive to instructional gains than would a fourth-grade measure. However, at least three times a year (beginning-, middle-, and end-of-year), the interventionist should administer the fourth-grade measure to evaluate progress toward grade-level learning. Schools often use progress monitoring data collected at Tier 2 to determine when students should be exited from Tier 2 or when the additional intensity of Tier 3 is necessary. Often, students who reach an appropriate grade-level benchmark (e.g., 40 words read correctly per minute on first-grade text during the last half of the first-grade year) are considered to have made sufficient response and then receive Tier 1 instruction only. During their planning for RTI implementation, schools need to determine how progress monitoring data will be used to determine response or nonresponse.

Making Adjustments

The notion of making adjustments to Tier 2 instruction is an issue that will require some school-level decision making. Many proponents of the standard protocol believe that Tier 2 interventions must be implemented as designed with minimal adjustments (e.g., Denton, 2012). The idea is that in determining which students are nonresponsive to intervention (and may have specific learning disabilities), all students need to receive the same intervention. If two interventionists implement very different Tier 2 interventions, it may be challenging to evaluate why students did not respond. It may be that an interventionist's chosen intervention was not focused enough on the right critical skills.

On the other hand, two students may have failed to respond to Tier 1 for different reasons and will need different Tier 2 interventions. For example, in second grade, some nonresponsive students may need remediation in basic word recognition skills while others need fluency practice and vocabulary instruction. Exposing both of these students to the same rigidly implemented Tier 2 program would likely not meet both of their needs. Thus, we recommend that schools discuss which types of adjustments are allowable at Tier 2 within their RTI system. As a rule of thumb, schools should select a set of evidence-based Tier 2 curricula that cover a range of critical skills and implement these by the book. We do, however, recommend making adjustments to improve student response. Here are some possibilities:

Reteach and review basic skills. If data suggest that a student has failed to master or maintain knowledge of critical skills, reteach them. For example, some reading interventions presume children know basic sound–symbol correspondences, but many children—even older struggling readers—have difficulty remembering short vowel sounds (e.g., *e* in *bet*). It is better to explicitly reteach and practice missing skills than continually correct the child every time she forgets the skill.

Add more opportunities for guided practice. Increasing the number of times a student can practice applying newly learned information is one effective method to increase mastery. Interventionists may determine that a Tier 2 program's effectiveness may be enhanced by integrating additional chances for students to practice applying newly acquired skills with immediate, corrective feedback.

Adjust the entry point on the scope and sequence. Each Tier 2 intervention has a specific scope and sequence that indicates which skills are to be taught in which order. Each intervention also often recommends a starting point for each child based on her age and skill level. However, schools have their own CBM data, and the starting point should be adjusted for students whose data suggest they will do too poorly or too well at the program's recommended entry point.

Move the students to a different, smaller Tier 2 group. Decreasing the number of students in a small group increases intensity of instruction by allowing additional opportunities for the student to engage with instruction. Moving a student who is performing poorly in Tier 2 to a smaller group may be all that is needed to improve responsiveness.

Increase student motivation. Motivation is an essential component of all instruction—however, it likely plays an even more important role for students who demonstrated insufficient response to previous instruction. Sometimes, it is not the instructional routine that needs to be revamped. Instead, students (and often interventionists) simply need to be reenergized to engage with the intervention. As we stated earlier, positive reinforcement can produce positive effects; in the studies of PALS (e.g., Fuchs et al., 1997), teachers and students found a points-based reinforcement system motivating. The Evidence Based Intervention network (http://ebi.missouri.edu at the University of Missouri is one place to get ideas for motivating students.

Place into a different Tier 2 curriculum. As we described earlier, schools should have Tier 2 programs for different skill levels. If other adjustments have not been successful for a child within one program, it is worth considering whether the school's other Tier 2 curriculum should replace or enhance intervention. If data indicate a student requires more complex or simpler skills, the interventionist can collaborate with the RTI team to change the student's program. To make this work, interventionists need to review their CBM data carefully to see if Tier 2 students require a change. As we stated earlier, however, schools should not have too many programs (two each for reading and mathematics are probably sufficient) because fidelity of implementation and consistency for students will be higher if there are fewer programs to manage.

The list shown in Rapid Reference 2.3 is not all-inclusive, and school teams should discuss which adjustments are allowable within Tier 2 at their school. Whatever adjustments the RTI team decides to implement, they should be (1) simple, (2) made based on students' CBM data, and (3) done while maintaining fidelity to the programs' methods for learning targeted skills. Interventionists should avoid rewriting, reorganizing, or picking and choosing parts of programs.

Rapid Reference 2.3 Adjusting Tier 2 to Improve Its Value

- Reteach and review basic skills.
- Add more opportunities for guided practice.
- Adjust the entry point on the scope and sequence.
- Move the students to a different, smaller Tier 2 group.
- Increase student motivation.
- Place into a different Tier 2 curriculum.

This kind of extensive modification is not appropriate for Tier 2. This work is, however, precisely the focus of Tier 3.

Considerations for Secondary Schools

Tier 2 in middle and high school differs in at least three important ways. First, students will need substantially more intervention time than that often provided in elementary school; one full class period of intervention daily is appropriate (Biancarosa & Snow, 2006) provided students are also receiving Tier 1 literacy instruction throughout the day. Second, the need to integrate Tier 1 and Tier 2 instruction is even more important for secondary school learners. Regardless of reading skill, students are responsible for mastering content area material. The closer aligned instruction is across the tiers, the greater the chances are that students will learn the content area information. Third, additional research is needed on progress monitoring measures for secondary school learners. Espin, Wallace, Lembke, Campbell, and Long (2010) demonstrated that struggling readers at the secondary level present very limited weekly growth on CBM. Less frequent monitoring (e.g., monthly) may be sufficient for older students, although additional research is still needed to determine the best interval of CBM administration.

Summary

Tier 2 intervention is intensive, meaning it is teacher (interventionist)-centered, explicit (i.e., direct rather than inferred), frequent, and in small groups. To select Tier 2 programs, schools should only consider programs that are intensive, that provide scripts or clear procedures for implementation (i.e., they are standardized), and address critical skills. To help select a program, government- and university-sponsored websites provide information about program foci, effectiveness, and cost. To implement Tier 2, schools should select interventionists who will work well with children, have patience with children who may not get concepts quickly, and have good common sense to make minor instructional decisions. In addition, schools should train interventionists to teach the program(s), monitor fidelity of implementation with checklists, and monitor students' progress with CBM. Make some limited adjustments if necessary, leaving the big changes for Tier 3. In secondary schools, be sure Tier 2 aligns with the content of Tier 1.

TIER 3 INTERVENTION

Tier 3 is designed for what some scholars call *treatment resisters* or *nonresponders*, "students who make minimal gains after being taught with high quality, validated classroom instruction (Tier 1) and additional intervention (Tier 2)" (Wanzek &

Vaughn, 2010, p. 306). Failure to reach all students through Tier 2 is not a failure of the system. Even in some of the most intensive and well-implemented interventions tested by researchers, students fail to respond (e.g., Denton, Fletcher, Anthony, & Francis, 2006; McMaster et al., 2005; Torgesen et al., 2001). Between 4 and 10% of students will not respond, even with very high-quality Tier 2 interventions (Al Otaiba & Fuchs, 2002; Torgesen, 2000). Unlike Tier 2, however, there is some ambiguity about the nature of Tier 3.

Overview of Tier 3: Special Education?

Whether Tier 3 should be considered special education is contested, and it is not the purpose of this chapter to review this important topic. Here is a summary of our position: Students who do not respond to Tier 2 need something different than what Tier 2 provides. The instructional tools that have been selected for Tier 1 and Tier 2 should be programs through which "most children are thriving" (Speece & Case, 2001, p. 736). Students who have failed to thrive under these conditions need the (1) individualization, (2) intensity, and (3) expert instruction that are the hallmark of an individualized Tier 3. If a school is able to provide these resources outside of special education, we have no quarrel with that (leaving aside the issue of federal allocation of special education resources). However, it is our experience that schools provide individualized, intensive, expert support mostly—or only—in special education.

Instructional Tools: Designing Data-Based, Individualized Instruction

Instructional tools are designed by highly qualified teachers—we still call them interventionists, but strong content and pedagogical knowledge are requisite—at Tier 3, as shown in Figure 2.1. Unlike Tier 2, Tier 3 instruction is individualized and carefully planned. The basic idea is to begin with an *instructional platform*, a research-validated program, and adapt it based on students' needs. Generally, Tier 3 is thought to be *extensive intervention*, defined by including more than 100 sessions over more than 20 weeks (Wanzek & Vaughn, 2007), or more time per day but for fewer weeks (e.g., 8 weeks of 2 hours per day with a 1:1 student–teacher ratio; Torgesen et al., 2001).

Experimental Teaching/Data-Based Individualization

Recently, Fuchs et al. (2010) argued that Tier 3 should include a return to a form of instruction known as *experimental teaching* or *data-based individualization* (Deno & Mirkin, 1977; Fuchs, Fuchs, & Fernstrom, 1993; Marston, 1987–1988). Under this model of instruction, interventionists make modifications to their instruction

Program

Child

- Strengths
  - What is **good about the program?**
  - *Continue doing things that...*
    - Are critical skills
    - Seem to be working for this child
- Challenges
  - What about the **program makes it ineffective for** *this child?*
    - Too many skills are taught
    - Too little time is spent on each skill
    - Instruction is too complex
    - Explanations are not simple and/or clear enough
    - It is not covering the critical skills the student needs
  - *Change things that...*
    - Plays to this student's strengths
    - Avoids this student's weaknesses

- Strengths
  - What strengths does the child have that facilitate learning?
  - *Adjust instruction so that...*
    - You emphasize elements to play to the child's strengths *and* improve skills
- Challenges
  - What about the **child makes him struggle?**
    - Needs more time/practice
    - Needs more help/explanation
    - Needs simpler tasks first
    - Struggles with attention, motivation, or behavior
  - *Change instruction so that...*
    - Instruction occurs at an appropriate rate
    - Difficult and critical parts are emphasized while others are skipped
    - A system to improve attention and motivation is used

Figure 2.2. Thinking About Data-Based Individualization

The left column contains ideas to consider about the *program* when making adjustments in Tier 3. The right column contains ideas to consider about the *child* when making adjustments in Tier 3.

based on the apparent needs of an individual student and track the student's progress in response to this instruction. If the data suggest the instruction is working, the interventionist continues with it. If not, he makes an adjustment to the instruction and continues to monitor progress. Data-based individualization involves the interventionist thinking about the program he will implement in Tier 3 and the needs of the student and figuring out how to adjust instruction in a way that (1) preserves the quality present in the program, (2) plays to the student's strengths, and (3) changes the program to make it fit the student's needs better. Figure 2.2 illustrates one way to think about this process.

The idea of data-based individualization has been around for many years and has extensive empirical support (see Fuchs et al., 2010, for a review), but doing it well can be difficult. Here are some guidelines for doing effective data-based individualization for students with the most severe learning needs.

Provide intensive instruction. At Tier 3, intensity in terms of time, group size, and explicitness increases. In terms of *time*, Tier 3 instruction will likely occur daily and for an extended period of time. It may be as long as two hours. It will probably occur across the entire school year. The *group size* should be very small. The idea of individualized instruction presupposes that instruction is delivered in a way that is appropriate for an individual student. So, tutoring is ideal for Tier 3 instruction. As we described above, RTI can help maximize resources to calibrate intensity across tiers. Accordingly, in a well-designed RTI model, one-to-one or dyadic instruction should be possible. We know from working in many schools that some resource room teachers who work with students with specific learning disabilities have as many as 15 students in their classroom at a time, often with a single paraprofessional to assist them. If students in Tier 3 are to make progress toward reaching ambitious grade-level goals, such schools must find ways to have far smaller groups. The failure to create such groups will certainly result in limited progress; a model without small Tier 3 groups is not a good model of RTI.

Teaching should be done by an *expert instructor*. The idea of data-based individualization relies on the interventionist making careful decisions about what instruction students require and how to execute it. These interventionists must have specialized knowledge of the needs of students in Tier 3 and the many instructional options available. Imagine a student who struggles to remember that *ch* says /ch/. The interventionist has many options for improving a student's *ch* knowledge, including methods that emphasize the spelling (e.g., the modified alphabet of *Reading Mastery*, SRA/McGraw-Hill, 2008), methods that focus on the pronunciation of the sounds (e.g., the articulatory features emphasized in the *Lindamood-Bell Phoneme Sequencing Program*, Lindamood & Lindamood, 1998), and methods that teach the student key words that include *ch* spellings (e.g., ATCH =/ach/in BATCH, LATCH, and MATCH; Lovett, Lacarenza, & Borden, 2000). All of these methods have instructional value. It is the role of the expert instructor to choose the one likely to work best for the individual student.

Explicitness is another key feature of Tier 3 instruction (Fuchs et al., 2008; Vaughn, Wanzek, Murray, & Roberts, 2012). As we described with Tier 2, the idea of explicit instruction is that the interventionist must be as clear and incisive as possible when explaining things to students, with no guessing and few inferences. It should be totally clear what the interventionist intends for them to learn and how they can demonstrate they have learned it. Explicitness at Tier 3 should be even greater than at Tier 2, and interventionists will be creating their own explicit language or modifying it from the program's (rather than following the language written by program authors with few changes, as in Tier 2), so we present here some guidelines for being explicit:

1. *Simplify* the content as much as possible so it has the fewest number of steps possible. As part of lesson preparation, the interventionist should take time to complete a task analysis, that is, determine all of the steps required to

complete an academic task (Swanson & Hoskyn, 1998). Then, he should figure out how to simplify those steps so only the most essential remain.

2. *Be consistent—use the same language* every time to discuss the content. It is easy for interventionists to change their words when explaining things. When teaching phonics, they may variously tell students to "sound it out," "say the sounds first," "say it slowly," or "stretch the sounds out." None of these is incorrect, but using them all is likely to confuse a student who needs Tier 3 instruction. Always tell students the same thing with the same language. Creating consistency requires great discipline (and often some handy reminder notecards), but it will help the student internalize the content more quickly.

3. *Use short sentences to explain concepts.* Students who require Tier 3 support are often overwhelmed by too much information, so short sentences help. It is also helpful to have students repeat what the interventionist says, making it more likely they will remember concepts.

4. *Gradually release responsibility.* The "I do, we do, you do" sequence we mentioned for Tier 2 is equally important here, and here it may require more steps and more time.

Teach basic skills first. Many students who reach Tier 3 do so because they have failed to master basic skills. By basic skills, we refer to foundational skills in reading and mathematics that provide access to more complex academic content but have limited utility on their own. In reading, phonological awareness (including phonemic awareness) and phonics instruction are basic skills. In mathematics, basic addition, subtraction, multiplication, and division facts and the ability to perform arithmetic computation (i.e., correctly use algorithms for the four problem types) are basic skills. Detailed descriptions of these basic skills are not the focus of this chapter, but other chapters in this book will provide this information. We also recommend several websites that provide excellent resources for teaching these skills (see Rapid Reference 2.4).

Rapid Reference 2.4 Websites for Teaching Basic Skills

- The Meadows Center at the University of Texas (www.meadowscenter.org)
- The Center on Instruction (www.centeroninstruction.org)
- The Florida Center for Reading Research (www.fcrr.org)

Fidelity at Tier 3

Some aspects of fidelity of implementation at Tier 3 may look very similar to those at Tier 2. In cases where an interventionist is implementing an evidence-based curriculum as it was intended to be implemented, fidelity monitoring will be the same. However, often at Tier 3 substantial adjustments are needed to improve student response. If schools are following a model of RTI in which data-based individualization is used to match intervention to student need, fidelity will likely involve a stronger evaluation of the decision-making process rather than examining if the lesson was delivered as recommended. In other words, at Tier 3, interventionists often start with a base program—an instructional platform—and, based on student response and related data will systematically adjust instruction to improve student performance. Implementing Tier 3 with fidelity means that the interventionist is using data to systematically make adjustments. Fidelity at this level is used to help understand whether the adaptations made to instruction were likely to be responsible for changes in student performance.

Progress Monitoring

Assessment of academic progress should be more intensive and individualized at Tier 3. The goals of progress monitoring in this tier are to evaluate student response and to provide data to make adjustments to the intervention. This progress monitoring should occur frequently. It should be more frequent than in Tier 2, at least weekly and possibly more because the interventionist will constantly assess whether instructional modifications are producing positive effects. Traditional CBM at the student's current grade level should be used, but this will not capture the academic growth of Tier 3 students significantly below grade level. Some suggestions for monitoring progress in Tier 3 are outlined next.

Begin with grade-level CBM. Students who are placed into Tier 3 are likely substantially below grade level. This may mean that a grade-level CBM may be very challenging. For example, consider Brooklyn, a fourth-grade student who is only able to read five words correctly in a minute on an end-of-fourth-grade-level oral reading fluency measure. In her case, we would recommend that the interventionist monitor progress on grade-level skills periodically throughout the year (e.g., every other month), but not any more frequently. This will decrease the number of times the student is exposed to the overly difficult measure, yet will allow the interventionist to regularly compare progress to the grade-level standard.

Supplement with below-grade-level CBM. High-frequency progress monitoring should occur at the student's instructional level. For our student, Brooklyn, an interventionist would be able to gain much better information for monitoring growth in oral reading fluency on her instructional level. If data collected on Brooklyn demonstrated that she read 18 words correctly on a first-grade level passage (which is below the grade-level benchmark), the interventionist would likely find CBM at this level captures improvements and feels less frustrating for Brooklyn. The interventionist could then move her up to the second-grade passage when she met the end-of-first-grade benchmark (i.e., 40 words correct). In addition, Brooklyn's interventionist is targeting phonics skills, and he would monitor Brooklyn's progress on first-grade nonsense-word fluency CBM because this measure provides an index of students' ability to use phonics skills.

Conduct an error analysis of CBM. Often, when CBM is used, interventionists only compare the student's score to a set of benchmarks. However, instructionally relevant information is also collected during CBM. An interventionist can review the errors made and use these to refine instruction. For example, if Brooklyn was unable to read the words *were* and *with* and she repeatedly read C-V-C words containing the vowel letter *i* (as in *bit*) with a "long I" (/ī/, the sound in *bite*), the interventionist could develop lessons to directly teach these skills.

Compare performance on untimed CBM measures. Some students in Tier 3 struggle substantially with fluency. If the timed nature of CBM appears to make it hard to show progress, interventionists can compare performance on timed and untimed versions of the measure. If a student's score is substantially higher on the untimed measure, this may indicate that the student requires additional fluency practice. For example, if Brooklyn was able to read a majority of the words correctly in the first-grade passage when provided additional time, this would indicate that Brooklyn has the skill to accurately identify the words but simply cannot do it quickly enough. The Tier 3 interventionist would then focus on word-reading fluency more than accuracy. This use of CBM is appropriate for diagnostic purposes, but it is not true CBM because the reliability and validity (that is, whether it measures what we want in the way we want) of CBM are based on its use as a timed measure. To measure progress, timed CBM should be used.

Mastery measurement. Interventionists may find it useful to collect what we call "mastery measurement" data as a supplement to CBM. By mastery measurement we mean that an interventionist will identify a limited set of items to be directly taught to a child. For example, Brooklyn needs to learn the words *were*, *with*, and 18 other high-frequency words. The interventionist may place these on flashcards and check to see which ones she can quickly read at the end of the lesson. Sometimes, these checks for understanding are done repeatedly during the lesson, perhaps at 5 and 15 minutes after initial instruction (O'Connor, Bocian, Beach, & Sanchez, in press). The words that Brooklyn reads correctly three days in a row could be considered mastered. The interventionist could then conduct a maintenance check on mastered words every week or two to determine if Brooklyn has maintained her new learning—if not, the words can be retaught.

Mastery measurement can be used as a part of the interventionist's treatment to evaluate how well the student is learning the exact skills taught. It may be particularly helpful when students repeatedly make little progress on grade- and instructional-level CBM, despite well-implemented Tier 3 instruction. It may also assist interventionists in planning future instruction. However, we emphasize that only timed CBM will provide an index of the child's overall progress in the academic area. Traditional CBM—on grade- and instructional-level measures—is necessary to monitoring progress over a period of time and for developing Individualized Education Program (IEP) goals (see, Yell & Stecker, 2003).

Making Adjustments

Put simply, Tier 3 is all about making adjustments. No longer are interventionists required to follow a script. Here, student progress is likely to be based on the interventionist's intimate knowledge of the student and the instructional tools available. Figure 2.2 illustrates how to make Tier 3 decisions, as we described earlier. Interventionists will necessarily go through a trial-and-error process to decide what instruction seems to work best. The critical idea is that they use data to determine response and make changes. We think of Tim Gunn, the *Project Runway* designer/mentor, when we say that sometimes interventionists just have to make it work. Like excellent designers, interventionists know their craft and use their judgment and professional experience to make decisions. There are fewer rules and guidelines for Tier 3, precisely because each child is unique and the prescriptive guidelines for Tier 2 did not produce success. So, use data, judgment, and professional experience, and make it work.

The only adjustment we do not endorse is a move toward "cognitively focused" interventions. There are programs purported to improve students' cognitive processing in areas like working memory (Holmes, Gathercole, & Dunning, 2009), motor processing (Reynolds, Nicolson, & Hambly, 2003), and visual processing (Iovino, Fletcher, Breitmeyer, & Foorman, 1998). In a review of 50 studies of such interventions, Kearns and Fuchs (2013) found tepid evidence for their ability to improve academics. Perhaps as technology improves, cognitively focused intervention may become important (see Turkeltaub et al., 2012), but for now, we recommend only academic intervention.

Considerations for Secondary Schools

There are few substantial differences in how Tier 3 should be implemented between elementary and secondary schools—interventionists at both levels need to use data to guide enhancements and refinements of instruction. Likely, as students age, the challenges of catching students up with grade-level peers will increase. Further, the closer students are to completing their secondary schooling, the more that interventionists (and IEP teams, if applicable) need to consider transition goals. Devoting the majority of instructional time to teaching basic reading and math skills may not be in the student's best interest. In other words, by high school, a broader picture of the student's post-secondary goals should be factored into determining what is included in the student's curriculum. If Brooklyn continues to read at an early elementary level throughout high school, decoding instruction should likely no longer be a priority (although reading instruction should be part of her schooling). Instead, the focus should be to assist her in preparing for transition to an adult life in which she can gain employment or further education, be productive, be independent, and be happy (Lemons, Kloo, Zigmond, Fulmer, & Lupp, 2012).

Summary

Tier 3 instruction should be differentiated. Tier 3 interventionists should consider the strengths and needs of each child and of programs relative to the child's strengths and needs. A highly qualified interventionist will create instruction that is intensive. It will be in very small groups and provided very explicitly, with simple, consistent, short language to explain concepts and a slow gradual release of responsibility. In Tier 3, basic skills come first, although more advanced skills are appropriate once a child masters the basics. Measuring fidelity will relate to the interventionist's use of data-based individualization rather than program adherence. Progress monitoring for Tier 3 will involve the use of out-of-grade passages and interventionists may also use error analysis, untimed measurement, and mastery measurement in addition to CBM. For secondary school students, life-skills instruction might supplant basic academics as they approach the end of high school. Tier 3, by definition, involves constant adjustment of instruction to meet students' needs, but beware programs that purport to teach cognitive processes directly. Based on our review of the research, cognitively focused intervention is not ready for primetime. However, others are more positive about cognitively focused intervention (see Hale et al., 2010 and Chapter 1, this volume).

CONCLUSION

RTI is one of the latest buzzwords in education, something almost everyone is talking about. We often hear school leaders say, "Oh, yes, we are doing RTI." However, their descriptions of RTI vary widely, and their descriptions tend to follow a few patterns:

1. "We're trying, but it's tricky": School leaders are implementing RTI following a standard protocol, much as we have described it. They have important and difficult questions about using resources and making things work under less-than-ideal circumstances (e.g., a Tier 2 program is needed but resources are very limited; it is difficult to find or designate interventionists).
2. "It's the same old thing": School leaders indicate they are using a problem-solving model, but they have really made no changes from the pre-referral intervention (e.g., "student study team") process that has long been a feature of the special education referral process. They often believe that RTI is merely a newly fashionable way of describing that process. RTI—even under the standard protocol—is more than that. Our description of Tier 3 should make this clear.
3. "We bought X for CBM and Y for Tier 2": School leaders have a progress monitoring system in place and they are collecting triennial screening data on all students. However, the data collected are examined by only a few people, and they are not used to determine students' response at each Tier. They have purchased and have asked classroom teachers to use a Tier 2 intervention program. However, there is little training and no requirement to implement with fidelity. Teachers implement the programs as they see fit, if at all.

In our work with schools and districts across the United States and Canada, we are seeing more and more pattern #1 schools, but there are still many school and district leaders whose discussions with us fit patterns #2 and #3. These patterns are problematic because they reflect serious misconceptions about the purpose and nature of RTI. However, we empathize with, admire, and support all education professionals engaged in implementation of RTI because we recognize that it is complex and ambitious work.

We hope, therefore, that the guidelines we have provided for all three tiers will clarify the nature of the system. We realize that the school- and district-specific conditions will make certain recommendations easier (e.g., there are funds for supplemental interventions) or harder (e.g., contract requirements place conditions on fidelity monitoring), but these are the general principles of effective RTI implementation. Schools are on the right track if they are (1) implementing evidence-based programs at Tier 1, research-validated programs at Tier 2, and data-based individualization at Tier 3, (2) maximizing resources to increase intensity across tiers to provide the "just right" amount of support each student needs, and (3) using data to make decisions about program value and student needs at each tier.

We recommend that school leaders resist the temptation to view RTI as pre-referral intervention warmed over or to implement RTI hastily without building systems to collect and disseminate data and implement programs effectively. Our experiences in doing research on RTI and our experiences working in many schools lead us to believe that following these guidelines has the potential to change the academic trajectories of many struggling students, reduce special education referrals, and improve system-wide instructional quality.

REFERENCES

Adams, G., & Carnine, D. (2003). Direct instruction. In H. L. Swanson, K. R. Harris, & S. Graham (Eds.), *Handbook of learning disabilities* (pp. 403–416). New York, NY: Guilford Press.

Akin-Little, K. A., Eckert, T. L., Lovett, B. J., & Little, S. G. (2004). Extrinsic reinforcement in the classroom: Bribery of best practice. *School Psychology Review, 33*, 344–362.

Al Otaiba, S., & Fuchs, D. (2002). Characteristics of children who are unresponsive to early literacy intervention: A review of the literature. *Remedial and Special Education, 23*, 300–316.

Anderson, R. C., Spiro, R. J., & Anderson, M. C. (1978). Schemata as scaffolding for the representation of information in connected discourse. *American Educational Research Journal, 15*, 433–440.

Archer, A. L., & Hughes, C. A. (2010). *Explicit instruction: Effective and efficient teaching.* New York: Guilford Press.

Baker, S. K., Fien, H., & Baker, D. L. (2010). Robust reading instruction in the early grades: Conceptual and practical issues in the integration and evaluation of Tier 1 and Tier 2 instructional supports. *Focus on Exceptional Children, 42*(9), 1–20.

Baumann, J. F., & Kameenui, E. J. (1991). Research on vocabulary instruction: Ode to Voltaire. In J. Flood, J. J. D. Lapp, & J. R. Squire (Eds.), *Handbook of research on teaching the English language arts* (pp. 604–632). New York, NY: MacMillan.

Bear, D., Invernezzi, M., Templeton, S., & Johnston, F. (2000). *Words their way: Word study for phonics, vocabulary, and spelling instruction.* Columbus, OH: Merrill/Macmillan.

Biancarosa, C., & Snow, C. E. (2006). *Reading next—a vision for action and research in middle and high school literacy: A report to Carnegie Corporation of New York.* Washington, DC: Alliance for Excellent Education.

Borko, H., Jacobs, J., Eiteljorg, E., & Pittman, M. E. (2008). Video as a tool for fostering productive discussions in mathematics professional development. *Teaching and Teacher Education, 24*, 417–436.

Brewer, W. F., & Nakamura, G. V. (1984). *The nature and functions of schemas.* Champaign, IL: University of Illinois at Urbana-Champaign, Center for the Study of Reading.

Brown, A. L., & Campione, J. C. (1996). Psychological theory and the design of innovative learning environments: On procedures, principles, and systems. In L. Schauble & R. Glaser (Eds.), *Innovations in learning: New environments for education* (pp. 289–325). Mahwah, NJ: Lawrence Erlbaum.

Cameron, J., & Pierce, W. D. (1994). Reinforcement, reward, and intrinsic motivation: A meta-analysis. *Review of Educational Research, 64*, 363–423.

Carnegie Council on Advancing Adolescent Literacy (CCAAL).(2010). *Time to act: An agenda for advancing adolescent literacy for college and career success.* New York, NY: Carnegie Corporation of New York.

Compton, D. L., Fuchs, D., Fuchs, L. S., & Bryant, J. D. (2006). Selecting at-risk readers in first grade for early intervention. *Journal of Educational Psychology, 98*, 394–409.

Connor, C. M., Morrison, F. J., Fishman, B. J., Schatschneider, C., & Underwood, P. (2007). Algorithm-guided individualized reading instruction. *Science, 315*, 464–465.

Connor, C. M., Morrison, F. J., & Petrella, J. N. (2004). Effective reading comprehension instruction: Examining child × instruction interactions. *Journal of Educational Psychology, 96*, 682–698.

Darch, C., & Gersten, R. (1985). The effects of teacher presentation rate and praise on LD students' oral reading performance. *British Journal of Educational Psychology, 55*, 295–303.

Davis, E. A., & Krajcik, J. S. (2005). Designing educative curriculum materials to promote teacher learning. *Educational Researcher, 34*, 3–14.

Deno, S. L. (1985). Curriculum-based measurement: The emerging alternative. *Exceptional Children, 52*, 219–232.

Deno, S. L., & Mirkin, P. K. (1977). *Data-based program modification: A manual.* Reston, VA: Council for Exceptional Children.

Denton, C. A. (2012). Response to intervention for reading difficulties in the primary grades: Some answers and lingering questions. *Journal of Learning Disabilities, 45*, 232–243.

Denton, C. A., Fletcher, J. M., Anthony, J. L., & Francis, D. J. (2006). An evaluation of intensive intervention for students with persistent reading difficulties. *Journal of Learning Disabilities, 39*, 447–466.

Eckert, T. L., Dunn, E. K., & Ardoin, S. P. (2006). The effects of alternative forms of performance feedback on elementary-aged students' oral reading fluency. *Journal of Behavioral Education, 15*, 148–161.

Elleman, A. M., Lindo, E. J., Morphy, P., & Compton, D. L. (2009). The impact of vocabulary instruction on passage-level comprehension of school-age children: A meta-analysis. *Journal of Research on Educational Effectiveness, 2*, 1–44.

Espin, C., Wallace, T., Lembke, E., Campbell, H., & Long, J. D. (2010). Creating a progress-monitoring system in reading for middle-school students: Tracking progress toward meeting high-stakes standards. *Learning Disabilities Research & Practice, 25*, 60–75.

Frykholm, J. A. (1998). Beyond supervision: Learning to teach mathematics in community. *Teaching and Teacher Education, 14*, 305–322.

Fuchs, D., Compton, D. L., Fuchs, L. S., Bryant, J., & Davis, G. N. (2008). Making "secondary intervention" work in a three-tier responsiveness-to-intervention model: Findings from the first-grade longitudinal reading study of the National Research Center on Learning Disabilities. *Reading and Writing, 21*, 413–436.

Fuchs, D., & Deshler, D. D. (2007). What we need to know about responsiveness to intervention (and shouldn't be afraid to ask). *Learning Disabilities Research & Practice, 22*, 129–136.

Fuchs, D., Fuchs, L. S., & Burish, P. (2000). Peer-assisted learning strategies: An empirically-supported practice to promote reading achievement. *Learning Disabilities Research and Practice, 15*, 85–91.

Fuchs, D., Fuchs, L. S., & Compton, D. L. (2012). Smart RTI: A next-generation approach to multilevel prevention. *Exceptional Children, 78*(3), 263–279.

Fuchs, D., Fuchs, L. S., & Fernstrom, P. (1993). A conservative approach to special education reform: Mainstreaming through transenvironmental programming and curriculum-based measurement. *American Education Research Journal, 30,* 149–177.

Fuchs, D., Fuchs, L. S., Mathes, P., & Simmons, D. (1997). Peer-assisted learning strategies: Making classrooms more responsive to diversity. *American Educational Research Journal, 34,* 174–206.

Fuchs, D., Fuchs, L. S., & Stecker, P. M. (2010). The "blurring" of special education in a new continuum of general education placements and services. *Council for Exceptional Children, 76*(3), 301–323.

Fuchs, D., McMaster, K., Saenz, L., Kearns, D. M., Fuchs, L. S., Yen, L., & Zang, W. (2010, February). *Bring educational innovation to scale: Top-down, bottom-up, or a third way?* Presentation at the Pacific Coast Research Conference, Coronado, CA.

Fuchs, D., Mock, D., Morgan, P. L., & Young, C. L. (2003). Responsiveness-to-intervention: Definitions, evidence, and implications for the learning disabilities construct. *Learning Disabilities Research & Practice, 18,* 157–171.

Fuchs, L. S., & Fuchs, D. (2002). Curricum-based measurement: Describing competence, enhancing outcomes, evaluating treatment effects, and identifying treatment nonresponders. *Peabody Journal of Education, 77,* 64–84.

Fuchs, L. S., Fuchs, D., & Karns, K. (2001). Enhancing kindergarteners' mathematical development: Effects of peer-assisted learning strategies. *The Elementary School Journal, 101,* 495–510.

Fuchs, L. S., Fuchs, D., Powell, S. R., Seethaler, P. M., Cirino, P. T., & Fletcher, J. M. (2008b). Intensive intervention for students with mathematics disabilities: Seven principles of effective practice. *Learning Disability Quarterly, 31,* 79–92.

Fuchs, L. S., Seethaler, P. M., Powell, S. R., Fuchs, D., Hamlett, C. L., & Fletcher, J. M. (2008a). Effects of preventative tutoring on the mathematical problem solving of third-grade students with math and reading difficulties. *Exceptional Children, 74,* 155–173.

Gersten, R., Beckmann, S., Clarke, B., Foegen, A., Marsh, L., Star, J. R., & Witzel, B. (2009a). *Assisting students struggling with mathematics: Response to intervention (RtI) for elementary and middle schools.* Washington, DC: Institute of Education Sciences.

Gersten, R., Compton, D., Connor, C. M., Dimino, J., Santoro, L., Linan-Thompson, S., & Tilly, W. D. (2009b). *Assisting students struggling with reading: Response to intervention and multi-tier intervention in the primary grades.* Washington, DC: Institute of Education Sciences.

Greenwood, C. R., Delquadri, J. C., & Hall, R. V. (1989). Longitudinal effects of classwide peer tutoring. *Journal of Educational Psychology, 81,* 371–383.

Hale, J., Alfonso, V., Berninger, V., Bracken, B., Christo, C., Clark, E., & Yalof, J. (2010). Critical issues in response-to-intervention, comprehensive evaluation, and specific learning disabilities identification and intervention: An expert white paper consensus. *Learning Disabilities Quarterly, 33,* 223–236.

Harris, K. R., Graham, S., & Mason, L. H. (2003). Self-regulated strategy development in the classroom: Part of a balanced approach to writing instruction for students with disabilities. *Focus on Exceptional Children, 35*(7), 1–16.

Hill, D., King, S., Lemons, C. J., & Partanen, J. N. (2012). Fidelity of implementation and instructional alignment in Response to Intervention research. *Learning Disabilities Research & Practice.*

Holmes, J., Gathercole, S. E., & Dunning, D. L. (2009). Adaptive training leads to sustained enhancement of poor working memory in children. *Developmental Science, 12,* F9–F15.

Hosp, M. K., Hosp, J. L., & Howell, K. W. (2007). *The ABCs of CBM: A practical guide to curriculum-based measurement.* New York, NY: Guilford Press.

Iovino, I., Fletcher, J. M., Breitmeyer, B. G., & Foorman, B. R. (1998). Colored overlays for visual perceptual deficits in children with reading disability and attention deficit/hyperactivity disorder: Are they differentially effective? *Journal of Clinical and Experimental Neuropsychology, 20,* 791–806. doi:10.1076/jcen.20.6.791.1113

Jitendra, A., DiPipi, C. M., & Perron-Jones, N. (2002). An exploratory study of schema-based word-problem-solving instruction for middle school students with learning disabilities. *Journal of Special Education, 36,* 23–38.

Kamil, M. L., Borman, G. D., Dole, J., Kral, C. C., Salinger, T., & Torgesen, J. (2008). *Improving adolescent literacy: Effective classroom and intervention practices: A practice guide* (NCEE#2008-4027) Washington, DC: National Center for Education Evaluation and Regional Assistance, Institute of Education Sciences, U.S. Department of Education.

Kearns, D., & Fuchs, D. (2013). Does cognitively-focused instruction improve the academic performance of low-achieving students? *Exceptional Children, 79,* 263–290.

Kearns, D. M., Fuchs, D., Fuchs, L. S., Compton, D. L., & Bouton, B. D. (2012, April). *Adaptive beginning reading intervention: The effects of rigor and individualized instruction.* Paper presentation at the annual conference of the Council for Exceptional Children, Denver, CO.

King, S., Lemons, C. J., & Hill, D. (2012). Response to intervention in secondary schools: Considerations for administrators. *National Association of Secondary School Principals Bulletin, 96*(1), 5–22.

Klingner, J. K., Vaughn, S., Arguelles, M. E., Hughes, M. T., & Leftwich, S. A. (2004). Collaborative strategic reading: "Real-word" lessons from classroom teachers. *Remedial and Special Education, 25,* 291–302.

Lemons, C. J., Kloo, A., Zigmond, N., Fulmer, D., & Lupp, L. (2012). Implementing an alternate assessment based on modified academic achievement standards: When policy meets practice. *International Journal of Disability, Development, and Education, 59*(1), 67–79.

Lienemann, T. O., & Reid, R. (2005). Self-regulated strategy development for students with learning disabilities. *Teacher Education and Special Education, 29,* 3–11.

Lindamood, P., & Lindamood, P. (1998). *The Lindamood Phoneme Sequencing Program for reading, spelling, and speech: LiPS: Teacher's manual for the classroom and clinic* (3rd ed.) Austin, TX: PRO-ED.

Lovett, M. W., Lacerenza, L., & Borden, S. L. (2000). Putting struggling readers on the PHAST track: A program to integrate phonological and strategy-based remedial instruction and maximize outcomes. *Journal of Learning Disabilities, 33*(5), 458–476.

Maag, J. W. (2001). Rewarded by punishment: Reflections on the disuse of positive reinforcement in schools. *Exceptional Children, 67,* 173–186.

Marston, D. (1987–1988). The effectiveness of special education: A time-series analysis of reading performance in regular and special education. *Journal of Special Education, 21,* 13–26.

Marston, D. (2005). Tiers of intervention in responsiveness to intervention: Prevention outcomes and learning disabilities identification patterns. *Journal of Learning Disabilities, 38,* 539–544.

McMaster, K. L., Fuchs, D., Fuchs, L. S., & Compton, D. L. (2005). Responding to nonresponders: An experimental field trial of identification and intervention methods. *Exceptional Children, 71,* 445–463.

National Mathematics Advisory Panel. (2008). Foundations for success: The final report of the National Mathematics Advisory Panel. Washington, DC: United States Department of Education.

O'Connor, R., Bocian, K., Beach, K., & Sanchez, V. (in press). Access to a Responsiveness to Intervention model: Does beginning intervention in kindergarten matter? *Journal of Learning Disabilities.*

Pany, D., & McCoy, K. M. (1988). Effects of corrective reading on word accuracy and reading comprehension of readers with learning disabilities. *Journal of Learning Disabilities, 21,* 546–550.

Peng, P., Fuchs, D., Cho, E., Compton, D. L., Fuchs, L. S., Kearns, D. M., & McMaster, K. L. (2011, July). Conceptual and practical implications of fidelity-of-treatment implementation: An IRT approach. Poster presentation given at the Annual Meeting of the Society for the Scientific Study of Reading, St. Petersburg, FL.

Reynolds, D., Nicolson, R. I., & Hambly, H. (2003). Evaluation of an exercise-based treatment for children with reading difficulties. *Dyslexia, 9,* 48–71. doi:10.1002/dys.235

Scammacca, N., Vaughn, S., Roberts, G., Wanzek, J., & Torgesen, J. K. (2007). *Extensive reading interventions in grades k-3: From research to practice.* Portsmouth, NH: RMC Research Corporation, Center on Instruction.

Scruggs, T. E., & Mastropieri, M. A. (1990). Mnemonic instruction for students with learning disabilities: What it is and what it does. *Learning Disability Quarterly, 13,* 271–280.

Seidel, T., Prenzel, M., Schwindt, K., Sturmer, K., Blomberg, G., & Kobarg, M. (2009). LUV and observe: Two projects using video to diagnose teacher competence. In T. Janik & T. Seidel (Eds.), *The power of video studies in investigating teaching and learning in the classroom* (pp. 161–180). New York, NY: Waxmann.

Slavin, R. E. (2006). *Educational psychology: Theory and practice* (10th ed.). Boston, MA: Allyn & Bacon.

Speece, D. L., & Case, L. P. (2001). Classification in context: An alternative approach to identifying early reading disability. *Journal of Educational Psychology, 93,* 735–749.

SRA/McGraw-Hill.(2008). *Reading mastery signature edition.* New York, NY: Author.

Stecker, P. M., Fuchs, L. S., & Fuchs, D. (2005). Using curriculum-based measurement to improve student achievement: Review of research. *Psychology in the Schools, 42,* 795–819.

Sutherland, K. S., Wehby, J. H., & Yoder, P. J. (2002). Examination of the relationship between teacher praise and opportunities for students with EBD to respond to academic requests. *Journal of Emotional and Behavioral Disorders, 10,* 5–13.

Swanson, H. L., & Hoskyn, M. (1998). Experimental intervention research on students with learning disabilities: A meta-analysis of treatment outcomes. *Review of Educational Research, 68,* 277–321.

Torgesen, J. K. (2000). Individual differences in response to early interventions in reading: The lingering problem of treatment resisters. *Learning Disabilities Research & Practice, 15,* 55–64.

Torgesen, J. K., Alexander, A. W., Wagner, R. K., Rashotte, C. A., Kytja, K. S., Voeller, K. K. S., & Conway, T. (2001). Intensive remedial instruction for children with severe reading disabilities: Immediate and long-term outcomes from two instructional approaches. *Journal of Learning Disabilities, 34,* 33–58.

Turkeltaub, P. E., Benson, J., Hamilton, R. H., Datta, A., Bikson, M., & Coslett, H. B. (2012). Left lateralizing transcranial direct current stimulation improves reading efficiency. *Brain Stimulation, 5,* 201–207.

Vadasy, P. F., Jenkins, J. R., & Pool, K. (2000). Effects of tutoring in phonological and early reading skills on students at risk for reading disabilities. *Journal of Learning Disabilities, 33,* 579–590.

Van Keer, H., & Verhaeghe, J. P. (2005). Effects of explicit reading strategies instruction and peer tutoring on second and fifth graders' reading comprehension and self-efficacy perceptions. *Journal of Experimental Education, 73,* 291–329.

Vaughn, S., Cirino, P. T., Wanzek, J., Wexler, J., Fletcher, C. D., Denton, C. D., . . . Francis, D. J. (2010). Response to intervention for middle school students with reading difficulties: Effects of a primary and secondary intervention. *School Psychology Review*, *39*, 3–21.

Vaughn, S., & Fletcher, J. M. (2012). Response to intervention with secondary school students with reading difficulties. *Journal of Learning Disabilities*, *45*, 244–256.

Vaughn, S., & Linan-Thompson, S. (2003). What is special about special education for students with learning disabilities? *Journal of Special Education*, *37*, 140–147.

Vaughn, S., Linan-Thompson, S., & Hickman, P. (2003). Response to instruction as a means of identifying students with reading/learning disabilities. *Exceptional Children*, *69*, 391–409.

Vaughn, S., Wanzek, J., Murray, C. S., & Roberts, G. (2012). *Intensive interventions for students struggling in reading and mathematics: A practice guide*. Portsmouth, NH: RMC Research Corporation, Center on Instruction.

Vellutino, F. R., Scanlon, D. M., Sipay, E. R., Small, S. G., Pratt, A., Chen, R., & Denckla, M. B. (1996). Cognitive profiles of difficult-to-remediate and readily remediated poor readers: Early intervention as a vehicle for distinguishing between cognitive and experiential deficits as basic causes of specific reading disability. *Journal of Educational Psychology*, *88*, 601–638.

Wanzek, J., & Vaughn, S. (2010). Is a three-tier reading intervention model associated with reduced placement in special education? *Remedial and Special Education*. Advance online publication. doi:10.1177/0741932510361267

Xin, Y. P., Jitendra, A. K., & Deatline-Buchman, A. (2005). Effects of mathematical word problem-solving instruction on middle school students with learning problems. *Journal of Special Education*, *39*, 181–192.

Yell, M. L., & Stecker, P. M. (2003). Developing legally correct and educationally meaningful IEPs using curriculum-based measurement. *Assessment for Effective Intervention*, *28*, 73–88.

Zimmerman, B. J. (2000). Attaining self-regulation: A social cognitive perspective. In M. Boekaerts, P. Pintrich, & M. Zeidner (Eds.), *Handbook of self-regulation* (pp. 13–39). San Diego, CA: Academic Press.

TEST YOURSELF

I. Under the standard protocol, which tier is part of special education?

a. Only and always Tier 1

b. Only and always Tier 3

c. Only Tier 1, but not always

d. Only Tier 3, but not always

2. The purpose of RTI is to

a. Place needy children in special education

b. Make it possible for all children to stay out of special education

c. Provide the correct level of support for each child

d. Collect progress monitoring data on all students

(continued)

(continued)

3. **Some critical features of an RTI system are (circle all that apply):**
   a. A system to monitor student progress
   b. A research-validated Tier 1 program
   c. A research-validated Tier 2 program, implemented in a standard way
   d. Monitoring of fidelity for all tiers of instruction
   e. A research-validated Tier 3 program, implemented in a standard way

4. **An evidence-based program:**
   a. Is a program researchers have studied carefully and continually changed and improved
   b. Includes components based on research but may not have been tested as a unit
   c. Includes components that program authors tested individually and put together
   d. Is evidence-based only if it has been endorsed by the What Works Clearinghouse or the Best Evidence Encyclopedia

5. **What are important characteristics of Tier 1 implementation? (Select all that apply.)**
   a. They are evidence-based
   b. They are research-based
   c. They do not include systematic, explicit instruction
   d. Fidelity is checked to assure the program is being used as designed
   e. They are designed to be most effective for students at-risk for academic problems

6. **Tier 2 instruction should be**
   a. Teacher-directed because children in Tier 2 are likely to make greater progress this way
   b. Teacher-directed because all children learn best when the teacher controls the instruction
   c. Independent because children in Tier 2 need more space to think about complex concepts
   d. Peer-mediated because peers provide support in a way that will be more logical than what the teacher does

7. **Under the standard protocol, which three are critical characteristics of Tier 2?**
   a. A highly expert instructor
   b. Research-validated academic programs
   c. Regular monitoring of students' progress
   d. Teacher-centered explicit, systematic instruction
   e. IQ testing to validate that low IQ is not causing poor reading

8. Which of the following are true of RTI? (Select all that apply.)

a. *All* children receive progress monitoring at regular intervals (e.g., weekly)

b. Only children schools consider at risk participate in universal screening

c. Intervention usually begins after a period of progress monitoring without intervention (although sometimes intervention will begin immediately)

d. RTI is part of general education

9. Tier 3 instruction is generally

I. Completely scripted

II. Provided in small groups, dyads, or one-to-one

III. Provided by a well-trained parent volunteer or paraprofessional

a. I only

b. II only

c. III only

d. I and II

e. II and III

10. For secondary school students, intervention can begin

a. After 4–6 weeks of progress monitoring

b. After 2–3 weeks of progress monitoring, provided students have low state test scores

c. Immediately if prior-year test scores indicate an academic need

Answers: 1. d; 2. c; 3. a, c, d; 4. b; 5. a, d; 6. a; 7. b, c, d; 8. c, d; 9. b; 10. c

Three

HOME–SCHOOL COLLABORATION FOR INTERVENTION PLANNING[1]

Michael J. Coutts
Susan M. Sheridan
Tara M. Sjuts
Tyler E. Smith

O
f all that is known about children's learning and behavior, one fact is
very clear: Opportunities to promote optimal educational experiences
are evident across many settings. The most influential environments
that predict and support learning are the home and school. Learning and
development do not occur in a vacuum; that is, events a child experiences in
one setting (e.g., at home) influence and are influenced by events in the other (e.g.,
the classroom). Given that adults in these complementary settings control the
events and conditions experienced by children, it follows that cooperation and
coordination (in fact, collaboration) between settings and the adults populating
and driving them is a reasonable goal.

WHAT IS COLLABORATION?

Collaboration is defined as the act of working together or cooperating with others
toward a common goal or set of goals. Identified goals within the educational context
are those associated with learning and development, and the primary players charged
with supporting these goals are teachers and parents, in the school and home settings,

1. The development of this chapter was supported by a grant awarded to Dr. Susan M. Sheridan
by the Institute for Educational Sciences (Grant #R324A100115). The opinions expressed herein are
those of the authors and do not reflect those of the funding agency.

respectively. As an extension, home–school collaboration is defined as "a reciprocal, dynamic process that occurs among systems . . . and/or individuals . . . who share in decision making toward common goals and solutions related to students (Cowan, Swearer Napolitano, & Sheridan, 2004, p. 201). Collaboration between families and schools extends the notion of family involvement, which describes activities prescribed by schools and practiced by parents, to a recognition of the importance of families and schools working together to achieve important goals.

Collaboration typically implies short-lived, targeted interactions to achieve pre-scribed goals. Programs that promote collaboration increase their sustainability by fostering cooperative *partnerships* between individuals. Contrary to an activity merely involving home–school collaboration to achieve a specific outcome, we prefer espousing a *partnership* orientation in working with families. This partnership is defined as a relationship that evolves over time and is characterized by shared responsibilities, reciprocal processes, complementary roles, and mutually determined objectives to jointly advance students' positive academic and social competence. Rapid Reference 3.1 outlines the principles and goals characterized by collaborative partnerships.

Rapid Reference 3.1 Principles and Goals of Collaborative Partnerships

Principles of Collaborative Partnerships	Goals of Collaborative Partnerships
• Requires that all team members want to work together toward a common goal • Based on a sense that all participants—parents, teachers, administrators, and students—are truly valued • Embraces the unique perspectives of all individuals comprising the educational team • Based on a strong sense of purpose • Requires trust and a sense of shared responsibility	• To promote optimal learning and social-emotional competencies of students • To provide a context for parents and educators alike to feel empowered as co-supporters and co-facilitators of students' learning • To actively invite and use parents' and educators' ideas and strengths to pro-mote students' educational outcomes • To develop constructive connections and linkages across home and school to create seamless learning experiences for students

WHY ESTABLISH PARTNERSHIPS ACROSS SCHOOL AND HOME?

Decades of research findings support the fact that partnerships between teachers and parents lead to several positive outcomes for students, families, and schools alike. Whereas the importance of effective teaching strategies and competent parenting practices cannot be overstated, the joint influence of what happens at home and at school together promotes the greatest possibilities for children (Barbarin, Downer, Odom, & Head-Reeves, 2010). A plethora of research has made one finding abundantly clear: The establishment of opportunities and structures for parents and teachers to work together (i.e., partner) and share responsibilities for setting children on a positive educational trajectory outweighs the power of efforts that occur within one individual setting only (Crosnoe, Leventhal, Wirth, Pierce, & Pianta, 2010).

Parent-and-teacher engagement as partners is essential in maximizing a child's educational experience. When parents are actively engaged in their child's learning and schooling, there are important benefits for children, families, and schools, such as increased student achievement and academic performance, stronger self-regulatory skills, fewer discipline problems, better study habits, more positive attitudes toward school, improved homework habits and work orientation, and higher educational aspirations (Aeby, Manning, Thyer, & Carpenter-Aeby, 1999; Galloway & Sheridan, 1994; Grolnick & Slowiaczek, 1994; Ma, 1999; Masten & Coatsworth, 1998; Trusty, 1999).

Benefits of family–school collaboration and partnerships are also evident for families and schools (Christenson, 1995; Davies, 1993; Epstein, 1986). A partnership orientation enhances communication between parents and educators, a desirable outcome for both parties (Christenson, Hurley, Sheridan, & Fenstermacher, 1997). Increased communication provides an opportunity for parents and educators to understand better the various environments in which a child learns and develops. Working together as partners improves relationships between teachers and parents; through collaborative partnership processes, they begin to understand one another's perspectives and feel supported by each other as they work toward goals. Joint ownership in the identification and generation of solutions to academic or social-behavioral challenges increases shared commitment to meeting educational goals for students (Becher, 1984; Epstein, 1995).

KEY COMPONENTS FOR COLLABORATIVE PARTNERSHIPS

Like many educational initiatives, establishing a culture of collaborative partnerships between families and schools is often easier said than done. Our research and experience have led us to identify several key components that characterize effective partnerships. They can be described using "the four *A*'s": Approach, Attitudes, Atmosphere, and Activities (Christenson & Sheridan, 2001). Effective implementation of the four *A*'s leads to a fifth *A*: Achievement for students.

Approach pertains to the framework used by schools as they prepare to interact with families. In a truly effective educational partnership, there is an explicit perception that the relationship between families and schools is a high priority. This perception is realized when individual members of the collaborative partnership let go of their individual agendas, recognizing the value of shared responsibility and decision making on behalf of students' opportunities and experiences. Likewise, a family–school partnership espouses full commitment by families and schools to the shared work related to education. There is a sense of interdependence, such that individual and personal priorities and responsibilities give way to a reliance on each other to achieve collective goals.

Attitudes are the values and perceptions held by families and schools about their relationship. In educational partnerships, parties establish genuine trust in each other. This includes confidence that the other person has the capacity to fulfill agreed-upon roles, and trust that the other is committed to the relationship. Over time and throughout the course of establishing collaborative partnerships, parents and teachers begin to share mutual beliefs about education and learning. A shared vision is adopted to achieve mutual as well as individual goals.

Atmosphere concerns the climate in schools for families and educators. It refers to the quality or character of a school's environment and is characterized by an attractive and inviting physical appearance; collaborative relationships among school staff members, students, and families; high expectations for students, educators, and parents; respectful and positive interactions; and opportunities for meaningful participation in social and academic functions (Bear, Blank, & Smith, 2009). A positive school atmosphere is one in which individuals are valued and respected, and it is essential to establishing successful collaboration between home and school. School atmosphere contributes to effective teaching, positive student learning, and open, two-way communication within and outside of the school.

Actions are the strategies used by educators and parents to build shared responsibility. By focusing on establishing shared responsibility for children's educational outcomes, actions help facilitate the relationship between families and schools. Successful actions involve effective problem solving across home and school settings, recognizing and managing conflict, and aiding teachers in increasing relations and communication with families. Increased communication between families and educators establishes the groundwork for creating a positive school atmosphere. Approach, attitudes, and atmosphere are essential components to developing and maintaining successful actions.

Strengths-Based Approach

Successful partnerships with families stem from a family strengths-based approach. Family strengths are the "competencies and capabilities of various individual family members and the family unit that are used in response to crisis and stress, to meet needs, and to promote, enhance, and strengthen the functioning of the family system" (Trivette, Dunst, Deal, & Hamer, 1990, p. 17). Educators may adopt a strengths-based approach by shifting the way they think about and approach families.

Specifically, it is important for educators to recognize that every family has unique strengths and that by supporting those strengths rather than focusing on weaknesses, the potential for creating positive changes is great. Additionally, when families fail, it is not due to family deficits; rather, social systems and institutions have failed to allow family competencies to be learned or displayed. Further, the goal for the educator is to build on family strengths, not to fix the family, and to strengthen families and help them become less dependent on professionals (Christenson, 2003; Trivette et al., 1990). Educators can further promote strengths-based attitudes by listening to parents, viewing differences as strengths, focusing on mutual interests, sharing information to foster shared understanding, respecting parent skills and knowledge, sharing planning and decision making, sharing resources, providing a common message about schoolwork and behavior, demonstrating willingness to address conflict, refraining from fault finding, and committing to shared successes (Christenson, 2003). Rapid Reference 3.2 provides strategies for establishing a family-strengths approach to partnerships.

DON'T FORGET

It is important for educators to recognize that every family has unique strengths and that by supporting those strengths, rather than focusing on weaknesses, the potential for creating positive changes is great.

≡ Rapid Reference 3.2 Goals and Actions of Establishing a Family-Strengths Approach to Partnerships

Goals	Actions
1. Address the needs that parents identify for their children.	• Use parent-identified, rather than professional-identified, desires to increase ownership. • Provide families with opportunities to voice concerns, desires, and goals. • Allow parents to describe and identify priorities to ensure that what is addressed is of greatest importance to the family. • Help parents stay focused on the main needs or concerns for the child. • Ensure you have an understanding of what the parent tells you so that you have a shared conversation.
2. Provide a context for families to feel empowered.	• Help family members acquire skills to proactively identify needs, mobilize resources, and accomplish goals by building on family capacities, strengths, and abilities. • Focus on the ability of families to meet their own needs, rather than meeting needs for families. • Respect family's rights, values, cultures, and abilities to make decisions. • Recognize the value of family-decided actions for ensuring follow through. • Notice beautiful moments between parents and children.
3. Actively invite and use parents' ideas and strengths to address concerns and goals.	• Recognize that parents are the experts about their child and their home. • Recognize that families have skills and resources that can be tapped. • Use active invitations to help family members feel validated. • Communicate belief and trust in parents' abilities. • Comment on what the parents have done thus far to build parent confidence.

(continued)

(*continued*)

4. Acknowledge competencies of parents and offer opportunities to enhance knowledge and skills.

- Enhance knowledge and skills by supporting engagement in the collaborative process.
- Highlight, reinforce, and build upon current practices used by parents.
- Validate parents' competencies by providing new opportunities to build on strengths and enhance the development of new knowledge and skills.
- Strengthen parents' confidence in their ability to note child strengths, preferences, and needs.

Healthy Relationships

Building on a strengths-based approach, it is critical that educators connect with parents and develop positive and healthy relationships. The first step toward supporting families is to form a connection with them—to develop an intentional and ongoing relationship to enhance the child's learning and to address any obstacles (Christenson, 2003). The family–school relationship is best based on two-way communication, cooperation, coordination, and collaboration. Through a collaborative relationship, parents and teachers have shared rights and responsibilities, and contribute to the process equally. This collaborative relationship is characterized by reciprocal respect for skills and knowledge, clear and authentic communication, open and bidirectional information sharing, conjointly agreed-upon goals, and shared decision making and planning (Adams & Christenson, 2000; Christenson, 2003). Parents and educators form healthy relationships when they believe that they share the same goals for the child (e.g., positive development and achievement), that home and school experiences are both important for the child to reach educational goals, and that schools and families have unique and important roles in facilitating child development. When schools and families act on those beliefs and commit to establishing and maintaining positive relationships and to following through on individual responsibilities, the relationship is strengthened. Finally, consistency across home and school settings, including consistent goals and shared expectations, strengthens and is strengthened by positive relationships (Clarke, Sheridan, & Woods, 2010).

Trust. Bidirectional trust is a key component of healthy relationships (Christenson, 2003; Christenson & Sheridan, 2001; Clarke et al., 2010), and many elements of effective family–school relationships are predicated on trust (Adams & Christenson, 2000). Trust within a family–school relationship is defined as "confidence that another person will act in a way to

CAUTION

The importance of attributing trust on a personal level is clear; without this attribution, trust is vulnerable to fluctuations in the behavior of the partners, with a false step jeopardizing the relationship (Adams & Christenson, 2000; Holmes & Rempel, 1989).

benefit or sustain the relationship, or the implicit or explicit goals of the relationship, to achieve positive outcomes for students" (Adams & Christenson, 2000, p. 480). The development of trust progresses across three hierarchical levels: predictability, dependability, and faith. Predictability refers to the reliability and stability of behavior. As trust progresses, it is conceptualized as a personal attribute, leading to dependability. At the dependability level, trust is placed less on concrete behaviors, and more on personal qualities. The final level, faith, occurs when one individual expects that his or her partner will follow through and be responsive to the individual's needs (Adams & Christenson, 2000). The importance of attributing trust on a personal level is clear; without this attribution, trust is vulnerable to fluctuations in the behavior of the partners, with a false step jeopardizing the relationship (Adams & Christenson, 2000; Holmes & Rempel, 1989).

When trust has been established and is present at a high level in a relationship, partners interpret the behavior of one another positively, and negative behaviors are downplayed in comparison to positive characteristics. Negative behaviors are given less threatening explanations, limiting the impact of their occurrence. High-trust relationships are conceptualized as long-term and stable, and trusting and non-trusting behaviors are thought to average out in the long run. Conversely, in lower-trust relationships, partners are defensive, and positive behaviors are interpreted as situation specific. Negative behaviors are viewed as a sign of deeper concerns. In low-trust relationships, the expectation from a partner is negative behavior and limited interaction (Holmes & Rempel, 1989).

Trust is developed over time in relationships based on the presence and interaction of several key components: respect, competence, personal regard for others, integrity (Bryk & Schneider, 2002; Minke, 2006), accountability, and consideration (Christenson, 2003; Clarke et al., 2010). Respect demonstrated in a parent–educator relationship conveys the understanding that both parties are necessary and important in promoting a child's positive development. Parents and educators may show respect by genuinely listening to, valuing, and considering each other's ideas, perspectives, experiences, and knowledge. Next, competence is shown when one fulfills his or her role obligations to the other as expected. Personal regard for others is demonstrated when educators strive to reduce feelings of vulnerability in parents and when parents and educators show caring attitudes or go beyond expectations (Clarke et al., 2010).

Integrity, another key component of trust, is shown through consistency between one's words and actions, whereas accountability is shown in one's dependability in meeting expectations. Consideration, a final component of trust, pertains to the voluntary giving of resources from one to another. This intentional act is based on five conditions. The first condition is the presence of empathy; the giver perceives the other's need. Second, the giver feels agency, or his or her ability to meet that need. Third, the effort to meet the need requires little sacrifice. Fourth, the action of meeting the need is clearly voluntary, and finally, the act is not routine or customary (Clarke et al., 2010).

Given the presence of respect, competence, personal regard for others, integrity, accountability, and consideration in a relationship, educators can further facilitate trust by considering how each interaction with a family will influence that family's ability to trust their child's school or teacher (Christenson & Sheridan, 2001). The nature of a parent–teacher interaction is a better predictor of trust than frequency of interactions (Adams & Christenson, 2000). Rapid Reference 3.3 provides strategies for building trust within a family–school partnership (Christenson & Sheridan, 2001; Clarke et al., 2010; Margolis & Brannigan, 1990).

Effective Communication

In addition to the trust necessary for healthy relationships, effective communication is essential to establishing and maintaining those relationships (Christenson, 2003) and is critical to cooperation and collaboration (Ulrich & Bauer, 2003). Furthermore, improving home–school communication is a primary way to enhance the trust in the family–school relationship (Adams & Christenson, 2000). In a healthy

DON'T FORGET
....
The nature of a parent–teacher interaction is a better predictor of trust than frequency of interactions (Adams & Christenson, 2000).

≡ Rapid Reference 3.3   Strategies for Building Trust within a Family–School Partnership

1. Accept parents as they are.
2. Share resources and information.
3. Seek information directly from families.
4. Attend to parents' goals.
5. Keep your word.
6. Discuss objectives openly.
7. Come prepared to meetings with families.
8. Respond to concerns promptly.
9. Share information from your own background and experiences.

relationship, participants communicate openly, frequently, constructively, and bidirectionally (Christenson & Sheridan, 2001; Clarke et al., 2010). Effective communication is particularly important in a school setting. It serves to increase understanding of the child, his or her support systems, and each party's expectations and goals. Additionally, it can improve parents' understanding of school rules and norms and teachers' knowledge of family cultural beliefs and situational demands. Further, it allows educators to demonstrate that families are instrumental in promoting educational success.

Healthy parent–educator communication is characterized by a focus on supporting a child to reach his or her goals (Christenson, 2003; Sheridan & Kratochwill, 2008). It conveys three overarching themes: (a) a desire to develop a partnership with families; (b) the vast importance of family input in children's educational progress; and (c) the importance of a partnership in taking effective steps toward identifying mutually advantageous solutions (Christenson & Sheridan, 2001). Educators can further promote healthy communication by taking a personal approach; using common and clear language (i.e., avoiding jargon); listening quietly when the parent is speaking, verbalizing initially only to convey understanding (e.g., through minimal encouragers) and using words that unify (e.g., *we, our, together*); and expressing shared ownership and joint responsibility for addressing

DON'T FORGET

Improving home–school communication is a primary way to enhance the trust in the family–school relationship (Adams & Christenson, 2000).

needs. Finally, educators can promote healthy communication by avoiding the tendency to dominate conversations or engage in emotionally charged interactions. Guidelines and practices for establishing effective communication are found in Rapid Reference 3.4 (Christenson & Sheridan, 2001, pp. 121–122).

Listening

One of the most important forms of effective communication is listening. Listening allows a person to demonstrate concern and a desire to understand and to obtain enough information to make well-reasoned decisions (Friend &

≡ Rapid Reference 3.4 Guidelines and Practices for Establishing Effective Communication

Effective Communication Guidelines	Effective Communication Practices
• Strive for a positive orientation rather than a deficit-based or crisis orientation.	• Good-news phone calls. • Invite and incorporate parent reactions to policies and practices. • Contact parents at the first sign of a concern. • Communicate an optimistic message about the child.
• Consider tone as well as the content of your communications.	• Reframe language from problems to goals for the student. • Focus on a parents' ability to help.
• Develop and publicize regular, reliable, varied two-way communication systems.	• Family–school communication/assignment notebooks. • Shared parent–educator responsibility for contacts. • Handbooks. • Newsletters. • "Thursday folders," including relevant home and school information. • Telephone tree. • Electronic communication technology.

- Emphasize a win-win orientation rather than placing blame.

- Keep the focus of communication on the child's performance.

- Ensure that parents have needed information to support children's educational progress.

- Create formal and informal opportunities to communicate and build trust between home and school.

- Underscore all communication with a shared responsibility between families and schools.

- Discuss and focus on mutual goals and interests.
- Use words such as *we*, *us*, and *our*, versus *you*, *I*, *yours*, and *mine*.
- Bidirectional communication regarding classroom activities, progress, suggested activities for parents.
- Home–school notebooks/notes.
- Family–school meetings with students present.
- Shared parent–educator monitoring system (e.g., educational file, contract).
- Several orientation nights, with follow-up contact for non-attendees.
- Parent support groups to disseminate information on school performance.
- Home visits.
- Home–school contracts with follow-up.
- Curriculum nights.
- Monthly meetings on topics of mutual interest.
- Multicultural potlucks.
- Grade-level bagel breakfasts.
- Family fun nights.
- Committees designed to address home–school issues.
- Workshops where parents and school personnel learn together.
- Principal's hour.
- Communicating the essential nature of family involvement.
- Sharing information about the curriculum of the home.
- Discussing co-roles (e.g., co-communicators) and implementing shared practices (e.g., contracts, common language about conditions for children's success).
- Back-to-school night.

Source: Christenson & Sheridan (2001, pp. 121–122). Reprinted with permission from Guilford.

DON'T FORGET

....

One of the most important forms of effective communication is listening.

Cook, 2010). There are two forms of listening: passive listening and active listening. Passive listening includes physical and psychological attending behaviors that demonstrate interest and involvement. Physical attending pertains to behaviors such as facing the other person, leaning slightly forward, and maintaining appropriate eye contact, whereas psychological attending involves behaviors such as providing undivided attention, using silence effectively (e.g., to gather thoughts, reflect, and engage in self-examination), and using minimal encouragers (e.g., head nods, saying "*Mm-hmm*"). Active listeners extend passive listening by engaging in problem solving and decision making while listening. Throughout the interaction, they convey understanding, acceptance, and acknowledgment, and reflect key comments and emotions to confirm their understanding. An active listener also uses open-ended questions to elicit and clarify information.

Nonverbal and Verbal Interpersonal Skills

In addition to listening, effective communicators use verbal and nonverbal interpersonal skills. Nonverbal skills include cues such as body movements (e.g., posture, eye contact, and facial expressions), vocal cues (e.g., voice tone, pacing of speech, voice quality), spatial relationships (e.g., physical distance, verbal space between statements), and use of silence (Friend & Cook, 2010). The use of silence allows a communicator to demonstrate interest, concern, empathy, and respect; allows others to think; and avoids interruptions and over-talking, which demonstrate one person's desire to control the conversation (Friend & Cook, 2010; Sheridan & Kratochwill, 2008).

Verbal interpersonal skills include open-ended questions, minimal encouragers, paraphrases/summarizations, and reflection. The first of these, open-ended questions, are questions for which there are an infinite number of potential responses. Open-ended questions cannot be answered through a single word or a yes/no response. They are beneficial for effective communication because they open up a conversation, encourage others to begin or continue speaking, and elicit personal perceptions of the concept in question. Minimal encouragers can be verbal or nonverbal in nature. Verbal minimal encouragers consist of statements or sounds such as "I see" or "*Uh-huh*." Nonverbal minimal encouragers can be shown through head nods or facial expressions that indicate that the conversation is being followed and understood.

School personnel can use paraphrasing and summarizing to restate the content of a parent's message. Through a paraphrase, educators immediately and briefly rephrase the parent's statement using his or her own language to communicate that the message was understood or to clarify the message. Summarizations are two or more paraphrases that recap the essential content of the parent's message. Used strategically and purposefully, summarizations may identify major themes or highlight key points. A final form of verbal interpersonal skills is reflection. Through reflection, school personnel restate key information to gain clarity and respond to the emotional tone of the parent's message. The stated or implied feelings embedded in the message are reiterated to communicate understanding and support for the parent (Sheridan & Kratochwill, 2008).

Conflict Management

Using the interpersonal skills discussed earlier, educators can take important steps toward fostering relationships with parents. However, parents and educators are likely to have differences in opinions as they work together. Through the use of effective conflict management strategies, educators can deter these differences from negatively influencing the home–school relationship. These strategies include maintaining constructive attitudes and respect, and engaging in negotiations emphasizing efforts toward mutual interests and benefits (i.e., positive outcomes for the child), instead of setting one party against the other (Christenson & Sheridan, 2001; Margolis & Brannigan, 1990).

Blocking blame is another conflict management strategy. When conflicts occur there is a tendency to place blame on someone or something; however, this can be counterproductive and lead to resistance or distrust within family and school relationships. When conflict occurs it is best to attempt to block the desire to assign blame. Blocking blame can be achieved in a variety of ways, including direct blocking, reframing, probing, refocusing, illustrating, validating, and agreeing. The first of these, direct blocking, involves explicitly stating that the purpose of the interaction is not to blame but rather to solve the problem at hand. Reframing provides an alternative point of view about a set of facts, giving facts a more positive and productive meaning. Through probing, blame can be blocked by eliciting additional information to clarify the context that led to the blaming. Next, refocusing can be used to redirect the discussion from a nonproductive or nonessential topic to one that is relevant to helping the child. Illustrating includes giving concrete examples of areas of concern, and by validating, one recognizes the validity of another's perception or efforts. Finally, by agreeing, blame can be blocked by confirming someone's perception of a situation (Christenson & Sheridan, 2001).

A structured problem-solving approach is useful in fostering constructive problem solving with families. It provides an effective means to address concerns

CAUTION

···

When conflicts occur there is a tendency to place blame on someone or something; however, this can be counterproductive and lead to resistance or distrust within family and school relationships. When conflict occurs it is best to attempt to block the desire to assign blame.

and reduce conflict, as it serves to separate people from the problem and minimize emotionally laden decision making (Christenson, 2003; Christenson & Sheridan, 2001). One such approach (conjoint behavioral consultation, CBC) is described next.

STRUCTURED PROBLEM SOLVING: CONJOINT BEHAVIORAL CONSULTATION

A collaborative model of problem solving requires that families and school personnel work together as co-equal partners and utilize the parity of strengths and information that each partner brings to the relationship (Sheridan & Kratochwill, 2008). Co-equal partners respect all other members and share ownership of the child's educational and social responsibilities. Partnership parity involves sharing information and skills and viewing differences as unique strengths to be shared. CBC (Sheridan & Kratochwill, 2008) represents one research-based collaborative (home–school) problem-solving approach that involves school personnel engaging families with the help of a trained consultant in a collaborative problem-solving process comprised of four stages: problem identification, problem analysis, plan implementation, and plan evaluation. In CBC, school personnel and families provide the majority of information during the collaborative problem-solving process; however, a trained consultant facilitates the steps of each stage of the process. The consultant's role is to guide school personnel and families through the process and empower them to develop effective skills and intervention plans for handling problem behaviors. A collaborative problem-solving model provides a structured plan for school personnel and families to develop and foster healthy family–school partnerships and allows a medium for all partners to use effective communication skills.

The problem identification stage of the problem-solving model involves school personnel and families jointly identifying their most pressing concern about the child's behavior. Once the concern has been agreed upon, information is collected about the behavior. Families and school personnel gather information about the concerning behavior in both settings that allows for the development of hypotheses about potential variables that may be serving the function of maintaining the problem behavior. This information is then used in the problem analysis stage where the information is brought together and findings are discussed. More information will be shared in the next section on the importance of identifying the function of the concerning behavior. After information on the concerning behavior has been gathered and analyzed, families and school personnel can jointly develop intervention plans for home and school that target the identified behavior using plan components that address the function of the child's behavior but also fit with the skills and cultural values, beliefs, and practices of the home and school, placing emphasis on those that are shared by both settings.

Once a plan is developed and agreed upon, the plan implementation stage begins. In this stage, plans at home and school are implemented and changes in the child's behavior are monitored. An important component during the plan implementation stage is treatment integrity, which is discussed in a following section. To draw conclusions about the child's performance, it is important that some data are collected before and after a plan is implemented. Excessive data on the concerning behavior is not necessary; however, it is important that pre- and post-plan data are collected in a similar manner and that enough data points (roughly 3–7) are collected for both pre- and post-plan periods. This information helps guide the final problem-solving stage, plan evaluation. The plan evaluation stage involves families and schools coming together again to discuss the progress made in the child's behavior. Collected data are compared to determine if satisfactory progress has been made and partners can share with each other their experiences of the process. Any changes needed to the plan can be made and partner members can determine what next steps they want to take. For instance, if satisfactory progress has not been made, partners can decide to go back to the problem analysis stage to obtain a better understanding of what is happening and determine how better to address the problem as a team. By using collaborative problem-solving to address child concerns, continuity between home and school intervention plans can have an additive effect on the plan's success by creating consistent messages and expectations for children between the two most important settings.

INTERVENTION PLANNING AND IMPLEMENTATION

Creating Continuity Through Home and School Plans

As previously described, family involvement in children's education is an important factor correlating with positive academic and behavioral outcomes for children. Children spend most of their time in the home or school setting,

DON'T FORGET

Family involvement in children's education is an important factor correlating with positive academic and behavioral outcomes for children.

and it is important for children to see a match, or continuity, between environments. Continuity between home and school settings is seen when there are similar and overlapping actions, beliefs, and values shared by the two environments. Continuity is more than individual practices, beliefs, and values displayed by parents and school personnel; it consists of those aspects being united together across settings to create a consistent and predictable message to children. Children's perception of continuity between school and home is an important aspect that impacts their educational success (Christenson & Sheridan, 2001).

High levels of continuity between home and school are positively linked to educational achievement (Hansen, 1986; Phelan, Davidson & Yu, 1998; Warzon & Ginsburg-Block, 2008) as well as positive behavioral and social outcomes (Galloway & Sheridan, 1994; Sheridan, Eagle, Cowan, & Mickelson, 2001; Sheridan, Kratochwill & Elliott, 1990). Intervention plans that promote continuity between settings can increase the magnitude of intervention effects by providing consistent messages and expectations to children across unique, but equally important settings. Achieving continuity when planning home–school interventions is an active and ongoing process.

Matching Function of Behavior to Interventions

Despite how it may seem at times, child behavior does not occur randomly; it is instead performed in response to environmental variables that cue and motivate children to act in a way that gets them what they want. In other words, children's behavior serves some type of function. Children will try many different behaviors over time. Once they identify one or several that effectively help them achieve what they desire, those behaviors are reinforced and it is likely that the child will perform them again at a later time for the same results. Often these behaviors are socially appropriate, such as in the case of a student asking a teacher kindly if he or she can play with a new toy. At times, however, they are less adaptive, such as when a child takes a new toy without asking permission. In each of these cases, the child was motivated by the desire to obtain a new toy, and each child found an effective method to attain the toy; however, only one of the behaviors would be considered acceptable to a teacher.

There are typically four types of functions that serve as motivators for children's behavior: escape or avoidance of an undesirable task, attention, access to desirable tangibles, and sensory reinforcement. Escape- or avoidance-motivated behaviors are those performed by a child when he or she wants to get away from a person, task, or environment. An example of escape might be a child engaging in disruptive behaviors (e.g., talking to others, bothering peers) to avoid completing a math assignment. Attention-motivated behavior occurs when there is a particular person or group of people (e.g., peers) present from whom a child would like to receive attention. Attention-seeking behavior is observed when a child blurts out often to obtain the attention of an adult or peers. Behavior motivated by a desire to access desired tangible objects occurs when something desirable is available to a child contingent on positive behavior, or when a desired object has been taken away or denied to a child. For instance, positive behavior can be emitted when a child believes it will result in receiving a special reward. Alternatively, hitting another child to take his or her toy could serve the function of gaining access to desirable tangible objects (in this case, the toy). Sensory reinforcement–motivated behavior can occur at any time or any location, but occurs because it feels good and meets a sensory need for the child. For example, a child might rock back and forth or bite his or her nails.

> **DON'T FORGET**
>
> There are typically four types of functions that serve as motivators for children's behavior: escape or avoidance of an undesirable task, attention, access to desirable tangibles, and sensory reinforcement.

When developing intervention plans to ameliorate problem behavior, it is vital that consideration be given to the function that the problem behavior serves. Identifying the function, or motivation, for a child exhibiting a problem behavior allows adults to modify the environment in such a way that the child learns appropriate behaviors to help him or her receive the same result. For instance, when a child takes a new toy without asking, it is clear that taking the toy served the function of helping the child attain a desired tangible item. In this case a possible intervention that matches the function of the behavior might be to teach the child to ask nicely for the toy and to reinforce the appropriate behavior by allowing the child to play with the toy. Additionally, child behaviors such as taking the toy without asking may be met with consistent undesirable consequences, such as denying the child access to the toy. This teaches and reinforces the child to use an appropriate action to get the desired outcome and extinguishes behaviors that do not achieve the desired goal.

> **DON'T FORGET**
>
> The best way to identify the function of a child's behavior and the variables that influence it is to conduct a functional assessment.

≡ Rapid Reference 3.5 Steps of a Functional Assessment

1. Collect information about the problem behavior through direct (e.g., observing the problem behavior in the target setting) and indirect (e.g., gathering information from records or parent reports) methods.

2. Based on the information collected, develop a hypothesis about what variables are thought to be maintaining the student's behavior.

3. Test the hypothesis by altering the antecedent or consequent variables that are thought to be maintaining the problem behavior.

   a. If behavior improves during step 3, proceed to step 4.

   b. If behavior does not improve or worsens, repeat steps 2 and 3 until behavior improves and the function is identified.

4. Develop and implement an intervention that targets the function of the student's behavior and manipulates the antecedent and consequent variables maintaining the behavior.

5. Evaluate intervention effectiveness and make any necessary changes.

The best way to identify the function of a child's behavior and the variables that influence it is to conduct a functional assessment. The steps of a functional assessment are provided in Rapid Reference 3.5 (McComas, Hoch, & Mace, 2000). When creating home–school intervention plans, it is important to investigate the function of the child's behavior at home and school as it may differ based on setting. Collaborating with and guiding parents through the process of investigating and identifying behavioral function is an important step of a structured problem-solving (e.g., CBC) process.

Maximizing Treatment Integrity with Parents

Implementing intervention plans at home and school requires attention to and monitoring of treatment integrity. In its most basic sense, treatment integrity is defined as the degree to which an intervention plan is implemented as intended (Gresham, 1989), or how closely parents and school personnel follow the steps outlined in an intervention plan. Reliable evaluation of the effectiveness of an intervention plan is impossible if a plan is not administered correctly or in its entirety. The purpose of implementing an intervention plan is to improve a child's behavior, and evaluating the effectiveness of an intervention plan thus requires determining whether the child's behavior improved, remained the same, or became worse. An essential step in validating the effectiveness of an intervention requires determining whether the intervention was appropriately administered. Effective intervention plans may be incorrectly or prematurely deemed ineffective and discarded if not administered as designed. For instance, if an intervention plan calls to reward a child contingent on appropriate behavior, but the child never receives the reward following the display of appropriate behavior, it would be impossible to state whether this particular intervention plan was effective.

> **CAUTION**
> Reliable evaluation of the effectiveness of an intervention plan is impossible if a plan is not administered correctly or in its entirety.

Adherence to a treatment protocol is one way to ensure treatment integrity. Adherence is generally calculated by dividing the number of steps completed by the total number of steps possible. Assessment of the number of steps completed can be done in three ways: direct observation, self-report, and permanent products. Direct observation requires that an independent observer assess the intervention in action and record the number of steps completed correctly by the intervention plan agent (usually a parent or teacher). In self-report measures, the intervention plan agent reports the number of steps they completed. Finally, permanent products include any hard-evidence documents that are outcomes of the intervention, such as a home–school note or a chart move that indicates that the child met his or her goal for that day. Assessing adherence to school-based intervention plans using any of these three forms can be relatively easy if resources are available. However, it can be challenging to measure treatment integrity in the home setting. In the home setting, reliance on self-reports or permanent products is often necessary to assess adherence.

Promoting Treatment Integrity
There are many ways in which school personnel can promote treatment integrity of home intervention plans. Two common methods used by school personnel include providing families with a copy of an intervention plan and explaining the importance of treatment integrity. These steps are necessary, but not sufficient for maximizing parent adherence to an intervention plan. School personnel should focus additional attention on teaching parents how to administer the plan steps, modeling the steps for them, and practicing the intervention plan steps with them until they have demonstrated the ability to implement the plan fully and independently. Providing feedback and support to parents over the course of intervention delivery is also recommended to promote home plan treatment integrity. Other suggestions that may be helpful to school personnel when collaboratively developing home intervention plans are found in Rapid Reference 3.6 (Swanger-Gagné, Garbacz, & Sheridan, 2009).

≣ Rapid Reference 3.6 Tips for Increasing Parent Treatment Integrity

1. Develop strategies collaboratively with the family that fit with their culture and values.
2. Clearly define expectations of intervention plan components (i.e., who does what, when, and how).
3. Create inexpensive and easy-to-implement intervention plans.
4. Train parents in intervention plan delivery.
5. Use permanent products as evidence of treatment integrity.
6. Provide specific feedback to parents on their integrity in the intervention steps.
7. Problem-solve with parents who struggle with implementing an intervention.
8. Communicate often with parents about intervention effects.

Source: Adapted from strategies outlined in Swanger-Gagné, Garbacz, & Sheridan (2009).

Example: Devon's Homework

The following example demonstrates a positive home–school intervention plan involving Devon, a third-grade male, his family, his teacher, Ms. Smith, and a CBC consultant. Devon was experiencing difficulty completing his math assignments at school and was not returning completed math homework each day. Ms. Smith decided she needed to try something new and contacted the school psychologist, who recommended CBC and a local consultant. After discussing CBC with the consultant, Ms. Smith contacted Devon's parents to discuss joining in the problem-solving process. A meeting was then scheduled with Devon's parents, Ms. Smith, and the CBC consultant. An early morning time was set to accommodate Devon's parents' work schedules.

Problem Identification
Ms. Smith's concerns focused on Devon's math work completion, and Devon's parents' concerns centered on the effort it took to focus Devon and to be productive during homework completion. Given the shared concerns, it was jointly determined that more information would be collected by everyone involved, and the group would focus on improving Devon's math work completion at home and at school. Devon's parents collected information about the homework time structure in the home, how much homework Devon completed each night, and what possible variables impacted Devon's homework completion.

Ms. Smith gathered information on the percentage of problems Devon completed during math independent work time, tracked the amount of time that Devon was on-task, and noted the activities in which he engaged other than math. Additionally, brief curriculum-based measurement (CBM) probes were administered to determine if Devon had the skills to complete the math work. A second meeting time was set for the following week to analyze the information.

Problem Analysis

In the second meeting, the collected information was discussed and hypotheses and functions were shared. This discussion led to the development of an intervention plan for home and school. Devon's parents described homework time as a 45-minute period immediately following dinner wherein Devon and his two siblings, ages 7 and 13 years, respectively, completed their homework at the living-room table. One parent was present intermittently to monitor behavior, but not consistently. There were no rewards or punishment for completion or non-completion of work, and homework was rarely checked for completion once the time period was over. Devon's parents also recorded that Devon completed an average of 44% of his homework problems each night and that he completed more work when one of his parents was present at the homework table. Ms. Smith's data revealed that Devon completed about 47% of his work during independent math time. Devon's CBM probes indicated that he was able to complete the work independently, demonstrating that Devon had the skills to complete the work but did not do so. Ms. Smith also found that Devon was on-task for only 53% of independent math time, took multiple bathroom/drink breaks, and doodled on scrap paper instead of working on math problems. With a classroom of 26 children, Ms. Smith was not able to redirect Devon back to his work often, but when she did, he complied right away but did not stay on-task for long.

Based on the information shared, the team determined that the function of Devon's behavior was escape-maintained and that he was not completing his work because he could avoid it with minor consequences. A plan for home and school was then developed to target Devon's math work completion and work avoidance. A goal of completing 60% of his work was established for home and school. At home, the team decided that one parent would be present throughout all of homework time to help prompt Devon to complete his work. To address the function of escaping from work, Devon was rewarded with a break at specified times contingent on work completion. When Devon completed 35% of his work he was allowed a five-minute break to draw or play with the family dog. To motivate and reinforce Devon's homework completion, a chart move was used. Devon enjoyed race cars so an oval racetrack was drawn on a chart with

20 checkpoints evenly spaced around the track, and a race car was drawn at the start line. If Devon met his goal of 60% math homework completed, he was able to make a chart move by drawing a line connecting the checkpoints in sequential order. If he finished 100% of his work, he could connect two checkpoints. Devon was rewarded with a prize from a reward menu comprised of his favorite activities for every four check points connected. Once Devon completed an entire lap (by connecting all 20 checkpoints) he was rewarded with dinner at his favorite restaurant. Similarly, at school, Devon was given one bathroom/drink pass per independent work time and was given a five-minute break to doodle after 35% of his work was completed. The same chart move reward system was used at school, with a chart move for 60% work completion and two chart moves for 100% work completion. Every fourth chart move resulted in Devon earning a reward, such as being line leader or running errands to the office. A completed lap resulted in lunch with the principal. In addition, a home–school note was passed back and forth between Ms. Smith and Devon's parents wherein daily goal status and reward options were recorded. Originally, Ms. Smith wanted to have a punishment system in place so that Devon would miss recess should he fail to meet his goal; however, Devon's parents were not comfortable with punishing Devon. Instead, the group decided that rewarding Devon's goal attainment was more acceptable.

Plan Implementation
During the plan implementation stage, home and school plans were implemented and communication was maintained through the daily home–school note.

Plan Evaluation
After two-and-a-half weeks of plan implementation at home and school, Ms. Smith, Devon's parents, and the CBC consultant met again to review progress and evaluate the effectiveness of the intervention plan. Home and school intervention plan data are presented in Figure 3.1. At home, Devon met his goal of 60% work completed on 11 of 14 days and raised his average of work completion from 44% to 85%. There were seven days in which he completed all of his math homework. At school, Devon met his goal on 9 of 14 days and raised his average work completion from 47% to 79%. Devon completed 100% of his schoolwork six times during the intervention plan period. Ms. Smith and Devon's parents were satisfied with the progress, and Devon's parents decided to maintain the homework plan for Devon and implement a similar plan for their oldest son. Devon's math assignments and the home–school note served as indicators of treatment integrity, and it was calculated that the intervention was implemented as intended at home for 13 of the 14 days, and 14 of the 14 days at school. These statistics

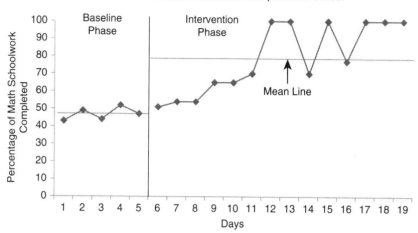

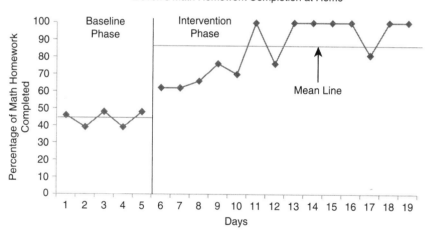

Figure 3.1. Devon's School and Home Intervention Plan Data

provided confidence that the intervention was responsible for the increase in Devon's work completion.

CONCLUSIONS

Developing collaborative family–school partnerships is an important mission for educators in today's schools. There are many benefits to children, families, and schools when such partnerships are established. This chapter began by discussing the importance of collaborating with families and introduced strategies and guidelines to engage families in meaningful partnerships. Next, a description of a structured problem-solving model was provided to give educators an empirical roadmap to help guide family–school partnerships to purpose-driven relationships that focus on supporting children in the two most important settings. Finally, strategies and guidelines for developing and implementing family–school interventions were provided, as well as a case study using conjoint behavioral consultation as an example of these strategies and guidelines in action. Combining the efforts of families and schools into a cohesive unit, building on family strengths, and establishing continuity between systems are powerful methods for increasing the impact of interventions developed to ameliorate child problems. The problem-solving approach described here provides a structured model for educators and families to follow when developing interventions at home and at school.

REFERENCES

Adams, K. S., & Christenson, S. L. (2000). Trust and the family–school relationship: Examination of parent–teacher differences in elementary and secondary grades. *Journal of School Psychology, 38*, 477–497.

Aeby, V. G., Manning, B. H., Thyer, B. A., & Carpenter-Aeby, T. (1999). Comparing outcomes of an alternative school program offered with and without intensive family involvement. *School Community Journal, 9*, 17–32.

Barbarin, O., Downer, J., Odom, E., & Head-Reeves, D. (2010). Home–school differences in beliefs, support, and control during public pre-kindergarten and their link to children's kindergarten readiness. *Early Childhood Research Quarterly, 25*, 358–372.

Bear, G. G., Blank, J., & Smith, D. C. (2009). *School climate.* Consortium to Prevent School Violence. Retrieved from www.preventschoolviolence.org.

Becher, R. M. (1984). *Parent involvement: A review of research and principles for successful practice.* Urbana, IL: ERIC Clearinghouse on Elementary and Early Childhood Education. (ERIC Document Reproduction Service No. ED 247-032).

Bryk, A. S., & Schneider, B. (2002). *Trust in schools: A core resource for improvement.* New York, NY: Russell Sage Foundation.

Christenson, S. L. (1995). Supporting home–school collaboration. In A. Thomas & J. Grimes (Eds.), *Best practices in school psychology III* (pp. 253–267). Washington, DC: National Association of School Psychologists.

Christenson, S. L. (2003). The family–school partnership: An opportunity to promote the learning competence of all students. *School Psychology Quarterly, 18*, 454–482.

Christenson, S. L., Hurley, C., Sheridan, S. M., & Fenstermacher, K. (1997). Parents' and school psychologists' perspectives on parent involvement activities. *School Psychology Review, 26*, 111–130.

Christenson, S. L., & Sheridan, S. M. (2001). *Schools and families: Creating essential connections for learning.* New York, NY: Guilford Press.

Clarke, B. L., Sheridan, S. M., & Woods, K. E. (2010). Elements of healthy family–school relationships. In S. L. Christenson & A. L. Reschly (Eds.), *Handbook of school–family partnerships* (pp. 61–79). New York: Routledge.

Cowan, R., Swearer Napolitano, S. M., & Sheridan, S. M. (2004). Home–school collaboration. In C. Spielberger (Ed.), *Encyclopedia of applied psychology* (Vol. 2, pp. 201–208). San Diego, CA: Academic Press.

Crosnoe, R., Leventhal, T., Wirth, R. J., Pierce, K. M., & Pianta, R. C. (2010). Family socioeconomic status and consistent environmental stimulation in early childhood. *Child Development, 81,* 972–987.

Davies, D. (1993). Benefits and barriers to parent involvement: From Portugal to Boston to Liverpool. In N. F. Chavkin (Ed.), *Families and schools in a pluralistic society* (pp. 53–72). Albany: State University of New York Press.

Epstein, J. L. (1986). Parents' reactions to teacher practices of parent involvement. *Elementary School Journal, 86,* 277–294.

Epstein, J. L. (1995). School/family/community partnerships: Caring for the children we share. *Phi Delta Kappan, 76,* 701–712.

Friend, M., & Cook, L. (2010). *Interactions: Collaboration skills for school professionals.* Boston, MA: Pearson.

Galloway, J., & Sheridan, S. M. (1994). Implementing scientific practices through case studies: Examples using home–school interventions and consultation. *Journal of School Psychology, 32,* 385–413.

Gresham, F. M. (1989). Assessment of treatment integrity in school consultation and prereferral intervention. *School Psychology Review, 18,* 37–50.

Grolnick, W. S., & Slowiaczek, M. L. (1994). Parents' involvement in children's schooling: A multidimensional conceptualization and motivational model. *Child Development, 65,* 237–252.

Hansen, D. A. (1986). Family–school articulations: The effects of interaction rule mismatch. *American Educational Research Journal, 23,* 643–659.

Holmes, J. G., & Rempel, J. K. (1989). Trust in close relationships. In C. Hendrick (Ed.), *Close relationships* (pp. 187–220). Newbury Park, CA: Sage.

Ma, X. (1999). Dropping out of advanced mathematics: The effects of parental involvement. *Teachers College Record, 101,* 60–81.

Margolis, H., & Brannigan, G. G. (1990). Strategies for resolving parent–school conflict. *Reading, Writing, and Learning Disabilities, 6,* 1–23.

Masten, A. S., & Coatsworth, J. D. (1998). The development of competence in favorable and unfavorable environments: Lessons from research on successful children. *American Psychologist, 53,* 205–220.

McComas, J. L., Hoch, H., & Mace, F. C. (2000). Functional analysis. In E. S. Shapiro & T. R. Kratochwill (Eds.), *Conducting school-based assessments of child and adolescent behavior* (pp. 78–120). New York, NY: Guilford Press.

Minke, K. M. (2006). Parent–teacher relationships. In G. G. Bear & K. M. Minke (Eds.), *Children's needs III: Development, prevention, and intervention* (pp. 73–85). Bethesda, MD: National Association of School Psychologists.

Phelan, P., Davidson, A. L., & Yu, H. C. (1998). *Adolescents' worlds: Negotiating family, peers, and school.* New York, NY: Teachers College Press.

Sheridan, S. M., Eagle, J. W., Cowan, R. J., & Mickelson, W. (2001). The effects of conjoint behavioral consultation: Results of a 4-year investigation. *Journal of School Psychology, 39,* 361–385.

Sheridan, S. M., & Kratochwill, T. R. (2008). *Conjoint behavioral consultation: Promoting family–school connections and interventions.* New York, NY: Springer.

Sheridan, S. M., Kratochwill, T. R., & Elliott, S. N. (1990). Behavioral consultation with parents and teachers: Delivering treatment for socially withdrawn children at home and school. *School Psychology Review, 19,* 33–52.

Swanger-Gagné, M. S., Garbacz, S. A., & Sheridan, S. M. (2009). Intervention implementation integrity within conjoint behavioral consultation: Strategies for working with families. *School Mental Health, 1,* 131–142.

Trivette, C. M., Dunst, C. J., Deal, A. G., & Hamer, A. (1990). Assessing family strengths and family functioning style. *Topics in Early Childhood Special Education, 10,* 16–35. doi: 10.1177/027112149001000103

Trusty, J. (1999). Family influences on educational expectations of late adolescents. *Journal of Educational Research, 91,* 260–270.

Ulrich, M. E., & Bauer, A. M. (2003). A closer look at communication between parents and professionals. *Teaching Exceptional Children, 35,* 20–23.

Warzon, K. B., & Ginsburg-Block, M. (2008). Cultural continuity between home and school as a predictor of student motivation: What we know, what we need to learn, and implications for practice. In C. Hudley & A. Gottfried (Eds.), *Academic motivation and the culture of school in childhood and adolescence* (pp. 121–145). New York, NY: Oxford University Press.

🐊 TEST YOURSELF 🐊

1. *True or false?*: Families and schools partnering together to help children has benefits for children, families, and schools alike.

2. Which of the following is *not* one of the four key components to collaboration?
   a. Atmosphere
   b. Attitude
   c. Actions
   d. Alertness
   e. Approach

3. Which of the following is *not* a strategy for building a trusting relationship?
   a. Respond to concerns promptly.
   b. Keep your background information and experiences to yourself.
   c. Accept parents as they are.
   d. Come prepared to meetings with families.
   e. Share resources and information.

4. Which of the following definitions best describes continuity?
   a. It is the degree that a parent implements an intervention as intended.
   b. It is the continuous assessment of a student's academic or behavioral skills over time.
   c. It is the degree of match between actions, values, and beliefs in the home and school settings.
   d. It is the process of identifying the function of a child's behavior.

5. Name the four typical functions that motivate children's behavior.

6. Which of the following strategies increases the likelihood of a parent implementing an intervention with good integrity?

a. Provide specific feedback to parents on their integrity in the intervention steps.

b. Clearly define expectations of intervention plan components (i.e., who does what, when, and how).

c. Provide parents training in intervention delivery.

d. Develop strategies collaboratively with the family that fit with their culture and values.

e. All of the above strategies increase that likelihood.

Answers: 1. True; 2. d; 3. b; 4. c; 5. escape-avoidance; attention; access to desirable tangibles; sensory reinforcement; 6. e

Part II

SELECTING AND TAILORING INTERVENTIONS AND INDIVIDUALIZING INSTRUCTION

Four

TAILORING INTERVENTIONS IN READING BASED ON EMERGING RESEARCH ON THE DEVELOPMENT OF WORD RECOGNITION SKILLS

David Kilpatrick

I magine taking your poorly running car to a mechanic. Your mechanic says he doesn't understand why the car has this problem, yet suggests different ways that the problem can be minimized or improved upon. However, because the mechanic cannot identify the cause of the problem, there is little hope of fixing it.

When it comes to word-level reading difficulties, those of us who conduct educational evaluations have often been functioning like that mechanic. That is, we tend to design interventions without knowing the nature or source of the reading difficulties. Two emerging sets of research, however, have demonstrated very clearly how we can understand the nature and sources of reading difficulties especially for students who have sufficient learning opportunities and exhibit good effort. First, research has demonstrated that *most* reading difficulties can be prevented or corrected (e.g., Torgesen et al., 2001; Vellutino et al., 1996). Second, the mystery surrounding the cause and nature of word-level reading difficulties has essentially been solved (e.g., Ehri, 1998, 2005; Ziegler & Goswami, 2005).

PREVENTING AND CORRECTING MOST READING DIFFICULTIES

Research over the last two decades has demonstrated that most reading difficulties can be corrected, or better yet, prevented in the first place. It is most unfortunate that the educational community appears to know nothing of these findings. In 1999, the American Federation of Teachers (AFT), the second largest teachers union, published *Teaching Reading IS Rocket Science*. On that document's first page, the AFT readily admitted that there was a large gap between the research findings on literacy and actual classroom practice (American Federation of Teachers, 1999). Ten years later, in 2009, a special issue of the *Journal of Learning Disabilities* was devoted to the question of why the important advances in our understanding of reading acquisition and reading difficulties have not made their way into our K–12 classrooms (Moats, 2009). Nelson and Machek (2007) have demonstrated that even school psychologists are not well acquainted with the major findings of reading research.

There have been many studies addressing the prevention and remediation of reading difficulties. However, two stand out in terms of significance: Vellutino et al. (1996) and Torgesen et al. (2001).

Prevention

In a large-scale study, Vellutino et al. (1996) conducted a 15-week intensive intervention in the spring of first grade for 74 students who represented the lowest 9% of students who were at risk for reading disabilities. By the end of the intervention, 67% scored at or above average on tests of word-level reading (above the 30th percentile), and these results were maintained a year after the intervention was discontinued (end of second grade) as well as three years later (Vellutino, Scanlon, & Lyon, 2000). Only 15% of the original 9% of at-risk students continued to earn scores below the 30th percentile at the end of second grade. Vellutino et al. (1996) projected this finding to the original population from which the at-risk students were drawn. Assuming their intervention would work with less involved cases (and research suggests it would, e.g., Fletcher et al., 1994; Stanovich & Siegel, 1994), they indicated that with such an intervention available, only 3% of the total population they drew from would earn scores below the 30th percentile and, of those, only half (1.5%) would earn scores below the 16th percentile. That projected figure represents a significant contrast to the annual reports of the *National Assessment of Educational Progress*, which indicate that 30 to 34% of fourth graders perform below a basic reading level. Most schools would not be able to implement the approach of Vellutino et al. (1996) for reasons discussed ahead. However, between Vellutino et al.'s (1996) ideal scenario of having only 1.5 to 3% of students with significant reading difficulties and the reality that 30 to 34% of students experience reading difficulties, there is room for substantial improvement.

Remediation

Torgesen et al. (2001) intervened with 60 fourth graders with very severe reading disabilities. Their mean IQ on the Wechsler Intelligence Scale for Children-Third

Edition (WISC-III, Wechsler, 1991) was 96 while their mean standard score for word-level reading on the Woodcock Reading Mastery Test–Revised (WRMT-R, Woodcock, 1987) was 68. Immediately after the intervention, as well as at one- and two-year follow-ups, these students maintained an average 20 standard score point gain on the WRMT-R Word Identification and Word Attack subtests.[1] Forty percent of these students required no ongoing reading help after the intervention ended, and nearly every student had WRMT-R standard scores within the average range after the intervention concluded and at the one- and two-year follow-ups. More surprising was the length of the intervention that produced these substantial, long-term results: eight weeks.

If the results from the two studies just described do not sound like a late-night television commercial for a product that is too good to be true, you may not have been reading carefully. These results are indeed remarkable. In fact, they would be difficult to accept were it not for the facts that they were (1) the result of large U.S. Government grants (NICHD), (2) conducted by world-renowned research teams, and (3) reported in top research journals (*Journal of Educational Psychology* and *Journal of Learning Disabilities*, respectively). More importantly, however, the highly successful techniques used in these studies were drawn from a rich empirical literature on reading acquisition and reading difficulties. For those familiar with this literature, the findings of these studies were very welcome, but not surprising. It is no wonder why the *Journal of Learning Disabilities* devoted a special issue to addressing the gap between findings like these and current classroom practice.

A caveat to these two studies is that they involved 1:1 tutoring for either 30 minutes per day for 15 weeks (Vellutino et al., 1996) or two 50-minute periods a day for 8 weeks (Torgesen et al., 2001). Most schools cannot afford such a remedial ratio. However, it could be argued that the *content*[2] rather than the delivery ratio was the most significant factor in these studies (though the ratio no doubt helped). Some research has suggested that if grouping is done carefully (i.e., students in the group have similar learning needs), small groups of 1:2 or 1:3 may yield nearly the same results as 1:1 remediation (Elbaum, Vaughn, Hughes, & Moody, 2000; Lennon & Slesinski, 1999). In fact, *School Psychology Review* reported on how the Vellutino et al. (1996) study was essentially replicated using 1:2 groups (Lennon & Slesinski, 1999).

---

1. To appreciate fully the magnitude of this effect, consider that research has shown the popular READ180 program averages approximately a three standard score point gain (Papalewis, 2004; Slavin, Lake, Chambers, Cheung, & Davis, 2009).

2. The content/curriculum of these studies involved intensive phonological awareness training, explicit phonics, and opportunities to apply these skills to reading connected text.

Due to the intensity of the intervention and size of the groups (i.e., 1:1 delivery system), it would not be appropriate to suggest that these two studies represent the new standard for common practice. However, as mentioned, they demonstrate that we have an incredible growth potential in terms of correcting or preventing a large portion of reading difficulties. We can do this by implementing the *content* of the instructional approaches used by these researchers, while doing our best to program small student groupings to maximize the learning opportunities. But none of these substantial changes can occur if educators are unaware that these findings exist, which unfortunately appears to be the case at the present time (Moats, 2009).

MYSTERY SOLVED: UNDERSTANDING WORD-LEVEL READING DIFFICULTIES

Reading progress is largely determined by how efficiently students build a sight vocabulary. A *sight vocabulary* refers to the pool of words students can recognize instantly and effortlessly, without having to guess or sound them out. Poor readers almost invariably have small sight vocabularies. Compared to their peers, there are fewer words they instantly recognize, so they must rely on phonic analysis and/or guessing. By contrast, accomplished readers have large sight vocabularies. Most of the words they encounter are instantly recognized, and only when encountering new words do they have to rely on phonics and/or guessing.

How do students quickly and efficiently build a sight vocabulary? In a sense, the answer to this question represents the proverbial Holy Grail of reading education. Students who can effortlessly identify words can focus all of their attention and working memory on reading *comprehension*. By contrast, students who have to guess at or sound out (i.e., decode) many of the words they read must allocate attentional and working memory resources to decoding, leaving fewer resources available for comprehending what they read.

First let's consider what skilled readers can do, ranging from second or third grade to adulthood (Crowder & Wagner, 1992; Rayner & Pollatsek, 1989). They can:

- Identify known words after an exposure of only 1/20 of a second.
- Learn new words after 1–5 exposures.

> **DON'T FORGET**
> ....
> Sight vocabulary refers to the pool of words that are familiar to the reader. Familiar words are recognized instantly and effortlessly. The more words that are recognized effortlessly, the more the reader can focus on comprehension.

- Remember the words they have learned without retrieval failures.
- Recognize words instantly, without the aid of context clues.

These skills do *not* characterize weak readers, who typically require many exposures to remember new words, read slowly and with much effort, forget words previously learned, and rely heavily on context cues. What makes the difference is sight vocabulary. So, how do students build a sight vocabulary?

Discovery of the Process Behind Sight-Word Learning

It is encouraging to note that researchers have largely discovered (1) how readers build a sight vocabulary, and (2) why some students have more difficulty building a sight vocabulary than others, including those with reading disabilities. At least in broad outline, the process is no longer a mystery. The problem is that outside the niche area in which these researchers work, few seem to be aware of this discovery (Moats, 2009; Nelson & Machek, 2007). Thus, educators have been making instructional decisions based upon one or two popular theories of word recognition, neither of which is consistent with the empirical findings (which are addressed ahead).

Dispelling Popular Theories That Are Inconsistent With Research

Arguably, the two most popular understandings about sight-word learning are (1) the Psycholinguistic Guessing Game and (2) the visual memory hypothesis.

Psycholinguistic Guessing Game

The *Psycholinguistic Guessing Game* (Goodman, 1976) has been the foundational theory of word perception within Whole Language. This theory claims that skilled readers identify words using three interactive cueing systems, graphophonemic (i.e., basic phonic), contextual, and linguistic. Developed in the 1960s–1970s, this theory has been impervious to the large body of empirical research that has accumulated since then. As it turns out, skilled readers can instantly identify any one of the thousands of words from their sight vocabularies, without recourse to context. While context is central to meaning, it is not necessary for recognizing familiar words. By contrast, weak readers rely heavily on context because of their limited sight vocabularies (e.g., Nation & Snowling, 1998). The Psycholinguistic Guessing Game assumes that words are not necessarily recalled from memory, but rather identified as the student moves through the text using the various cues. This theory essentially downplays or denies the existence of an efficient sight vocabulary.

The Psycholinguistic Guessing Game advocates teaching all children to use the three cueing systems from the beginning of reading instruction. For example, a student sees the sentence, "The boy is waiting for his ___." The student comes to that last word and notes it is a small word beginning with the letter *b*. That information combined with the context allows him to *guess* that the word is *bus*. Also, linguistically, a noun is called for at this point, which helped limit the possibilities. Further analysis of the word may confirm the guess (e.g., noticing the *–us* part of the word *bus*), but this is hardly necessary because the sampling of the phonic aspect (in this case the first letter) along with context and the linguistic parameters allow him to correctly derive meaning from the sentence. So in the Psycholinguistic Guessing Game, decoding is to a large extent the *product* of comprehending what you read, rather than considering comprehension as being largely informed by decoding. Rather than reading words based on instant access of known words from long-term memory (LTM), words are continually guessed at as students move through text using the three cueing systems. It is presumed that skilled readers use these three cueing systems very efficiently, and poor readers are basically poor guessers.[3]

However, as mentioned, skilled readers can instantly identify tens of thousands of words in the absence of any context. There is an abundant amount of research supporting the notion that skilled readers have a vast pool of words stored in LTM (Crowder & Wagner, 1992; Rayner & Pollatsek, 1989). Students destined to be good readers develop a large sight vocabulary whether or not they receive this guessing-type of instruction (Liberman & Liberman, 1990), while poor readers latch onto the contextual guessing because they are inefficient at building a sight vocabulary (Nation & Snowling, 1998). The extensive scientific research into the reading process is inconsistent with the Psycholinguistic Guessing Game, despite the very bold and confident pronouncements from its developers (Ehri, 1998; Liberman & Liberman, 1990). However, as the mechanism for decoding within the Whole Language approach to literacy, it has enjoyed wide popularity for well over two decades, despite its inconsistency with the empirical findings.

Visual Memory

Until recently, almost everyone implicitly assumed that visual memory was the mechanism for sight-word learning. This assumption is based upon strong, intuitive evidence. However, contrary to our intuitions, we do not store words visually. Because this assumption seems so pervasive in education, I will spend some time describing why scientists reject this highly intuitive notion.

Two concepts must be clearly distinguished to understand how we remember words: *input* and *storage*. When we read, we obviously *input* words visually.

---

3. For a helpful, accessible, and detailed critique, see Dr. Kerry Hempestall's online review at http://www.educationnews.org/articles/the-three-cueing-model-down-for-the-count.html.

But that does not mean that our LTM for words involves visual *storage*. In fact, research suggests otherwise. For example, consider the simple working memory task of looking up a number in a telephone directory. That involves visual input

> ## CAUTION
> •••
> *Input* and *storage* must not be confused. Printed words are input *visually*, but are stored linguistically (i.e., *phonologically* and *semantically*).

and visual-motor output (via the keypad). Despite the visual input (and output), we do not *store* that information visually. Rather, we store it *auditorily/phonologically*.[4] We verbally repeat the number a few times, either aloud or silently. Thus, we are *storing* the number phonologically, even though it was *input* visually. While this illustration involves working memory, the same can be said about LTM—input and storage are not the same process.

To lay to rest the pervasive misunderstanding that visual memory is the mechanism of word storage, the following are several reasons why we now know that sight vocabulary is not based on visual memory:

1. Results of "mixed-case" studies do not support the visual memory hypothesis. Researchers exposed adults to words in mixed case (i.e., every other letter was uppercase: yEsTeRdAy; hAPpY). They assumed these would not match a stored visual memory. Not surprisingly, mixed-case words slowed reaction times. However, when the adults had ample exposure to words printed in this unusual manner, they could read a fresh batch of words they had never seen in mixed case as quickly and accurately as words printed normally (Adams, 1990). This finding demonstrated that readers were not matching those mixed-case words to visual memories because they had never seen those particular words printed that way before.

2. Related to the mixed-case finding is the observation that we read words in many different fonts, uppercase, lowercase, and innumerable variations among people's manuscript and cursive handwriting. We do not have a visual memory for tens of thousands of words multiplied by the countless different ways they are visually presented in print.

3. Over 120 years ago, Cattell (1886) discovered that reaction times to written words (e.g., *chair*) were faster than for drawings (e.g., of a chair),

---

4. *Auditory* refers to all sound input while *phonological* refers to the auditory information related to the sounds in spoken language. Those with reading disabilities do not have strictly auditory difficulties. Their difficulties are phonological in nature (Share, Jorm, MacLean, & Matthews, 2002).

suggesting that word recognition and visual memory might represent different processes.

4. Since the 1970s researchers have known that the visual memory skills of students with reading disabilities (i.e., no concurrent math disabilities) are comparable to typical readers (Swanson, 1978; Vellutino et al., 1996; Vellutino, Steger, DeSetto, & Phillips, 1975). This would not make sense if visual memory is central to skilled word reading.

5. Many studies have shown high correlations between word-level reading skills and phonological awareness yet very low correlations (typically not significant) with visual memory tasks. (Adams, 1990; Vellutino et al., 1996). These findings seem inconsistent with the notion that visual memory is the basis of sight-word learning.

6. Don't those who are deaf read by visual memory? Actually, research does not support this intuitive assumption (Hanson, 1991; Leybaert, 2000). Many individuals who are deaf never read higher than the third- or fourth-grade reading level (Leybaert, 2000). Over 95% of those who are deaf wear hearing-aids, which means they have at least some residual sound input. As a result, the correlation between phonological awareness and reading is similar in deaf and hearing populations (Hanson, 1991).

≡ Rapid Reference 4.1 Some Reasons We Know Words Are Not Stored via Visual Memory

- MiXeD cAsE sTuDiEs.
- High correlation between sight-word learning and phonological awareness.
- Exclusively students with reading disabilities (i.e., no math problems) have average visual memory but weak orthographic memory.
- With the help of hearing-aids, individuals who are deaf can develop the phonological structure of the spoken language and can learn to read while those who do not develop phonological awareness struggle in reading—there is no efficient visual alternative for readers who are deaf.
- Naming speed for written words is faster than for objects, suggesting printed word memory and visual memory involve different processes.
- We sometimes fail to retrieve the names of familiar objects and people (temporary visual-association memory failure), but never fail to retrieve the written words we have learned.

While visual memory is not the primary mechanism for sight-word storage, that does not mean it is unrelated to reading acquisition. Common sense and empirical research (Crowder & Wagner, 1992; Vellutino et al., 1996) suggest visual memory affects the process of learning letter names and sounds. However, visual memory is not the basis of sight-word reading for the reasons outlined earlier.

> **CAUTION**
>
> While visual memory is not the mechanism for sight-word storage, it is very important for letter-sound learning.

Neither visual memory nor the Psycholinguistic Guessing Game can provide an adequate explanation of word-level reading acquisition or reading difficulties. Neither correctly explains how readers establish a sight vocabulary.

HOW WE STORE WORDS

Though largely unknown outside a limited circle of researchers, scientists have developed a fairly well established understanding of how we store words in LTM for fast, accurate retrieval. In the research literature, this understanding is referred to by various terms, including *bonding* (Ehri, 2005), the *representation hypothesis* (Perfetti, 1991), *direct mapping* (Rack, Hulme, Snowling, & Wightman, 1994), *unitization* (Treiman, Sotak, & Bowman, 2001), the *lexical tuning hypothesis* (Castles, Davis, Cavalot, & Forster, 2007), the *self-teaching hypothesis* (Share, 1999), or simply *mapping*[5] (e.g., Landi, Perfetti, Bolger, Dunlap, & Foorman, 2006). In what follows, we will be using the terms *orthographic memory, orthographic mapping*, or simply *mapping* to refer to the process researchers have discovered that explains how individuals store words for fast, accurate retrieval.

Orthographic mapping is the mental process we use to store permanently words for immediate, effortless retrieval. It is the process that transforms an unfamiliar printed word into an instantly recognizable sight-word. Thus, orthographic mapping is the mechanism we use to develop a sight vocabulary.

But precisely what does *orthographic* mean? The word *orthography* is based on two Greek words, *orthos* ("straight," "correct") and *graphos*

> **DON'T FORGET**
>
> *Orthographic mapping* is the mental process we use to store words for instant, effortless retrieval. It is our mechanism for developing our sight vocabulary.

---

5. This simple term, *mapping*, is also used as a synonym for *phonic decoding words* (e.g., Landi et al., 2006; Stahl & Murray, 1994), which adds imprecision to the term's usage.

DON'T FORGET

Orthography refers to the precise/correct spelling of words. The sequence of letters in words becomes bonded to the spoken pronunciation and meaning. Thus, orthographic memory, not visual memory, is the basis for sight-word learning.

("writing"). Orthography refers to the correct spellings of specific words. A sight vocabulary refers to a memory for specific words whose spellings have been committed to recognition memory.[6]

The process of orthographic mapping occurs quite naturally for students who have the prerequisite skills of letter-sound knowledge, phonemic awareness, and oral vocabulary (Ehri, 1998, 2005; Laing & Hulme, 1999) see, Rapid Reference 4.2. For students who lack one or more of these component skills, mapping is very inefficient and a sight vocabulary grows very slowly. Understanding this process of sight-word storage is essential for addressing the reading acquisition of all learners. It will assist educators in determining what to teach and how to teach it.

Orthographic Mapping Process

Our oral lexicons involve a lightning-fast lookup system allowing us to comprehend instantly the words we hear. As it turns out, sight-word learning piggybacks on this existing system of instantaneous oral recall. When reading, we do not use a separate visual lookup system that parallels our oral one. This unified system is

≡ *Rapid Reference 4.2 Key Elements of Sight-Word Learning*

- Sound-symbol skills
- Phonemic awareness
- Oral vocabulary

---

6. Orthographic memory (i.e., the memory for specific spellings of specific words) appears to operate on two broad levels. Orthographic *recognition* memory allows a reader to distinguish instantly that *pear* is a fruit while *pair* refers to two things. The reader does not have to produce those spellings, only *recognize* them. Orthographic *recall* memory seems to be a more rigorously encoded form of orthographic memory. It allows us to correctly spell words. There are, no doubt, more readers who can instantly recognize words like *tongue, bouquet, colonel, rendezvous,* or *licorice* than can consistently spell them.

Table 4.1 Examples of Types of Letter Sequences

Random Letter Sequences (Not Meaningful or Familiar)		Meaningful Letter Sequences			
		Familiar		Unfamiliar	
NZQ	SRTE	CIA	USMC	IEEE	UMWA
SBMR	QWS	NCAA	YMCA	SBE	TAOM

why word recognition is so quick for competent readers. The *input* is visual, but the *storage* is linguistic (i.e., phonological and semantic). To understand this process, it may be helpful to use terms that focus on the mechanics behind orthographic mapping, namely *meaningful letter sequences* and *familiar letter sequences*. Consider the acronyms in Table 4.1.

The letter strings in the first set are meaningless—they were made up for this table. Thus, they are not likely to be familiar to the reader. The second two sets of letter sequences are all meaningful. They are all acronyms for organizations in the United States. Acronyms are *meaningful* because each letter represents the first letter in the words in the organization's name (e.g., CIA = Central Intelligence Agency). But both sets of meaningful acronyms are not likely to be *familiar* to the reader. The first set is more common and familiar, but the second set includes organizations less well known to the average reader (e.g., SBE = Society of Broadcast Engineers). But all of these acronyms are equally *meaningful*, even if they are not equally *familiar*.

It is the precise order of the letters that make acronyms meaningful. The National Basketball Association is referred to as the *NBA*. Neither NAB nor BNA are likely to activate "National Basketball Association" in the minds of those familiar with the acronym NBA. The precise order is needed to do that. After a few exposures, the acronym becomes familiar. So when someone sees *NBA*, he or she does not say "*Hmm, N – B – A*. Oh, *NBA!*" Rather, he or she instantly knows it upon seeing it and no longer has to focus on the parts of that letter sequence. Once familiar, the letter sequence is recognized *as a unit*. Any change in that sequence throws off the reader as the examples NAB and BNA illustrate. So, the precise order of letters in meaningful letter sequences becomes familiar, that is, the sequence becomes *unitized* for instant recognition. By contrast, meaningless letter strings are very difficult to remember. There is little or nothing we can use to anchor them in memory.

This analogy using acronyms helps illustrate the concepts of *meaningful* and *familiar* when it comes to letter sequences. In a similar sense, written words in alphabetic languages are meaningful sequences of letters *because the letter sequences are designed to represent the oral sequences of phonemes in spoken words.* *Phonemes* are the smallest units of spoken language. For example, the word *red* has three phonemes (/r//ĕ//d/)[7] while the word *shoe* has two (/sh//ū/). Written words are not random letter sequences to be memorized. Rather, each phoneme in a spoken word is represented by a letter or digraph (e.g., *ch, sh, ee, oa*).[8] So there is a meaningful connection between the spoken sequence of phonemes and the written sequence of letters.[9] This is the whole idea behind alphabetic writing systems.

Two of the major components necessary for this orthographic memory process to work are (1) sound-symbol skills (e.g., knowing *t* says/t/and *m* says/m/) and (2) phonemic awareness. *Phonemic awareness* is the most advanced form of phonological awareness. *Phonological awareness* is the ability to notice the sound structure within spoken words. It may involve rhyming or alliteration, but also the ability to segment, blend, or manipulate syllables, onsets and rimes,[10] and phonemes (Scarborough & Brady, 2002). Phonemic awareness is thus a subcategory of phonological awareness. However, *phonemic* awareness is the level of awareness necessary to interact with an alphabetic writing system, because written *letters* represent oral *phonemes*.

Students with poor phonemic awareness do not notice the phoneme structure within spoken words. Thus, they have a difficult time recognizing that the specific letter sequences within written words are *meaningful.* They do not naturally notice the precise relationship between the sounds in spoken words and the letters used to represent those sounds due to the fact that they cannot attune themselves to the sounds/phonemes in spoken words. The exception to this is the first sound in a word, which even the most disabled readers seem to get.

Consider an imaginary study with two groups of adults who have to memorize a set of 15 sequences of random letters. In one group are American sports fans while in the other group are Australians who know nothing about American sports. The 15 "random" letter strings are comprised of sequences like NFL, NBA, LPGA,

---

7. Letters printed between slash marks (e.g., /t/) represent sounds, not letters.

8. Exceptions to this are *extremely* rare. The only common words violating this pattern are *one* and *once*, neither of which has a letter to represent the/w/sound at the beginning. Virtually all other irregular words represent every sound in the word; they just do so irregularly.

9. The problem of irregular words will be addressed ahead.

10. An *onset* is the consonantal portion of a syllable before the vowel (e.g., *c-ap*, *bl-ink*, *scr-eech*). *Rime* is not a misspelling of *rhyme*, but an obscure alternative spelling that reading researchers use to refer to the part of the syllable that includes the vowel and anything after the vowel sound in that syllable (e.g., *m-ake*, *f-eet*, *g-o*). Rimes can be oral or written (Scarborough & Brady, 2002).

≡ Rapid Reference 4.3 Key Phon-Terms

Phonics: "An approach to, or type of, reading instruction that [promotes] . . . the correspondences between phonemes and graphemes [i.e., letters and digraphs]."

Phonological awareness: Involves "attending to, thinking about, and intentionally manipulating the phonological aspects of spoken language."

Phonemes: "The smallest units into which speech can be divided."

Phonemic awareness: "The particular kind of phonological awareness that involves attending to, thinking about, and intentionally manipulating the individual *phonemes* [my emphasis] within spoken words and syllables."

Source: Scarborough & Brady (2002, pp. 326, 312, 303, and 313).

MLB, WNBA, PGA, NHL, NCAA, and so on. Because these strings are not really random and represent American sports leagues, we can be sure the American sports fans would remember more sequences. Also, when asked to reproduce the sequences, who might get the letter order mixed up? We could imagine seeing some of the Australians remembering NFL as NLF, but could not imagine a single American sports fan transposing any letters.

By analogy, the American sports fans are like students who begin their literacy careers with sufficient phonological awareness and sound-symbol skills. The Australians in our make-believe study are like students who lack adequate phonological awareness and/or sound-symbol skills. For this latter group, letter strings have to be memorized *as if* they were random, even though they are not. The former group, by contrast, can recognize that the sequences are meaningful, which greatly facilitates the process of making them familiar.

Students who struggle with phonemic awareness and/or sound-symbol skills struggle in reading. Why is this so? Because *the letter strings they see are not particularly meaningful to them, which makes them very difficult to remember.* Unless these foundational skills are developed, a student will not have an efficient way to make letter sequences familiar. Students with good phonemic awareness and phonics skills naturally associate the sounds in spoken words with the letter sequences used to represent those spoken words. As a result, they remember the words they read. Phonemic awareness allows students to effectively key letter strings into the lightning-fast oral lexicon they use for spoken language.

Identification Versus Recognition

Given proper clues, we can identify people and things we have never seen before. If I tell you there is a group of 30 people in the next room and I want you to give a

> ## DON'T FORGET
> ....
> Word *identification* could involve phonic decoding, visual feature memorization, contextual guessing, or instant recognition of stored words. In each case, the word is *identified*. Word *recognition*, however, is a subcategory of word identification that refers to instant, effortless recall of known words (i.e., words in the reader's pool of sight-words).

message to a tall man with red hair and glasses, you could identify him without having seen him before. Yet if I tell you to deliver a message to your best friend, no clues are needed. Recognition presumes previous experience and memory, while identification does not. The focus of phonic decoding is on identification of unknown words. If you have sufficient sound-symbol skills and *blending* skills (i.e., when you hear the sounds /r//ĕ//d/ separately, it activates the oral word *red*), you can identify words you have never seen before. You can also identify words based on guessing from context. Or, you can combine phonics and contextual guessing. But these are *identification* approaches that presume the word is unfamiliar. If the word were familiar, there would be no need for guessing or phonic decoding.

With orthographic mapping, we are not talking about identifying unfamiliar words. Rather we are talking about storing words so they immediately activate the pronunciation of the oral word. With word recognition, the precise letter order becomes consolidated in memory in a unitized fashion, just like NFL will not be confused with NLF or FNL.

Orthographic Mapping Versus Phonic Decoding

Orthographic mapping must not be confused with phonic decoding. Phonic decoding is a strategy to identify unfamiliar words. By contrast, orthographic mapping is the process that produces a unitized memory for specific letter sequences. It involves bonding the specific letter sequence to the word's pronunciation and meaning. So, rather than a visual memory lookup process, instant recognition involves rapid access to familiar letter sequences that are visually input into the linguistic system. This means that sound-symbol skills are necessary for word identification (via phonic decoding) and permanent word storage (via orthographic mapping). The same sound-symbol skills are used for two different and complementary aspects of word-level reading (see Figure 4.1).

> ## CAUTION
> ....
> Orthographic mapping must not be confused with phonic decoding. Each involves sound-symbol skills. However, phonic decoding is a strategy to identify *unfamiliar* words while orthographic mapping is the process that makes words *familiar* for instant recognition.

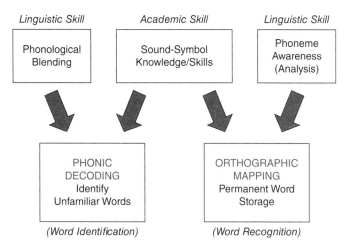

Figure 4.1. Relationships Among Some of the Components of Word-Level Reading

To read efficiently in an alphabetic script, particularly English, orthographic memory is absolutely essential (Ziegler & Goswami, 2005). The word *make* is spelled *m-a-k-e*, not *m-a-k*. Homophonic words (e.g., *right/write, see/sea, stair/stare*) are words that are pronounced the same, but are spelled differently. This means they share the same *phonology*, but differ in their *orthography*. We must therefore develop a memory for the precise spellings of words, which instantly activates the pronunciations and meanings of those words. But to anchor that orthographic sequence into our memory system, we participate in a connection-forming process that aligns or *maps* the sequence of oral phonemes in a spoken word onto the actual orthographic sequence used to spell that word. So, with orthographic memory, *visual* characteristics of the word (uppercase or lowercase, handwriting, differing fonts, etc.) are not the least bit important, as long as the letters are legible. Once that letter sequence enters the system via visual input, the previous connections between orthography and phonology allow our phonological/pronunciation system and our semantic system to take over for instant recognition.

CAUTION

••

Orthographic memory must not be confused with *visual memory*. *Visual memory* involves memory for objects, people, numbers, letters of the alphabet, and so on. *Orthographic memory* is memory for the specific letter combinations that form written words. The *visual* characteristics of words, such as uppercase, lowercase, varying fonts, and handwriting, are not important for orthographic memory.

The Formative Research on Orthographic Mapping

What is here called *orthographic mapping* represents the theory developed by Linnea Ehri in the late 1970s.[11] Ehri has called this process *sight-word learning, bonding, amalgamation*, and *graphophonemic awareness* (Ehri, 1998, 2005). Ehri provided tentative empirical support for her theory in the late 1970s and 1980s (e.g., Ehri & Wilce, 1985). However, the theory seemed to gain broader acceptance among reading researchers following confirmation via a series of studies by British researchers (Laing & Hulme, 1999; Rack et al., 1994). Since then, further support has come in English and in other languages (e.g., Cardoso-Martins, Mamede Resende, & Assunção Rodrigues, 2002; Dixon, Stuart, & Masterson, 2002; Share, 1999).

Ehri and Wilce (1985) taught preschoolers and kindergarteners two different types of words. They compared modified phonetic forms of words (e.g., TRDL for *turtle* and NE for *knee*) with visually distinctive forms of words with no phonetic correspondence (e.g., Y^MP for *turtle* and Fo for *knee*). They found that non-readers with minimal letter-sound knowledge remembered the visually distinctive forms more easily, while those with good letter-sound knowledge found the phonetic spellings easier to remember. This suggested that as soon as they gain letter-sound knowledge, beginning readers use that knowledge in a process of creating a bond or map between the sequence of phonemes in the oral word and the sequence of letters used to represent that oral word. Such connections make those letter sequences familiar.

Rack et al. (1994) improved Ehri's methodology by controlling for the look of the words. They taught five-year-old non-readers and beginning readers two types of modified words, varying the degree of phonetic correspondence in the spellings. For example, the word *farmer* was represented as *vmr* or *zmr*, the former being closer phonologically to *fmr*. The sounds /f/ and /v/ differ only in voicing (i.e., whether vocal cords vibrate), while /f/ and /z/ differ in voicing and place of articulation. Their results were similar to Ehri and colleagues. Readers with letter-sound knowledge made use of the letter sequences to *remember* words. This was word memory, not phonic decoding, because they prescreened these children and they could not yet sound out words. Others have replicated this finding (Cardoso-Martins et al., 2002; Dixon et al., 2002), including Laing and Hulme (1999), who demonstrated the importance of phonemic awareness in producing this effect. They found that the more skilled the students were in phonemic awareness, the more efficiently they mapped the words to memory.

---

11. For a historical perspective on the origin and development of the theory, see Ehri (1998).

How Orthographic Mapping Works

Consider an example to understand this mapping process. Two students in late first grade see the word *sent* for the first time. The first student has good phonemic awareness and sound-symbol skills while the second does not. The first student notices that the spelling of *sent* aligns with the sequence of phonemes in the spoken word (i.e., /s//ĕ//n//t/). For this student, it will be easy to remember that sequence, and distinguish it from similar-looking sequences (e.g., *set*, *send*). However, the second student will not be aware of the phonemes in the spoken word *sent*. He will not notice why the spelling *s-e-n-t* is any more meaningful than *s-n-e-t* or *s-e-t-n*. If there is nothing meaningful about the letter order, then only an inefficient, raw memorization strategy is possible, and sight vocabulary growth will be dramatically hindered.

Irregular Words

English has many words in which the phonemes and letters are not tightly aligned. Consider the word *island*. When a student first sees it, he may say "iz-land." He eventually learns the *s* is silent (not common in English). He is able to recognize the logical connection between the oral phonemes and the letters in the *rest* of the word, with a mental note about the irregularity. A more subtle example is *put*. It does not use the short *u* sound as in the word *but*. The student with adequate orthographic mapping skills can notice how the oral sequence maps onto *that particular written sequence*, as each sound aligns with a particular letter, even if the vowel connection is not typical (see Figure 4.2). After a few exposures, the sequence becomes a fully automatic sight-word. In a sense, the student says to himself, "Oh, *that's* how the word *put* is represented in print." If he can attune himself to the sounds in the spoken word, he is prepared to see how those sounds map onto the written form of the word. Then when he sees the orthographic sequence (i.e., the particular spelling of that word), he can notice how the sounds align with that particular sequence. This mapping process makes the sequence meaningful, even if not phonically regular. Once meaningful, the sequence can more easily become familiar.

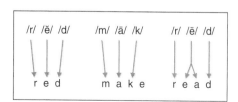

Figure 4.2. Examples of How Phonemes Map onto Letters

Consider the word *take*. Like *island*, but unlike *put*, there is not a one-to-one correspondence between letters and sounds. The student notices connections to the meaningful parts of the sequence, but adjusts for the irregular part. The silent-*e* pattern may be "phonically regular," but with orthographic mapping it presents a problem because it is an extra letter not connected with a phoneme. But if the student is aware of the "silent-*e* rule," he can more quickly appreciate the meaningfulness of this sequence. Once familiar, *take* becomes unitized and not confused with *tame, tape*, or *tack*.

The Graphophonemic Connection-Making Process

Let's further examine how the orthographic mapping process creates unitized orthographic sequences. When letter-sound knowledge becomes automatic, the sight of a letter activates the associated sound instantly.[12] As skills develop, a sequence of two or more letters can activate the sounds associated with that two-letter sequence. For example, when we see *ip* within a word, we do not have to determine its pronunciation by sounding out each letter separately. Rather we treat that letter sequence and its pronunciation together, simply as /ĭp/. There are many common word parts, such as rime units (e.g., *–et, –ig, –ake, –ot,*), beginning and ending blends (e.g., *tr–, bl–, str–, –nd, –rt,*), suffixes (e.g., *–ing, –ed, –tion*), and prefixes (e.g., *re–, con–, un–, dis–*). When we see these letter sequences in the context of words, their respective pronunciations are activated. We no longer need to break them apart letter-by-letter (Kilpatrick & Cole, 2013).

But how do words or word parts become familiar? Here is where phoneme awareness is very important. While oral word parts such as /ĭp/ are not words, they are part of our existing oral language system and familiar to us if we have adequate phonological awareness. That's because /ĭp/ appears in many oral words such as *dip, hip, lip, rip, sip, trip, zip*, and so on. If a student does not have phonological awareness, the letter sequence *ip* will not anchor to anything in particular in his memory. For him, *ip* represents two letters to memorize. If we have phonemic awareness we can use a connection-forming process between the letter combination and its pronunciation. The oral pronunciation of the sub-word sequence /ĭp/ is already stored in the linguistic system and we map the specific sequence of letters (*i-p*) to that pronunciation. We cannot do that without adequate sound-symbol skills and phonemic awareness. We can extend this multi-letter bonding process to larger letter sequences and words, based on reading experience.

---

12. Technically, it can activate more than one sound, if the letter has more than one sound associated with it. The context of that letter allows us to determine the correct sound and the others get discarded (Crowder & Wagner, 1992; Rayner & Pollatsek, 1989).

Contrary to a popular "e-mail forward" that has circulated for several years, we attend to virtually every letter of every word we read[13] (Crowder & Wagner, 1992; Rayner & Pollatsek, 1989). This has been demonstrated using various experimental paradigms. If we did not attend to every letter of the words we read, we could not instantly recognize any one of the thousands of words we know that differ from another word by a single letter (e.g., *strand/stand, black/block, send/sent*). When we see a word, our perceptual span can take in all of the letters simultaneously (Rayner & Pollatsek, 1989). Because we are able to attend to every letter in the word, the orthographic sequence representing that word will immediately be recognized as familiar or unfamiliar, depending on past learning.

Consider your web browser. As you type a web address, the browser tries to "guess" what you are intending to type based on addresses already stored in the browser's memory. With each letter you type, the guesses get more limited and refined, because more information is available for its "guess." Each new letter you type *constrains* the possibilities of what word you are intending. Our brains seem to work in a similar way, but with much greater efficiency because our eyes see *all* of the letters in the word simultaneously. Thus, our word perception is not limited to a letter-by-letter refinement process like the web browser. Nor is it like phonic decoding, which deals with one letter or digraph at a time. Rather the entire string is perceived simultaneously, and this immediately *constrains* the possibilities down to the specific word with that specific letter sequence. Our simultaneous perception of all the letters in printed words allows recognition to be instantaneous. To push the analogy further, the letter order of a printed word represents the "address" in our brains to the specific pronunciation and meaning of the oral word, like the precise web address takes you to a specific site.

So, *familiar* letter sequences are *unitized* letter sequences. When we see *spend*, we don't say, "*Hmm, s – p – e – n – d*. Oh, *spend*!*" Rather, we instantly recognize that letter sequence as familiar. *Spend* is familiar to us, while *stend* or *slend* are not. And, we do not confuse the letter order in *spend* with words like *spent* or *send* because those are different sequences of letters that have been unitized in their own right. Thus, we no longer have to focus consciously on the parts of the letter string, because the precise sequence has been unitized, just like we don't focus on the parts of IRS, FBI, or NFL. The individual letters are still perceived (that's how we

13. Those adhering to the Psycholinguistic Guessing Game have widely promoted the mistaken notion that we don't attend to every letter of every word we read. While this may be true for weak readers or good readers who are skimming, it is not true for typical readers. The popular e-mail mentioned here purports to prove this (by jumbling the order of letters). But that e-mail demonstrates a phenomenon called *contextual facilitation* and does not represent our normal word recognition processes, contrary to its claims.

tell similar looking words apart), but are not separately processed, like in phonic decoding. This unitization phenomenon is why our intuitions mislead us to think we are reading words based upon some sort of visual memory bank. We know we are not phonically decoding words that quickly, so we mistakenly think that the only other alternative is visual memory.

Letter Transpositions and "Dyslexia"

The previous information makes clear why children with reading difficulties sometimes transpose letters (e.g., spelling *said* as *siad* or reading *form* as *from*) during reading and spelling—a symptom more common among dyslexics than typical readers and spellers. These transpositions are not due to poor visual-spatial processing. It happens because specific letter sequences are not well established in the LTM of dyslexics. Their poor phonemic awareness and poor orthographic mapping skills make it difficult to anchor the precise letter order into LTM. Incidentally, *dyslexia* is defined by many researchers and *Webster's Collegiate Dictionary* as simply referring to individuals with reading difficulties.[14] Because the phonological-core deficit is so common with word-level reading difficulties, transpositions become associated with dyslexia. This has become part of the popular lore that dyslexia is based on visual-spatial deficits.

Traditional Instructional Practices and Sight-Word Learning

The traditional whole-word, phonics, and Whole Language approaches were formalized in the 1800s (Adams, 1990). We have learned a lot since then and need to make use of recent findings rather than rely, as we do, on prescientific approaches to teaching reading (AFT, 1999; Moats, 2009). None of the classic approaches adequately addresses orthographic mapping. This is understandable because they all predate its discovery. The Whole Language approach mistakenly assumes that contextual guessing is an important part of mature word recognition while the whole-word method assumes visual memory is the mechanism for skilled reading. As a result, these approaches have not incorporated the kinds of instructional activities that would promote sight-word development in all students. In a sense, most kids learn to read *in spite of* these methods. Liberman and Liberman (1990) estimate that 75% of children will develop the skills needed for reading, "no matter how unhelpful the instruction is" (p. 54). We do not have that

---

14. Dictionary.com and the *American Heritage Dictionary* (upon which dictionary.com is based), include a definition of dyslexia hinting at popular misunderstandings about visual processing. However, dictionaries *reflect* usage, so the eventual inclusion of this popular misunderstanding is inevitable.

room for error with struggling readers. In fact, some instructional activities (e.g., contextual guessing or
drawing attention to visual features
of words) actually direct attention
away from the connection between
the orthographic and phonological
properties of words—the very properties central to the mapping process.

CAUTION

Phonics and phonological awareness
must not be confused. Phonological
awareness pertains to *oral* language
while phonics pertains to *written* language. Just remember: You can do
phonological awareness with your eyes
closed.

While most kids figure this all out naturally, struggling readers do not.

Phonics instruction promotes sound-symbol skills as a word identification
strategy. Such skills must be coupled with phonemic awareness to allow students
to make orthographic sequences meaningful and familiar. Thus, while phonics
takes us part-way there, it needs to be supplemented, particularly for students with
weak phonological awareness skills.

The author has presented this information about orthographic mapping to
hundreds of teachers, administrators, and school psychologists and realizes that it
is not always understood the first time through. If you find this to be the case, a
careful re-reading of this chapter may help. Also, another presentation of mapping
is provided on the supplemental CD.

RECOMMENDATIONS BASED ON CURRENT KNOWLEDGE

The research findings about sight-word learning and the studies on effective
prevention and intervention have led to specific ways we can dramatically improve
our ability to prevent and/or correct most reading difficulties and reading
disabilities.

Prevention

To prevent reading difficulties, we must make certain that all students arrive at the
beginning of reading instruction with the skills needed for mapping. This means
letter names and then letter sounds in kindergarten (e.g., Treiman, et al., 2001),
along with phonological awareness at the syllable and onset-rime levels. Basic
phoneme-level awareness needs to be developing adequately throughout first grade
in order for the mapping process to take hold. Without this, students are likely to
develop compensating habits inconsistent with efficient sight-word development.
For students who develop these skills early, success in reading is nearly assured
(Liberman & Liberman, 1990; McInnis, 1999). All kindergarten teachers work on

letter names and sounds. But comprehensive phonological awareness training of all students in kindergarten must become standard practice to prevent reading difficulties. This would be an integral part of using scientifically validated approaches to reading instruction that is called for by the National Reading Panel (NRP, 2000) and by Tier 1 of the Response to Intervention (RTI) approach.

Intervention 1: Before They Fail

All students should be screened in the fall of kindergarten for letter-name and letter-sound knowledge and phonological awareness.[15] For those with low skills, additional intervention in these skills is essential. The clock is ticking and reading instruction will soon commence. To be sure that these at-risk students will be successful, they will need to get up-to-speed on these basic sound-symbol and phonological awareness skills. Additional intervention (Tier 2 of RTI) is needed for these students before reading instruction begins (Vellutino et al., 2000).

Intervention 2: Students With Reading Difficulties

For students who display reading difficulties in grades 1–12, assessment of sound-symbol skills (using a nonsense word task from a commercially available test), phonological awareness, rapid automatized naming (RAN), and working memory (WM) will invariably suggest a problem in one or more of these lower-level linguistic skills. The *Comprehensive Test of Phonological Processing, Second Edition* (CTOPP-2, Wagner, Torgesen, & Rashotte, 2013) assesses these latter three skills. In most cases, phonological awareness will be an issue. The supplemental materials on the CD include a sensitive phonological awareness test.

The statute of limitations never runs out on phonemic awareness (e.g., Bruck, 1992). If 3rd, 8th, or 12th graders struggle in reading and have poor phonemic

---

15. Not all phonological awareness tasks/tests are equally sensitive to phonological awareness difficulties. It is unfortunate that until recently there has been no research comparing among the various phonological awareness tasks to answer the practical question of which task is most well suited for practitioners to use to determine if a student has a phonological awareness problem. All phonological awareness tasks *correlate* with reading, but those correlations vary widely (.3 to .8). The question of which is/are the most sensitive to reading difficulties has only recently been examined (Kilpatrick, 2012a, 2012b). Due to this lack of comparative research, one of the *least* sensitive tasks has become the one most commonly incorporated into the comprehensive screening batteries (e.g., DIBELS, AIMSweb, easyCBM), namely phonological *segmentation*. Phonological *manipulation* tasks such as deleting a sound from a word (found on the CTOPP-2 and PAT-2 and on the supplementary CD) appear to be more sensitive to reading difficulties (see Kilpatrick, 2012a, 2012b, and Chapter 7 on the supplementary CD) and should be preferred when seeking to determine the presence of phonological awareness difficulties.

awareness, they will not likely display much reading improvement until the phonemic awareness difficulty is corrected (e.g., Swanson, Hodson, & Schommer-Aikins, 2005). The same could be said regarding phonics skills (Rack, Snowling, & Olsen, 1992). In addition, students will need to be retrained to approach words to counteract the years of compensating strategies (Kilpatrick, 2013). The supplementary CD provides several approaches for doing this.

The recommendations included on the CD match the types of interventions that were used by Vellutino et al. (1996) and Torgesen et al. (2001). You may remember that these studies had very substantial results. These researchers made no mention of Ehri's theory of sight-word learning in their articles. Rather, they were drawing upon earlier, smaller-scale studies that had demonstrated success with at-risk and struggling readers that validated the approaches they used. However, Ehri's theory can now explain *why* those studies were so successful. The techniques used by Vellutino et al. and Torgesen et al. directly promoted orthographic mapping. They specifically addressed the reasons these students were struggling and fixed those problem areas. These studies relied heavily on sound-symbol learning and phonological/phonemic awareness training. As a result, they produced successful orthographic mappers who were then able to efficiently build a sight vocabulary. Follow-up showed that these results continued long after the intervention was over. For the most part, they solved the reading problem of most of these students who were (1) most seriously at-risk (Vellutino et al.), or (2) most seriously reading disabled (Torgesen et al.). Thus, while these important studies made no reference to our current understanding of sight-word learning, their interventions match the kind of recommendations that are suggested based on the more recent findings regarding permanent word storage.

SUMMARY

Research has demonstrated that we can prevent or correct most reading difficulties, though currently, educators do not appear to be familiar with this research. Scientists have developed an understanding of how we store sight-words for instant, effortless retrieval, which allows readers to focus on comprehension. This process is not based on visual memory. Rather, it involves forming connections between the precise sequence of phonemes in the spoken words and the letters used to represent those phonemes in printed words. Sequences become familiar and unitized for instant recognition. It is now incumbent upon school personnel to make use of this research to enhance the educational success of students who struggle in reading or who are at risk for reading difficulties or disabilities.

REFERENCES

Adams, M. J. (1990). *Beginning to read: Thinking and learning about print*. Cambridge, MA: MIT Press.

American Federation of Teachers (1999). *Teaching reading IS rocket science*. Washington, DC: AFT.

Bruck, M. (1992). Persistence of dyslexics' phonological awareness deficits. *Developmental Psychology, 28*, 874–886.

Cardoso-Martins, C., Mamede Resende, S., & Assunção Rodrigues, L. (2002). Letter name knowledge and the ability to learn to read by processing letter-phoneme relations in words: Evidence from Brazilian Portuguese-speaking children. *Reading and Writing: An Interdisciplinary Journal, 15*(3–4), 409–432.

Castles, A., Davis, C., Cavalot, P., & Forster, K. (2007). Tracking the acquisition of orthographic skills in developing readers: Masked priming effects. *Journal of Experimental Child Psychology, 97*, 165–182.

Cattell, J. M. (1886). The time taken up by cerebral operations. *Mind, 44*, 524–538.

Crowder, R. G., & Wagner, R. K. (1992). *The psychology of reading: An introduction*. New York: Oxford University Press.

Dixon, M., Stuart, M., & Masterson, J. (2002). The relationship between phonological awareness and the development of orthographic representations. *Reading and Writing: An Interdisciplinary Journal, 15*(3–4), 295–316.

Ehri, L. C. (1998). Research on learning to read and spell: A personal-historical perspective. *Scientific Studies of Reading, 2*(2), 97–114.

Ehri, L. C. (2005). Learning to read words: Theory, findings, and issues. *Scientific Studies of Reading, 9*(2), 167–188.

Ehri, L. C., & Wilce, L. S. (1985). Movement into reading: Is the first stage of printed word learning visual or phonetic? *Reading Research Quarterly, 20*, 163–179.

Elbaum, B., Vaughn, S., Hughes, M. T., & Moody, S. W. (2000). How effective are one-to-one tutoring programs in reading for elementary students at risk for reading failure? A meta-analysis of the intervention research. *Journal of Educational Psychology, 92*(4), 605–619.

Fletcher, J. M., Shaywitz, S. E., Shankweiler, D. P., Katz, L., Liberman, I. Y., Steubing, K. K., . . . Shaywitz, B. A. (1994). Cognitive profiles of reading disability: Comparisons of discrepancy and low achievement definitions. *Journal of Educational Psychology, 86*, 6–23.

Goodman, K. S. (1976). Reading: A psycholinguistic guessing game. In H. Singer & R. B. Ruddell (Eds.), *Theoretical models and processes of reading* (2nd ed.), pp. 497–508. Newark, DE: International Reading Association.

Hanson, V. L. (1991). Phonological processing without sound. In S. A. Brady & D. P. Shankweiler (Eds.), *Phonological processes in literacy: A tribute to Isabelle Y. Liberman* (pp. 153–161). Hillsdale, NJ: Erlbaum.

Kilpatrick, D. A. (2012a). Not all phonological awareness tests are created equal: Considering the practical validity of phonological manipulation vs. segmentation. *Communiqué, 40*(6), 31–33.

Kilpatrick, D. A. (2012b). Phonological segmentation assessment is not enough: A comparison of three phonological awareness tests with first and second graders. *Canadian Journal of School Psychology, 27*(2), 150–165.

Kilpatrick, D. A. (2013, in press). *Equipped for reading success: A comprehensive, step-by-step program for developing phonemic awareness and fluent word recognition*. Syracuse, NY: Casey & Kirsch. (Portions included on the supplemental CD).

Kilpatrick, D. A., & Cole, L. A. (2013). Exploring the development of sight-word learning in second and fifth graders using rimes, pseudorimes, and real-word rimes. *Reading and Writing: An Interdisciplinary Journal*. (submitted).

Laing, E., & Hulme, C. (1999). Phonological and semantic processes influence beginning readers' ability to learn to read words. *Journal of Experimental Child Psychology, 73*, 183–207.

Landi, N., Perfetti, C. A., Bolger, D. J., Dunlap, S., & Foorman, B. R. (2006). The role of discourse context in developing word form representations: A paradoxical relation between reading and learning. *Journal of Experimental Child Psychology, 94*, 114–133.

Lennon, J. E., & Slesinski, C. (1999). Early intervention in reading: Results of a screening and intervention program for kindergarten students. *School Psychology Review, 28*(3), 353–364.

Leybaert, J. (2000). Phonology acquired through the eyes and spelling in deaf children. *Journal of Experimental Child Psychology, 75*, 291–318.

Liberman, I. Y., & Liberman, A. M. (1990). Whole language vs. code emphasis: Understanding assumptions and their implications for reading instruction. *Annals of Dyslexia, 40*, 51–76.

McInnis, P. J. (1999). *A guide to readiness and reading: Phonemic awareness and blending* (3rd ed.). Penn Yan, NY: ARL.

Moats, L. (2009). Still wanted: Teachers with knowledge of language. Introduction to special issue. *Journal of Learning Disabilities, 42*(5), 387–391.

Nation, K., & Snowling, M. J. (1998). Individual differences in contextual facilitation: Evidence from dyslexia and poor reading comprehension. *Child Development, 69*(4), 996–1011.

National Institute of Child Health and Human Development. (2000). Report of the National Reading Panel. Teaching children to read: An evidence-based assessment of the scientific research literature on reading and its implications for reading instruction (NIH Publication No. 00-4769). Washington, DC: U.S. Government Printing Office.

Nelson, J. M., & Machek, G. R. (2007). A survey of training, practice, and competence in reading assessment and intervention. *School Psychology Review, 36*(2), 311–327.

Papalewis, R. (2004). Struggling middle school readers: Successful, accelerating intervention. *Reading Improvement, 41*(1), 24–37.

Perfetti, C. A. (1991). Representations and awareness in the acquisition of reading competence. In L. Rieben & C. A. Perfetti (Eds.), *Learning to read: Basic research and its implications* (pp. 33–44). Hillsdale, NJ: Erlbaum.

Rack, J., Hulme, C., Snowling, M., & Wightman, J. (1994). The role of phonology in young children's learning of sight words: The direct mapping hypothesis. *Journal of Experimental Child Psychology, 57*, 42–71.

Rack, J. P., Snowling, M. J., & Olsen, R. K. (1992). The nonword reading deficit in developmental dyslexia: A review. *Reading Research Quarterly, 27*, 28–53.

Rayner, K., & Pollatsek, A. (1989). *The psychology of reading*. Hillsdale, NJ: Erlbaum.

Scarborough, H. S., & Brady, S. A. (2002). Toward a common terminology for talking about speech and reading: A glossary of the "phon" words and some related terms. *Journal of Literacy Research, 34*(3), 299–336.

Share, D. L. (1999). Phonological recoding and orthographic learning: A direct test of the Self-Teaching Hypothesis. *Journal of Experimental Child Psychology, 72*, 95–129.

Share, D., Jorm, A. F., MacLean, R., & Matthews, R. (2002). Temporal processing and reading disability. *Reading and Writing: An Interdisciplinary Journal, 15*(1–2), 151–178.

Slavin, R. E., Lake, C., Chambers, B., Cheung, A., & Davis, S. (2009). Effective reading programs for the elementary grades: A best-evidence synthesis. *Review of Educational Research, 79*(4), 1391–1466.

Stahl, S. A., & Murray, B. A. (1994). Defining phonological awareness and its relationship to early reading. *Journal of Educational Psychology, 86*(2), 221–234.

Stanovich, K. E., & Siegel, L. S. (1994). Phenotypic performance profile of children with reading disabilities: A regression-based test of the phonological-core variable-difference model. *Journal of Educational Psychology, 86*(1), 24–53.

Swanson, L. (1978). Verbal encoding effects on the visual short-term memory of learning disabled and normal readers. *Journal of Educational Psychology, 70*(4), 539–544.

Swanson, T. H., Hodson, B. W., & Schommer-Aikins, M. (2005). An examination of phonological awareness treatment outcomes for seventh-grade poor readers from a bilingual community. *Language, Speech, and Hearing Services in Schools, 36*(3), 336–345.

Torgesen, J. K., Alexander, A. W., Wagner, R. K., Rashotte, C. A., Voeller, K. K. S., & Conway, T. (2001). Intensive remedial instruction for children with severe reading disabilities: Immediate and long-term outcomes from two instructional approaches. *Journal of Learning Disabilities, 34*(1), *33*, 58–78.

Treiman, R., Sotak, L., & Bowman, M. (2001). The roles of letter names and letter sounds in connecting print to speech. *Memory & Cognition, 29*(6), 860–873.

Vellutino, F. R., Scanlon, D. M., & Lyon, G. R. (2000). Differentiating between difficult-to-remediate and readily remediated poor readers: More evidence against the IQ–achievement discrepancy definition of reading disability. *Journal of Learning Disabilities, 33*, 223–238.

Vellutino, F. R., Scanlon, D. M., Sipay, E. R., Small, S. G., Pratt, A., Chen, R., & Denkla, M. B. (1996). Cognitive profiles of difficult-to-remediate and readily remediated poor readers: Early intervention as a vehicle for distinguishing between cognitive and experiential deficits as basic causes of specific reading disability. *Journal of Educational Psychology, 88*, 601–638.

Vellutino, F., Steger, J., DeSetto, L., & Phillips, F. (1975). Immediate and delayed recognition of visual stimuli in poor and normal readers. *Journal of Experimental Child Psychology, 19*, 223–232.

Wagner, R. K., Torgesen, J. K., & Rashotte, C. A. (2013). *The Comprehensive Test of Phonological Processing (CTOPP)–Second edition.* Austin, TX: Pro-ED.

Wechsler, D. (1991). *Wechsler Intelligence Scale for Children* (3rd ed.). San Antonio, TX: Psychological Corporation.

Woodcock, RN. (1987). *Woodcock Reading Mastery Tests-revised examiner's manual.* Circle Pines, MN: American Guidance Service.

Ziegler, J. C., & Goswami, U. (2005). Reading acquisition, developmental dyslexia, and skilled reading across languages: A psycholinguistic grain size theory. *Psychological Bulletin, 131*(1), 3–29.

🐟 TEST YOURSELF 🐟

1. **According to the NAEP, about what percentage of fourth graders in the United States read below a basic level?**
   a. 30–34%
   b. 22–25%
   c. 16–18%
   d. 10–11%

2. **Reading researchers used to assume that visual memory was the mechanism for sight-word storage. Which of the following types of research demonstrates why they no longer accept that?**
   a. Studies show that linguistic skills strongly predict sight vocabulary.
   b. Research shows LD readers have fairly normal visual memory.
   c. Mixed-case experiments (using words like: tAbLe, eLePhAnT, etc.) where adults learned to quickly read words even though the visual image was disrupted.
   d. All of the above are correct.

3. **All of the following statements about competent readers are true *except*:**

   a. They can identify a word in 1/20 of a second.

   b. They can read 150–250 words per minute.

   c. They can identify tens of thousands of words immediately by sight, without a context.

   d. They require 10–20 exposures to new words in order to permanently store those words.

4. **Orthographic mapping (also called *bonding, direct mapping, self-teaching hypothesis*, etc.) is:**

   a. The mental process we use to store words for immediate retrieval.

   b. A learning strategy using children's literature to motivate interest in reading.

   c. A method of evaluating which words children have learned.

   d. A method of determining which types of words children learn most quickly.

5. **Orthographic mapping involves:**

   a. Applying phonemic awareness to the phonic aspects of words.

   b. Hearing the sounds in spoken words and noticing how they relate to their printed forms.

   c. Connecting printed forms of words to a child's existing oral/mental dictionary.

   d. All of the above

6. **What is phonological awareness?**

   a. It is an awareness that oral words are made up of smaller sound parts.

   b. It is a teaching strategy that emphasizes the differences between regular and irregular words.

   c. It is when children read aloud, they notice when they have misread a word.

   d. It is the ability to answer comprehension questions when a passage is read to the student.

7. **The American Federation of Teachers and a 2009 special issue of the *Journal of Learning Disabilities* pointed out that:**

   a. Reading difficulties are genetic and can be helped only to a limited degree.

   b. The only effective way to remediate reading is with 1:1 instruction.

   c. There is a gap between scientific research on reading and classroom practice.

   d. Reading scores have consistently improved over the last 30 years.

8. **Large-scale U.S. government–funded studies (e.g., Torgesen et al., 2001; Vellutino et al., 1996) have suggested that**

   a. Reading progress in reading disabilities is limited because of the genetic/neurological origin of this condition.

   b. With the right kind of prevention and remediation opportunities, *all* children can become skilled readers.

   c. With the right kind of prevention and remediation opportunities, *most* reading disabilities can be prevented or corrected.

   d. Success with overcoming reading difficulties is directly keyed to a student's IQ.

(continued)

(continued)

9. To prevent reading disabilities, we must be sure that students begin their reading careers with:

a. Sufficient phonological awareness to begin mapping words to permanent memory.

b. Sufficient sound-symbol skills to begin mapping words to permanent memory.

c. Sufficient graphophonemic awareness to allow students to notice the relationship between the sounds in spoken words and the letters used to spell them.

d. All of the above will prevent reading disabilities.

Answers: 1. a; 2. d; 3. d; 4. a; 5. d; 6. a; 7. c; 8. c; 9. d

Five

SELECTING AND TAILORING INTERVENTIONS FOR STUDENTS WITH READING DIFFICULTIES

Steven G. Feifer

For many cognitive neuroscientists, literacy is often viewed as a novel and a rather essential leap in the evolution of human cognitive processing. After all, the ability to capture, transcribe, and decipher human intellectual thought through an alphabetic code encompasses just a scant 6,000-year history. Yet in many ways, literacy has spearheaded the cognitive advancement of our species in an exponential fashion. For instance, the development of an alphabetic code made possible the ability to transcribe the collective knowledge, skills, and abilities of previous generations for each successive generation. Hence, the cumulative knowledge of humankind finally had a vehicle for growth; literacy was born.

Recently, neuroscientists have explored an even greater implication of literacy, particularly the impact of reading on the working brain (Ardila et al., 2010). In other words, does the development of literacy skills actually forge novel and more robust neural pathways in the brain in order to tackle the information processing demands brought on by such a newfound skill? The answer appears to be yes. Multiple studies from a variety of cultures and languages, including Brazil (Deloche, Souza, Braga, & Dellatolas, 1999), China (Li et al., 2006), and the United States (Carreiras et al., 2009), have revealed startling differences in the functional integrity of inter-hemispheric connectivity in the brain between literate versus illiterate subjects. Startling results have suggested that literacy fundamentally alters the architecture of the brain as more efficient and voluminous neural circuits emerge between the hemispheres in order to process the alphabetic code in a more automatic fashion. Perhaps these new information highways, known as *fasciculi*, in the brain are created because they are essential to traverse the cerebral cortex in order to digest the rapid consumption of information brought to the brain through reading. As Ardila et al. (2010) noted, the impact of literacy is reflected in multiple spheres of cognitive functioning, as learning to read reinforces certain fundamental abilities such as working memory skills, phonological awareness skills, language abilities, as well as executive functioning skills. Therefore, the importance of literacy in our culture not only remains a critical component of academic success, but also may play a role in the evolution of cognition itself. In essence, literacy allows individuals to extend cognition and acquire new information more readily, reliably, and rapidly. As Elkonon Goldberg stated in his seminal work, *The New Executive Brain* (2009):

> In human societies, a low acquired-to-inherited knowledge ratio found in traditional cultures is associated with the cult of the elders as the repositories of accumulated wisdom. By contrast, a high acquired-to-inherited knowledge ratio found in modern societies is associated with the cult of the young as the vehicle of discovery and progress. (p.137)

LITERACY DEVELOPMENT

Currently, illiteracy remains present among one-fifth of the world's adult population, as nearly 800 million adults lack minimal reading skills, of which two-thirds are women (UNESCO, 2012). There are significant diversity rates among countries, ranging from 99% literacy rates in Japan, Canada, and Finland to below 20% for countries such as Mali and Niger. Though elusive to measure and plagued by definitional inconsistencies, some estimates have suggested that one in seven adults in the United States is functionally illiterate (UNESCO, 2012). With respect to children, a recent 2009 study by the Program for International Student Assessment (PISA) reported the performance of 15-year-old students in reading literacy in over 65 countries and other education systems (USDOE, 2009a). The U.S. students' average score on the combined reading literacy scale (500) was not measurably different from the average score of the rest of the countries (493). In all 65 participating countries, female students scored higher than male students, with the average difference between U.S. males and females approximately 25 scaled points.

Despite the relative proficiency of U.S. students with respect to literacy skills, there still remain a substantial number of children eligible for special education services in our public schools. According to the National Center for Educational Statistics (2009), approximately 6.5 million children ages 3–21 currently receive special education services, which corresponds to approximately 13% of all public school enrollment (USDOE, 2009b). Among those receiving special education services, 42% have been found eligible for services due to a specific learning disability, more than for other educational disability codes (see Figure 5.1). Notwithstanding, approximately 80% of those children manifesting a specific learning disability have a language-based deficit hindering reading and/or written language skills (National Association of School Psychologists [NASP], 2011). Simply put, more students receive special education services due to deficits with reading than for any other learning, behavioral, or emotional condition (http://www.edsource.org/data-students-special-education-types-disabilities.html).

Neuroscientific research has revealed considerable evidence that developmental dyslexia reflects specific neurological abnormalities underlying the reading circuitry in the brain (Gaab, Gabrieli, Deutsch, Tallal, & Temple, 2007; Kronbichler et al., 2008; McCandliss & Noble, 2003; Pugh et al., 2000; Sandak et al., 2004; Shaywitz, 2004). According to Reynolds (2007), the biological basis of learning disabilities has clearly been demonstrated through various neuropsychological studies of brain functioning, with various subtypes and precise diagnostic markers clearly emerging. As Temple (2002) observed, most individuals with dyslexia have difficulty with phonological processing that may stem from disorganization of white matter tracts connecting the temporal-parietal regions

Students in Special Education: Types of Disabilities

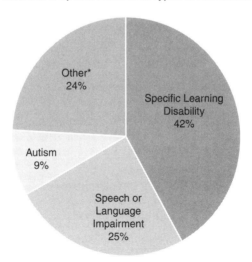

Figure 5.1. Special Education Disability Categories

*Other includes 10 less-common categories.

Source: California Department of Education (CDE) (February 2011).

≋ *Rapid Reference 5.1 NASP Position Statement on Students With Learning Disabilities (2011)*

- Specific learning disabilities are endogenous in nature and are characterized by neurologically based deficits in cognitive processes.
- These deficits are specific; that is, they impact particular cognitive processes that interfere with the acquisition of academic skills.
- Specific learning disabilities are heterogeneous in that there are various types of learning disabilities, and there is no single defining academic or cognitive deficit common to all types of specific learning disabilities.
- Specific learning disabilities may coexist with other disabling conditions.
- The manifestation of a specific learning disability is contingent to some extent upon the type of instruction, supports, and accommodations provided, and the demands of the learning situation.
- Early intervention can reduce the impact of many specific learning disabilities.
- Multi-tiered systems of student support have been effective as part of a comprehensive approach to meet student academic needs.

with other cortical areas involved in the reading process. In fact, Ramus (2004) suggested that micro-lesions in the perisylvan cortex along the left temporal regions were responsible for deficits in phonological processing, and may be the primary cause of most reading disorders. However, not all individuals with reading disorders suffer from deficits with phonological processing, and therefore do not necessarily profit equally from all remediation techniques (Ramus, 2003). Recently, NASP (2011) issued a position statement for practitioners working with children and adolescents in the identification and remediation of specific learning disabilities to yield optimal student outcomes. As can be seen in Rapid Reference 5.1, some of the key provisions acknowledge that learning disorders are neurologically based deficits, are heterogeneous in nature, consist of multiple subtypes, differ in degree, and require evidence-based multitier service delivery systems.

A NEUROPSYCHOLOGICAL PERSPECTIVE

Considering there are approximately 1.1 trillion cells in the human brain, including some 100 billion neurons averaging 5,000 synaptic connections per neuron (Hanson & Mendius, 2009), the task of evaluating reading disabilities from a neuropsychological perspective can seem rather daunting. Most neuropsychologists find that a more palatable form of analyzing brain functions involves taking a macro-level perspective that focuses upon specific neural structures in the brain. Therefore, neuropsychological research involving reading does not necessarily occur at the cellular or microbiological level, but instead accentuates specific neural pathways supporting selected aspects of cognition. For instance, specific cognitive constructs such as phonemic awareness, rapid and automatic naming skills, visual perceptual skills, language, working memory, and executive functioning skills are of particular importance in the development of literacy. Still, there have been differing opinions as to the most efficacious manner to catalog reading deficits based on the aforementioned cognitive constructs. In fact, the literature is rife with multiple classification schemes purported to describe how reading is best represented in the brain (Heim et al., 2008).

Perhaps the multiplicity of theories, be they neuropsychological, educational, or genetic, aimed at developing a universal explanation of dyslexia is still incomplete, due in part to the heterogeneity of the disorder itself. In all likelihood, dyslexia is probably not a unique entity, but rather reflects various neurocognitive pathologies expressed as various phenotypes (Pernet, Poline, Demonet, & Rousselet, 2009). After all, effective reading involves developing proficiency in skills such as phonemic awareness, automaticity, fluency, comprehension, and vocabulary knowledge, and the ability to rapidly self-organize incoming verbal information. As most educators are aware, a breakdown in any of these areas can lead to a bevy of academic difficulties. Therefore, using monolithic terms such as *learning disabled* to represent, categorize, and label such a heterogeneous set of cognitive attributes may be in part why so many neuroimaging studies of reading and literacy have produced rather conflicting results (Kronbichler et al., 2008). Nevertheless, there are certain brain regions associated with dyslexia that tend to show similar functional abnormalities despite the confusion surrounding the nomenclature of the term *learning disabled*. At present, some of the primary neural correlates associated with dyslexia include the superior temporal and temporal-parietal cortices, both of which play a crucial role in the phonological assembly of words for beginning readers; the inferior frontal gyrus, which represents the inner articulation network for spoken words; and the cerebellum, which fine tunes movement, coordination, and may be related to some of the underlying cognitive processes in word identification (Kronbichler et al., 2008). In addition, the occipital-temporal cortices, or what is often referred to as the *fusiform gyrus*, appears vital to the reading process since it houses the visual word-form area, a key aspect of reading fluency (Shaywitz & Shaywitz, 2005).

Since there are various neural systems involved in the reading process, it remains questionable as to whether one unifying theory can best capture the dynamic properties of this skill. According to Grizzle and Simms (2009), the most

≡ Rapid Reference 5.2 Five Big Ideas of the Reading Process (National Reading Panel, 2000)

1. **Phonemic awareness:** Ability to detect, manipulate, and process acoustical information in words.
2. **Alphabetic principle:** Associating sounds with letters, and blending graphemes into words.
3. **Reading fluency:** Ability to automatically read words within text using minimal effort.
4. **Vocabulary:** A working knowledge of word meanings also mapped to oral vocabulary.
5. **Reading comprehension:** Ability to derive meaning from text.

broadly accepted model of reading is simply referred to as the *connectionist model*, and is often used to understand how the brain manages to bring into fruition the five "big ideas" of the reading process as initially outlined by the National Reading Panel (2000) in Rapid Reference 5.2. The connectionist model is merely a summary of the four main cognitive processes used by skilled readers. These processes represent the underlying constructs necessary for reading to develop and consist of *phonology* (assembling letter sounds), *orthography* (recognition of visual contour and shapes of words), *meaning* (semantic cues), and *context* (background knowledge providing frame of reference). Ultimately, skilled reading involves each of these processes working smoothly and efficiently and effortlessly.

SUBTYPES OF READING DISORDERS

Consistent with both the connectionist model and the aforementioned NASP (2011) position paper on the identification and remediation of specific learning disabilities, Feifer and Della Toffalo (2007) have summarized four general subtypes of reading disorders stemming from the contribution of multiple brain regions and the functional interplay of each.

1. The first reading disorder subtype is called *dysphonetic dyslexia* and is characterized by an inability to utilize a phonological route to successfully bridge letters and sounds successfully. Instead, there tends to be an over-reliance on visual and orthographic cues to identify words in print. Since there is little reliance on letter-to-sound conversions, these readers tend to frequently guess on words based on the initial letter observed. For instance, the word *cat* may be read as *couch* or *corn*. These students have difficulty incorporating strategies to allow them to crash

through words in a sound-based manner, are inaccurate oral readers, and tend to approach reading by simply memorizing whole words. According to Noble and McCandliss (2005), poor phonological processing in the early years leads to inefficient neural mappings between letters and sounds. As noted by Grizzle and Simms (2009), children do not perceive sounds as discrete entities, but rather as overlapping bursts that must be painstakingly deciphered at the metacognitive level. The supramarginal gyrus, located at the juncture of the temporal and parietal lobes, is a key brain region responsible for the temporal ordering of phonological information (McCandliss & Noble, 2003; Sandak et al., 2004; Shaywitz, 2004). However, the angular gyrus is more of a cross-modal association area presumed to be involved in mapping visually presented inputs onto linguistic representations (McCandliss & Noble, 2003). The eventual formation of the *visual word-form area* may underscore the orthographic representation of words. Therefore, early intervention emphasizing the development of phonemic awareness (manipulation of sounds) and phonological processing (manipulation of sounds to the printed word form) remains vital to remediating this type of reading deficiency.

2. The second reading disorders subtype is sometimes referred to as *surface dyslexia* and is the sheer opposite of the dysphonetic subtype. These students are readily able to sound out words, though they lack the ability to recognize automatically and effortlessly words in print. Consequently, there is a tendency to read in a letter-by-letter fashion because there is an *over-reliance* upon the phonological properties of the word, and an *under-reliance* upon the orthographical or spatial properties of the visual word form. Since the English language has over 1,100 different variants to map out each of the 44 phonemes (Uhry and Clark, 2005), surface dyslexia is basically an inability to map out phonologically irregular words, such as *yacht*, which cannot be decoded in a one-to-one correspondence. Therefore, there is a certain symbiosis between the phonological and orthographical processors of the brain to identify automatically words in print. With surface dyslexia, most phonologically irregular words are painstakingly broken down to individual phonemes and read very slowly and laboriously and often inaccurately. Fluency tends to suffer the most, though phonological processing skills remain relatively intact. Simply put, the underlying deficit impeding the reading process lies more with faulty orthographical processing.

Emerging studies have highlighted weaker functional connectivity in the left posterior region of the brain with orthographic processing. For instance, Cao, Burman, & Booth (2006) found that rhyming judgment on visually presented word pairs (i.e., *pint-mint, has-jazz*) requires the ability to map orthographic features of words with phonological features, with children with reading disabilities often showing abnormal activation in the left fusiform gyrus. According to

Shaywitz (2003) and Cao et al. (2006), the left fusiform gyrus represents a key brain region that automatically recognizes words in print, and tends to be weaker for children with reading disabilities. Furthermore, this brain region is particularly sensitive toward the orthographic representation of words, and is pivotal in developing fluency, speed, and automaticity. Therefore, specific interventions should focus on automaticity and fluency goals, and not necessarily an explicit phonological approach tediously combining families of sounds.

3. The third reading disorders subtype is often referred to as *mixed dyslexia*, and constitutes the most severe type of reading disability for students. Generally, these readers have difficulty across the language spectrum, and are characterized by a combination of poor phonological processing skills, slower rapid-and-automatic word recognition skills, inconsistent language comprehension skills, and bizarre error patterns in their reading (Feifer & Della Toffalo, 2007). The *double-deficit hypothesis* often applies here, as there are numerous deficits that disrupt the natural flow of rapidly and automatically recognizing words in print. According to Cao et al. (2006), multiple functional connectivity deficits including the left fusiform gyrus and left angular gyrus hinder the integration of *both* phonological and orthographical representation of words.

There are two essential aspects needed to assist readers with mixed dyslexia in developing functioning reading skills. First, most interventions should focus on a *balanced literacy* approach, which targets multiple aspects of the reading process in order to yield the best opportunity for success. Often, these students have had years of instruction utilizing a monolithic approach, such as a phonological type of intervention, with limited success derived. In Rapid Reference 5.2, Grizzle and Simms (2009) outlined the five big ideas of the reading process—phonemic awareness, the alphabetic principle, fluency, vocabulary, and comprehension—as being the core of a balanced literacy approach.

Second, there should also be a greater emphasis on the explicit teaching of morphological rules, instead of an over-reliance upon phonological cues. *Morphology* refers to the smallest unit of sound that still conveys meaning when isolated from other phonemes, and represents more of a *top-down* or semantic cueing approach to recognize words in print. According to Senechal and Kearnan (2007), children learn to anticipate words through a combination of phonological, orthographic, and morphological strategies. Consequently, explicit teaching of morphological rules is vital because knowledge of morphology contributes to individual differences in reading and spelling that cannot be entirely attributed to orthographic and phonological processing (Senechal & Kearnan, 2007). Specific examples of morphological cues are noted in Rapid Reference 5.3.

≡ Rapid Reference 5.3 Morphological Cueing Examples

Prefixes	Suffixes	Latin Roots
ante	able	cent
extra	tion	extra
mis	ment	hemi
para	ness	meta
pre	ship	therm
retro	tude	ultra

4. The final reading disorders subtype involves deficits in *reading comprehension skills*. It has been estimated that some 10% of all school-aged children have good decoding skills but possess specific difficulties comprehending the text (Nation & Snowling, 1998). In essence, these readers struggle to derive meaning from print despite good reading mechanics. Specific cognitive constructs underlying reading comprehension include *executive functioning*, which involves the strategies students use to organize incoming information with previously read material; *working memory*, which is the amount of memory needed to perform a given cognitive task; and *language foundation skills*, which represent the fund of words with which a student is familiar (Feifer & Della Toffalo, 2007). According to Cutting, Materek, Cole, Levine, & Mahone (2009), executive functioning skills are particularly important attributes influencing comprehension, especially traits such as verbal and visual memory, as well as the capacity to plan, organize, and continuously monitor a steady influx of verbal information. In fact, these researchers noted that beyond reading fluency and oral language, top-down executive processes modulated by frontal lobe functioning play a significant role in the comprehension process. Clearly, the ability to self-organize verbal information in a logical, sequential, and meaningful manner lies at the heart of effective recall.

Perhaps the most crucial component of executive functioning skills that tends to be impaired in children with developmental dyslexia is working memory (Reiter, Materek, Cole, Levine, & Mahone, 2001; Willcutt et al., 2001). Working memory involves the ability to hold representational knowledge of the world around us in mind, coupled with the mental flexibility to manipulate this knowledge in whatever manner we choose (Levine & Reed, 1999). Hence, working memory subserves the reading process by temporarily suspending previously read information while simultaneously allowing the reader to acquire new information. Deficits in working memory can certainly disrupt a student's ability to make appropriate linkages between

DON'T FORGET

....

1. **Dysphonetic dyslexia:** Difficulty sounding out words in a phonological manner.
2. **Surface dyslexia:** Difficulty with the rapid and automatic recognition of words in print.
3. **Mixed dyslexia:** Multiple reading deficits characterized by impaired phonological and orthographic processing skills. This is the most severe form of dyslexia.
4. **Comprehension deficits:** The mechanical side of reading is fine but difficulty persists deriving meaning from print.

information in the text. In summary, executive functions are involved with, but not limited to, the *direction* of multiple cognitive processes toward the pursuit of a goal-directed academic task for a successful learning outcome. The specific role of executive functioning with respect to reading comprehension and self-organizing the rapid flux of incoming verbal information is outlined and summarized in Rapid Reference 5.4.

≋ *Rapid Reference 5.4 Executive Functioning Characteristics in Reading Comprehension*

....

Executive Functioning Trait	Reading Attribute
Planning skills	Read with a specific question or purpose in mind when seeking specific information. Also involves strategic manner the reader uses to process new information.
Organization skills	Stitch together text in a cohesive manner. Also, when distracted, the ability to return back to the text and resume the story flow.
Working memory	Temporarily suspending previously read information in mind while simultaneously linking to new information being read.
Cognitive flexibility	Shifting patterns of thought processes to the organizational parameters of the text being read, and not perseverating on material.
Verbal fluency	Speed of processing linguistic information at the word level to facilitate passage comprehension at the text level.
Concept formation	Depth of understanding of the text.
Response inhibition	Refraining from jumping ahead when reading text and missing salient aspects of the passage.
Sustained attention	The ability to stay focused on the text for prolonged periods of time and resist distractions.

CHOOSING AN INTERVENTION

Certainly, the question remains as to whether neuroscience can define various pathways concomitant to the reading process and also assist in determining a child's response to a particular reading intervention. Furthermore, can knowledge about a particular aspect of a child's brain actually yield useful information toward the selection of an intervention as well? According to Hoeft et al. (2011), recent neuroimaging data are beginning to show the answer is yes! In a groundbreaking longitudinal study designed to uncover whether behavioral or brain measures could best predict student outcome toward improved reading gains, neurocognitive brain measures were the clear winner. In fact, few of the behavioral tests, including the popular Woodcock Reading Mastery Tests (Woodcock, 2011), were capable of successfully predicting which students would respond best to a given reading intervention. Using diffusion tensor imaging (DTI), which involves mapping water molecules in the brain to reveal subtle abnormalities in white matter fiber structure and neural connectivity, significant results were revealed (Hoeft et al., 2011). In fact, students capable of recruiting neurons from additional brain regions normally not dedicated to the reading process exhibited the greatest gains. Specifically, students who activated the right prefrontal cortex, as well as the language centers in the right hemisphere, particularly along the arcuate fasciculus (white matter tract connecting anterior and posterior speech zones) were found to have the greatest reading gains. Subsequent research is needed to replicate and extend these findings, especially with younger students, yet the significance of such a study remains unparalleled. Reading is a reflection of the relative integrity and interplay of various neural pathways in the brain. Therefore, developing a working knowledge of these pathways should not only allow practitioners the opportunity to diagnose various types of reading disorders, but also direct interventions toward developing alternative pathways to support the reading process. Rapid Reference 5.5 provides a brief overview of key reading pathways and appropriate intervention strategies.

PHONOLOGICAL PROGRAMS

Feifer and Della Toffalo (2007) referred to the acquisition of phonological skills as being more of a bottom-up or synthetic method of teaching reading because most programs are hierarchically structured and sequenced based on a set of learned rules and correspondences for letters and sounds that underscore whole words. Phonological programs are based on the assumption that 80% of the 30,000 most

≡ Rapid Reference 5.5 Summary of Reading Pathways and Keys to Intervention (Davis et al., 2010)

Reading Pathways	Intervention Strategy
1. Temporal-parietal juncture: Slower pathway involved with word assembly based on sound structures of words.	Phonemic awareness and explicit phonological processing strategies.
2. Insular cortex–angular gyrus: Important neural pathway involved with the lexical process and identifying features of whole words.	Fluency- and orthography-building strategies to develop word automaticity.
3. Occipital temporal juncture: Visual word-form association area responsible for rapid and automatic recognition of words.	Balanced literacy approach. Emphasize morphological cues.
4. Inferior frontal gyrus: Pathway connecting posterior speech zones to anterior speech zones for text comprehension and deriving meaning from print.	Enhance executive functioning skills related to self-organization of verbal information. Increase vocabulary knowledge.

commonly used English words follow a predictable code and are therefore phonologically consistent or regular (Uhry & Clark, 2005). According to the National Reading Panel (2000), most explicit phonics programs tend to yield the most success with younger readers, especially in the early elementary grades. The following programs are recommended for students who have difficulty acquiring the basic tenets of phonological processing (Subtype I):

Alphabetic Phonics

The Alphabetic Phonics program is basically a derivative of the traditional Orton-Gillingham multisensory approach to reading. Alphabetic Phonics is a comprehensive bottom-up approach to reading specifically geared toward strengthening phonological awareness and the temporal ordering of sounds. The emphasis on automaticity allows students to map sounds in words, and progress monitoring is documented by benchmark measures examining letter knowledge, alphabetizing skills, reading, spelling, and handwriting. The structured daily lessons can take up to an hour to complete, and include 11 fast-paced activities (Uhry & Clark, 2005). The program can be administered individually or in a small group, and used as a supplemental intervention to assist students with their language arts core curriculum.

1. *Language building (5 minutes):* Warm-up activity fostering language development skills.
2. *Alphabet recognition (5 minutes):* Rapid recognition of the sequence and directionality of the alphabet.
3. *Reading decks (3 minutes):* Drill cards to develop rapid and automatic sight-word skills.
4. *Spelling decks (3 minutes):* Students listen, echo a phoneme, say the letter names, and write the sounds in words.
5. *New learning (5 minutes):* A new sound is introduced through a combination of multisensory activities, including monitoring mouth movements and using diacritical marks as visual cuing codes to auditory rules.
6. *Reading practice (5 minutes):* Reading words (as opposed to texts or stories) that are phonetically controlled.
7. *Handwriting practice (5 minutes):* Cursive writing taught to reinforce directionality.
8. *Spelling practice (10 minutes):* Spelling of sounds using printed letters, as well as simultaneous oral spelling.
9. *Verbal expression (2–5 minutes):* Use "parts of speech" cards to introduce the beginning of a lesson.
10. *Review (5 minutes):* Review index cards with learning cues about each lesson.
11. *Reading comprehension (5 minutes):* Choose material on the student's cognitive level, not reading level, to listen and then reflect on specific questions.

Fundations

A downward extension of the Wilson Reading System, Fundations is designed for students in kindergarten through third grades. The primary focus of the program is to develop both phonemic awareness and phonology as well as develop spelling rules and boundaries in young children. Similar to the Wilson Reading System, Fundations is a multisensory phonics model of teaching reading and spelling in a very structured and systematic approach. Fundations is intended to serve as a prevention program to help reduce reading and spelling failure in the general curriculum. There are 15 sequenced activities intended to be rotated throughout the week for instruction. Teachers are encouraged to follow a specific script, though the program is flexible enough to be taught in a whole-group or one-on-one setting. The authors recommended that general education teachers incorporate a 30-minute daily Fundations lesson into their language arts classroom instruction. Specific lessons focus on carefully sequenced skills that include print knowledge, alphabet awareness, phonological awareness, phonemic awareness, decoding, vocabulary, fluency, and spelling. Critical thinking and speaking and listening skills are practiced during story-time activities. The program can be either embedded within a general education curriculum or used as a supplemental intervention to assist students with their language arts core curriculum.

SRA Corrective Reading

The SRA Corrective Reading program allows students to work in a decoding program, a comprehension program, or both. Each program has four levels, and placement tests are provided so students may enter the program at their appropriate instructional level. The decoding and the comprehension programs are designed for students in grades 4 through 12, as the context of the reading material is geared more for secondary-level students. In Corrective Reading, daily programs can take up to 45 minutes with the goal being to accomplish one reading lesson per day. The first three levels take approximately a half-year to complete, and the fourth level takes approximately one year. There are benchmark mastery tests built into the program as well. Corrective Reading uses an approach called *direct instruction*, a highly scripted reading program that allows teachers to work with students in small groups of up to 10 students. Students are asked to respond to teacher-directed questions in unison, with as many as 10 oral responses per minute required. This allows instructors to pinpoint immediately which students may be struggling with a specific sound or word pattern. Corrective Reading is a synthetic type of phonics program that carefully scaffolds sounds by building upon previously learned sounds and words. Long- and short-vowel sounds are presented in mixed order together in the scripted presentation. Corrective Reading is not a multisensory program and there are no diacritical markers used to assist with sound patterns. At the elementary level, the program is often used as a supplemental intervention to assist students with their language arts core curriculum. Corrective Reading can be used as a student's language arts curriculum at the secondary level.

Horizons Fast Track A-B

There are numerous versions of the Horizons program, including Horizons A and Horizons B, and Horizons Fast Track A-B, which is an accelerated program designed to accomplish two years of reading growth in just one academic year. The Horizons Fast Track A-B program has 150 lessons, with each lesson taking approximately 50 minutes. The time is divided between 30 minutes of reading instruction, 10 minutes of spelling instruction, and 10 minutes of independent seatwork. Horizons Fast Track A-B is a highly scripted program geared for first-grade students, or children in grades 2 or above who are nonreaders and have weak decoding skills. There is an initial placement test as well. The initial 30 lessons of the Fast Track program primarily focus on phonemic awareness and learning left-to-right sequencing conventions for letters in words. During lessons 31–70, children are reading short stories up to 90 words in length, with numerous promptings taking place to call attention to various letter combinations.

Horizons uses a unique approach to teaching letter sounds as most letters are grouped into two families. For instance, letters such as F, L, M, N, R, S, X, and Y are consonant letters as the last part of the letter name is essentially the same as the letter sound it makes. However, letters such as B, D, J, K, P, T, V, and Z have the first part of the letter name that corresponds to the letter sound. After consonants are learned, orthographic prompts that color-code sounds are used to guide the student in developing an appropriate strategy to decode words. These colors are gradually faded out once more advanced decoding activities are integrated into the lessons. By color-coding these diacritical markers, Horizons essentially minimizes the working memory demands of decoding words in print and avoids more abstract diacritical markers. Word-attack activities emphasizing decoding and critical vocabulary prepare students for upcoming stories. The program is often used as a supplemental intervention to assist students with their language arts core curriculum.

Saxon Phonics and Spelling

Saxon is designed for students in kindergarten through third grade, with daily lessons consisting of three main parts; a warm-up, introducing new material, and application of new concepts. It is essentially a supplemental phonics-based program, often used in conjunction with a more traditional core reading program. Unlike many of the aforementioned reading programs, Saxon is not scripted and offers teachers much more flexibility to deliver their own presentation format. Each lesson is highly interactive and there is a multisensory component as well. For instance, most lessons begin with a warm-up activity using kinesthetic activities to practice learning the alphabet. There are also sequenced activities designed for developing phonemic awareness using Saxon cards, tile sets, worksheets, and picture card sets. In addition, there is a portion of the lesson called a *new increment*, which includes handwriting and spelling rules, skywriting activities, a spelling dictionary, and handwriting strips to reinforce learned skills through writing activities. The third part of each lesson involves a continual review of skills, including daily homework sheets and decodable readers. Every fifth lesson includes a written and oral assessment component.

Lindamood Phoneme Sequencing Program (LiPS)

The LiPS program uses a unique approach to teaching phonemic awareness systematically. Instead of linking sounds to letters, the program links sounds to *articulatory gestures*, or movements of the face and mouth involved in producing speech sounds. Therefore, the program is a multisensory model of teaching reading through five developmental levels. The first level is called *Setting the Climate for Learning*, and the activities include auditory perception and sequencing sounds. The second level involves matching speech sounds with articulatory gestures based on the shape and position of the lips, teeth, and tongue. For instance, when teaching a *b* or a *p* sound, there are photographs of a mouth position with lips pursed, and a puff of air blowing outward, to illustrate the mouth position when making these sounds. The third level teaches students to identify various sound categories by representing them with colored blocks. The fourth level involves students associating sounds with letters printed on tiles, and there is a clear distinction made between phonologically consistent words versus phonologically inconsistent words. The final level involves spelling and decoding skills. There is a heavy emphasis on using spelling to teach reading very early in the program as well. The program is often used as a supplemental intervention to assist students with their language arts core curriculum.

FLUENCY PROGRAMS

Some children struggle with reading fluency skills and have difficulty rapidly and automatically recognizing words in print. These students are readily able to sound out individual phonemes embedded within words, but tend to have poor orthographic processing skills, slowing down the pace of word recognition. Consequently, there is a tendency to over-rely on a decoding strategy, which is often a very slow and methodical approach to reading and tends to be confusing when presented with more phonologically irregular words. For instance, words such as *debt, yacht,* and *ocean* can be very difficult to decode since these words are among the 20–25% of English words that do not follow the standard phonological conventions (Uhry & Clark, 2005). The following interventions are more suitable for students who have difficulty with reading fluency but may not necessarily struggle with phonological aspects of reading.

Read Naturally

Read Naturally emphasizes reading fluency and speed as well as fostering more accurate comprehension skills. The program uses repeated exposures to modeled reading and progress monitoring to increase overall fluency skill. It is designed for students who fall below the mean-level oral fluency rates for second grade (51 wpm) through eighth grade (133 wpm). There is an initial placement test that dictates the level at which each student will begin the program. All Read Naturally tasks follow a structured sequence whereby the student first selects a story of interest, subvocalizes vocabulary terms and meanings, and formulates a prediction about the story. Second, the student attempts a *cold-read* of the story, and then graphs the number of words read correctly in one minute. It should be noted that in the Read Naturally Software Edition, the computer calculates and graphs the cold-timing score automatically. Next, each student reads the story aloud three times along with the tape recording in order to hear proper pronunciation, expression, and phrasing. The rate of the recorded reading level increases with each successive reading. The student then attempts a *hot-read* of the passage as the teacher records errors, monitors prosody, and times the pace of reading. A variety of comprehension questions, including main idea, details, vocabulary, drawing inferences, and a short-answer question, are presented as well. Finally, the student is then given 5–8 minutes to retell the story either orally or in writing. Read Naturally is usually recommended for a minimum of 30 minutes per day, three to five days per week, and used as a supplemental intervention program.

RAVE-O

*R*etrieval, *A*utomaticity, *V*ocabulary, *E*ngagement, *O*rthography is a comprehensive fluency program developed by Maryanne Wolf at Tufts University. The goal of the program is to expand upon fluency skills, increase comprehension, and develop confidence with both oral and written language. RAVE-O is a 16-week program with daily lessons averaging between 30–45 minutes. Each week, students learn a series of words at the phonemic, orthographic, morphological, and semantic levels. The format of each lesson involves a warm-up activity to review previously taught words, introduction to core words, continued practice of speed and accuracy, and an assessment of newfound skills. There is also a "game-like" atmosphere embedded within the lessons, including a Speed Wizard computer program for letter-and-word-recognition games. The overarching philosophy of RAVE-O is the more in-depth a student knows a word, the faster the word is retrieved and comprehended, which ultimately leads to greater automaticity and fluency.

Great Leaps Reading

Great Leaps Reading is a supplementary reading program that requires just 10 minutes per day, for a minimum of three days per week. The program is divided into three major sections: (1) *phonics* for developing basic sound awareness skills; (2) *sight-phrases* for mastering sight-word skills; and (3) *fluency*, which uses age-appropriate stories designed to build oral reading fluency and automaticity, as well as to enhance student motivation. Great Leaps does not teach high-frequency words in isolation, and instead relies upon sight-phrases to be mastered within the context of a story. The program is highly *scaffolded*, meaning that one skill mastered leads to the next. In fact, students literally leap to the next page once mastery on timed tests is attained. The goal of Great Leaps is to develop fluent and independent reading skills up to the fifth-grade level. Great Leaps requires little formal training, thus making it accessible to an instructional assistant, tutor, or school volunteer. The program is used as a supplemental intervention to assist students with their language arts core curriculum.

Balanced Literacy Programs

As previously noted, students with mixed dyslexia generally have the most severe forms of reading disorders and consequently need the most intensive types of interventions. However, intensity should not be confused with inflexibility. In other words, simply increasing the same unsuccessful intervention will not necessarily lead to improved reading performance. As noted by Grizzle and Simms (2009), there is scant research to suggest that children in special education actually close the gap on peers, despite the service delivery model. Therefore, it does not behoove students to increase time in special education if the appropriate reading interventions are not put in place. According to Berninger and Richards (2010), phonological awareness is not sufficient in and of itself to develop effective reading skills for disabled readers; rather, an emphasis on morphological and orthographical awareness is also necessary to learn to read and spell. Furthermore, Grizzle and Simms (2009) noted that a focus on reading comprehension and vocabulary instruction is essential at all levels of reading instruction as well. Hence there is need for a balanced literacy model utilizing multiple bottom-up (phonological) as well as top-down (morphological) strategies to meet the challenges of our most disabled readers.

Read 180

Read 180 is a balanced literacy program designed for students in late elementary through high school, and focuses on the development of fluency, vocabulary and language building, and comprehension skills. This is not an explicit phonics model of teaching reading; therefore, it may be better suited for students at the secondary level. Read 180 uses effective metacognitive strategies, including main idea, summarizing, sequencing, and self-monitoring, to assist with comprehension, and may be particularly effective for students with executive functioning types of deficits (see Rapid Reference 5.4).

The 90-minute instructional model essentially serves as a student's language arts curriculum, and begins with 20 minutes of instruction before students rotate between three smaller groups, including an adaptive software station. This software is highly interactive and systemically directs the learner though the four learning zones. The *Reading Zone* includes phonics, fluency, and vocabulary instruction as students read through passages. The *Word Zone* provides systemic instruction in decoding and word recognition skills as 6,000 words are defined and analyzed. The *Spelling Zone* allows students to practice spelling and receive immediate feedback, and the *Success Zone* focuses on comprehension once the other zones have been mastered. The software component of the program is highly adaptive as opportunities are provided for repeated oral reading, hearing models read with fluency, and using videos to provide background knowledge and introduce vocabulary. Based on how the student reads, the software continually adjusts the level of instruction to adapt to the individual learner.

Wilson Reading System

The Wilson Reading System is one of the few reading programs developed specifically for adolescents and adults with dyslexia. It was initially designed for students in grades 2 through 12 and may also be appropriate for bilingual students. The program is comprised of 12 steps consisting of decoding, advanced word analysis, vocabulary development, comprehension, and metacognition. According to Uhry and Clark (2005), there are three unique features of the Wilson program that can be extremely helpful for older students with dyslexia. First, there is an immediate emphasis on the six syllable types comprising English orthography, though complex diacritical markers are not a component of the program. Instead, students create their own system of coding syllables using underlines instead of slash marks. A second feature of the program is the use of a unique finger-tapping system to analyze spoken words into phonemes to assist with spelling. Finally, the Sound Cards in the program are color-coded, with consonants being yellow, vowels being orange, and word families green. It is recommended that students receive 45–90 minutes of instruction per day, and all steps in the program are laid out in a very structured and ordered format, with students starting at the same level. The program is often used as a supplemental intervention to assist students with their language arts core curriculum, and can also be paired effectively with fluency-based intervention programs to create a more balanced mode of instruction.

COMPREHENSION PROGRAMS

It has been estimated that some 10% of all school-aged children have good decoding skills but possess specific difficulties with reading comprehension skills (Cutting et al., 2009; Nation & Snowling, 1998). As previously discussed, executive functioning skills such as planning, organizing, and self-monitoring, as well as verbal and visual working memory skills, are crucial to the comprehension process (Cutting et al., 2009). Certainly, students with conditions such as *hyperlexia* (advanced word-reading skills in spite of significant language limitations) or *attention-deficit/hyperactivity disorder* are among those who suffer from significant reading comprehension difficulties. However, the majority of students with reading comprehension deficits do not necessarily have other comorbid conditions, but rather struggle to derive meaning from print despite good reading mechanics. Though most of the discourse in reading research is centered around teaching skills and strategies to foster the phonological processing, it is important to note that the ultimate goal of reading is to teach students how to derive meaning from print. Hence, the following strategies and interventions are offered to assist students with their passage comprehension skills:

Soar to Success

The Soar to Success program is a relatively fast-paced, small-group instructional program for students in grades 3 through 6. The program mainly focuses on

DON'T FORGET

Four Keys to Reading Comprehension:
1. **Content affinity:** Attitude and interest toward specific material. Students should practice reading high-interest material to foster comprehension.

2. **Working memory:** Ability to temporarily suspend previously read information while simultaneously reading new information. Students should learn to take notes and highlight key points while reading.

3. **Executive functioning:** Strategies used to self-organize verbal information to facilitate retrieval. Students should learn to skim through the text by looking at topic headers and reviewing questions prior to reading the text.

4. **Language foundation:** Having the prerequisite core vocabulary knowledge to develop a semantic understanding of the text. Therefore, specific terms should be defined and discussed prior to reading the passage.

metacognitive strategies aimed at improving reading comprehension skills. Specific instructional strategies involve the use of graphic organizers and story maps to help students visually construct meaning from print. Story maps outline the main characters, setting, time of day, sources of conflict, and so forth prior to reading the passage. In addition, reciprocal teaching techniques (a dialogue between the student and teacher for the purpose of constructing meaning from text) emphasize four strategies—*summarize-clarify-question-predict*—as teachers model the use of these strategies while text is being read. There are 18 books, sequenced from simple to complex, and a typical lesson is approximately 30–35 minutes.

Lindamood Visualization and Verbalization Program

This program is designed to improve reading comprehension, oral expression, and critical thinking skills in a rather unique and innovative fashion. It was initially designed by Nancy Bell, and recommended for 30 minutes a day, three to five times per week for approximately 12 weeks. The essence of the program is for teachers to ask directed questions to assist students in forming a concept image about specific attributes of each story. The program consists of nine specific steps. At the beginning levels, 12 "structure words" (*what, size, color, number, shape, where, movement, mood, background, perspective, when,* and *sound*) are used to help the child learn to visualize words. Writing skills, vocabulary development, and higher-order thinking questions are introduced in later steps. The scope and sequence of the program also includes sentence imaging, sentence-by-sentence imaging, paragraph imaging, and paragraph-by-paragraph imaging. Consideration for the program should be given for students who have weaker language skills, second-language-learner students, students with a pervasive developmental disorder, and students with hyperlexia.

SQ3R

The SQ3R method is a five-step technique that teaches students how to Survey, Question, Read, Recall, and Review. Students are initially taught to scan and survey the content of the chapter and focus on the introduction and summary sections to become familiar with the text. Next, students are encouraged to make a note of specific questions, which in part serve as study goals. Third, students begin to read through the chapter and to take notes in a *mind-map* format. A mind map is a type of note-taking technique where students diagram important points in a particular shape, using colors and symbols to organize information around central themes. Next, students are asked to recall isolated facts about the passage. Finally, the review stage involves re-reading the story, expanding notes, and then discussing with someone else. Rapid Reference 5.6 provides additional classroom strategies to enhance reading comprehension skills.

≡ Rapid Reference 5.6 Ten Strategies to Enhance Reading Comprehension

1. Review vocabulary daily, but avoid rote memorization of terms.
2. Provide preferential seating closer to instructor and check on student progress every five minutes. Have the student paraphrase verbally what was read.
3. Make real-life connections with the material to increase motivation and interest.
4. Assign more projects than tests to assess knowledge.
5. Have student underline all topic sentences prior to reading the text.
6. Use a tracking bar to guide reading and eliminate page distractions.
7. Modify text to student's basic reading level.
8. Reciprocal teaching—students work in small groups and follow a protocol for predicting, questioning, clarifying, and summarizing information.
9. Visualize the reading process.
10. Use structured note-taking while reading, not highlighting.

SUMMARY

Cognitive neuroscience has begun to emerge as the leading discipline in forging the inevitable alliance between science and education. Whether shaped by political forces such as the 2002 No Child Left Behind policy, or fashioned by neuroscientific discoveries in the learning arena, public schools have made a renewed commitment toward using evidence-based instructional techniques as the foundation for sound educational practice. It stands to reason that evidenced-based assessment techniques should follow as well. Therefore, it is incumbent upon psychologists and educational diagnosticians to begin interpreting assessment data from a brain-based educational perspective in order to enhance their diagnostic precision. The ability to pinpoint underlying constructs impeding the learning process remains a vital component to fortify instruction and guide the intervention process. In summary, the application of neuroscientific research to both diagnose and remediate learning disorders in children remains our greatest mountain to climb, but the peak is no doubt within reach.

REFERENCES

Ardila, A., Bertolucci, P. H., Braga, L. W., Castro-Caldas, A., Judd, T., Kosmidis, M. H., . . . Rosselli, M. (2010). Illiteracy: The neuropsychology of cognition without reading. *Archives of Clinical Neuropsychology*, 25, 689–712.

Berninger, V., & Richards, T. (2010). Inter-relationships among behavioral markers, genes, brain and treatment in dyslexia and dysgraphia. *Future Neurology*, 5(4) 597–617.

Cao, F., Bitan, T., Chou, T. L., Burman, D. D., & Booth, J. R. (2006). Deficient orthographic and phonological representations in children with dyslexia revealed by brain activation patterns. *Journal of Childhood Psychology and Psychiatry*, 47(10), 1041–1050.

Carreiras, M., Seghier, M. L., Baquero, S., Estevez, A., Lozano, A., Devlin, J. T., & Price, C. J. (2009). An anatomical signature for literacy, *Nature*, 461(7266), 983–986.

Cutting, L. E., Materek, A., Cole, C. A. S., Levine, T. M., & Mahone, E. M. (2009). Effects of fluency, oral language, and executive function on reading comprehension performance. *Annals of Dyslexia*, 59(1), 34–54.

Davis, N., Fan, Q., Compton, D. L., Fuchs, D., Fuchs, L. S., Cutting, L. E., . . . Anderson, A. W. (2010). Influences of neural pathway integrity on children's response to reading instruction. *Frontiers in Systems Neuroscience*, 4(150), 1–11.

Deloche, G., Souza, L., Braga, L. W., & Dellatolas, G. (1999). A calculation and number processing battery for clinical application in illiterates and semi-literates. *Cortex*, 35, 503–521.

Feifer, S. G., & Della Toffalo, D. (2007). *Integrating RTI with cognitive neuropsychology: A scientific approach to reading*. Middletown, MD: School Neuropsych Press.

Gaab, N., Gabrieli, J. D., Deutsch, G. K., Tallal, P., & Temple, E. (2007). Neural correlates of rapid auditory processing are disrupted in children with developmental dyslexia and ameliorated with training: An fMRI study. *Restorative Neurology and Neuroscience*, 25(3–4): 295–310.

Goldberg, E., (2009). *The new executive brain: Frontal lobes in a complex world.* New York, NY: Oxford University Press.

Grizzle, K. L., & Simms, M. D. (2009). Language and learning: A discussion of typical and disordered development. *Current Problems in Pediatric Adolescent Health Care, 39,* 168–189.

Hanson, R., & Mendius, R. (2009). *The practical neuroscience of Buddha's brain: Happiness, love & wisdom.* Oakland, CA: New Harbinger.

Heim, S., Tschierse, J., Amunts, K., Wilms, M., Vossel, S., Willmes, K., . . . Huber, W. (2008). Cognitive subtypes of dyslexia. *Acta Neurobiologiae Experimentalis, 68,* 73–82.

Hoeft, F., McCandliss, B. D., Black, J. M., Gantman, A., Zakerani, N., Hulme, C., . . . Gabrieli, J. D. E. (2011). Neural systems predicting long-term outcome in dyslexia. *Proceedings of the National Academy of Sciences of the United States of America, 108*(1), 361–366.

Kronbichler, M., Wimmer, H., Wolfgang, S., Hutzler, F., Mair, A., & Ladurner, G. (2008). Developmental dyslexia: Gray matter abnormalities in the occipitotemporal cortex, *Human Brain Mapping, 29,* 613–625.

Levine, M. D., & Reed, M. (1999). *Developmental variation and learning disorders.* Cambridge, MA: Educators Publishing Services.

Li, G., Cheung, R. T., Gao, J. H., Lee, T. M., Fox, P. T., Jack, C. R., & Yang, E. S. (2006). Cognitive processing in Chinese literate and illiterate subjects: An fMRI study. *Human Brain Mapping, 27*(2), 144–152.

McCandliss, B. D., & Noble, K. G. (2003). The development of reading impairment: A cognitive neuroscience model. *Mental Retardation and Developmental Disabilities, 9,* 196–205.

Nation, K., & Snowling, M. J. (1998). Individual differences in contextual facilitation: Evidence from dyslexia and poor reading comprehension. *Child Development, 69,* 994–1009.

National Association of School Psychologists: Position Statement. (2011). *Identification of students with specific learning disabilities:* Retrieved July 14, 2012, from http://www.nasponline.org/about_nasp/position_paper.aspx.

National Reading Panel. (2000). *Teaching children to read: An evidence-based assessment of the scientific research literature on reading and its implications for reading instruction.* Washington, DC: National Institutes of Child Health and Human Development.

Noble, K. G., & McCandliss, B. D. (2005). Reading development and impairment: Behavioral, social, and neurobiological factors. *Developmental and Behavioral Pediatrics, 26*(5), 370–376.

Pernet, C. R., Poline, J. B., Demonet, J. F., & Rousselet, G. A. (2009). Brain classification reveals the right cerebellum as the best biomarker of dyslexia. *BMC Neuroscience, 10,* 67.

Pugh, K. R., Mencl, W. E., Jenner, A. R., Katz, L., Frost, S. J., Lee, J. R., . . . Shaywitz, B. A. (2000). Functional neuroimaging studies of reading and reading disability (developmental dyslexia). *Mental Retardation and Developmental Disabilities Research Reviews, 6,* 207–213.

Ramus, F. (2003). Developmental dyslexia: Specific phonological deficit or general sensorimotor dysfunction? *Current Opinion in Neurobiology, 13,* 212–218.

Ramus, F. (2004). Neurobiology of dyslexia: A reinterpretation of the data. *Trends in Neurosciences, 27,* 720–726.

Reiter, A., Tucha, O., & Lange, K. W. (2004). Executive functions in children with dyslexia. *Dyslexia, 11,* 116–131.

Reynolds, C. R. (2007). RTI, neuroscience, and sense: Chaos in the diagnosis and treatment of learning disabilities. In E. Fletcher-Janzen & C. R. Reynolds (Eds.), *Neuropsychological perspectives on learning disabilities in the era of RTI* (pp. 14–27). Hoboken, NJ: John Wiley & Sons.

Sandak, R., Mencl, W. E., Frost, S., Rueckl, J. G., Katz, L., Moore, D. L., . . . Pugh, K. R. (2004). The neurobiology of adaptive learning in reading: A contrast of different training conditions. *Cognitive, Affective, & Behavioral Neuroscience, 4*(1), 67–88.

Senechal, M., & Kearnan, K. (2007). The role of morphology in reading and spelling. *Advances in Child Development and Behavior, 35,* 297–325.

Shaywitz, S. E. (2003). *Overcoming dyslexia: A new and complete science-based program for reading problems at any level.* New York, NY: Alfred A. Knopf.

Shaywitz, S. (2004). *Overcoming dyslexia.* New York, NY: Random House.

Shaywitz, S., & Shaywitz, B. (2005). Dyslexia: Specific reading disability. *Biological Psychiatry, 57,* 1301–1309.

Temple, E. (2002). Brain mechanisms in normal and dyslexic readers. *Current Opinion in Neurobiology, 12,* 178–193.

Uhry, J. K., & Clark, D. B. (2005). *Dyslexia: Theory and practice of instruction.* Baltimore, MD: York.

United Nations Educational Scientific and Cultural Organization: UNESCO. (2012). Retrieved July 14, 2012, from http://www.uis.unesco.org/literacy/Pages/adult-youth-literacy-data- viz.aspx.

U.S. Department of Education. (2009a). *Highlights from PISA 2009: Performance of U.S. 15- year-old students in reading, mathematics, and science literacy in an international context.* Washington, DC: National Center for Educational Statistics.

U.S. Department of Education: Institute of Educational Sciences. (2009b). *Children and youth with disabilities.* Washington, DC: National Center for Educational Statistics.

Willcutt, E. G., Olson, R. K., Pennington, B. F., Boada, R., Ogline, J. S., Tunick, R. A., & Chabildas, N. A. (2001). Comparison of the cognitive deficits in reading disability and attention deficit hyperactivity disorder. *Journal of Abnormal Psychology, 110,* 157–172.

Woodcock, R. (2011). *Woodcock reading mastery tests,* Third Edition (WRMT-III). San Antonio, TX: Pearson.

🦔 TEST YOURSELF 🦔

1. **Which of the following statements is *true* regarding literacy rates?**

   a. Illiteracy remains prevalent among one-fifth of the world's population.

   b. Approximately one in seven adults in the United States is functionally illiterate.

   c. Illiteracy is more prevalent among females worldwide, though in the United States, females score higher than males on standardized reading measures.

   d. All of the above are true.

2. **Which type of reading disability is characterized by an over-reliance on sound patterns, poor fluency and speed, and difficulty reading phonologically irregular words?**

   a. Mixed dyslexia

   b. Surface dyslexia

   c. Phonological dyslexia

   d. Deep dyslexia

(continued)

(continued)

3. *True or false?*: According to the National Association of School Psychologists, learning disabilities are neurologically based deficits, heterogeneous in nature, consist of multiple subtypes, differ in degree, and require evidence-based multitier service delivery systems.

4. **What should interventions for mixed dyslexia should consist of?**
   a. Phonology and audiology
   b. Balanced literacy and morphology
   c. Morphology and word cueing
   d. Comprehension and recall strategies

5. **According to Grizzle and Simms (2009), what do the "five big ideas" of reading involve?**
   a. Phonemic awareness, rapid naming, comprehension, working memory, and spelling
   b. Phonemic awareness, alphabetic principle, reading fluency, vocabulary, comprehension
   c. Alphabetic principle, spelling, prosody, orthography, executive functioning
   d. Phonemic awareness, alphabetic principle, automaticity, decoding, whole words

6. **What are the three main cognitive constructs involved with reading comprehension skills?**
   a. Executive functioning, sensory motor skills, vocabulary
   b. Working memory, visual memory, verbal memory
   c. Executive functioning, working memory, vocabulary skills
   d. Visual-spatial skills, memory, processing speed

7. **Which of the following reading programs are primarily geared toward the development of phonological processing skills?**
   a. Alphabetic phonics
   b. Great Leaps
   c. RAVE-O
   d. Lindamood Visualization and Verbalization Program

8. **Which type of reading disability is characterized by deficits in acquiring basic sound-symbol relationships necessary to decode words?**
   a. Mixed dyslexia
   b. Surface dyslexia
   c. Phonological dyslexia
   d. Deep dyslexia

9. **Which reading program is recommended for a 6-year-old student with poor decoding skills and limited phonological processing abilities?**
   a. Fundations
   b. Read Naturally
   c. Read 180
   d. Alphabet Scanning

10. **Which reading program is not geared specifically toward the improvement of reading comprehension skills?**

a. SQ3R

b. Soar to Success

c. Saxon Phonics

d. Lindamood Verbalization and Visualization

Answers: 1. d; 2. b; 3. True; 4. b; 5. b; 6. c; 7. a; 8. c; 9. a; 10. c

Six

SELECTING AND TAILORING INTERVENTIONS FOR STUDENTS WITH MATHEMATICS DIFFICULTIES

Diane Pedrotty Bryant
Kathleen Hughes Pfannenstiel
Brian R. Bryant
Jessica Hunt
Mikyung Shin

According to the National Mathematics Advisory Panel (NMAP, 2008), the U.S. workforce must be capable of understanding and applying quantitative concepts to remain competitive in a global economy. Yet, findings from international studies (e.g., *Trends in International Mathematics and Science Study* [TIMSS]; Gonzales et al., 2004; *Program for International Student Assessment* [PISA]; Organization for Economic Cooperation and Development, 2009) show that students from the United States continue to be outperformed on mathematics tests by their peers in many developed countries. Additionally, findings from the National Assessment of Educational Progress (NAEP; National Center for Education Statistics, 2011) indicate a persistent problem of under-achievement (i.e., scoring below the *basic* level) for students with mathematics difficulties (MD) and for students with mathematics learning disabilities (MLD).

Underachievement suggests gaps in understanding fundamental content. Unfortunately, lacking a solid mathematics foundation impedes successful per-formance in higher-level mathematics courses, such as algebra, and contributes to lifelong difficulties in employment and meeting the demands of daily living (Aunola, Leskinen, Lerkkanen, & Nurmi, 2004; Geary, 2011; NMAP, 2008).

The purpose of this chapter is to provide (1) an overview of MD and MLD, (2) a summary of common reasons for MD and MLD, (3) cases of students with MD and MLD, and (4) examples of interventions for the cases of students with MD and MLD.

OVERVIEW OF MATHEMATICS DIFFICULTIES AND MATHEMATICS LEARNING DISABILITIES

The Individuals with Disabilities Education Improvement Act (IDEIA, 2004) indicated that students with MD and MLD experience difficulties in the area of math calculations and/or math problem solving. Studies have shown that difficulties with math calculations are a defining characteristic of students with mathematics difficulties or disabilities (e.g., Gersten, Jordan, & Flojo, 2005; Hanich, Jordan, Kaplan, & Dick, 2001; Jordan, Kaplan, & Hanich, 2002), and are an important contributor to students' inability to solve whole-number computation and word problems (Fuchs et al., 2005) (see Rapid Reference 6.1 for prevalence figures).

Mathematics Domains and Mathematics Difficulties

The National Council of Teachers of Mathematics (NCTM, 2000, 2006) identified five domains that are most critical for mathematics instruction: *number and operations, algebra, geometry, measurement,* and *data analysis.* These domains have been incorporated into the more recent (National Governors Association Center for Best Practices [NGA Center] & Council of Chief State School Officers [CCSSO], 2010). Moreover, the CCSS (2010) provides Standards for Mathematical Practice that focus on critical "processes and proficiencies," including the NCTM process standards (i.e., problem solving, reasoning and proof, communication, representation, and connections). Thus, standards and policy recommendations to inform instruction in mathematics domains are pervasive.

≋ *Rapid Reference 6.1 Prevalence Studies of MLD and LA*

Prevalence studies have shown that 7% of the school-aged population has MLD (Barbaresi, Katusic, Colligan, Weaver, & Jacobsen, 2005; Geary, 2011; Shalev, Manor, & Gross-Tsur, 2005); further, 5 to 10% of the school-aged population may be classified as having persistent low achievement in mathematics (Berch & Mazzocco, 2007; Geary, 2011; Geary, Hoard, Byrd-Craven, Nugent, & Numtee, 2007). Undoubtedly, a significant number of students demonstrate poor mathematics achievement (Swanson, 2006) that is persistent and pervasive with potentially long-term mathematics difficulties (Geary, 2004; Murphy, Mazzocco, Hanich, & Early, 2007).

Critical Mathematics Skills and Concepts

Research on specific mathematical domains (e.g., number and operations, algebra) and the performance of students with MD and MLD has been slow to emerge and restricted in focus in domains and across age groups. Primarily, research has focused on younger at-risk students' performance in the areas of number and arithmetic (e.g., Bull & Scerif, 2001; D. Bryant et al., 2011b; Fuchs et al., 2005; Geary, Bailey, & Hoard, 2009) and to a lesser degree on older students' performance on rational numbers (Hecht & Vagi, 2010; Mazzocco & Devlin, 2008) and word problem solving (e.g., Swanson, Jerman, & Zheng, 2008). Overall, findings show that students with MD and MLD perform less well than age- or grade-matched students who do not have mathematics calculation difficulties (e.g., number facts) and who have arithmetic strategies, word problem-solving skills, and number-sense activities (e.g., identifying the ranking of proportions) (Bryant, Bryant, & Hammill, 2000; Bryant, Smith, & Bryant, 2008; Shin & Bryant, 2013). Noticeable, is the limited research base in other mathematics domains (e.g., algebra, measurement, geometry).

Number facts retrieval (i.e., addition and subtraction facts and multiplication and related division facts) is a critical ability for students with MD to master; yet, for many students with MD and MLD, fluency is not often achieved because of lack of sufficient practice, immature counting strategies (e.g., counting all, counting on fingers), and difficulty understanding properties that can facilitate fluency (Geary, 1990, 2004; Jordan et al., 2003). Persistent deficits in number facts retrieval is a defining feature of students with MD and MLD (Gersten et al., 2005; Hanich et al., 2001; Jordan, Kaplan, & Hanich, 2002), and is an important contributor to students' inability to solve whole-number computation and word problems (Fuchs et al., 2005).

Rational numbers is another area that is critical for more advanced mathematics success, especially in algebra (NMAP, 2008). Research has shown that most young students have a practical knowledge of fractions, sometimes referred to as *informal knowledge* (Mack, 1995) that allows them to problem-solve (Kieren, 1988; Mack, 1990). For instance, the concept of dividing something in half is a relatively easy one that most young students understand and can demonstrate with pictures and concrete objects. However, results from a

DON'T FORGET

Persistent deficits in number facts retrieval is a defining feature of students with mathematics learning disabilities and contributes to the inability to solve whole-number computation and word problems.

study of older students with MLD revealed gaps in conceptual understanding of fractions and decimals. Findings from Mazzocco and Devlin's (2008) longitudinal study with 147 sixth-, seventh-, and eighth-grade students with MLD and MD and with typical achievers (TA) found students with MLD performing poorly on ranking proportions with fractions and decimals (e.g., ranking smallest to largest decimals [numerically displayed] and fractions [pictorially displayed]) as compared to the other two groups of students. Additionally, students with MLD manifested significantly more difficulties in identifying fraction and decimal equivalence $(.50 = \frac{5}{10})$ as compared to students with MD and students who were TA. Mazzocco and Devlin attributed poor conceptual understanding of rational numbers (i.e., weak number sense) as a possible explanation for low performance in basic tasks (i.e., equivalence of rational numbers and comparing and ordering fractions and decimals), which are associated with earlier grades' content.

Mathematical problem solving has been conceptualized as a multi-componential task that involves five types of knowledge (see Rapid Reference 6.2). These types of knowledge are engaged when representing problems and executing the steps to solve the problems (Mayer, 1998). Problem representation involves helping students comprehend the problem by translating and transforming linguistic, semantic, and schematic knowledge into various mathematical representations (e.g., graphic, symbolic) to illustrate the relationship among the elements of the problem. Problem execution requires the application of strategic and procedural knowledge as students identify the solution strategy and calculate the answer to the problem (Jitendra, Griffin, Deatline-Buchman, & Sczesniak, 2007; Montague, Enders, & Dietz, 2011).

Findings from studies on mathematical problem solving have shown that younger (e.g., Jitendra et al., 2007) and older (e.g., Montague et al., 2011)

≡ *Rapid Reference 6.2 Types of Knowledge in Math Problem Solving*

One model of problem solving includes five types of knowledge: linguistic (i.e., language and syntax), semantic (i.e., mathematical structure of problems, type of word problem), schematic (i.e., framework, outline, or plan), strategic (i.e., planning and monitoring cognitive and metacognitive processes), and procedural (i.e., performing a sequence of steps and operations) (Mayer, 1985).

students with MD and MLD have weak problem-solving capabilities that are linked to difficulties with comprehending problem-solving processes for representing problems and in terms of determining efficient solution strategies. For example, Montague (1997) found that middle school students differed from their typically achieving peer group quantitatively and qualitatively in *types* of cognitive strategies they used to solve word problems. Given the difficulties students with MD and MLD manifest in learning mathematics, evidence-based interventions are needed to promote understanding and accuracy with whole-number operations, rational numbers, and mathematical problem solving. These interventions must be linked to helping students overcome mathematics difficulties while being cognizant of possible reasons for the difficulties.

SUMMARY OF COMMON REASONS FOR MATHEMATICS DIFFICULTIES AND MATHEMATICS LEARNING DISABILITIES

Research in understanding the reasons for MD and MLD can be characterized as in the early stages of development (Swanson & Jerman, 2006), focusing on difficulties exhibited primarily by elementary-aged students in specific mathematical domains, such as number, arithmetic, and mathematical problem solving. Geary (2011) discussed the causes of mathematics difficulties in elementary-aged children as related to mathematical domains of number and arithmetic and general domains of intelligence, working memory, and processing speed. Accordingly, when examining the relationship of these variables to mathematics achievement, his findings showed that:

[C]hildren with MLD and their [low-achieving] LA peers have deficits in understanding and representing numerical magnitude, difficulties retrieving basic arithmetic facts from long-term memory, and delays in learning mathematical procedures. These deficits and delays cannot be attributed to intelligence but are related to working memory deficits for children with MLD, but not LA children. These individuals have identifiable number and memory delays and deficits that seem to be specific to mathematics learning. (p. 250)

Cognitive Variables Related to Mathematics Achievement

Research on cognitive variables related to mathematics achievement has been conducted notably in the areas of early numeracy, arithmetic calculations, and word problem solving to examine individual differences across groups (e.g., MLD, low math performance). In the area of early numeracy, Geary et al. (2007) have examined the relationship of working memory to early numeracy performance. They found that kindergarten children with MLD demonstrated deficits across specific early numeracy math cognition tasks (number and counting), and on measures of processing speed and working memory (e.g., Phonological Loop Storage [PL], Central Executive Function [CE], and Visuospatial Sketch Pad Storage [VSPP]). Compared to the typically achieving group, low-achieving children showed math deficits only on specific math tasks (i.e., fluency of processing numbers, making number line estimates, and fact retrieval), moderate differences for processing speed, and no differences in working memory. In another recent study, Geary, Hoard, Nugent, and Byrd-Craven (2008) examined the ability of first- and second-grade students with MLD and low math performance to show magnitude representations on a number line (i.e., mental number line). Results showed that students with MLD performed significantly poorer than low-performing students without MLD and that this performance was related to a deficit in WM (i.e., central executive function attentional and inhibitory control).

In the area of arithmetic calculations and computational fluency with basic facts, processing speed has been linked to math skills requiring automaticity, such as fact retrieval (Fuchs et al., 2005; Geary, 2004). Speed of processing potentially can facilitate fluent counting for calculating answers, thus promoting associations between problems and answers in WM. For example, findings have shown that students with poor mastery (accuracy and fluency) of arithmetic combinations compared to students who demonstrated mastery of arithmetic combinations showed little progress over a two-year period in retrieval of basic combinations in a timed condition (Geary, 2004; Jordan et al., 2003). According to Geary, this deficit appears to be persistent and characteristic of a developmental difference, suggesting that these children may have some form of memory or cognitive deficit that may lead to the identification of a mathematics learning disability (Gersten et al., 2005).

CAUTION

Compared to reading research, research in mathematics and struggling students is in the early stages of development; thus, more studies are needed to confirm characteristics and validate interventions.

DON'T FORGET

Studies have shown that processing speed is a strong predictor of arithmetic competence (Bull & Johnston, 1997) and may be a stronger predictor of mathematics performance than WM (Fuchs et al., 2005).

Finally, regarding word problem solving, Swanson et al. (2008) found that the central executive function and phonological system accounted for substantial variance in problem-solving accuracy. Theoretically, WM performance is related to one's ability to access relevant information related to solution accuracy on word problems from long-term memory (LTM). A word problem introduces information into WM, and the contents of WM are compared with possible action sequences (e.g., associative links) in LTM (Ericsson & Kintsch, 1995). When a match is found (recognized), the contents of WM are updated and used to generate a solution. Swanson et al., found that when the mediating effects of skill (e.g., reading, math computation) and cognitive variables (e.g., phonological coding, inhibition) were partialed out, WM performance contributed substantial and significant variance to children's ability to identify later the question and operations of a word problem as well as their ability to access the correct algorithm.

Instructional Variables

For many students with MD and MLD, their difficulties may be linked to a variety of instructional factors. One such factor is inadequate development of foundational understandings of whole numbers, the relationships among the four operations, and whole-number properties. For instance, students may not understand the relationship between multiplication and division (e.g., multiplication and division as inverse operations; multiplication facts and related division facts). Lack of understanding of inverse relationships inhibits the ability to recognize number families (e.g., $5 + 6 = 11$, $6 + 5 = 11$, $11 - 6 = 5$, $11 - 5 = 6$) as a strategy for solving arithmetic combinations.

A second factor that may influence fluency or automatic retrieval is a limited understanding of the meaning and application of arithmetic properties. For example, students may lack an understanding of the commutative (i.e., $A + B = B + A$; $A \times B = B \times A$) and associative (i.e., $[A + B] + C = A + [B + C]$; $[A \times B] \times C = A \times [B \times C]$) properties of addition and multiplication, and the distributive property (i.e., $A \times [B + C] = [A \times B] + [A \times C]$). Knowledge about and application of these properties can help students solve more number facts successfully (e.g., $5 \times 3 = 3 \times 5$) and derive answers more efficiently for more difficult problems (e.g., $4 \times 8 = 4 \times 6 + 4 \times 2 = 24 + 8 = 32$).

DON'T FORGET

Lack of an understanding of whole-number properties hinders the ability to recognize number families successfully as a strategy for solving arithmetic combinations (NRC, 2009).

≣ *Rapid Reference 6.3 Strategy Use for Solving Math Problems*

Geary (1990) found that students did not differ significantly from typically achieving peers in the *types* of strategies (e.g., counting on, use of fingers, verbal counting, retrieval) used to solve problems. Rather, students with mathematics difficulties made more errors in the *use* of these strategies than the typically achieving peer group.

A third factor relates to the design and delivery of explicit, systematic instruction. Modeling and multiple opportunities to practice and engage in meaningful ways with the mathematical ideas (i.e., concepts) using mathematically precise language are critical aspects of instruction. MLD and MD students must master effective and efficient procedures with deep conceptual understanding to improve their mathematics performance. For example, students with MD and MLD are not fluent in using more advanced counting strategies (e.g., count-on strategy) and derived strategies (e.g., $9 + 6 = 9 + [1 + 5] = [9 + 1] + 5 = 10 + 5 = 15$) to solve addition, subtraction, multiplication, and division problems. Without focused practice and review that leads to mastery, students do not know how to use the strategies correctly (Woodward & Rieth, 1997; see Rapid Reference 6.3).

In summary, findings from current cognitive science research provide evidence for a relationship between cognitive variables (e.g., working memory, including attention, inhibition, and task switching, and processing speed) and the mathematics performance of students with a broad range of low performance.

Additionally, consistent application of explicit, systematic practices is well supported in the research as necessary for struggling students (Swanson, Hoskyn, & Lee, 1999) and thus is the approach widely cited in our intervention examples.

CAUTION

Students whose mathematics performance was in the lowest end of the performance continuum demonstrated more cognitive processing deficits (e.g., working memory, processing speed) compared to students who scored higher in the range of low performance. Also, these findings focused predominantly on primary-age students and performance in early numeracy concepts, basic facts, and, to a lesser extent, word problem solving with elementary students (grades 1–3; Swanson et al., 2008).

CASES OF STUDENTS WITH MATHEMATICS DIFFICULTIES AND MATHEMATICS LEARNING DISABILITIES

Case Study I

Sidney Nguyen is a student with MD who attends a general education fifth grade at Forest Hills Elementary School. During fourth grade, Sidney began to fall behind because the mathematics curriculum started to focus on domains (e.g., fractions, problem solving) that required mastery of previously taught knowledge. Unfortunately, Sidney's mathematics performance on previously taught concepts and skills often had failed to reach mastery. The school's Child Study Team decided to review Sidney's mathematics performance on the beginning-of-the-year (BOY) assessments in fifth grade to determine next steps to support Sidney. Forest Hills Elementary School uses its own curriculum-based measures (CBM), as well as state assessment results, to identify those students who need intensive intervention. The school administers CBM in basic facts and word problem solving. The fact probes, which include 100 items, test students' fluency to solve basic facts in addition, subtraction, multiplication, and division in a one-minute time period. The word-problem-solving assessment is given during a one-hour period and contains 20 questions, which include different types of semantic structures (e.g., change, equal-groups problems). Sidney's test results are found in Table 6.1.

Sidney's results showed that she was performing below the benchmark level of proficiency for grade level in subtraction, multiplication, and division. Proficiency was defined as 30 digits correct (i.e., 90% accuracy). On the word-problem-solving assessment, Sidney drew some pictures to illustrate the problem situation but they were often incorrect representations, which contributed to her weak word-problem-solving performance. Mrs. Harrison, Sidney's teacher, reported that she completed the assessment in 30 minutes but appeared very frustrated. When asked if she needed more time, Sidney reported that she was done.

Based on Sidney's performance on the assessments and work completed in class, Mrs. Harrison determined that Sidney did use some strategies to solve basic facts, but her response rate was quite slow; thus, she needed to increase fluency across all operations. She also required support in the application of the operations within a word problem. Moreover, Sidney did not understand how to determine the semantic structure of the problems and translate the situation into a representation, as evidenced by the limited pictures she drew; she drew only two pictures—a dog (the story mentioned buying dog food) and a family (following a word problem about a family trip). She was recommended for intensive intervention mathematics instruction in a small group.

Table 6.1 Participant Demographics and Assessment Information

Name	Age	Gender	Ethnicity/Language					
Sidney	10	F	Asian/Pacific Islander	BOY Addition Probe: Digits correct for problems attempted: 28 Accuracy: 90%	BOY Subtraction: Digits correct for problems attempted: 20 Accuracy: 80%	BOY Multiplication: Digits correct for problems attempted: 18 Accuracy: 75%	BOY Division: Digits correct for problems attempted: 5 Accuracy: 10%	BOY WPS: 20 problems: 8 out of 20 problems correct
Mario	12	M	Hispanic English first language	WASI FS IQ 94 SS 34th percentile	WJ-III Calculation 80 SS 9th percentile	KeyMath3 Calculation 73 SS 4th percentile	KeyMath3 Numeration 77 SS 6th percentile	Math Goals in IEP
Cooper	14	M	African American	WISC IV FS IQ 85 SS 16th percentile	WISC IV Processing Speed Index 75 SS 5th percentile	WIAT III Mathematics Total 68 SS 2nd percentile	WIAT III Reading Total 80 SS 9th percentile	WIAT III Written Expression Total 80 SS 9th percentile
Harper	7	F	Caucasian	Fall M-CAP 10th percentile Total Score: 2	Fall M-COMP 12th percentile Total Score: 7	Winter M-CAP 11th percentile Total Score: 7	Winter M-COMP 3rd percentile Total Score: 8	

Note: BOY = Beginning of Year; WPS = Word Problems; SS = Standard Score; WASI = Wechsler Abbreviated Scale of Intelligence; WJ III = Woodcock Johnson Tests of Achievement–Third Edition; IEP = Individual Education Program; WISC IV = Wechsler Intelligence Scale for Children–Fourth Edition; WIAT III = Wechsler Individual Achievement Test–Third Edition; M-CAP = Mathematics Concepts and Applications; M-COMP = Mathematics Computation.

Case Study 2

Mario Peña is a sixth grader and has been identified as having MLD. He began receiving special education services for mathematics at Longhorn Elementary School in the latter half of the third grade to work on fluent retrieval of basic facts and to build conceptual understanding of whole-number computation (e.g., regrouping, place value). His services continued in fourth and fifth grade, where instruction focused on developing conceptual understanding of fractions (e.g., comparisons, unit fractions) and calculating answers to fraction problems. Now in the sixth grade, Mario's special education teacher, Mr. Medley, is concerned about whether Mario is benefiting from his small-group instruction. The group is on the fourth lesson in ratios and equivalency, the first unit of the school year. So far, Mario's first three homework scores were below 30% correct. Mr. Medley reviewed the mathematics assessment results from recent testing (see Table 6.1); he already knew that Mario scored at the 45th percentile in reading and the 8th percentile in mathematics on the fifth-grade state assessment test.

Mr. Medley decided to use a clinical interview approach to understand better Mario's thinking with the current instructional topic. He created three problems that were representative of the next several lessons in the ratio unit and gave them to Mario to assess his understanding of ratio and equivalency concepts. Mario's work for one of these problems is shown in Figure 6.1.

Mr. Medley asked Mario questions as he solved the problem:

MR. MEDLEY: How many cartons would you need?

MARIO: So I need to draw the thirty classrooms, right? [Draws 30 classrooms, counts, then crosses out 6 as he counts down to arrive at 24] I counted all of these and then I took six of them away and I got twenty-four.

2. If two cartons of paper are enough to supply 6 classrooms, how many cartons of paper are needed to supply 30 classrooms?

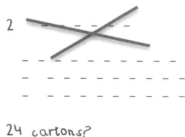

Figure 6.1. Mario's Work

MR. MEDLEY: Why did you take six away?

MARIO: It's thirty classrooms and then six classrooms, so I find out how many. So, it's plus—no, wait—*minus*, right?

From the student's work, Mr. Medley determined that Mario did not understand the ratio relationship implied in the problem. When talking through his work, Mario did not use ratio language to describe the ratio relationship, and he was unable to use the ratio relationship (in this case, 2 to 3) to understand notions of ratio equivalence. Moreover, Mario's representation of the problem was not beneficial in helping him to understand the underlying ratio relationship.

Mario's standardized assessment scores showed difficulties with calculations and numeration. Closer examination revealed a lack of understanding with multiplication representations (e.g., area models) and limited accuracy with multiplication and related division facts. Moreover, Mr. Medley determined that Mario's present instructional difficulties stemmed from his incomplete background knowledge about concepts related to ratios and insufficient strategies for answering basic facts accurately and fluently (a problem associated with MLD).

Case Study 3

Cooper Davidson is a ninth-grade student with MLD and reading difficulties at Drake High School. Cooper has been receiving special education resource services since fourth grade. The most recent assessment scores from his reevaluation are shown in Table 6.1. The reading and written expression scores fall in the descriptive category of low average and the mathematics results fall in the descriptive category of very poor performance. His teacher also analyzed the state alternative assessment results to identify any patterns in questions missed. Overall, the analysis showed that Cooper could solve basic operations, but lacked fluency with basic facts. Understanding and applying proportionality to linear equations and using expressions, equations, and functions within word problems were the areas in which intensive intervention would be necessary. He also often struggled with reading and comprehending word problems. When asked to verbalize how he solved a problem, Cooper was often scattered in his thoughts and would often forget how to apply the multistep problem strategy, including translating the semantic structure into a visual representation. Also, his slow processing speed made it difficult for him to finish multistep problems in the allotted time. Furthermore, it took Cooper a much longer time than his peers to fully understand and use the vocabulary correctly to explain how to generalize a pattern for a set of equations using a variable.

Case Study 4

Harper Giese is a student with mathematics difficulties in the second grade at Bright Oaks Elementary school. At the beginning of second grade, the district required the administration of AIMSweb® as its universal screener to identify mathematics performance of all students and to determine those students who were at-risk for mathematics difficulties. Based on her assessment scores (see Table 6.1), Harper was identified as at-risk and began receiving supplemental support from her classroom teacher in 20-minute sessions, three days per week. The classroom teacher just completed the winter benchmark assessment and is concerned because Harper made very little progress and lacks the understanding of fundamental knowledge related to the core mathematics curriculum.

Showing little progress after one semester of intervention, the school interventionist, Mr. Weiss, decides to complete a clinical interview with Harper to determine what prerequisite knowledge is lacking as one explanation of minimal growth. Mr. Weiss shows Harper a card with *2 + 7*. She holds up two fingers and then seven more fingers and counts all of her fingers to get 9.

MR. WEISS: Can you show how you just solved two-plus-seven using these cubes? [Harper pulls out cubes and makes a pile of two cubes. She then makes a straight line of seven cubes and counts all] What if I took two cubes away, how many cubes are left? [She waits until Mr. Weiss removes two cubes and then counts all]

HARPER: There are now seven cubes left.

MR. WEISS: What happened to the total amount of cubes? What can you tell me about the numbers two, seven, and nine?

HARPER: You took the cubes. Those are all numbers—see I can make piles. [She then proceeds to make piles of two cubes, seven cubes, and nine cubes]

MR. WEISS: What is the answer to nine-minus-seven? Can you solve this quickly using the last problem, two-plus-seven, to help?

Looking at the AIMSweb® assessments and the clinical interview data with Harper, Mr. Weiss concluded that she is lacking number knowledge and the ability to understand inverse operations and the commutative property. For example, 2 and 7 are parts of a greater whole number, 9. A typical student sees that 2, 7, and 9 are members of a number family, meaning two addition and two subtraction equations can be written. It appears that Harper lacks an understanding of how numbers are related and sees each problem as separate. Harper also lacks efficiency in counting; rather than counting on from the larger number, for example, she counts the quantity of each number both with her fingers and concrete manipulatives. Mr. Weiss also had Harper compare numbers; she was able to identify the greater- or less-than number, except when the two numbers compared were similar, as in 13 and 31. Harper lacks fluency in counting on from a number greater than 1 (e.g., start counting at 22) and in counting back (e.g., count back from 47). Mr. Weiss is planning on increasing the amount of intervention time from three days to five days per week with 30-minute sessions.

INTERVENTIONS FOR STUDENTS WITH MATHEMATICS DIFFICULTY AND MATHEMATICS LEARNING DISABILITIES

The NMAP and NRC (2001) recommended three aspects of mathematical learning that should be emphasized during instruction: conceptual understanding (comprehension of mathematical concepts, operations, and relations), computational fluency, and problem-solving skills. Additionally, we know that certain principles of instruction, self-regulation and motivation, and progress monitoring are critical aspects of teaching students who struggle in learning mathematics.

Principles of Effective Instructional Design and Delivery

Findings from a recent meta-analysis on teaching mathematics to students with learning disabilities (LD) found the following practices to have a moderate-to-high effect on students' mathematical learning: (a) explicit instruction on a frequent basis, (b) multiple instructional examples, (c) student verbalizations about decisions and solutions to problem solving, (d) multiple/heuristic strategies, (e) ongoing formative assessment with feedback to teachers, and (f) peer-assisted instruction (Gersten et al., 2009; Jayanthi, Gersten, & Baker, 2008). Moreover, we know that students with MD and MLD benefit from a combined approach of explicit instruction with strategy instruction (B. Bryant et al., 2008; Bryant, Kim, Hartman, & Bryant, 2006; Swanson et al., 1999). See the Evidence-Based Instructional Practices on the CD for more examples of recommended practices.

Self-regulation and Motivation

One means of reinforcing mastery of foundational number skills and facts is using *self-regulation strategies* within academic interventions. The combination of academics and self-regulation strategies may contribute to increased academic achievement and decrease the time needed to master specific skills (Rock, 2005) because it "enhances learning by helping students take control of their actions and move toward independence as they learn" (Montague, 2007, p. 76). By involving students in the process of data collection within self-regulation, the students decreased disengaged time and increased time on task, as well as productivity across "new versus previously learned material" (Rock, 2005, p. 13). Konrad and Test (2007) found similar results by including students as active participants in educational goal setting and planning. Konrad and Test found that self-regulation strategies play a significant role in improving academic outcomes.

Progress Monitoring

Progress monitoring plays a vital role in any educational program (Office of Public Instruction, 2009; Shinn, 2010). Although progress monitoring can take many forms, we consider this component of assessment to be fundamental to answering four academic-related questions (see Figure 6.2).

In our work, universal screening takes the form of Benchmark Checks by which all students are tested to determine whether they are below-average mathematics achievers and are in need of supplemental instruction to bolster their mathematical skills and concepts (Cuillos, SoRelle, Kim, Seo, & Bryant, 2011). Benchmark Checks are administered in the fall, winter, and spring of the academic year. Students' test scores are compared to a benchmark to determine whether students qualify for supplemental instruction or can exit instruction if they are already receiving services.

We assign Benchmark Check scores to three levels: A, B, and C. Those who score above the 35th percentile are assigned to the A level, which stands for "All ahead full." Because they are doing well, students should continue to receive whatever core instruction has been given by their teachers, which may or may not include supplemental assistance when they struggle with a specific concept or skill. Students falling in the 25th through the 35th percentile range are assigned to the B level, which stands for "Be alert." These students, although they score at or above the benchmark, may be at risk for later failure. So we urge teachers to check for students' understanding even more so than they would for A-level students, because B-level students may require assistance when learning new skills and concepts to ensure that they continue to meet benchmarks. The final group, C-level students, fall below benchmark. C stands for "Change," because what is being done thus far is not working. In most instances, change means Tier 2 supplemental instruction or Tier 3 intensive intervention, depending on the severity of student struggles.

Once supplemental instruction begins, interventionists require information about the effectiveness of the supplemental instruction or intervention. At the end

Progress Monitoring Tool	Purpose	Administration	Examples
Benchmark check	To answer the questions, "Where does the student fall in comparison to his or her peers?" and "Does the student qualify for intervention?"	Benchmark checks are given to all students in the fall, winter, and spring of the year.	Four, 2-minute timed tests assessing number and operation skills (e.g., magnitude comparisons, number sequences, place value, addition/subtraction combinations), which are summed to form a total score.
Daily check	To answer the question, "Did the student meet the objective of the day's lesson?"	Daily checks are administered only to students receiving intervention at the end of each day's lesson.	Several items that assess the content of the lesson. Administered as part of independent practice, the daily check total score should allow for one mistake, yet still achieve mastery (e.g., for a five-item daily check, mastery is set at 80% correct).
Unit check	To answer the questions, "Has the student mastered the content of the unit/chapter as presented across a 2-week (or so) period?" and "Has the student maintained daily learning across an elongated time frame?"	Unit checks are administered only to students receiving intervention at the end of the 2-week intervention unit or chapter.	Ten to 20 items that assess the content taught during the unit/chapter. Tests can be a pregenerated component of the commercial or research intervention, or unit checks can be created using items from the daily checks. With at least 10 items, mastery can be set at 90%.
Aim checks	To answer the question, "Is the student making progress towards his or her intervention goal?"—which is usually the next benchmark.	Aim checks are administered twice per week to students receiving intervention. Some teachers choose to administer aim checks to all students once every week or 2 weeks.	Aim checks should be alternate forms of benchmark checks. It is best to create four or five forms of the aim checks to ensure that students do not remember answers from a single form.

Figure 6.2. Description of Progress Monitoring Tools

Source: Reprinted with permission from Sage Publications. *Description of Progress Monitoring Tools* from Cuillos, SoRelle, Kim, Seo, & Bryant (2011, p. 121).

of each day's lesson, a Daily Check, in the form of independent practice items, is administered to determine whether the student met the lesson's objective as illustrated in our case study lessons. At the end of a unit or chapter, usually over a period of two to three weeks, a Unit Check is administered that covers the content taught in the unit's or chapter's lessons. If the student is meeting the objective based on Daily Check performance, the next question asked is: "Are those skills and concepts maintained across the length of the unit or chapter?" Many struggling students fail to maintain learning even over a short period of time. When this occurs, Unit Checks may capture that possibility.

During intervention, Aim Checks, usually in the form of curriculum-based measures, can be administered to determine whether the supplemental intervention is helping students' progress toward their semiannual or annual goal. Aim Checks can be administered anywhere from once a week to once a month, depending on school policy. In our work, students are administered Aim Checks once every week or two (more frequently for some seriously struggling students). As alternative forms of the Benchmark Checks (Bryant, Roberts, Pfannenstiel, & Porterfield, 2011a), Aim Checks are administered and their scores plotted from baseline (the previous Benchmark Check score) to the next goal (the winter or spring Benchmark Check raw score that corresponds to the 25th percentile).

A critical component of progress monitoring is the creation of decision rules. What happens when a student does not show mastery on Daily Checks or Unit Checks? What if the student's Aim Check score does not keep pace with the Aim Line? Is regrouping necessary? Does the intervention need to be modified? Is intervention continued until a specified time period of mastery failure occurs? These are complex issues, but the unique relationship between intervention and progress monitoring dictates that data-based decisions be made and implemented. See the Progress Monitoring section on the CD for an example of graphing student scores (see Rapid Reference 6.4).

≡ Rapid Reference 6.4 Progress Monitoring Resources

National Center on Student Progress Monitoring: http://www.studentprogress.org/

National Center on Response to Intervention: http://www.rti4success.org/ progressMonitoringTools

Research Institute on Progress Monitoring: http://www.progressmonitoring.org/

National Research Center on Learning Disabilities: http://www.nrcld.org/rti_manual/ pages/RTIManualSection2.pdf

Case Study 1: Intervention for Sidney

Mrs. Harrison and the mathematics interventionist developed a plan to target Sidney's fluency with basic facts and understanding of how to solve word problems. Sidney participated in 30-minute sessions, four days per week with Mrs. Harrison. During intervention, approximately 10 minutes were devoted to reviewing previously taught strategies and practicing with facts. Rather than focus on all four operations, Mrs. Harrison began with addition and related subtraction facts until Sidney demonstrated mastery. Mastery had been defined as 30 digits correct or better in one minute, based on the district's guidelines and recommendations from the research. Once Sidney reached mastery in addition and related subtraction, the instruction transitioned to multiplication and related division.

The next 20 minutes of intervention focused on word problem solving. Sidney was taught specific problem-solving steps using a cognitive strategy: underlining or highlighting the question, circling important information, crossing out extra information not needed, completing a diagram that represents the problem's semantic structure, and writing a number equation to solve the problem. Particular emphasis was placed on the use of a diagram to represent the problem situation. She first practiced using the strategy in easier problems to reach mastery without the distraction of solving more complex problems, and she was allowed to use the number line and hundreds chart to compute calculations in the problems as needed. Mrs. Harrison had Sidney verbalize the steps of the strategy as she solved the problem and explain how to use the schema diagram to set up and solve the problem (see Instructional Practices on the CD for an example of a schematic diagram). Mrs. Harrison already had introduced the use of graphing as a motivational tool, so Sidney was able to graph her word-problem-solving accuracy score after each independent practice activity (see Instructional Practices on the CD for an example of a word-problem-solving cognitive strategy with the modeling sheet and answer sheet).

Case Study 2: Intervention for Mario

Mr. Medley developed a series of mini-lessons focused on building a stronger conceptual understanding of multiplication and fluency with multiplication and related division facts. He also wanted Mario to develop an understanding of ratio concepts and equivalency, including the use of mathematically precise language to describe the ratio concepts (e.g., "For every two blue marbles in the jar there are four red marbles").

To help develop Mario's understanding of multiplication, his teacher began a series of explicitly delivered mini-lessons. Mr. Medley used models to illustrate to

Mario how to show different equal groups (e.g., using an area model to represent seven sets of four) and how he could use skip-counting and tabular representations to keep track of the "double count" involved (e.g., 4 [one group], 8, [two groups], 12 [three groups], 16 [four groups] . . . 28 [seven groups]).

To transition from using counting strategies to number properties in conceptualizing multiplication, Mario's teacher delivered a second series of mini-lessons that provided demonstration and practice on break-apart strategies for multiplication based on the distributive property. Throughout both series of mini-lessons, Mr. Medley tracked Mario's performance with progress monitoring probes measuring multiplication of basic facts. Satisfied that Mario's understanding of multiplication had increased, Mr. Medley implemented a set of mini-lessons on teaching ratio equivalency using explicit, systematic practices, mathematically precise language, and word problems (see Instructional Practices on the CD for an example of a lesson to teach ratio equivalency).

Case Study 3: Intervention for Cooper

Cooper receives resource class services for language arts and mathematics. The special educators have determined that because of his severe weaknesses in algebra-readiness concepts and procedures, he would receive a double dose of mathematics intervention by also attending a mathematics lab during an elective period. Thus, he received two 45-minute blocks of mathematics instructional time to bolster prerequisite knowledge for algebra. Systematic, explicit instruction was used to teach Cooper how to set up equations and ratios from a word problem, as well as how to describe the steps needed to solve the problem. An understanding of rates and ratios had to be mastered prior to proportionality. The instruction included multiple representations (including concrete, pictorial, and abstract/symbolic) to model, generate, and simplify ratios and rates, and generate equivalency. Also, the pace of the lesson was modified to enable Cooper more processing time with the content. He used a calculator for basic operations to compensate for difficulties quickly retrieving basic multiplication and related division facts; however, he often forgot the calculator entry steps for more complex functions (e.g., graphing). Thus, he and his teacher wrote up the steps as a cue card to help him recall the procedures. To promote understanding of mathematics vocabulary terms, during mathematics lab time he worked with another special educator to illustrate and provide examples for the vocabulary. The special educator knew that Cooper was motivated to pass Algebra I; she thought a self-regulation component (i.e., checklist) would allow him to monitor his own progress in solving problems and encourage his progress.

Case Study 4: Intervention for Harper

To help develop Harper's number knowledge, Mr. Weiss began a series of systematic, explicit lessons on part-part-whole concepts with numbers 1–10, magnitude comparisons, and counting forward and backward. Mr. Weiss used counters and a part-part-whole mat to build Harper's understanding of decomposing numbers by identifying the whole number and breaking apart this whole number into two parts. By using the counters and the part-part-whole mat Harper was able to move the counters to see that the total number did not change (e.g., $5 + 4 = 6 + 3$ because the total number was 9). Mr. Weiss presented different equations, both addition and subtraction, and had her model them using concrete materials and mathematically precise vocabulary to describe her actions. As Harper made progress in connecting the operations to the part-part-whole language and model building, Mr. Weiss transitioned to pictorial representations (having Harper draw dots if needed) and then just abstract (i.e., numbers and symbols) representations. Following this progression, Mr. Weiss taught Harper strategies for solving addition and related subtraction, linking the strategies (count on, count back) to the part-part-whole concept.

SUMMARY AND CONCLUSIONS

The purpose of this chapter was to provide information about how to tailor mathematics interventions for students who exhibit mathematics difficulties. We considered students who had identified MD and MLD. We examined mathematics interventions by first providing an overview of the difficulties students demonstrate when learning math in various settings across specific domains (i.e., arithmetic calculations, word problem solving, and rational numbers). We were guided by the fact that the IDEIA (2004) identified MLD in calculations and math problem solving; undoubtedly these are the areas that have received the most research attention in recent years. Clearly, research endeavors in other mathematics domains (e.g., geometry, measurement) is warranted and with other age groups besides primarily elementary students.

Research findings have focused on the relationship of general domain areas, such as intelligence, working memory, and speed of processing, and mathematics domain–specific areas. Evidently, findings about these relationships vary depending on the students' level of mathematics performance (e.g., very low performance) and the types of strategies students choose to solve whole-number computation and word problem solving.

For those students who require intensive intervention, evidence-based practices are emerging to support classroom teachers' efforts to supplement core instruction with interventions that must be implemented with struggling students. Practices that support strong instructional design and delivery plus mathematics practices that are supported by research findings together provide some of the best practices available for classroom teachers. The field of mathematics intervention continues to benefit from research findings that unveil promising practices that could potentially impact the mathematics performance of students who are most in need of instructional support.

REFERENCES

AIMSweb. NCS Pearson, Inc. All Rights Reserved (2012). http://aimsweb.com/.

Askey, R. (Fall, 1999). Knowing and teaching elementary mathematics. *American Educator/ American Federation of Teachers.*

Aunola, K., Leskinen, E., Lerkkanen, M-K., & Nurmi, J-E. (2004). Developmental dynamics of math performance from preschool to grade 2. *Journal of Educational Psychology, 96*(4), 699–713. doi: 10.1037/0022-0663.96.4.699

Barbaresi, W. J., Katusic, S. K., Colligan, R. C., Weaver, A. L., & Jacobsen, S. J. (2005). Math learning disorder: Incidence in a population-based birth cohort, 1976–82, *Ambulatory Pediatrics, 5*(5): 281–289. doi: 10.1367/A04-209R.1

Berch, D. B., & Mazzocco, M. M. M. (Eds.). (2007). *Why is math so hard for some children? The nature and origins of mathematical learning difficulties and disabilities.* Baltimore, MD: Paul H. Brookes.

Brown, G., & Quinn, R. J. (2007). Investigating the relationship between fraction proficiency and success in algebra. *Australian Mathematics Teacher, 63*(4), 8–15.

Bryant, B. R., Bryant, D. P., Kethley, C., Kim, S., Pool, C., & Seo, Y. (2008). Preventing mathematics difficulties in the primary grades: The critical features of instruction in textbooks as part of the equation. *Learning Disability Quarterly, 31*(1, Special series), 21–35.

Bryant, D. P., Bryant, B. R., & Hammill, D. D. (2000). Characteristic behaviors of students with learning disabilities who have teacher-identified math weaknesses. *Journal of Learning Disabilities, 33*(2), 168–177, 199. doi: 10.1177/002221940003300205

Bryant, D. P., Bryant, B. R., Roberts, G., Pfannenstiel, K. H., & Porterfield, J. (2011a, September). Effects of early intervention for second grade students at-risk for mathematics difficulties. Session presented at the Society for Research on Educational Effectiveness, Washington, DC.

Bryant, D. P., Bryant, B. R., Roberts, G., Vaughn, S., Pfannenstiel, K., Porterfield, J., & Gersten, R. (2011b). Early numeracy intervention program for first-grade students with mathematics difficulties. *Exceptional Children, 78*(1), 7–23.

Bryant, D. P., Kim, S.A., Hartman, P., & Bryant, B. R. (2006). Standards-based mathematics instruction and teaching middle school students with mathematical disabilities. In M. Montague & A. Jitendra (Eds.), *Teaching mathematics to middle school students with learning difficulties* (pp. 7–28). New York, NY: Guilford Press.

Bryant, D. P., Smith, D. D., & Bryant, B. R. (2008). *Teaching students with special needs in inclusive settings.* Boston, MA: Allyn & Bacon.

Bull, R., & Johnston, R. S. (1997). Children's arithmetical difficulties: Contributions from processing speed, item identification, and short-term memory. *Journal of Experimental Child Psychology, 65,* 1–24.

Bull, R., & Scerif, G. (2001). Executive functioning as a predictor of children's mathematics ability: Inhibition, switching, and working memory. *Developmental Neuropsychology, 19*(3), 273–293. doi: 10.1207/S15326942DN1903_3

Council of Chief State School Officers & National Governors' Association. (2010, June). *Common Core Sate Standards for Mathematics.* Common core state standards initiative. Retrieved from http://www.corestandards.org/assets/CCSSI_Math%20Standards.pdf.

Cuillos, S., SoRelle, D., Kim, S. A., Seo, Y. J., & Bryant, B. R. (2011). Monitoring student response to mathematics intervention: Using data to inform tier 3 intervention. *Intervention in School and Clinic, 47,* 120–124.

Ericsson, K. A., & Kintsch, W. (1995). Long-term working memory. *Psychological Review, 102,* 211–245. doi: 10.1037/0033-295X.102.2.211

Fuchs, L. S., Compton, D. L., Fuchs, D., Paulsen, K., Bryant, J., & Hamlett, C.L. (2005). Responsiveness to intervention: Preventing and identifying mathematics disability. *Teaching Exceptional Children, 37*(4), 60–63.

Geary, D. C. (1990). A componential analysis of an early learning deficit in mathematics. *Journal of Experimental Child Psychology, 49,* 363–383. doi: 10.1016/0022-0965(90)90065-G

Geary, D. C. (2004). Mathematics and learning disabilities. *Journal of Learning Disabilities, 37,* 4–15. doi: 10.1177/00222194040370010201

Geary, D. C. (2011). Consequences, characteristics, and causes of mathematical learning disabilities and persistent low achievement in mathematics. *Journal of Developmental & Behavioral Pediatrics, 33*(30), 250–263. doi: 10.1097/DBP.0b013e318209edef

Geary, D. C., Bailey, D. H., & Hoard, M. K. (2009). Predicting mathematical achievement and mathematical learning disability with a simple screening tool: The number sets test. *Journal of Psychoeducational Assessment, 27,* 265–279. doi: 10.1177/0734282908330592

Geary, D. C., Hoard, M. K., Byrd-Craven, J., Nugent, L., & Numtee, C. (2007). Cognitive mechanisms underlying achievement deficits in children with mathematical learning disability. *Child Development, 78,* 1343–1359. doi: 10.1111/j.1467-8624.2007.01069.x

Geary, D. C., Hoard, M. K., Nugent, L., & Byrd-Craven, J. (2008). Development of number line representations in children with mathematical learning disability. *Developmental Neuropsychology, 33,* 277–299. doi: 10.1080/87565640801982361

Gersten, R., Beckmann, S., Clarke, B., Foegen, A., Marsh, L., Star, J. R., & Witzel, B. (2009). *Assisting students struggling with mathematics: Response to Intervention (RtI) for elementary and middle schools* (NCEE 2009-4060). Washington, DC: Institute of Education Sciences What Works Clearinghouse, U.S. Department of Education.

Gersten, R., Jordan, N. C., & Flojo, J. R. (2005). Early identification and intervention for students with mathematics difficulties. *Journal of Learning Disabilities, 38*(4), 293–304. doi: 10.1177/00222194050380040301

Gonzales, P., Guzman, J. C., Paretlow, L., Pahlke, E., Jocelyn, L., Kastberg, D., & Williams, T. (2004). Highlights from the *trends in international mathematics and science study.* Washington, DC: National Center for Education Statistics.

Hanich, L. B., Jordan, N. C., Kaplan, D., & Dick, J. (2001). Performance across different areas of mathematical cognition in children with learning difficulties. *Journal of Educational Psychology, 93,* 615–626. doi: 10.1037//0022-0663.93.3.615

Hecht, S. A., & Vagi, K. J. (2010). Sources of group and individual differences in emerging fraction skills. *Journal of Educational Psychology, 102*(4), 843–858. doi: 10.1037/a0019824

Hecht, S. A., Vagi, K. J., & Torgesen, J. K. (2007). Fraction skills and proportional reasoning. In D. B. Berch & M. M. M. Mazzocco (Eds.), *Why is math so hard for some children? The nature and origins of mathematical learning difficulties and disabilities* (pp. 121–132). New York, NY: Brookes.

Individuals with Disabilities Education Improvement Act of 2004. Pub. L. No. 108–446.

Jayanthi, M., Gersten, R., & Baker, S. (2008). *Mathematics instruction for students with learning disabilities or difficulty learning mathematics: A guide for teachers.* Portsmouth, NH: RMC Research Corporation, Center on Instruction.

Jitendra, A. K., Griffin, C., Deatline-Buchman, A., & Sczesniak, E. (2007). Mathematical word problem solving in third grade classrooms. *Journal of Educational Research, 100*(5), 283–302. doi: 10.3200/JOER.100.5.283-302

Jitendra, A. K., Star, J., Starosta, K., Leh, J., Sood, S., Caskie, G., . . . Mack, T. (2009). Improving students' learning of ratio and proportion problem solving: The role of schema-based instruction. *Contemporary Educational Psychology, 34*(9), 250–264.

Jordan, N. C., Hanich, L. B., & Kaplan, D. (2003). Arithmetic fact mastery in young children: A longitudinal investigation. *Journal of Experimental Child Psychology, 85*, 103–119. doi: 10.1016/S0022-0965(03)00032-8

Jordan, N. C., Hanich, L. B., & Uberti, H. (2003). Mathematical thinking and learning disabilities. In A. J. Baroody & A. Dowker (Ed.). *The development of arithmetic concepts and skills: The construction of adaptive expertise* (pp. 359–383). Mahwah, NJ: Erlbaum.

Jordan, N. C., Kaplan, D., & Hanich, L. B. (2002). Achievement growth in children with learning difficulties in mathematics: Findings of a two-year longitudinal study. *Journal of Educational Psychology, 94*, 586–597. doi: 10.1037//0022-0663.94.3.586

Kieren, T. E. (1988) Personal knowledge of rational numbers: Its intuitive and formal development. In J. Hiebert and M. Behr (Eds.), *Research agenda for mathematics education: Number concepts and operations in the middle grades* (Vol. 2, pp. 162–181). Reston, VA: National Council of Teachers of Mathematics.

Konrad, M., & Test, D. W. (2007). Effects of GO 4 IT . . . NOW! Strategy instruction on the written IEP goal articulation and paragraph-writing skills of middle school students with disabilities. *Remedial and Special Education, 28*, 277–291. doi: 10.1177/07419325070280050301

Mack, N. K. (1990). Learning fractions with understanding: Building on informal knowledge. *Journal for Research in Mathematics Education, 21*, 16–32. doi: 10.2307/749454

Mack, N. K. (1995). Critical ideas, informal knowledge, and understanding fractions. In J. T. Sowder & Bonnie P. Schapple (Eds.), *Providing a foundation for teaching mathematics in the middle grades* (pp. 67–84). Albany: State University of New York Press.

Mayer, R. E. (1985). Mathematical ability. In R. J. Sternberg (Ed.), *Human abilities: Information processing approach* (pp. 127–150). San Francisco, CA: Freeman.

Mayer, R. E. (1998). Cognitive, metacognitive, and motivational aspects of problem solving. *Instructional Science, 26*, 49–63.

Mazzocco, M. M. M., & Devlin, K. T. (2008). Parts and holes: Gaps in rational number sense in children with vs. without mathematical learning disability. *Developmental Science, 11*(5), 681–691. doi: 10.1111/j.1467-7687.2008.00717.x

Milgram, R. J. (2005). *What is math proficiency?* Retrieved September 10, 2012, from ftp://171.64.38.20/pub/papers/milgram/milgram-msri.pdf.

Montague, M. (2007). Self-regulation and mathematics instruction. *Learning Disabilities Research & Practice, 22*, 75–83. doi: 10/1111/j.1540-5826.2007.00232.x

Montague, M. (1997). Cognitive strategy instruction in mathematics for students with learning disabilities. *Journal of Learning Disabilities, 30*(2), 164–177. doi: 10.1177/002221949703000204

Montague, M., Enders, C., & Dietz, S. (2011). Effects of cognitive strategy instruction on math problem solving of middle school students with learning disabilities. *Learning Disability Quarterly, 34*(4), 262–272.

Murphy, M. M., Mazzocco, M. M. M., Hanich, L. B., & Early, M. C. (2007). Cognitive characteristics of children with mathematics learning disability (MLD) vary as a function of the cutoff criterion used to define MLD. *Journal of Learning Disabilities*, *40*, 458–478. doi: 10.1177/00222194070400050901

National Center for Education Statistics. (2011). *The Nation's report card mathematics 2011*. Institute of Education Sciences, U.S. Department of Education, Washington, DC. Retrieved September 10, 2012, from http://www.nationsreportcard.gov/math_2011/summary.asp

National Council of Teachers of Mathematics. (2000). *Principles and standards for school mathematics*. Reston, VA: Author.

National Council of Teachers of Mathematics. (2006). *Curriculum focal points for pre-kindergarten through grade 8 mathematics: A quest for coherence*. Reston, VA: Author.

National Mathematics Advisory Panel. (2008). *Foundations for success: The final report of the National Mathematics Advisory Panel*. Washington, DC: U.S. Department of Education.

National Research Council (U.S.). (2009). *Mathematics learning in early childhood: Paths toward excellence and equity*. Washington, DC: National Academies Press. A comprehensive review of research on young children's mathematics development, learning, and education.

National Research Council (U.S.). (2001). *Adding it up: Helping children learn mathematics*. Washington, DC: National Academies Press.

Office of Public Instruction. (2009). *Montana response to intervention framework*. Retrieved September 10, 2012, from http://opi.mt.gov/pub/RTI/Framework/RTIFramework-GUIDE.pdf.

Organization for Economic Cooperation and Development (OECD). (2009). *Program for international student assessment: What students know and can do: Student performance in reading, mathematics and science*. Paris, France: Author.

Rock, M. L. (2005). Use of strategic self-monitoring to enhance academic engagement, productivity, and accuracy of students with and without exceptionalities. *Journal of Positive Behavior Interventions*, *7*(1), 3–17.

Shalev, R., Manor, O., & Gross-Tsur, V. (2005). Developmental dyscalculia: A prospective six-year follow-up. *Developmental Medicine and Child Neurology*, *47*, 121–125.

Shin, M. & Bryant, D. P. (2013). *Mathematical performance and cognitive characteristics of students with mathematics learning disabilities*. (Manuscript submitted for publication.)

Shinn, M. R. (2010). Building a scientifically based data system for progress monitoring and universal screening across three tiers including RTI using curriculum-based measurement. In M. R. Shinn & H. M. Walker (Eds.), *Interventions for achievement and behavior problems in a three-tier model, including RTI* (pp. 259–292). Bethesda, MD: National Association of School Psychologists.

Siegler, R., Carpenter, T., Fennell, F., Geary, D., Lewis, J., Okamoto, Y., . . . Wray, J. (2010). *Developing effective fractions instruction for kindergarten through 8th grade: A practice guide* (NCEE #2010-4039). Washington, DC: National Center for Education Evaluation and Regional Assistance, Institute of Education Sciences, U.S. Department of Education. Retrieved from whatworks.ed.gov/publications/practiceguides.

Star, J. R. (2005). Reconceptualizing procedural knowledge. *Journal for Research in Mathematics Education*, *36*(5), 404–411.w

Swanson, H. L. (2006). Cognitive processes that underlie mathematical precociousness in young children. *Journal of Experimental Child Psychology*, *93*, 239–264. doi: 10.1016/j.jecp.2005.09.006

Swanson, H. L., Hoskyn, M., & Lee, C. (1999). *Interventions for students with learning disabilities. A meta-analysis of treatment outcomes*. New York, NY: Guilford Press.

Swanson, H. L., & Jerman, O. (2006). Math disabilities: A selective meta-analysis of the literature. *Review of Educational Research*, *76*(2), 249–274. doi: 10.3102/00346543076002249.

Swanson, H. L., Jerman, O., & Zheng, X. (2008). Growth in working memory and mathematical problem solving in children at risk and not at risk for serious math difficulties. *Journal of Educational Psychology, 100*(2), 343–379. doi: 10.1037/0022-0663.100.2.343

Wechsler, D. (1999). *Wechsler Abbreviated Scale of Intelligence.* San Antonio, TX: Psychological Corporation.

Wechsler, D. (2003). *Wechsler intelligence scale for children, Fourth Edition.* San Antonio, TX: Psychological Corporation.

Wechsler, D. (2009). *Wechsler Individual Achievement Test (WIATT-III)—Third Edition.* San Antonio, TX: Psychological Corporation.

Woodcock, R. W., McGrew, K. S., & Mather, N. (2001). *Woodcock-Johnson III Tests of Achievement.* Itasca, IL: Riverside Publishing.

Woodward, J., & Rieth, H. (1997). A historical review of technology research in special education. *Review of Educational Research, 67*(4), 503–536.

Wu, H. (2005, September). *Key mathematical ideas in grades 5–8.* Retrieved September 10, 2012, from http://math.berkeley.edu/~wu/NCTM2005a.pdf.

Wu, H. (2006, October). *Professional development: The hard work of learning mathematics.* Presentation at the fall southeastern section meeting of the American Mathematical Society, Johnson City, TN.

🐊 TEST YOURSELF 🐊

1. **Which of these is *not* a content domain identified by the National Council of Teachers of Mathematics (NCTM, 2000, 2006) as the most critical for mathematics instruction?**

   a. Number and operations

   b. Algebra

   c. Geometry

   d. Communication

2. **___ is a critical basic ability for students with MD to master; yet, fluency is not often achieved because of lack of sufficient practice, immature counting strategies, and difficulty understanding properties that can facilitate fluency.**

   a. Number fact retrieval

   b. Rational numbers

   c. Mathematical problem solving

   d. Number sense

3. **Which of the following statements is supported by recent research on rational numbers?**

   a. Most young students do not have a practical knowledge of fractions (e.g., dividing something in half).

   b. Students with MLD manifest significantly more difficulties in identifying fraction and decimal equivalence ($.70 = \frac{7}{10}$) as compared to students with MD and students with TA.

c. Poor procedural knowledge of rational numbers is a possible explanation for low performance in equivalence of rational numbers and comparing and ordering fractions and decimals.

d. All of the above.

4. **Which of the following is *not* a type of knowledge involved in mathematical problem solving?**
   a. Linguistic
   b. Semantic
   c. Pragmatic
   d. Schematic

5. **Which of the following domains has been examined in terms of its relationship with mathematics difficulties?**
   a. Intelligence
   b. Working memory
   c. Processing speed
   d. All of the above

6. ***True or False?*: Compared to the typically achieving group, low-achieving children show significant deficits on working memory tasks.**

7. **__ enhance(s) learning by helping students take control of their actions and move toward independence as they learn.**
   a. Self-regulation strategies
   b. Progress monitoring
   c. Fluency practice
   d. Scaffolds

8. **According to a recent meta-analysis, which of these is *not* supported as effective mathematics practices in teaching students with learning disabilities?**
   a. Explicit instruction
   b. Multiple instructional examples
   c. Discovery learning
   d. Student verbalizations

9. **__ answers the question, "Did the student meet the objective of the day's lesson?"**
   a. Benchmark Check
   b. Daily Check
   c. Unit Check
   d. Aim Check

10. ***True or False?*: The Individuals with Disabilities Education Improvement Act (2004) indicated that MLD consists of difficulties in algebra *and* mathematical problem solving.**

Answers: 1. d; 2. a; 3. b; 4. c; 5. d; 6. False; 7. a; 8. c; 9. b; 10. False

Seven

SELECTING AND TAILORING INTERVENTIONS FOR STUDENTS WITH WRITTEN EXPRESSION DIFFICULTIES

Tanya Santangelo
Steve Graham

THE NEWS

When it comes to tailoring instruction for students who experience difficulty with written expression, we have good and bad news to share with you. Let's get the bad news out of the way first: Simply put, there is a pressing need to improve writing instruction in the United States. Evidence for this need can be found in several recent national surveys suggesting not only is little time devoted to teaching writing, but when writing is taught, the use of research-based instructional practices is uncommon (Applebee & Langer, 2011; Cutler & Graham, 2008; Gilbert & Graham, 2010; Graham, Harris, MacArthur, & Fink-Chorzempa, 2003; Kiuhara, Graham, & Hawken, 2009). Moreover, although some teachers differentiate their writing instruction to meet the needs of academically diverse students, many others do not. Given this picture, the fact that the majority of students are not skillful writers should not be particularly surprising. For example, on the most recent National Assessment of Educational Progress (NAEP), only 33% of 8th graders and 24% of 12th graders scored high enough to be classified as proficient writers—meaning they met or exceeded grade-level writing expectations (Salahu-Din, Persky, & Miller, 2008). The NAEP data for students with disabilities is even more sobering, with proficiency rates of only 6% and 5%, respectively. Given that writing is an essential skill for educational and occupational success, it is hard to characterize the current state of writing instruction and outcomes as anything other than bad news. Fortunately, however, that's not the end of the story; we also have good news to share.

The convergence of several factors has us very optimistic about the future of writing instruction. First, although much remains to be learned about evidence-based practices (readers interested in this topic are encouraged to see Cook & Cook, in press and Cook, Smith, & Tankersley, 2012), knowledge of what techniques are (and are *not*) effective for promoting students' writing development has expanded greatly in recent years. Second, whereas writing has historically been viewed as a "second-tier" area of academic focus behind reading and mathematics, this, too, is changing. This is perhaps best illustrated by the Common Core State Standards (National Governors Association Center for Best Practices [NGA Center] & Council of Chief State School Officers [CCSSO], 2010) as they clearly communicate the necessity for writing to be a central element of education reform. In the CCSS, students are expected to learn how to write for a variety of authentic purposes and to use writing for the purpose of acquiring, organizing, and analyzing information across disciplines, such as history/social studies, science, and technical subjects. Indeed, it is not an overstatement to say the CCSS aims to revolutionize how writing is taught and used in schools.

Taken together, our growing understanding of what constitutes effective writing instruction and the new priority placed on writing in schools represent a truly unique opportunity to ensure not only that all students consistently receive a sufficient quantity of high-quality instruction across curricular areas and grade-levels, but also that students who struggle with writing are provided with instruction and interventions that are tailored to meet their needs and proven to be effective. In the remainder of this chapter, we explore a few of the elements that will help realize this goal.

WHAT DOES IT TAKE TO BECOME A GOOD WRITER?

In this section, we provide an overview of four factors that research shows are important elements of skillful writing. Students who demonstrate proficiency in these areas tend to be good writers. Conversely, when a student struggles with writing, it is often because of difficulty in one or more of these areas. Research suggests skillful writing is related to four factors: (1) writing approach, (2) relevant knowledge, (3) foundational skills, and (4) motivation.

Strategic Approach to Writing

Writing is a complex, challenging, and time-consuming process—even for those considered to be experts at the craft. For example, Ernest Hemingway

DON'T FORGET

....

Research suggests skillful writing is related to four factors: (1) writing approach, (2) relevant knowledge, (3) foundational skills, and (4) motivation.

indicated he wrote the last page of *Farewell to Arms* 39 times, whereas Dorothy Parker quipped: "I can't write five words but I change seven" (Gordon, 2000). The idea that writers go through multiple rounds of planning, drafting, and revising is so common today that some of the terminology surrounding these processes is integrated into our routine discourse. For example, when a father asked his 8-year-old daughter, "You call that a made bed?," she retorted, "No, Dad, it's only a rough draft!" (Loranger, 2000). Although employing a recursive and strategic approach to writing is commonplace among good writers, it is elusive for many students who struggle with writing—particularly in regard to planning, revising, and self-regulation.

Planning

Planning is a fundamental and essential part of the writing process (Torrance & Galbraith, 2006). Good writers typically begin planning by critically considering or "dissecting" the particular writing task at hand and then formulating goals and a plan of action that reflect crucial elements such as the rhetorical purpose, perceived audience needs, genre demands, and appropriate linguistic style. As part of planning, skilled writers draw upon a variety of strategies that help them generate and organize ideas, which can subsequently be translated into text. Importantly, planning continues throughout the composition process, as evidenced by the fact that good writers frequently pause to reflect upon and change their developing text.

There are at least two significant differences between the planning behaviors displayed by skilled writers and by students who struggle with writing. First, unlike skilled writers, who typically engage in thoughtful and conceptual-level planning before they begin to draft their text, students who struggle with writing typically devote less than one minute to advanced planning—even when they are explicitly prompted to do so (De La Paz, 1999; Lienemann, Graham, Leader-Janssen, & Reid, 2006; Troia, Graham, & Harris, 1999). Second, whereas skilled writers continue to plan while they draft and revise their text, struggling writers often rely on an approach called *knowledge telling* (Bereiter & Scardamalia, 1987). That is, they write down all the information they can think of that seems somewhat related to the topic, and each idea, phrase, or sentence spawns the one that follows. They rarely (if ever) critically evaluate their initial ideas, reorganize their text, or reflect on whether their writing is harmonious with important considerations such as the purpose of the task, the needs of their intended audience, or the demands of the genre. As a fourth-grade student who struggles mightily with writing recently explained to us, "I just want to get stuff down and fill my paper so I get this stupid writing thing done!"

Although multiple factors likely contribute to struggling writers' minimization of planning (for instance, a lack of knowledge and difficulties with foundational skills—two topics discussed later in this section—can hinder planning), one primary reason is they do not approach planning strategically, like skilled writers do (Graham, 2006). Evidence of this comes from multiple studies showing that when struggling writers are explicitly taught about the importance of planning and provided with a strategy to guide their planning behaviors, meaningful improvements are seen in the amount of time they devote to planning, as well as in the length and quality of their compositions (for a summary of this research, interested readers are encouraged to see Graham, Harris, & McKeown, in press). A sample planning strategy represented by the mnemonic *POW + TREE* can be found in Rapid Reference 7.1.

≡ Rapid Reference 7.1 Sample Strategy for Planning and Drafting a Persuasive Essay

POW + TREE

POW (Strategy for Planning)
Pick my ideas
Organize my notes
Write and say more

TREE (Strategy for Drafting)

(for younger students)		(for older students)	
Topic Sentence	Tell what you believe!	Topic Sentence	Tell what you believe!
Reasons (3 or more)	Why do I believe this? Will my readers believe this?	Reasons (3 or more)	Why do I believe this? Will my readers believe this?
Ending	Wrap it up right!	Explain Reasons	Say more about each reason.
Examine	Do I have all my parts?	Ending	Wrap it up right!

Source: Harris, Graham, Mason, & Friedlander (2008).

Revising

Revising is another important and multidimensional component of the writing process (Hayes, 2004). Among skilled writers, revision is an ongoing and strategic activity that requires the coordination and management of several cognitive skills and draws upon the resources of working and long-term memory. Guided by their overarching goals for a particular writing task (e.g., reflecting rhetorical purpose, intended audience, and genre expectations), skillful writers iteratively improve the overall quality of their compositions by attending to the conceptual and linguistic aspects of their developing text. Underlying the success of this process is their ability to identify what needs to be improved and make beneficial changes.

There is a notable contrast between the revising behaviors of good and struggling writers. For example, whereas skilled writers spend significant time revising the conceptual and rhetorical aspects of their compositions, many struggling writers focus their efforts almost exclusively on changing surface-level features such as punctuation, capitalization, and spelling (MacArthur & Graham, 1987; MacArthur, Graham, & Schwartz, 1991). Moreover, revisions they do make typically do not improve the overall quality of their writing. Often, the only improvement is handwriting legibility and, although a necessary and important accomplishment for some students, it is by no means sufficient.

As with planning, one reason struggling writers have difficulty with revising is because they do not employ the strategic approach that skilled writers use to improve iteratively the quality of their text. Support for this claim is found in research demonstrating that when students who struggle with writing are explicitly taught about the elements of revising and provided with a strategy to facilitate their revising routine, the amount of time spent revising and the quality of their revisions improve (interested readers are encouraged to see Graham, Harris, & McKeown, in press, for a summary of this research). Rapid Reference 7.2 contains an example of a revising strategy represented by the mnemonic *REVISE*.

Self-Regulation

In addition to being strategic when they plan, draft, and revise, good writers are also self-regulated—meaning, they consciously direct, monitor, and evaluate their thoughts and behaviors (readers interested in detailed discussions of self-regulation as it relates to writing are encouraged to see Graham & Harris, 1997, and Harris, Santangelo, & Graham, 2010). Among the multitude of self-regulation techniques good writers use to help successfully manage and complete various composing tasks, three that are particularly salient include: goal-setting, self-monitoring (which involves self-assessment and self-recording), and self-instructions (see Rapid

≡ *Rapid Reference 7.2 Sample Strategy for Revising Text*

REVISE

With this strategy, students are given two sets of cue cards (six Evaluate cards and four Verbalize cards) that guide and prompt their use of the strategy. Prior to using the strategy, they establish one or two individualized goals (e.g., add more details and examples so my paper is more convincing to the reader).

Read Your Essay	Read your essay aloud softly. Highlight places where you think changes should be made and ask yourself if you need more ideas. Use a caret [^] to indicate where you will add something.
Evaluate the Problems	Use the *six Evaluate cards* to evaluate the problems. <ul><li>This doesn't sound quite right.</li><li>Part of the essay isn't in the right order.</li><li>People may not understand what I mean.</li><li>I'm getting away from my main point.</li><li>This is a weak or incomplete idea.</li><li>The problem is: _____ .</li></ul>
Verbalize What You Will Do	Use the four *Verbalize cards* to decide how you will fix each problem. <ul><li>ADD: Include more information, examples, details, etc.</li><li>DELETE: Take something (a word, phrase, sentence) out.</li><li>REWRITE: Say it (a word, phrase, sentence) in a different way.</li><li>MOVE: Rearrange information (a word, phrase, sentence) in a different way.</li></ul>
Implement the Changes	Implement the changes in your draft.
Self-Check Your Goals	Self-check the goals you set for yourself. Make other revisions based on these goals.
End by Rereading and Making More Changes	Read your revised essay aloud softly. Make additional changes that will make it even better.

Source: Harris, Graham, Mason, & Friedlander (2008).

≡ *Rapid Reference 7.3 Overview of Self-Instructions*

Skilled writers often have running conversations with themselves to monitor and direct the composing process. For example, they consider where they are in the writing process, what needs to be done next, options for accomplishing a particular task, whether ideas are relevant, how the audience might interpret the text, and so on. Although excerpts from this dialogue may occasionally be spoken aloud, it is not typically intended for others to hear. The table here provides student-generated examples of different types of self-instructions that can be used to guide the writing process.

Define the Task	• What kind of writing is this and what does that mean?
	• If I'm the reader, what would make me think this is the *best paper ever?*
	• My goals are . . .
Hatch a Plan	• What are all the things I need to do? Number them: 1, 2, 3 . . .
	• What will likely trip me up? What can I do to head it off?
Check How I'm Doing	• Plan check: Am I doing what's on my list?
	• Will this introduction grab my reader, or is it lame?
	• Am I doing what it takes to make this awesome?
Overcome Challenges	• Oops—my mind was wandering! I need to stay focused.
	• Getting ideas down is tough, but I can do it. Brrreeeaathhhe, and try again.
	• I'm stuck and need to phone a friend for help. I think I'll call—and ask . . .
Celebrate!	• Wow—these are rockin' words!
	• Shout out to *me*—I knew I could write something tight!
	• Super-awesome job!

Reference 7.3). Seasoned writers have exemplified each self-monitoring task. For instance, when Robert Benchley was a college student, he took an exam asking him to discuss issues involving international fisheries from the point of view of the United States and England (Hendrickson, 1994). Instead, he reset the goal to address the question from the point of view of fish! Self-monitoring ruled Anthony Trollope's writing life, as he counted the number of words produced every 15 minutes to ensure he wrote regularly and productively (Trollope, 1946). Finally, skilled writers constantly direct the process of writing by talking to themselves. While waiting on a student to finish an exam, J. R. R. Tolkien randomly jotted down a sentence about a hobbit living in a hole in the ground (Bernard, 1996). He then told himself

he needed to find out what hobbits were like, leading to one of the most beloved books of all time (i.e., *The Hobbit*).

Many students who struggle with writing do not utilize the self-regulation techniques that good writers draw

> **DON'T FORGET**
> ....
> Many students who struggle with writing need to learn how to plan and revise their text, as well as how to use self-regulation techniques to manage the writing process.

upon to facilitate the writing process (Graham, 2006; Hooper, Swartz, Wakely, de Kruif, & Montgomery, 2002). For instance, when skilled writers become frustrated while drafting—certainly not an uncommon scenario—they might take a deep breath and a short walk, and think something such as, "Okay, I need to put this down and clear my head so I can come back with fresh ideas." Conversely, when students who struggle with writing encounter frustration, they would be much more likely to give up and conclude, "I just can't do this!" Importantly, however, when struggling writers are explicitly taught how to use self-regulation techniques to guide the writing process, their approach to writing and the text they produce improve (see, for example, Graham & Harris, 2000).

Knowledge

Skillful writing requires the integration of several types of knowledge, including general writing knowledge, genre-specific knowledge, and topic-related knowledge. In terms of the first category, good writers have a solid understanding of the general characteristics and processes associated with high-quality text, such as conveying ideas in an organized and engaging manner and writing in a style that is harmonious with the intended audience (Graham, 2006). Many struggling writers, in contrast, lack essential knowledge of what constitutes good writing (Saddler & Graham, 2007). This pattern is clearly documented in Lin, Monroe, and Troia's (2007) study that involved interviews with typically developing and struggling writers in second through eighth grade. Older, typically developing writers had a solid understanding of abstract and concrete elements of writing and a repertoire of strategies to help them accomplish a variety of different writing tasks. For instance, one student explained:

> Good writing is when you write, you stay on topic, don't go off. . . . You can also graph it out, and write your draft and write the final draft and you look at it and have other people read it to make sure it's good. . . . Good writing also needs right punctuation. . . . It's like, when you read something, you want to get pulled into it. Yeah, you want the person that's reading to get really hooked. You can also have a really good paragraph, maybe some excitement.

You definitely want the person who reads it to know who you are, how you feel. (p. 217)

In contrast, younger typically developing writers and struggling writers of all ages possessed minimal and superficial writing knowledge that focused almost exclusively on physical aspects of writing products, such as handwriting and appearance. To illustrate, when asked to describe good writing, these students offered responses such as: "Looks really neat"; "Skip lines"; and "They sit on the chair. Sometimes they get some water and a pencil" (pp. 212, 218). In addition to documenting the significant differences between skilled and struggling writers' knowledge, Lin et al.'s findings also revealed that the knowledge gap widens as students progress through school.

Along with having a solid base of general writing knowledge, good writers have a solid understanding of the specific structures and attributes associated with various genres (Graham, 2006; Olinghouse, Graham, & Gillespie, 2012). Struggling writers, on the other hand, often have limited genre knowledge, even with familiar formats such as narrative writing. The following explanations of what should be included in a story from a typically developing and from a struggling writer, respectively, illustrate this pattern (Lin et al., 2007, p. 221):

- It has to have a good ending. You need to know what your readers want because you want your audience to be happy, know who the characters are, and you don't want them to have question marks on their face and wonder what the story is about. You want to be with the story at all times. You also need to have characters because people are just part of the world and if there's no characters, the story won't be so good . . . . Got to have a good plot and setting to tell readers where the story takes place. Usually there is a conflict like a problem because every story needs a problem . . . . Finally there is a resolution. That's like the solution to the problem. If you have a problem in the story, you need a solution.
- It's like a fight, you know, aliens or something like that. Add more details.

Unfortunately, although perhaps not surprisingly, a lack of genre knowledge negatively impacts students' writing products. For instance, MacArthur and Graham (1987) found that stories written by fifth- and sixth-grade struggling writers typically included a main character, some information about the setting, and some type of action on the part of the characters. They rarely established a starter event, included goals for the characters, described characters' reactions, or offered a summative conclusion. Likewise, De La Paz (1999) reported that most of the persuasive essays written by struggling writers in seventh and eighth grade contained a basic premise, but fewer than half included a conclusion, and nearly 15% did not offer even one reason to support their opinion. The good news is that research shows that when struggling writers are provided with explicit instruction targeting genre structures and characteristics, their compositions become longer, more complete, and qualitatively better (Boscolo, Gelati, & Galvan, 2012; Fitzgerald & Teasley, 1986).

Finally, it is important to consider topic knowledge—that is, how much a writer knows about the specific topic(s) featured in a particular composition (Graham, 2006; Olinghouse et al., 2012). Whereas skilled writers have a solid base of relevant topical knowledge, this is not true for many students who struggle with writing. In some cases, this is because they just do not have adequate background knowledge and/or experiences to include in their text. In other instances, however, struggling writers actually have relevant information, but experience difficulty retrieving it from memory when they compose. Support for this premise comes from research showing that when struggling writers are given visual and/or verbal prompts to help them recall information, the length and quality of their writing increases. For example, in a study by Graham (1990), the persuasive essays initially written by fourth- and sixth-grade students consisted of a simple *yes*-or-*no* opinion statement, with little (if any) support or elaboration. But, when students were given a series of three verbal prompts designed to help them recall information and expand their drafts, they generated up to four times more content—the majority of which was substantive because it represented additional reasons or elaboration to support their opinion.

Foundational Skills

To produce text, a writer needs to translate his or her ideas into linguistic messages (e.g., words, phrases, and sentences) and then transcribe those units into connected written text (McCutchen, 2006). Underlying the text production process are several foundational skills, such as sentence and paragraph construction, grammar, spelling, punctuation, capitalization, and handwriting/keyboarding. Whereas good writers evidence proficiency and automaticity with these skills, this is not the case for many students with written language difficulties (Graham, 2006). Their writing is often characterized by a lack of linguistic and syntactic complexity and an abundance of spelling, grammar, capitalization, and punctuation errors. Handwriting is also extremely challenging for many struggling writers, as it often takes them twice as long to produce letters that are often less legible (MacArthur & Graham, 1987; Weintraub & Graham, 1998).

CAUTION

Don't overlook difficulties with foundational skills, such as spelling and handwriting, because they can have negative *reader* and *writer* affects. Try the activity on CD file 1 to experience this for yourself.

Difficulties with foundational skills have several negative implications, which can be conceptualized broadly as *reader* and *writer* affects. When a piece of writing contains numerous errors, such as those related to spelling, grammar, punctuation, and capitalization, and/or the handwriting is difficult to decipher, it hinders readability. For the author of the text, this impedes the ability to review and revise the text. It also negatively impacts others' perceptions of the writing. Recent research by Graham, Harris, and Hebert (2011b), for example, revealed that if a legibly written composition is scored at the 50th percentile for writing quality, the score for the exact same composition written with poor—but readable—handwriting would be between the 10th and 22nd percentile. If a paper has a modest number of spelling or grammar errors, the respective percentile point decreases associated are 8–21 and 14–28. Again, the precipitous drops for quality scores result solely from changes in the readability of the text—the content is identical.

Along with negative reader effects, difficulties with foundational skills have a detrimental impact on the writing process (Graham, 2006). Put simply, when a writer needs to devote conscious attention and cognitive resources to handwriting, spelling, and other similar skills, it greatly interferes with the ability to carry out other essential processes, such as planning and revising. Evidence for this statement can be found in three strands of research. First, it has been shown that handwriting fluency and spelling are powerful predictors of writing achievement (Graham, Berninger, Abbot, Abbot, & Whitaker, 1997; Jones & Christensen, 1999). Second, when the demands associated with foundational skills are removed for struggling writers (for example, through the use of dictation or speech recognition technology), significant increases are seen in the length and quality of their writing (e.g., MacArthur & Graham, 1987; Quinlan, 2004). Finally, when struggling writers are provided with explicit instruction targeting handwriting, spelling, or sentence construction skills, this, too, enhances their writing in meaningful ways (Graham, Harris, & Fink, 2000; Graham, Harris, & Fink-Chorzempa, 2002; Graham, McKeown, Kiuhara, & Harris, in press; Rogers & Graham, 2008; Santangelo & Graham, 2011, 2012). To help the reader better understand and appreciate the impact of foundational skills, we encourage the reader to complete a quick—but extremely powerful—activity featured on CD file 1.

Motivation

Thus far, we have highlighted what many think of as the nuts-and-bolts of writing development: approach to writing, knowledge, and foundational skills. A fourth element, motivation, is also important (Troia, Shankland, & Wolbers, 2012). Although much still remains to be understood about the relationship between motivation and writing, research in this area has revealed some important information about different aspects of motivation, particularly in regard to students who struggle with writing.

Perception of value is a critical motivational variable; when we believe a task or activity is important and worthwhile, we are much more likely to devote time and effort to completing it (Bruning & Horn, 2000). Research suggests most typically developing writers perceive writing as being useful (at least for achieving academic and vocational goals) by the time they reach upper-elementary school and they maintain this belief through college (Pajares & Valiante, 2006). Unfortunately, this finding does not hold true for students who struggle with writing. For example, based on interviews with fourth-graders, Saddler and Graham (2007) reported that skilled writers were more than twice as likely as struggling writers to articulate how writing benefited them in school (e.g., "will help when we go to college," "helps the teacher understand you") and more than four times as likely to describe how writing could promote future occupational success (e.g., "Make more money," "You might be a lawyer and have to write a persuasive story," "If you want to be a doctor, you could take special notes") (p. 241). Collectively, the data suggest that struggling writers believe writing has little personal relevance or value.

Attitude is another important motivational variable. For example, a study by Graham, Berninger, and Fan (2007) that included a large sample of first- and third-grade students empirically documented a direct relationship between writing attitudes and the development of writing competence. Despite this understanding, we know surprisingly little about struggling writers' attitudes toward composing. Anecdotal reports and personal experiences have led to the general assumption that students who experience writing difficulties have negative attitudes toward writing; however, this is not consistently supported in the literature (e.g., Graham, Schwartz, & MacArthur, 1993). It is, therefore, important to understand each student's personal attitude toward writing and intervene as needed.

Motivation is also influenced by self-efficacy—that is, our personal beliefs and judgments about our ability to perform at a certain level (Pajares & Valiante, 2006). Self-efficacy is derived from multiple sources, such as interpretations of previous performance, vicarious observations of others performing the task, and reactions from others; it affects, for example, choices of activities, effort, perseverance, resiliency, and performance. It is reasonable to expect that struggling writers have a lower sense of self-efficacy than good writers, but this is not consistently borne out through the available research. Indeed, elementary- and middle school–aged skilled and struggling writers have been found to be equally confident in their ability to generate and organize ideas for compositions, transcribe ideas into sentences, sustain their writing effort, and correct mistakes on their paper (Graham et al., 1993; Graham, Harris, & Mason, 2005). This finding begs the question: Why do struggling writers seem to have an inflated sense of self-efficacy? Although the answer is not yet fully understood, one possible explanation is that struggling writers have difficulty accurately assessing their skills and/or comparing them to a benchmark, such as grade-level standards or peers' performance. Struggling writers' unexpectedly high perceptions of competence may also stem from a desire to disguise embarrassment about their writing difficulties. Ultimately, although a robust sense of self-efficacy may promote persistence, it is also concerning because students who overestimate their capabilities may not devote the necessary time and effort to improve their writing.

WRITING INSTRUCTION

In this section of the chapter, we focus on how to tailor writing instruction to optimize the growth of students who struggle with written language. Before delving into this important topic, however, we want to highlight two ideas. First, it is essential that the core writing program provided to all students be comprised of instructional practices that have been validated as effective through sound research (Graham & Perin, 2007). Second, as is true with all academic subjects, writing instruction must be integrally linked with effective assessment practices. Indeed, only when students' progress as writers is monitored carefully, can the content and format of writing instruction be differentiated to meet their individual and collective needs (Graham, Harris, & Hebert, 2011a). Assessment also allows students who need more intensive writing interventions to be identified. As described in the beginning of this chapter, writing development and, on the flipside, writing difficulties, are heavily dependent on approach to writing, knowledge, foundational skills, and motivation; thus, assessment should target each of these areas to understand individual students' strengths and needs. A list of resources related to core writing instruction and writing assessment can be found on CD file 2.

We now turn to tailoring writing instruction by offering three illustrative case studies. By no means are these cases fully representative of the range of needs posed by struggling writers, nor are they exhaustive with regard to the possibilities for effective instruction and intervention. They should, however, offer a starting point for understanding and addressing students' written language difficulties.

Illustrative Case Study 1: Second Grade
Meet Aaliya

Aaliya is a second-grade student in Ms. Hickman's classroom. Based on observations of Aaliya when she writes and a careful review of Aaliya's writing products, Ms. Hickman has identified several strengths with regard to written language. For example, Aaliya's handwriting and spelling skills are developmentally appropriate and her vocabulary is quite advanced. Aaliya also has a notably positive attitude toward writing, as evidenced by her frequent proclamation, "I love being an author!" What concerns Ms. Hickman is Aaliya's knowledge-telling approach to writing. For instance, when asked to describe the process she uses to write a story, Aaliya explained: "I take what's in my mind and I put all the ideas on my paper and then I color it to jazz it up and make it look fancy and then I share it with someone." Unlike some students, Aaliya does not have difficulty generating ideas or text—in fact, her papers are often the longest in the class. However, her writing lacks organization and consists of essentially unrelated ideas. She also typically omits most, if not all, of the basic genre elements.

Meet Sydney

Sydney is also a student in Ms. Hickman's second-grade class. As a writer, Sydney has some commonalities with Aaliya, but he also differs in a few important ways. One of Sydney's strengths is his knowledge of what constitutes an exemplary story, which likely developed through his voracious reading of comic books and graphic novels. Sydney is also very creative and imaginative. Indeed, his classmates often say things such as, "Need a cool or freaky idea? Go see Sydney!" Ms. Hickman has two primary concerns about Sydney's writing. First, like Aaliya, Sydney's approach to writing is not very strategic. He typically does little (if any) planning and rarely makes any changes to his text. As a result, his compositions are a short series of unconnected, and often irrelevant, ideas. Moreover, even though Sydney can talk at length about features and characteristics that make the stories he reads engaging, this wealth of genre knowledge is not reflected in his own writing. Ms. Hickman suspects this is related to her second concern about Sydney: difficulties with foundational skills. Specifically, Sydney's spelling and handwriting skills are at least one year below grade level, which hinders his ability to plan, draft, and revise text.

Ms. Hickman's Plan

Ms. Hickman's first priority for Aaliya and Sydney is to help them develop a more strategic approach to planning and drafting text. Therefore,

DON'T FORGET

Each student has a unique profile of writing-related strengths and needs that should be used to plan instruction.

she decides to teach them a strategy using the Self-Regulated Strategy Development (SRSD) model (Harris, et al., 2008). Because narrative writing is a primary area of focus in the second-grade writing curriculum, Ms. Hickman selects a story-writing strategy represented by the mnemonic *POW + WWW* (see Rapid Reference 7.4). Since Ms. Hickman believes all of her students will benefit from becoming more strategic writers, she decides to use SRSD to teach the strategy to her entire class. Although a comprehensive description of SRSD is beyond the scope of this chapter, interested readers will find additional information about SRSD, including resources containing narrative examples of how to tailor SRSD instruction to meet students' individual needs, on CD file 3.

In addition to helping Sydney and Aaliya develop a more strategic approach to writing, Ms. Hickman takes several steps to address Sydney's difficulties with spelling and handwriting (Aaliya does not need these interventions because she does not struggle in these areas). At Ms. Hickman's school, all second-graders participate in 20 minutes of daily spelling instruction using a commercially published curriculum. Since Sydney is not making adequate growth with the core program alone, Ms. Hickman provides him with a structured supplemental spelling intervention. The program she selects has eight units, each of which teaches a few powerful spelling rules through a predictable set of activities, such as

---

≡ Rapid Reference 7.4 POW + WWW What = 2 How = 2

Strategy for Planning and Drafting Stories

POW (Strategy for Planning)
  Pick my ideas
  Organize my notes
  Write and say more

WWW What = 2 How = 2 (Strategy for Drafting)
  Who is the main character?
  When does the story take place?
  Where does the story take place?
  What does the main character do or want to do? What do other characters do?
  What happens then? What happens with other characters?
  How does the story end?
  How does the main character feel? How do other characters feel?

Source: Harris, Graham, Mason, & Friedlander (2008).

phonics warm-ups, word sorting, word hunting, and practice games (for a detailed description of this spelling program, see Graham et al., 2002). Since three other students in Ms. Hickman's class are also experiencing difficulty with spelling, she forms a small group for the intervention. She integrates the 20-minute lessons into the class's center time, three days per week. During the other two days of centers, Ms. Hickman gives Sydney and his peers practice activities that guide them to use their spelling words in authentic writing contexts.

To address Sydney's difficulties with handwriting, Ms. Hickman assists in two ways. First, because formal handwriting instruction is not part of the second-grade writing curriculum, Ms. Hickman selects an intervention program to supplement her existing writing instruction. The program targets legibility and fluency and consists of 27 short lessons (for a detailed description of the handwriting program, see Graham et al., 2000). For efficiency, a small group that includes Sydney and four students from other second-grade classes who also struggle with handwriting is created. One of the school's parent volunteers welcomes the opportunity to become familiar with the supplemental program and provide the small-group instruction. Second, Ms. Hickman gives Sydney the opportunity to draft and revise his text using one of the class computers. This is beneficial for Sydney because it reduces the burden associated with forming letters and spelling words and allows him to focus on important processes, such as generating ideas. Since Sydney is proficient with keyboarding and word processing software, the transition to composing on a computer is essentially seamless. If Sydney had not already mastered these prerequisites, Ms. Hickman would have helped him develop basic typing and computer skills. Readers interested in learning more about how technology can be used to bolster writing are encouraged to see Goldberg, Russell, and Cook (2003) and Morphy and Graham (2012).

Illustrative Case Study #2: Fourth Grade
Meet Hafiz

Hafiz is a student in Mr. Campbell's fourth-grade classroom. Hafiz excels in math and sports and is known throughout his school as the "resident sports statistician." Reading, in contrast, has been extremely challenging for Hafiz since kindergarten and he was identified as having a specific reading disability at the end of third

CAUTION

Sometimes it takes creative thinking and flexible use of resources to ensure students' needs are met. For example, Sydney's spelling intervention group is comprised of students from different classrooms and is taught by a parent volunteer.

grade. Hafiz participates in core literacy instruction with Mr. Campbell for 90 minutes a day. Four days a week, he receives intensive reading intervention support from Ms. Shelby, a special education teacher. Although Hafiz had not previously experienced significant difficulty with writing, it is not long into the school year before Mr. Campbell and Ms. Shelby notice he is struggling with the shift from narrative to expository writing and the increased expectations that accompany fourth grade. For example, when asked to write in response to an expository prompt, Hafiz's compositions typically include a few relevant ideas, but lack essential elements, such as a thesis statement, supporting details, and a conclusion. Additionally, his text contains only a few simple types of sentences and very basic vocabulary. This lack of linguistic sophistication puzzles Hafiz's teachers because it stands in stark contrast with the way he expresses himself orally. As Mr. Campbell noted, "If you listen to Hafiz talk and then read something he writes, it's like two completely different students!"

To understand better Hafiz's writing difficulties, Mr. Campbell and Ms. Shelby carefully review his compositions and have him complete three writing probes. They also have several informal conversations with Hafiz to learn more about his writing approach, knowledge, and motivation. Mr. Campbell and Ms. Shelby determine that Hafiz does not employ a strategic approach when writing expository text writing and lacks essential genre knowledge. He also has significant difficulty formulating his ideas into different types of sentence structures and spelling words he would like to include in his text (which is resulting in his intentionally limiting his vocabulary to that which he can spell correctly). Finally, after hearing Hafiz make comments such as, "So much for my career with *Sports Illustrated*," Mr. Campbell and Ms. Shelby are concerned his writing motivation in general, and self-efficacy, in particular, are decreasing.

Mr. Campbell and Ms. Shelby's Plan

Mr. Campbell and Ms. Shelby collaboratively develop a plan to address Hafiz's difficulties with writing. To bolster Hafiz's approach to, and knowledge of, expository writing, Ms. Shelby uses SRSD to teach him a planning and drafting strategy represented by the mnemonic *PLAN + WRITE* (see Rapid Reference 7.5). Throughout instruction, Ms. Shelby draws on Hafiz's interest in sports and goal of being a sportswriter. For instance, she helps him brainstorm interesting and authentic sports-related prompts to use when learning and practicing the strategy. Collaboratively, Ms. Shelby and Hafiz also create a self-monitoring graph that allows him to track his progress by coloring in baseballs. Once Hafiz is able to compose using PLAN + WRITE without support from Ms. Shelby, he uses the strategy to guide the writing he does in Mr. Campbell's class.

≡ Rapid Reference 7.5 PLAN + WRITE

Strategy for Planning and Drafting Expository Essays

How do you plan a good essay? Follow the steps in PLAN:

Pay Attention to the Prompt	Read the prompt. Decide what you are being asked to write about and how you will develop your essay.
List Main Ideas	Brainstorm possible responses to the prompt. Decide on one topic and then brainstorm at least ___ main ideas for the development of your essay. (*The targeted number of ideas is determined by each student, in collaboration with the teacher.*)
Add Supporting Ideas	Think of details, examples, or elaborations that support your main ideas.
Number Your Ideas	Number major points in the order you will use them.

How do you plan more as you go? Follow the steps in WRITE:

Work from your plan to develop a thesis statement.

Remember your goals.

Include transition words for each paragraph.

Try to use different kinds of sentences.

Exciting, interesting million-dollar words.

Source: Harris, Graham, Mason, & Friedlander (2008).

To address Hafiz's difficulties with spelling, Ms. Shelby supplements Mr. Campbell's core instruction with a word study intervention that is individualized for Hafiz based on data from a comprehensive, computerized assessment system called Spelling Performance Evaluation for Language and Literacy (for detailed descriptions of the spelling assessment and intervention program, see Apel, Masterson, & Niessen, 2004; Masterson & Apel, 2000, 2010; Masterson, Apel, & Wasowicz, 2006; and www.learningbydesign.com). Ms. Shelby also helps Hafiz learn to spell high-frequency writing words using the Basic Spelling Vocabulary List. This list represents 80% of the words students use in their writing and can be

DON'T FORGET

Collaboration is a powerful tool for helping students become better writers.

downloaded for free at http://www.readingrockets.org/article/22366. To determine which words Hafiz does not yet know how to spell, Ms. Shelby gives him a pretest. Every Monday, Hafiz selects six words he wants to learn that week and studies them using a five-step strategy:

1. Study the letters in the word.
2. Close your eyes. See the word in your mind and say each letter quietly.
3. Restudy the letters.
4. Write the word three times from memory. See how you did and correct any errors.
5. If you need more practice, start back with step 1.

Ms. Shelby also helps Hafiz learn sports-related words he often wants to include in his writing, but avoids because he does not know how to spell them (e.g., umpire, league). Together, Ms. Shelby and Hafiz generate a list of 25 words that he refers to as "My Top Clunkers." Each week, Hafiz selects two *clunker words* he wants to learn and studies them using the five-step strategy. He also keeps a copy of the word list in his binder to use as a reference when writing.

Mr. Campbell also takes steps to help Hafiz develop the foundational skills he needs to write successfully. For example, after Mr. Campbell notices that several of his students—including Hafiz—do not use technology to help them spell when they write, he creates a series of mini-lessons to teach them how to use the spelling features in their word processing software, as well as student-friendly Internet dictionaries (e.g., www.wordcentral.com and www.wordsmyth.net). To help Hafiz write more complex and varied sentences, Mr. Campbell opts to use sentence-combining instruction (for detailed discussions of the benefits associated with sentence combining, as opposed to traditional grammar instruction, see Graham, McKeown et al., in press, and Graham & Perin, 2007). Because all of his students can benefit from increasing the syntactic complexity of their writing, albeit in different ways, Mr. Campbell adds a 20-minute sentence-combining lesson to his core literacy instruction, three days a week (for detailed descriptions of sentence-combining instruction, including how it can be tailored to meet students' needs, see Saddler, 2007; Saddler, Behforooz, & Asaro, 2008; and Saddler & Graham, 2005).

CAUTION

Don't assume that just because a particular kind of instruction is common practice it is also the most effective approach. For example, traditional grammar instruction is used in many classrooms, but findings from a recent meta-analysis suggest it may actually have a *negative* impact on the overall quality of students' writing (Graham & Perin, 2007).

Illustrative Case Study #3: Seventh Grade
Meet Mya

Mya is an outgoing and kindhearted seventh-grader in Mrs. Bornstein's social studies class. Mya is very interested in social studies because, as she explains, "Being the class president, I need to know all about government. I also *love* History Hunters!" What concerns and perplexes Mrs. Bornstein is Mya's writing. Every time she gives an activity or assignment that requires writing more than a few sentences, Mya has a demonstrably negative reaction. Sometimes she sighs loudly and makes a comment such as, "Why do we have to do *another* paper? I mean, really, Mrs. B.—this is getting ridiculous!" On other occasions, she gets an anxious look on her face and puts her head down on her desk. Mya's writing products fit her reactions; she typically writes nothing and when she does produce text, it is short and incomplete. To learn more about why Mya struggles with writing, Mrs. Bornstein invites her back to the classroom for lunch and an informal, private conversation. Ultimately, Mrs. Bornstein determines that Mya's difficulties emanate from a lack of knowledge about what constitutes effective expository writing. As Mya explained, "I can write stories just fine, but I never learned how to do the types of papers that need facts, facts, and more facts. Last year I tried hard, but I still got bad grades, so now I'm like, why should I even try?"

Mrs. Bornstein's Plan

Although Mya has difficulty with several types of expository writing, Mrs. Bornstein knows that she will learn more—and thus, feel more successful—if she focuses on one at a time. Based on where the class is in the curriculum, Mrs. Bornstein starts with writing persuasive arguments (CD file 4 contains the relevant Common Core State Standard). Because all of the students in Mya's class can improve their persuasive writing skills (albeit in different ways), she designs two lessons for the whole class.

During the first lesson, students analyze model texts to identify the essential characteristics and features of effective persuasive arguments. Although different kinds of texts can serve as models (e.g., compositions written by teachers specifically for the purpose of modeling and students' own writing samples), to promote engagement, Mrs. Bornstein opts to use authentic products focused on a topic of high interest and personal relevance to her students: whether it is constitutional

DON'T FORGET

Content-area teachers play a unique and important role in helping students overcome difficulties with written language and learn to write like historians, mathematicians, scientists, and so on.

for schools to monitor and/or restrict students' use of social media. She selects three model texts: (1) the board of education's policy and accompanying rationale, (2) a newspaper editorial written by a parent organization, and (3) a series of blog posts written by teenagers.

During the first half of the lesson, Mrs. Bornstein helps the class dissect the three model texts by thinking aloud and posing questions to focus students' attention on key ideas:

- I see the author of this editorial included several questions in the introduction. Why do you think she did that? What other techniques might she have used?
- Think about how facts are used in the paper written by the school board and in the blogs. In what ways are they similar and how are they different? Are they equally effective? Why or why not?

Throughout this activity, Mrs. Bornstein strategically calls on students to ensure that each has an opportunity to offer a meaningful contribution. For instance, she asks Mya, "Did the author of this piece change your opinion in any way? Why or why not?" In the next part of the lesson, Mrs. Bornstein facilitates a class discussion that results in the creation of a list of features and characteristics found in high-quality persuasive essays. Finally, she helps students divide those ideas into two categories they refer to as "Must Haves" and "Bonus Features" (see Rapid Reference 7.6). CD file 5 contains the homework assignment Mya and her classmates complete after the first lesson.

During the second lesson, Mrs. Bornstein introduces students to three strategies—setting specific writing product goals, self-assessment, and self-recording—to help reinforce and extend what they learned the previous day. Mrs. Bornstein begins the lesson by leading a class discussion about goal setting, in general, and, in particular, the benefit of setting goals that are specific and at a level of difficulty that is personally challenging, yet attainable. Because the students in Mya's class differ in regard to their writing proficiency, Mrs. Bornstein next helps each student develop five to seven individualized goals, using the "Must Haves" and "Bonus Features" lists as a beginning framework. CD file 6 contains the goals Mya and one of her classmates (who is a more advanced writer) establish. Next, Mrs. Bornstein introduces students to the concept of self-assessment and models how to translate their personal goals into a self-assessment rubric. She then works with students individually and in small groups to help them create individualized self-assessment rubrics. Finally, Mrs. Bornstein explains that some writers find it beneficial to keep track of their performance (i.e., self-recording) and shows the

≡ Rapid Reference 7.6 "Must Haves" and "Bonus Features" for Persuasive Arguments

Five "Must Haves"

1. An introduction that states your position
2. Multiple reasons that make sense and have details
3. Evidence and examples for each reason
4. Possible arguments against your position
5. A convincing conclusion

Examples of "Bonus Features"

- Different kinds of sentences to keep the reader interested
- Graphics to "show" your position
- Powerful vocabulary
- An argument that is personal to the reader
- A variety of transition words

class several ways this can be done (e.g., using a graph or chart). To promote students' independence, she allows each student to decide whether self-recording is likely to be personally beneficial and, if so, what method to use. Mya decides to graph the number of essay elements she includes in each draft because, as she explains, "It will help me see for myself if I am improving." CD file 7 contains Mya's self-assessment rubric and self-recording system. As the semester proceeds, Mrs. Bornstein creates authentic opportunities for students to practice writing and self-evaluating persuasive arguments.

CONCLUSION

When we conduct workshops with teachers about how to teach writing, we commonly ask the participants how many of them had one really good writing teacher when they were in school. Somewhere between one-half to two-thirds of their hands go up. When we up the ante to two teachers, most of the hands drop, and when we go to three good writing teachers, it is a rare situation in which any hands are still left standing.

These simple questions illustrate part of the challenge in delivering high-quality writing instruction to typically developing and struggling writers. Teachers often do not have multiple models for how to teach writing effectively. We hope that the information presented in this chapter, as well as the material available on the accompanying CD, provide you with relevant and beneficial tools and information for teaching writing. We also hope they serve to whet your appetite to acquire even more knowledge in this area.

REFERENCES

Apel, K., Masterson, J. J., & Niessen, N. L. (2004). Spelling assessment frameworks. In C. A. Stone, E. R. Silliman, B. J. Ehren, & K. Apel (Eds.), *Handbook of language and literacy: Development and disorders* (pp. 644–660). New York, NY: Guilford Press.

Applebee, A., & Langer, J. (2011). A snapshot of writing instruction in middle and high schools. *English Journal, 100*, 14–27.

Bereiter, C., & Scardamalia, M. (1987). *The psychology of written composition*. Hillsdale, NJ: Erlbaum.

Bernard, A. (1996). *Now all we need is a title*. New York, NY: Norton.

Boscolo, P., Gelati, C., & Galvan, N. (2012). Teaching elementary students to play with meanings and genre. *Reading & Writing Quarterly, 28*, 29–50.

Bruning, R., & Horn, C. (2000). Developing motivation to write. *Educational Psychologist, 35*, 25–37.

Cook, B. G., & Cook, S. C. (in press). Unraveling evidence-based practices in special education. *Journal of Special Education*. doi: 10.1177/0022466911420877.

Cook, B. G., Smith, G. J., & Tankersley, M. (2012). Evidence-based practices in education. In K. R. Harris, S. Graham, & T. Urdan (Eds.), *APA educational psychology handbook: Theories, constructs, and critical issues* (Vol. 1). Washington, DC: American Psychological Association.

Cutler, L., & Graham, S. (2008). Primary grade writing instruction: A national survey. *Journal of Educational Psychology, 100*, 907–919.

De La Paz, S. (1999). Self-regulated strategy instruction in regular education settings: Improving outcomes for students with and without learning disabilities. *Learning Disabilities Research & Practice, 14*, 92–106.

Fitzgerald, J., & Teasley, A. B. (1986). Effects of instruction in narrative structure on children's writing. *Journal of Educational Psychology, 78*, 424–432.

Gilbert, J., & Graham, S. (2010). Teaching writing to elementary students in grades 4 to 6: A national survey. *Elementary School Journal, 110*, 494–518.

Goldberg, A., Russell, M., & Cook, A. (2003). The effect of computers on student writing: A meta-analysis of studies from 1992 to 2002. *The Journal of Technology, Learning, and Assessment 2*. Retrieved from http://escholarship.bc.edu/jtla/vol2/1/.

Gordon, W. (2000). *The quotable writer*. New York, NY: McGraw-Hill.

Graham, S. (1990). The role of production factors in learning disabled students' compositions. *Journal of Educational Psychology, 82*, 781–791.

Graham, S. (2006). Writing. In P. Alexander & P. Winne (Eds.), *Handbook of educational psychology* (pp. 457–478). Mahwah, NJ: Erlbaum.

Graham, S., Berninger, V. W., Abbot, R. D., Abbot, S. P., & Whitaker, D. (1997). The role of mechanics in composing of elementary school students: A new methodological approach. *Journal of Educational Psychology, 89*, 170–182.

Graham, S., Berninger, V., & Fan, W. (2007). The structural relationship between writing attitude and writing achievement in young children. *Contemporary Educational Psychology, 32*, 516–536.

Graham, S., & Harris, K. R. (1997). Self-regulation and writing: Where do we go from here? *Contemporary Educational Psychology, 22,* 170–182.

Graham, S., & Harris, K. R. (2000). The role of self-regulation and transcription skills in writing and writing development. *Educational Psychologist, 35,* 3–12.

Graham, S., Harris, K. R., & Fink, B. (2000). Is handwriting causally linked to learning to write? Treatment of handwriting problems in beginning writers. *Journal of Educational Psychology, 93,* 620–633.

Graham, S., Harris, K. R., & Fink-Chorzempa, B. F. (2002). Contribution of spelling instruction to the spelling, writing, and reading of poor spellers. *Journal of Educational Psychology, 94,* 669–686.

Graham, S., Harris, K. R., & Hebert, M. (2011a). *Informing writing: The benefits of formative assessment.* Washington, DC: Alliance for Excellence in Education. Retrieved from http://www.carnegie.org/fileadmin/Media/Publications/InformingWriting.pdf.

Graham, S., Harris, K. R., & Hebert, M. (2011b). It is more than just the message: Presentation effects in scoring writing. *Focus on Exceptional Children, 44*(4), 1–12.

Graham, S., Harris, K. R., MacArthur, C., & Fink-Chorzempa, B. (2003). Primary grade teachers' instructional adaptations for weaker writers: A national survey. *Journal of Educational Psychology, 95,* 279–293.

Graham, S., Harris, K. R., & Mason, L. (2005). Improving the writing performance, knowledge, and self-efficacy of struggling young writers: The effects of self-regulated strategy development. *Contemporary Educational Psychology, 30,* 207–241.

Graham, S., Harris, K. R., & McKeown, D. (in press). The writing of students with LD and a meta-analysis of SRSD writing intervention studies: Redux. In L. Swanson, K. R. Harris, & S. Graham (Eds.), *Handbook of learning disabilities* (2nd ed.). New York, NY: Guilford.

Graham, S., McKeown, D., Kiuhara, S., & Harris, K. R. (in press). A meta-analysis of writing instruction for students in the elementary grades. *Journal of Educational Psychology.*

Graham, S., & Perin, D. (2007). A meta-analysis of writing instruction for adolescent students. *Journal of Educational Psychology, 99,* 445–476.

Graham, S., Schwartz, S., & MacArthur, C. (1993). Knowledge of writing and the composing process, attitude toward writing, and self-efficacy for students with and without learning disabilities. *Journal of Learning Disabilities, 26,* 237–249.

Harris, K. R., Graham, S., Mason, L., & Friedlander, B. (2008). *Powerful writing strategies for all students.* Baltimore, MD: Brookes.

Harris, K. R., Santangelo, T., & Graham, S. (2010). Metacognition and strategies instruction in writing. In H. S. Waters & W. Schneider (Eds.), *Metacognition, strategy use and instruction* (pp. 226–256). New York, NY: Guilford.

Hayes, J. (2004). What triggers revision? In L. Allal, L. Chanquoy, & P. Largy (Eds.), *Studies in writing: Vol. 13. Revision: Cognitive and instructional processes* (pp. 9–20). Norwell, MA: Kluwer.

Hendrickson, R. (1994). *The literary life and other curiosities.* San Diego, CA: Harcourt.

Hooper, S., Swartz, C., Wakely, M., de Kruif, R., & Montgomery, J. (2002). Executive functioning in elementary school children with and without problems in written expression. *Journal of Learning Disabilities, 35,* 57–68.

Jones, D., & Christensen, C. (1999). The relationship between automaticity in handwriting and students' ability to generate written text. *Journal of Educational Psychology, 91,* 44–49.

Kiuhara, S., Graham, S., & Hawken, L. (2009). Teaching writing to high school students: A national survey. *Journal of Educational Psychology, 101,* 136–160.

Lienemann, T. O., Graham, S., Leader-Janssen, B., & Reid, R. (2006). Improving the writing performance of struggling writers in second grade. *The Journal of Special Education*, *40*, 66–78.

Lin, S. C., Monroe, B. W., & Troia, G. A. (2007). Development of writing knowledge in grades 2–8: A comparison of typically developing writers and their struggling peers. *Reading & Writing Quarterly*, *23*, 207–230.

Loranger, D. (2000, December). *Reader's Digest*, *110*, 126.

MacArthur, C., & Graham, S. (1987). Learning disabled students' composing with three methods: Handwriting, dictation, and word processing. *Journal of Special Education*, *21*, 22–42.

MacArthur, C., Graham, S., & Schwartz, S. (1991). Knowledge of revision and revising behavior among students with learning disabilities. *Learning Disability Quarterly*, *14*, 61–74.

Masterson, J. J., & Apel, K. (2000). Spelling assessment: Charting a path to optimal assessment. *Topics in Language Disorders*, *20*(3), 50–63.

Masterson, J. J., & Apel, K. (2010). Linking characteristics discovered in spelling assessment to intervention goals and methods. *Learning Disability Quarterly*, *33*, 185–198.

Masterson, J. J., Apel, K., & Wasowicz, J. (2006). SPELL: Spelling Performance Evaluation for Language and Literacy (2nd ed.) [Computer software]. Evanston, IL: Learning by Design.

McCutchen, D. (2006). Cognitive factors in the development of children's writing. In C. A. MacArthur, S. Graham, & J. Fitzgerald (Eds.), *Handbook of writing research* (pp. 115–130). New York, NY: Guilford.

Morphy, P., & Graham, S. (2012). Word processing programs and weaker writers/readers: A meta-analysis of research findings. *Reading and Writing: An Interdisciplinary Journal*, *25*, 641–678.

National Governors Association Center for Best Practices, Council of Chief State School Officers. (2010). *Common core state standards*. Washington, DC: Author. Retrieved from http://www.corestandards.org

Olinghouse, N., Graham, S., & Gillespie, A. (2012). *The role of content and discourse knowledge in three writing genres*. Manuscript submitted for publication.

Pajares, F., & Valiante, G. (2006). Self-efficacy beliefs and motivation in writing development. In C. A. MacArthur, S. Graham, & J. Fitzgerald (Eds.), *Handbook of writing research* (pp. 158–170). New York, NY: Guilford.

Quinlan, T. (2004). Speech recognition technology and students with writing difficulties: Improving fluency. *Journal of Educational Psychology*, *96*, 337–346.

Rogers, L., & Graham, S. (2008). A meta-analysis of single subject design writing intervention research. *Journal of Educational Psychology*, *100*, 879–906.

Saddler, B., Behforooz, B., & Asaro, K. (2008). The effects of sentence-combining instruction on the writing of fourth-grade students with writing difficulties. *Journal of Special Education*, *42*, 79–90.

Saddler, B., & Graham, S. (2005). The effects of peer-assisted sentence combining instruction on the writing performance of more and less skilled young writers. *Journal of Educational Psychology*, *97*, 43–54.

Saddler, B., & Graham, S. (2007). The relationship between writing knowledge and writing performance among more and less skilled writers. *Reading and Writing Quarterly*, *23*, 231–247.

Salahu-Din, D., Persky, H., & Miller, J. (2008). *The nation's report card: Writing 2007* (NCES 2008-468). Washington, DC: National Center for Education Statistics, Institute of

Education Sciences, U.S. Department of Education. Retrieved from http://nces.ed.gov/nationsreportcard/pubs/main2007/2008468.asp.

Santangelo, T., & Graham, S. (2011, February). *Does explicit spelling instruction make students better spellers, readers, and writers?* Poster presented at the Pacific Coast Research Conference, Coronado, CA.

Santangelo, T., & Graham, S. (2012, February). *Handwriting instruction: A comprehensive meta-analysis.* Poster presented at the Pacific Coast Research Conference, Coronado, CA.

Torrance, M., & Galbraith, D. (2006). The processing demands of writing. In C. A. MacArthur, S. Graham, & J. Fitzgerald (Eds.), *Handbook of writing research* (pp. 67–80). New York, NY: Guilford.

Troia, G. A., Graham, S., & Harris, K. R. (1999). Teaching students with learning disabilities to mindfully plan when writing. *Exceptional Children, 65,* 235–252.

Troia, G. A., Shankland, R. K., & Wolbers, K. A. (2012). Motivation research in writing: Theoretical and empirical considerations. *Reading & Writing Quarterly, 28,* 5–28.

Trollope, A. (1946). *An autobiography.* London, UK: Williams & Norgate.

Weintraub, N., & Graham, S. (1998). Writing legibly and quickly: A study of children's ability to adjust their handwriting to meet common classroom demands. *Learning Disabilities Research and Practice, 13,* 146–152.

🐾 TEST YOURSELF 🐾

1. **Which of the following statements is *false*:**
   a. Survey data suggest many teachers do not commonly use practices supported by research to teach writing.
   b. Students' performance on the NAEP writing test is very concerning.
   c. There is little reason to believe writing instruction and performance will improve any time in the foreseeable future.
   d. The NAEP writing scores of students with disabilities are lower than those of students without disabilities.

2. **Students' writing development and performance are influenced by:**
   a. Approach to writing
   b. Writing-related knowledge
   c. Foundational skills
   d. Motivation
   e. All of the above

3. **Which self-regulation techniques do skilled writers use to help manage the writing process?:**
   a. Goal-setting
   b. Self-monitoring
   c. Self-instructions
   d. All of the above
   e. All of the above and more

(continued)

(*continued*)

4. **Which of these statements is supported by research?:**
   a. Struggling writers' performance improves when teachers let them listen to music while writing.
   b. Struggling writers' performance improves when they are explicitly taught writing strategies.
   c. Struggling writers who do not overcome their difficulties with written language by fourth grade are unlikely ever to do so.
   d. Struggling writers' performance improves when they are allowed to use special paper.

5. *True or False?*: **Research has recently confirmed the commonsense belief that students who struggle with writing almost always have negative attitudes toward writing and a low sense of writing self-efficacy.**

6. *True or False?*: **Teachers interested in effectively tailoring instruction to meet the needs of students who struggle with writing should first ensure that their core writing instruction and assessment practices have been validated through sound research.**

7. **Which of the following instructional arrangements is/are beneficial when addressing the needs of struggling writers?:**
   a. 1:1 instruction
   b. Small group instruction
   c. Whole-class instruction
   d. All of the above, depending on the situation

8. *True or False?*: **Because nearly all students who struggle with writing have difficulties with writing approach, knowledge, foundational skills, and motivation, it is really not necessary to do a comprehensive assessment of each student's strengths and needs.**

9. **Which of the following individuals can help address the needs of struggling writers?:**
   a. General and special education teachers
   b. Specialists (e.g., speech and language pathologists, curriculum coordinators, librarians)
   c. Trained parent volunteers
   d. All of the above, depending on the situation
   e. All of the above, and more, depending on the situation

10. **Tailoring instruction for struggling writers is most effective when the intervention plan is developed by:**
    a. Teachers and other school professionals
    b. Family members
    c. Students
    d. All of the above, collaboratively

Answers: 1. c; 2. e; 3. e; 4. b; 5. False; 6. True; 7. d; 8. False; 9. e; 10. d

Eight

INDIVIDUALIZING INSTRUCTION FOR STUDENTS WITH ORAL AND WRITTEN LANGUAGE DIFFICULTIES[1]

Virginia W. Berninger
Jasmin Niedo

This chapter is divided into five sections. In the first section, we use an evidence-based conceptual framework for functional language systems and levels of language to define language and explain what oral and written language difficulties may occur in individual students. In the second section, we provide a brief overview of the tools for assessing the four language systems and their levels, with focus on new research developments. In the third section, we discuss biological and environmental variables that are relevant to tailoring instruction individually and monitoring response to instruction for students with language difficulties. In the fourth section, we discuss the historical context in which educational professionals and researchers have grappled with meeting the language learning needs of students with developmental and learning disabilities and propose a proactive, best professional practices model for the future. In the fifth section, we offer general guidelines for tailoring instruction individually for oral and written language difficulties and describe case examples that illustrate these for students with pervasive (case 1) or specific (case 2) developmental disabilities or specific learning disabilities, despite otherwise normal development, in multi-word-level oral and written language learning disabilities (case 3), word-level reading and writing disabilities (case 4), and subword-level writing disabilities (case 5).

1. Acknowledgment: Grant P50HD071764 from Eunice Kennedy Shriver National Institute of Child Health and Human Development supported preparation of this chapter.

I. EVIDENCE-BASED, CONCEPTUAL FRAMEWORK FOR FUNCTIONAL LANGUAGE SYSTEMS

What Is Language?

Functional Language Systems

Language is a set of internal codes for storing and processing representations of words, their parts, and their combinations. Language is not a single skill. Rather, four language systems (see Figure 8.1)— Language by Ear (Listening), Language by Mouth (Oral Expression), Language by Eye (Reading), and Language by Hand (Written Expression)—develop as children interact with the social and physical world; and individuals may show differences in terms of the level to which each of these separate language systems is developed (Berninger & Abbott, 2010).

Each language system is connected to a different input system (ears or eyes) or output system (mouth or hand), each of which has direct links to the external world. Language has only indirect contact with the external world through the sensory input and motor output systems. Each of the language systems is separate or distinct from the others, but also can work with one or more of the others through executive functions that develop to integrate the systems. The language systems, alone and collaboratively, also have connections with the internal cognitive systems supporting thinking (see Figure 8.1 and Fayol, Alamargot, and Berninger, 2012, Chapters 1, 3, 4, and 5) and social behavior (Troia, 2011), and the limbic systems that regulate emotions and motivation. The motor components of the functional language systems receive sensory feedback, and the sensory components of the functional language systems receive motoric feedback. Thus, children with language learning difficulties need more than multisensory instruction: They need multisensory-motor-language instructional approaches that engage and coordinate their cognitive, executive, and limbic (emotional and motivational) systems (Berninger & Wolf, 2009a, 2009b).

Levels of Language

Each of the functional language systems is organized by levels of language and these levels need to be able to communicate with each other for a language system to function well (see Figure 8.1). Individual students may have relative strengths or weaknesses in these various levels or units of language, ranging from subword to word to syntax to text, within and across

DON'T FORGET
....
Children with language learning difficulties need multisensory-motor-language instructional approaches, not just multisensory.

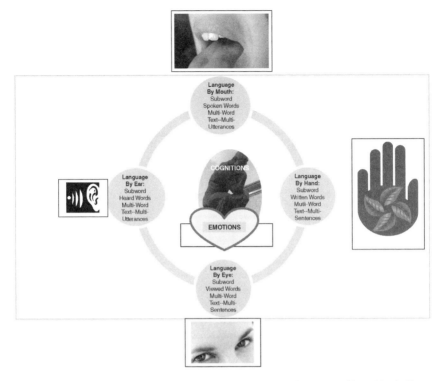

Figure 8.1. Four Language Systems, by Ear (Listening), Mouth (Speaking), Eye (Reading), and Hand (Writing), With Four Levels Each, Interacting With Each Other and With Cognitive Systems

Mouth and hand are larger than ear and eyes because a larger area of the brain is devoted to representing sensory input received via mouth and hand and producing output via mouth and hand than is the case for ears and eyes.

Source: Copyrighted June 24, 2012, by V. W. Berninger, UW Center for Oral and Written Language Learners (OWLS). Permission granted by V.W. Berninger to reproduce this figure in this chapter.

functional language systems that affect language learning (e.g., Abbott, Berninger, & Fayol, 2010). For example, a student may have age-appropriate vocabulary understanding for heard words but not for analyzing sounds in heard words. Alternatively, a student may demonstrate age-appropriate functioning in analyzing sounds at the subword or word level in spoken language but not in analyzing corresponding spelling units at the subword or word level in written language.

A. Input through ears (feedback from vestibular sense—position of body in space—and oral motor system/mouth).

Auditory processing—Sound wave through outer, middle, and inner ear (peripheral nervous system) to thalamus to primary auditory area in temporal lobe (BA 41) (central nervous system)

Sound pattern processing in secondary association areas of temporal lobe for both music and speech—Amplitude, frequency, duration, stress, sequencing, rhythm

Phonetic processing in secondary association areas of temporal lobe (speech-specific)—Perceiving coarticulated speech patterns within and across syllables—segmental consonant sounds and distributed vowel sounds

Phonemic processing in tertiary association areas of temporal, parietal, frontal lobes—Abstracting phonemes, which are the smallest units of sound that make a difference in meaning and correspond to one- or two-letter spelling units in alphabetic principle, but are not speech production units to which they have to be converted (see Language by Mouth)

B. Output through mouth (vocal tract/voice, tongue movements, lip movements). Feedback through ear and vestibular system (place and manner of articulation).

Language production—Frontal regions (inferior frontal gyrus and dorsal lateral prefrontal gyrus and supplementary and premotor areas) for words, syntax, and discourse (conversational turns or academic instructional register)

Speech production:

Oral motor planning—Executive functions for speech in left inferior frontal gyrus/ Broca's Area and premotor areas of frontal lobe

Oral motor control—Premotor and supplementary motor areas of frontal lobe

Oral motor output—Primary motor area (BA 4) in frontal lobe to lower pathways involving basal ganglia and eventually peripheral nervous system related to mouth (vocal tract/voice, tongue movements, lip movements)

Related nonverbal production—Facial expressions, hand gestures, and torso and limb movements

C. Input through the visual sensory sense (eyes) working with motor control systems (binocular coordination and saccadic eye movements), which receive feedback from both the eyes and the vestibular sense in the ears.

Visual processing—From retina to optic nerve to thalamus to primary visual area in BA 17 in occipital lobe

Visual perception in secondary association areas (nonlinguistic)—Pathways involving occipital and parietal lobes

Figure 8.2. Pathways from Sensory and Motor Systems in Language by Ear, Mouth, Eye, and Hand

Visible language analysis in secondary association areas (linguistic)—Occipital and parietal lobes, including visual motion, fusiform, and lingual areas

Word form, syntax, and semantic regions in tertiary association areas in temporal-parietal-frontal pathways—Storage and processing units for written words, spoken words, and morphological structures and their interrelationships, syntax (accumulating words), and text (accumulating syntactic units), and semantic and cognitive processors

D.    **Output by hand (feedback from sensory systems for touch, kinesthesia—movement, vision and vestibular system for position in space).**

Access to the mind's eye, which has links to different levels of language representations and their corresponding cognitive representations, including the morpho-orthographic and phonological regularities of word-specific spellings linked to word meanings, supported by posterior and frontal cortex and cerebellum

Orthographic loop for integrating the mind's eye and output through hand grapho-motor planning—Supplementary motor and premotor frontal areas and superior parietal areas for *coordinating orthographic loop of working memory* linking word-specific spellings and sequential finger movements and text generation

Grapho-motor control—Premotor and supplementary motor frontal areas and superior parietal areas for preparing and coordinating written symbols during production

Grapho-motor output—Production processes supported by central nervous system pathways from primary motor area (BA 4) in frontal lobe to lower output pathways in basal ganglia to peripheral nervous system output through nerves and muscles of hand and fingers

Figure 8.2.   Continued

What Are Language Difficulties?

In rare cases all language systems are impaired. More typically one level is impaired (and sometimes more than one level) within a system and sometimes across systems, thus interfering with language learning, which requires that all the systems work in a coordinated fashion (see Figure 8.2 for pinpointing where processing might break down in the language by ear, language by mouth, language by eye, and language by hand systems—at initial input or subsequent processing or output). To make the determination of where language processing has broken down, appropriately trained and credentialed teachers, psychologists, speech and language specialists, audiologists, neuropsychologists, developmental pediatricians, and pediatric neurologists on the multidisciplinary team in schools or clinics in the community should assess those aspects of language for which they have expertise and consult with each other. Ideally, some of their training should include supervised work on interdisciplinary teams serving students with both developmental and learning disabilities and other brain-related disorders.

CAUTION

Instead of just identifying language impairment, specify which level of language is impaired in which language system—language by ear, language by mouth, language by eye, or language by hand.

Language by Ear

All initial auditory input is sound waves, first processed in the peripheral nervous system, but subsequently in the central nervous system, in specific pathways depending on the nature of the auditory stimuli— noises like thunder, music, or heard speech. Some students are deaf due to impairments in either the peripheral nervous system (ear only) or central nervous system (brain). Other students may have auditory processing problems that involve the central, but not peripheral nervous system. Exactly how to show that impaired central auditory processing is not specific to speech and/or subsequent language processing has been fraught with controversy that has not yet been resolved.

Some students have central nervous system difficulties that affect abstraction of sound patterns in heard music and/or heard speech. Speech-specific processing is referred to as *phonetic* and typically emerges during infancy, and the toddler and preschool years for both heard words through ears and spoken words through mouth. A variety of phonetic difficulties may occur in speech-sound disorders through the auditory channel, that is, our ears: (a) identifying segmental consonants or continuous vowels within a syllable (subword level), (b) transitioning across syllables (subword level), (c) detecting patterns in speech sounds within syllables, including place and manner of articulation, and voicing (subword level), (d) discriminating among heard words (word level), or (e) abstracting phonotactic patterns of identity, positioning, and sequencing of sounds within and across syllables (subword and word levels), and/or rhythms across syllables within words and/or across words within multi-word units—timing and stress patterns (word, syntax, and text levels). Currently, research is advancing our knowledge about speech-sound disorders due to efforts of Pennington and colleagues at the Colorado Learning Disabilities Center, Pugh and colleagues at the Haskins Laboratory in Connecticut, Rice in Kansas, Treiman in Missouri, Storkel in British Columbia, and others throughout the world (see Arfé, Dockrell, & Berninger, in press). At an even higher level of central processing, language input by our ears is processed as language beyond speech alone—that is, phonemes are abstracted, which are the smallest units of sound that make a difference in meaning and correspond to graphemes (one or more alphabet letters) in the alphabetic principle. Thus, this higher level of sound processing is abstract and referred to as *phonemic*, which requires phonological awareness that is necessary for learning to decode written words—turn them into spoken words—in

≡ Rapid Reference 8.1 Phonetic Difficulties in Speech-Sound Disorders

A variety of phonetic difficulties may occur in speech-sound disorders through the auditory channel, that is, our ears: (a) identifying segmental consonants or continuous vowels within a syllable (subword level), (b) transitioning across syllables (subword level), (c) detecting patterns in speech sounds within syllables, including place and manner of articulation, and voicing (subword level), (d) discriminating among heard words (word level), or (e) abstracting phonotactic patterns of identity, positioning, and sequencing of sounds within and across syllables (subword and word levels), and/or rhythms across syllables within words and/or across words within multi-word units—timing and stress patterns (word, syntax, and text levels).

the beginning stages of learning to read. In turn, phonological awareness develops further as children gain practice pronouncing decoded words, which increase in phonological complexity across the grades (see Rapid Reference 8.1).

CAUTION

Don't confuse phonetic, phonotactic, and phonemic—they refer to different aspects of speech processing.

Alvin Liberman, a pioneer in speech science who articulated the Motor Theory of Speech Perception—producing speech by mouth enhances the perception of the speech sounds—laid the conceptual framework for helping students overcome *speech-sound disorders* by feeling their mouths produce speech sounds to develop articulatory awareness of how language by ear and language by mouth work together at the *phonetic* level (Liberman, 1999). However, his wife, Isabelle Liberman, and her colleague, Donald Shankweiler, pioneered in showing that children with impaired *phonemic awareness* need a different instructional approach such as counting or deleting syllables and phonemes to become aware of the abstract sound units in heard spoken words that relate to other aspects of language relevant to translating written words into spoken words (Liberman, Shankweiler, Fischer, & Carter, 1974). Nevertheless, by themselves, these segmental sound units do not fully specify the oral speech production through mouth, which involves coarticulated segmental and continuous sounds in accented syllables in whole words.

Language by Mouth

Speech production is necessary, but not sufficient, for language by mouth, which also draws on different levels of language—subword, word, and multi-word.

CAUTION

Don't confuse speech and language, which are different processes. Although they normally work together, in some children there is an impairment in the one but not the other. In other children, especially those with developmental disabilities, both may be impaired but each requires a different kind of treatment.

Appropriate individually tailored instruction depends on which processes break down—oral-motor production of speech sounds and/or oral language units at one or more levels of language. Disorders in oral-motor processes may result in a student who (a) is nonvocal (e.g., due to severe cerebral palsy) but may be able to use alternative communication devices to express language, (b) cannot produce speech that others can understand, (c) stutters, (d) exhibits abnormal intonation for single words or combined words, as some students with autism do, and/or (e) produces involuntary verbal and nonverbal vocalizations due to obsessive compulsive disorder. In other cases, oral language problems at the one-word or combined-word levels of language are observed during the preschool years and then during schooling in learning to use oral language in academic register of language, which differs from conversational register (Silliman & Scott, 2009), learning interrelationships among oral and written language (Silliman & Berninger, 2011; Silliman & Mody, 2008), and using language for social acts (Troia, 2011). This difficulty in language learning is called selective language impairment (SLI), language learning disability (LLD), or oral and written language learning disability (OWL LD). See Rapid Reference 8.2.

Language by Eye

When reading language by eye, light waves stimulate the retina in the peripheral nervous system, which transmits neural signals to the central nervous system for processing of visual features and configuration and their conversion to visible language representations. Students who are blind or partially sighted can learn

≡ Rapid Reference 8.2 Disorders in Oral-Motor Processes

Disorders in oral-motor processes may result in a student who (a) is nonvocal (e.g., due to severe cerebral palsy) but may be able to use alternative communication devices to express language, (b) cannot produce speech that others can understand, (c) stutters, (d) exhibits abnormal intonation for single words or combined words, as some students with autism do, and/or (e) produces involuntary verbal and nonverbal vocalizations due to obsessive compulsive disorder.

to read, but require alternative approaches: using braille to receive and send somatosensory input to language processing centers, or larger print, respectively. However, perception of incoming visual stimuli alone is not sufficient for reading.

> **DON'T FORGET**
> ....
> Although during reading the eye receives visual input, that information is then transmitted to higher level language processing centers, which process the language at the word, sentence, and text level and translate the language into cognitions, with support from working memory. Thus, reading is not just a visual process.

The initial sensations have to be segmented into sequential letters (or subword braille units), which must then be processed in sequential order, mapped onto corresponding sound and morphological units in word form coding (storage and processing units) in working memory, and linked to other levels of language, including words—their meaning and word-specific spellings, multiword units in sentences, and multi-sentence units in paragraphs and texts. In addition, these various levels of language have to be held in working memory while translated into a variety of cognitive representations that are explicitly stated or must be inferred (see Cain & Oakhill, 2007).

Language by Hand

Written expression begins with access to the mind's eye, which has links to the cognitive and language systems, via vocabulary meaning and word-specific spellings, and also to the output systems through hand movements and their interface with writing tools.

The orthographic loop of working memory, which integrates the mind's eye and sequential organization of finger movements, plays a special role in idea expression through language by hand (Berninger, 2012). Thus, language by hand involves not only motor processes but also cognitive, written language, working memory, and executive functions, all of which should be taken into account when tailoring instruction individually for students with writing difficulties.

II. ASSESSMENT AND ASSESSMENT-INSTRUCTION TOOLS

An essential starting point in tailoring instruction for individuals with language difficulties is assessing each level of language within each of the four language systems. Thirty years ago, few assessment resources were available with norms so results could be interpreted in reference to age or grade peers. Such tools are now

> **DON'T FORGET**
> ....
> There is more to writing than motor skills.

available (e.g., Carrow-Woolfolk, 2011; Goldblatt, 2011; Kaufman & Kaufman, 2004; Psychological Corporation, 2005; Seml, Wiig, & Secord, 2004; Wagner, Torgesen, & Rashotte, 1999; Woodcock, McGrew, & Mather, 2001) and more are being developed with research funding from federal agencies such as the Institute of Educational Science (IES). However, assessment results are most likely to generate instructionally useful information if organized according to the four language systems and their levels in Figure 8.1 and interpreted in reference to the model in Figure 8.2 to identify the nature of the difficulty. Given that measurement models based on categorization only are being replaced with hybrid dimensional and categorical approaches (e.g., Widiger & Trull, 2007), in this section we feature a new test under development based on levels of language and language systems (modalities) and dimensions (continuous scores on these level-modality combinations), with the goal of differentiated categories of normal or disabled language learners. We also feature an evolving approach to computerized assessment-intervention for writing, and instructional tools based on programmatic research for teaching oral and written language in the early and later grades.

The *Test of Integrated Language and Literacy Skills* (TILLS SV2) (Nelson, Helm-Estabrooks, Hotz, & Plante, 2011) is being standardized (expected completion, 2014) in IES-funded research for the dual purposes of differential diagnosis of oral and written language disorders and informing instructional plans for students ages 6 to 18 years who do and do not struggle with language learning. The 15 subtests are based on a *model of two language levels* (sound/word and sentence/discourse) *by four language modalities* (listening, speaking, reading, and writing). For Listening, Phoneme Awareness and Vocabulary Awareness assess Sound/Word Levels, and Story Questions and Listening Comprehension assess Sentence/Discourse Levels. For Speaking, Nonword Repetition assesses Sound/Word Levels, and Story Retelling and Social Communication assess Sentence/Discourse Levels. For Reading, Nonword Reading and Reading Fluency assess Sound/Word Levels, and Reading Comprehension assesses Sentence/Discourse Levels. For Writing, Nonword Spelling assesses Sound/Word Levels, and Written Expression assesses Sentence/Discourse Level. In addition, for Memory that supports all language modalities, Digits Forward and Digits Backwards assesses Sound/Word Levels, and Following Directions and Delayed Story Telling assess the Sentence/Discourse Levels.

This model is consistent with current research that shows that oral and written language difficulties are explained better by a language-levels-by-modalities theoretical model than a receptive/expressive one (Bishop & Snowling, 2004; Catts & Kamhi, 2005; Rice & Warren, 2004; Snowling & Hayiou-

≡ *Rapid Reference 8.3 Language-Levels-by-Modalities Model*

....

The language-levels-by-modalities model predicts four diagnostic groups, each with different implications for intervention: Dyslexia (low sound/word level skills, but high sentence/discourse; listening comprehension better than reading comprehension), Normal Language (at least average skills in all components), Oral and Written Language Impairment (low skills in all components), and Specific Comprehension impairment (high sound/word level skills and low sentence/discourse level skills across modalities).

Thomas, 2006; Tomblin, Zhang, Weiss, Catts, & Ellis Weismer, 2004). The language-levels-by-modalities model predicts four diagnostic groups (see Rapid Reference 8.3), each with different implications for intervention: Dyslexia (low sound/word level skills, but high sentence/discourse; listening comprehension better than reading comprehension), Normal Language (at least average skills in all components), Oral and Written Language Impairment (low skills in all components), and Specific Comprehension impairment (high sound/word level skills and low sentence/discourse level skills across modalities). Other researchers have reported similar profiles (Catts, Hogan, & Adlof, 2005; Nation & Snowling, 2004; Scarborough, 2005; Silliman & Berninger, 2011). Discriminant function analysis results for the preliminary data set were statistically significant with sensitivity and specificity both within target range of > 80% (83% sensitivity and 97% specificity) (Nelson, Anderson, & Applegate, 2011). Additional special population studies are underway with students with autism spectrum disorders, intellectual developmental disabilities, and deafness/hard-of-hearing.

McNamara and colleagues have developed a number of computerized tools for assessing and teaching composing. Writing PAL (e.g., McNamara & CSEP Lab, 2010; McNamara, Graesser, Cai, & Kulikowich, 2011) is a writing strategy tutoring program that includes nine modules of writing strategy training geared toward writing prompt-based essays in the style of SAT tests. It includes training, game-based practice, and also essay writing with automated feedback. The automated feedback focuses on higher-level aspects of the essay, and on guiding feedback relevant to the strategy modules. Coh-Metrix (e.g., Jarvis et al., 2012; McNamara, & CSEP Lab, 2005; McNamara & Graesser, 2012; McNamara et al., 2011) was developed to assess text difficulty for instructional purposes rather than the individual student's text composing skill. Coh-Metrix can be used to analyze writing variables such as lexical diversity, word frequency, and syntactic complexity reliably and validly; for example, better writers use more sophisticated language at these levels, which explains about 20–30% of the variance in their writing skills. Other tools are under development for computerized assessment of other levels of language contributing to overall text quality.

Other programmatic research programs have developed instructional tools for oral language (e.g., Beck & McKeown, 2006; Beck, McKeown, & Kucan, 2008) and reading comprehension (e.g., Denton, Vaughn, Wexler, Bryan, & Reed, 2012; O'Connor, & Vadasy, 2011) that provide important supplements to the earlier instructional tools that were research-generated for phonological skills in reading. In addition, researchers are generating advances in effective instruction for struggling writers (e.g., Nelson, Bahr, & Van Meter, 2004; Troia, 2009).

III. BIOLOGICAL AND ENVIRONMENTAL INFLUENCES ON LANGUAGE

Biological Bases of Individual Differences
Genetic Variables

Genetic differences account for normal variation among all students and also for severe developmental disabilities (associated with large deletions in the gene sequencing of base chemicals; Batshaw, Pellegrino, & Roizen, 2007) and specific learning disabilities but otherwise normal development (associated with small genetic variations, referred to as *alleles*; see Berninger & Richards, 2010). Researchers in the longest-standing NICHD-funded learning disability center, at the University of Colorado with collaborating sites in Denver and Nebraska in the United States, and in Australia, England, and Northern Europe, have published extensive twin studies showing that reading disability has genetic as well as environmental influences (e.g., Byrne et al., 2009; Olson, Byrne, & Samuelson, 2009; Pennington et al., 2008; Plomin & Bergeman, 1991). Also see Lyytinen et al. (2004) for similar findings in Finland. Just because a specific learning disability has a genetic basis, it does not follow that an individual with a specific learning disability is not responsive to instruction. In fact, instructional studies in the Colorado research center (e.g., Wise, Rogan, & Sessions, 2009) and elsewhere have shown that individuals with a genetically based learning disability can be responsive to instruction. Now that the sequencing of the four base chemicals in the human genome has been completed, the cutting edge of genetics research is *epigenetics*, that is, how environmental influences alter the behavioral expression of the underlying genetic code (for general introduction, see Cassiday, 2009;

Riddihough, & Zahn, 2010; for application to SLDs, see Berninger & Richards, 2010). At the same time, instruction does not alter the underlying gene sequencing, which means that a student with SLD may experience ongoing oral and/or written language learning difficulties as the curriculum changes across the

> **DON'T FORGET**
> ....
> Both genes and teaching influence language learning. The brain, which has the genetic code in each neuron, interacts with both the physical and social environment in school settings. See Berninger & Richards (2010).

grades and becomes increasingly more complex and demanding. Indeed, the nature of the genetic bases may change across grades (e.g., Plomin, DeFries, McClearn, & McGuffin, 2008). For students with more constraining developmental disabilities, instruction may result in varying degrees of developmental change and learning, but at a rate and on a trajectory limited by underlying genetic abnormalities that make full normalization unrealistic (Berninger & Miller, 2011).

Brain Variables

Since brain imaging became widely available during the last two decades of the 20th century, there has been an explosion of knowledge of brain-behavior relationships in typical oral and written language development and specific kinds of difficulties. For students with SLDs the findings generally support nature-nurture interactions in that students with oral and language difficulties may normalize in brain function in specific brain locations following language-based instruction (for a recent review, see Pugh & McCardle, 2009). However, researchers are still investigating whether functional connectivity, that is, which brain regions coactivate in time, fully normalizes following instruction for specific learning disabilities.

Environmental Bases of Individual Differences
Language

One issue that may contribute to language difficulties is language(s) spoken at home and at school. Even if some students speak the same language at home as at school, depending on the parents' first language, level of parent(s)' education, and dialect, the student may not hear the same version of the language at home and at school. Students who are good "code-switchers" between language or dialect spoken at home and at school are more likely to be successful in academic learning than those who are not (Washington & Thomas-Tate, 2009). Also, students with oral and written language difficulties have difficulty with academic register (instructional language), which differs from conversational register (Silliman &

Scott, 2009). Although some English-language learners with working memory difficulties (see research by Swanson in Swanson and Berninger, in press) may struggle with second-language learning, for others, speaking more than one language has an advantage for language learning (Petitto, 2009). Also, introducing a second language early in language development rather than during adolescence has an advantage because the second language is learned more easily earlier in development (Kovelman, Baker, & Petitto, 2008).

Culture

Race is not the same as culture, which varies across socioeconomic groups and educational levels for the same race. Immigrant populations bring diverse cultural backgrounds to the schooling of their children, but so do those who have been the involuntary immigrants across multiple generations (Native Americans and African Americans) for whom the cultural aftermath of past injustices continues to affect current generations of school-age children and youth and needs to be addressed (e.g., Ladson-Billings, 2006).

Family Systems

Families have stressors that can affect their children's performance in school. However, experience in problem-solving consultation and supervising trainees shows that reaching out to parents and helping them find support services in the community can have beneficial effects on their child's schooling.

School Systems

Schools, like individuals, differ in how they are structured and how they function. Systems-level variables, ranging from the single classroom level (teacher-student and student-student relationships) to the building level (e.g., climate of the school promoted by the principal) to the district level (policies and procedures) can all affect student learning and ability of a multidisciplinary team to support classroom teachers in providing individually tailored instruction for students with language difficulties.

Instruction

Individually tailored instruction does not mean that instruction has to be delivered to one student at a time. There is no evidence that students with language difficulties learn more in individual tutoring; in fact, students in the University of Washington intervention studies reported preferring participating in groups with others. Slavin (1987) reviewed research on the most effective delivery systems for individually tailored instruction. Assignment to a self-contained classroom based on achievement or ability was not found to be effective. However, what is now called the "walkabout" model and then was called the Joplin Plan, which regroups children across grade levels to provide reading instruction at the students' instructional level, was found to be effective. In general, students bene-fited from remaining in heteroge-neous classes for most of the day and being regrouped only for a sub-ject like reading, as long as classroom

> **DON'T FORGET**
> ....
> Children benefit from written language instruction at their current instructional level, but also from interaction with other students with diverse abilities and interests.

teachers provided the instruction for each smaller instructional group with a more restricted range of instructional levels.

IV. MODELS FOR INTERVENTION

Historical Context for Current Challenges
Legal Approaches
Before the 1960s, it was common for children with severe developmental disabilities to be placed in institutions or kept at home rather than receiving educational services in schools. Other children were normally developing, but had extreme difficulty learning specific academic skills and often were not receiving effective help at school. Parents of children with these two contrasting sources of learning difficulties joined forces to lobby at the national level to remedy this situation. The result was legislation that would guarantee the civil rights of their children to receive free and appropriate public education (FAPE). However, the professionals could not agree on how to define precisely these developmental disabilities, specific learning disabilities, or other medical conditions associated with educationally handicapping conditions. Thus, children and youth with educationally handicapping conditions have civil rights for FAPE, but the educational handicapping conditions are *not* identified in the same way in each state in the United States—either in the original legislation that passed in 1975 or in the reauthorizations in 1989 and 2004. Eligibility criteria for services are not the same as instructionally relevant, evidence-based definitions of specific educational handicapping conditions that identify what specific learning disabil-ities are and what they are not in a treatment-relevant way.

Research-Identified Problems With the Federal Definition of Educational Handicapping Conditions
The original federal guidelines used scores on IQ tests as an approximation of whether development was in the normal range to differentiate those who had developmental disabilities in cognition and those whose cognitive development

was at least in the normal range despite specific learning disabilities. However, over three decades of research has shown that no specific amount of discrepancy between full-scale IQs and reading, writing, or math achievement identifies a specific learning disability. Also, the IQ-discrepancy approach led to a wait-and-fail model. Many struggling students in the early grades did not show a large enough IQ-achievement discrepancy until fourth grade or above to receive specialized instruction. Two of the well-established NICHD-funded research centers for specific learning disabilities in Tallahassee, Florida, and Houston, Texas, have conducted substantial research on response to early Tier 1 intervention and supplemental ongoing Tier 2 intervention for those who fail to respond to the initial intervention in general education, and Tier 3 pull-out special education for those who fail to respond to Tier 2 intervention.

Although current research on response to intervention (RTI), beginning in the early grades, has shown it is effective in increasing the reading achievement of many students, to date no RTI study has yielded a reliable and valid way to classify students for purposes of special education services or defining SLDs (e.g., see Fletcher, Barth, & Stuebing, 2009; Fletcher et al., 2011; Stuebing; Fletcher, Marin, & Francis, 2012; Waesche, Schatschneider, Maner, Ahmed, & Wagner, 2011). Thus, neither IQ-achievement discrepancy nor RTI alone is sufficient for defining the oral and written language difficulties many school-age children and youth face.

Current Challenges

Without clear, evidence-based definitions of what educationally handicapping conditions are, the implementation of federal special education legislation in each state has become a system for deciding whether a student meets eligibility criteria for *categories of special education services* rather than for truly diagnosing individual instructional needs so that teachers can deliver differentiated instruction in general education. With substantial cuts in federal funding for special education, many schools in the current economically challenging times do not have the resources to perform legally mandated multidisciplinary assessments. Increasingly, parents who can afford to do so are turning to the private sector for these evaluations and sometimes taking legal action, but as a result, trust between parents and educators and home-school

DON'T FORGET

Accurate diagnosis of well-defined language learning difficulty plays a role in identifying and implementing effective instruction. Also, response to instruction should be monitored for all students on a daily, weekly, monthly, and annual basis—early, middle, and late in school year. And RTI results should be used to modify instruction if reasonable progress is not being made.

relationships suffer. Students whose parents cannot afford private assessments and who do not receive them at school may be at higher risk for school dropout and chronic academic struggles, and in some cases, getting in trouble with the law because they are not supervised. Moreover, there is no evidence that pull-out services are more effective than appropriate, differentiated instruction in the general education program. In sum, current practices are not cost effective for schools or society.

Proactive Approach and Best Professional Practices

Although FAPE has served an important role in guaranteeing civil liberties for individuals with educationally handicapping conditions, implementation of FAPE requires more than legal procedures. There is nothing in the federal law or the state implementations of it that prohibits educational professionals from proactively assessing and providing differentiated instruction for evidence-based developmental and learning disabilities and other conditions in general education, that is, FAPE for all students. Educational professionals should be allowed to implement best professional practices with flexible professional judgment. Research at the University of Washington from 1989 to 2007 supported a model of assessment-instruction delivery with three tiers that are implemented in parallel as needed to tailor instruction individually. The first Tier 1 component involves reaching out to parents of students at transition to formal schooling in kindergarten and first grade through questionnaires about developmental, medical, family, and preschool educational history and concerns. For students whose parents report concerns or risk factors, the interdisciplinary team meets to decide if Tier 1, Tier 2, and/or Tier 3 approaches are warranted and, if so, plan and implement them. The goal is to build healthy, productive working relationships from the beginning between parents and schools, both of whom play an important role in a student's learning outcomes (Alston-Abel, 2009). The second Tier 1 component is screening select children using evidence-based methods to assess those target skills research has shown to place students at risk for specific oral and written language learning outcomes. Those students found to be the lowest achievers on target skills receive evidence-based instruction. Students receiving this instruction, which is based on research findings conducted with children in grades K through 4, have shown improvements such that they were brought up to at least average range for grade level on the target skills (see Berninger, 2008, and Berninger, 2009 for overviews).

DON'T FORGET

Many specific language difficulties can be prevented with early identification and intervention.

Tier 2 is problem-solving consultation with parents, whose responses to the questionnaire suggest that their child is at risk and who are invited to have a face-to-face interview with school personnel to discuss issues related to preschool developmental, medical, and educational history, languages spoken in the home, culture, family stressors, and family history of developmental and/or learning disabilities, as may be relevant. Also at weekly meetings of classroom teachers and the multidisciplinary team, teachers are encouraged to bring to the attention of the team individual students who are struggling in the classroom, who may subsequently be observed in the classroom during instruction and receive modified instruction that is monitored for effectiveness. Also, based on parent questionnaires and follow-up interviews and teacher input, decisions are made about which students should receive comprehensive assessment to determine if they have a developmental or specific learning disability that should be addressed. Research-generated resources and guidelines for implementing each of these three tiers within a proactive, preventative model are provided in a CD in Berninger (2007).

DON'T FORGET

Problem-solving consultation assists teachers in helping more students in general education.

DON'T FORGET

Sometimes comprehensive assessment and differential diagnosis and treatment planning is warranted. The most appropriate place for implementing that differentiated instruction may be the general education classroom. Special education pull-out services are not necessarily the solution.

DON'T FORGET

Berninger, 2007.

Developmental Profiles

Eunice Kennedy Shriver's pioneering vision resulted in University Affiliated Programs (UAPs) for training professionals in multiple disciplines in diagnostic and treatment services for developmental and learning disorders. Regrettably, now that the funding for these interdisciplinary training programs is no longer available, many professionals are not receiving preservice training in cross-disciplinary collaboration for assessing students with developmental and learning disabilities and developing individually tailored treatment plans.

One UAP training program at the Boston Children's Hospital taught a multidisciplinary approach that is both evidence-based and best practice and may inspire others to learn from their groundbreaking training program. Both team members with the most expertise for each domain (in parentheses) and another team member assigned for cross-checking purposes assessed each of these five domains of development: cognition and memory (psychologists), language (speech and language specialists), sensory and motor (occupational and physical therapists, neuropsychologists, developmental pediatricians, and pediatric neurologists), social-emotional (psychologists and psychiatrists), and attention/executive functions (psychologists and neuropsychologists). Parents/legal guardians were interviewed to determine if there was evidence of a disability in one or more domains of development in the preschool years. For students who had sustained brain-related injuries, the same domains of development were assessed. Also, it was noted if toxins (environmental poisons such as lead or ingested substances such as methadone or alcohol) may be affecting prenatal or postnatal development.

Assessment results were summarized by domain and presented to the parents at the time of assessment, with focus on current functioning. No predictions or promises were made about the future. If, however, after three repeated assessments at least six months apart in the preschool years or a year apart in the school years, a child fell outside the normal range in all domains of development, a diagnosis of *pervasive developmental disability* (PDD) was made. If a child repeatedly fell outside the normal range in one or more, but not all, domains of development, a diagnosis was made of either a *specific developmental disability* (SDD) or *specific developmental disabilities* (SDDs). The word *delay*, which implies *catch-up*, was not used because that may give false hope for future development. If there were one or more splinter skills in the normal range, no predictions were offered that the child would eventually function fully in the normal range—because if that did not happen, the false hope harbored by the parents would interfere with dealing with the grief of the loss of a normal child.

Brain systems corresponding to each of the five developmental domains must function together in coordinated fashion, but that may not be possible if one or more of these systems or domains of development is not within the normal range. Just as all the musical instruments in the orchestra or band must function in synchrony to produce music rather than noise, uneven development of one or more domains in the developmental profile can interfere with age-appropriate learning or behavior. Professionals can explain to parents that the child will probably continue to

CAUTION

Students with developmental disabilities typically also have language difficulties, but of a different kind and requiring different instructional interventions than do those whose development is entirely within the normal range except for specific language difficulties.

develop at his or her own rate and pattern across the domains even if it is not the typical rate and pattern for children of the same age. A learning profile should also be described for specific reading, writing, and math skills. Oral and written language disabilities, which occur in many students with specific developmental disabilities and always occur in pervasive developmental disabilities, are likely to affect learning academic skills and are relevant to instructional planning. The oral language difficulties can affect ability to understand instructional talk of teachers across the curriculum and to participate in classroom discussions with classmates and the teacher. Also, for many of the neurogenetic and developmental disorders, research is generating a wealth of knowledge about the phenotypes (behavioral markers) of PDD and SDD or SDDs (e.g., see Batshaw et al., 2007), which are relevant to individualizing instruction and providing feedback to parents who seek information about etiology of a disorder. For further guidelines in assessing developmental profiles to identify students with pervasive or specific developmental disorders, other medical conditions affecting development, or normal development, see Silliman and Berninger (2011, especially Figure 2) and Berninger (2011a).

Specific Learning Disabilities

To identify students with specific learning disabilities (SLDs), it is necessary to rule out pervasive developmental disability (PDD) or specific developmental disability (SDD) or disabilities (SDDs) (Berninger, 2011a; Silliman & Berninger, 2011). Currently, researchers have begun to investigate academic learning problems of students with autism; but because the majority of children with autism have PDD or SDDs, it is important not to confuse these children and youth with those who have normal development across all five developmental domains but specific learning disabilities in oral and/or written language. The research on differential diagnosis and effective instruction for students with specific learning disabilities does not generalize to those with pervasive developmental disability or specific developmental disability/disabilities, including autism.

DON'T FORGET
....
The research on differential diagnosis and effective instruction for students with specific learning disabilities does not generalize to those with pervasive developmental disability or specific developmental disability/disabilities, including autism.

Over 20 years of research (e.g., for overview, see Berninger & Richards, 2010) has identified the skills in learning profiles and working memory phenotype profiles (Berninger, 2010–present; Berninger et al., 2006; Berninger, Raskind, Richards, Abbott, & Stock, 2008) associated with specific kinds of SLDs in children whose development is otherwise normal, such as dysgraphia, dyslexia, and oral and written language learning disability (OWL LD, also SLI or LLD). See Figures 9.1a and 9.1b in Berninger (2011a) for a graphic portrayal of the working memory architecture, which has storage and processing units for single spoken and written words and accumulating words, a phonological loop for naming through mouth and an orthographic loop for writing through hand the letters and words in the mind's eye, and a panel of executive functions for supervisory attention in working memory (focusing attention, switching attention, sustaining attention, and self-monitoring). Research has shown that specific kinds of SLDs can be defined on the basis of which skills in the learning profiles and phenotype profiles are impaired relative to the others (see Silliman & Berninger, 2011, Table 1, and Rapid Reference 8.4 herein); but students with any kind of SLD are likely to be impaired in one or more of the supervisory attention phenotypes (e.g., Berninger, 2008; Berninger et al., 2006, 2008).

≡ *Rapid Reference 8.4 Learning and Phenotype Profiles of Specific Learning Disabilities*

- The *learning profile for dysgraphia, a subword SLD*, shows hallmark impaired handwriting, for example, in automaticity, which is producing legible letters in alphabetic order from memory in the first 15 seconds before strategic processing takes over for finding, retrieving, and producing alphabet letters, and/or in sustaining strategic legible, fast letter writing.

- The *phenotype profile for dysgraphia* shows hallmark impaired (a) orthographic coding (storage and processing) of letter forms and/or written words in working memory, and/or (b) finger sequencing on imitative finger task (the planning and execution of serial movements of orthographic loop).

- The *learning profile for dyslexia, a word-level SLD*, shows hallmark impaired oral phonological decoding and written spelling words.

- The *phenotype profile for dyslexia* shows hallmark impaired (a) phonological coding (storage and processing of sounds and spoken words in working memory), (b) orthographic coding (storage and processing of letter forms and/or written words in working memory), (c) phonological loop, and/or (d) orthographic loop.

- The *learning profile for OWL LD, a multi-word-level SLD*, shows hallmark impaired (a) listening comprehension, (b) reading comprehension, and/or (c) written expression.

- The *phenotype profile for OWL LD* shows hallmark impaired (a) morphological and syntactic coding (storage and processing) in working memory, (b) word retrieval, and/or (c) bidirectional cognitive ← → linguistic translation underlying inferential thinking.

The *learning profile for dysgraphia, a subword SLD*, shows hallmark impaired handwriting, for example, in automaticity, which is producing legible letters in alphabetic order from memory in the first 15 seconds before strategic processing takes over for finding, retrieving, and producing alphabet letters, and/or in sustaining strategic legible, fast letter writing. The *phenotype profile for dysgraphia* shows hallmark impaired (a) orthographic coding (storage and processing) of letter forms and/or written words in working memory, and/or (b) finger sequencing on imitative finger task (the planning and execution of serial movements of orthographic loop). The *learning profile for dyslexia, a word-level SLD*, shows hallmark impaired oral phonological decoding and written spelling words. The *phenotype profile for dyslexia* shows hallmark impaired (a) phonological coding (storage and processing of sounds and spoken words in working memory), (b) orthographic coding (storage and processing of letter forms and/or written words in working memory), (c) phonological loop, and/or (d) orthographic loop.

The *learning profile for OWL LD, a multi-word-level SLD*, shows hallmark impaired (a) listening comprehension, (b) reading comprehension, and/or (c) written expression. The *phenotype profile for OWL LD* shows hallmark impaired (a) morphological and syntactic coding (storage and processing) in working memory, (b) word retrieval, and/or (c) bidirectional cognitive ← → linguistic translation underlying inferential thinking (Silliman & Scott, 2009). Students with OWL LD typically have a preschool history of late talking and/or other indicators of difficulties in language-learning (Silliman & Berninger, 2011). For other research-supported models, see Pennington (2006) for dyslexia, and Connelly, Dockrell, and Barnett (2012) for dyslexia, SLI, dysgraphia, and developmental motor disorder.

Predicting Reasonable Level of Written Language Achievement

Given the normal variation in oral and written language learning in the general population, the issue of what is a reasonable level of achievement in oral and written language has not been resolved—only in Lake Wobegon can we expect all children to be above average. Recent research by Niedo (submitted) evaluated whether verbal reasoning and specific components of the working memory architecture supporting language learning were correlated with specific reading and writing outcomes, and then, for those that were, whether each contributed uniquely to specific reading and writing outcomes. Beta weights for the multiple regression were used to model expected academic achievement for cases of students with and without SLDs.

Consistently, when measures of verbal working components supporting language learning were included along with *verbal reasoning* as predictors in the multiple regressions for real word reading, reading comprehension, spelling, and written expression, verbal reasoning explained unique variance (and so did orthographic coding in working memory). Phonological coding in working memory, but not verbal reasoning, explained unique variance in pseudoword decoding, with which some, but not all, students with specific learning disabilities have difficulty. Thus, just because IQ-achievement discrepancy is not a reliable and valid measure for identifying SLD, it does not follow that verbal reasoning ability, when combined with evidence-based indicators of the verbal working memory architecture supporting language learning, is not relevant to determining a reasonable expected learning outcome for students with and without SLDs in reading and writing real words and text.

V. GENERAL GUIDELINES FOR INDIVIDUALIZING INSTRUCTION AND ILLUSTRATIVE CASES

General Instructional Guidelines

For students with PDD, it is important to provide language instruction at their overall developmental level. For students with SDD in oral language, it is important to provide language instruction that takes into account their developmental level in language as well as the nature of their disabilities in language by ear and by mouth. For students with OWL LD, dyslexia, and dysgraphia, it is important to provide instruction that is individually tailored for their instructional and phenotype profiles, including the specific levels of language and language systems with which they have difficulty. In all cases, it is important to monitor response to instruction on target probes in each session during intervention and at immediate posttest and, if possible, long-term follow-up. Single-subject design methods (Kratochwill et al., 2009; White, 2009) are ideally suited for this purpose of addressing the research-into-practice question, "What works for whom?," which is as important as the research question, "What works?" (Berninger & Dunn, 2012). The following cases illustrate each of these instructional principles.

Case 1

A 9-year-old girl in fourth grade was referred because in addition to not making progress in reading she appeared to be regressing and was becoming withdrawn. Her mother

DON'T FORGET

Single-subject design methods are ideally suited for the purpose of addressing the research-into-practice question, "What works for whom?"

brought her for the evaluation, which the school team had recommended because they could not figure out why she was having problems or what to do to help her. The mother shared prior preschool and school assessments. The father, however, did not come because he was angry that, although his daughter had participated in a preschool program for autism, and he was told her IQ increased 6 points, the school psychologist now thought his daughter had intellectual disability. A comprehensive assessment at the university showed that not only was the girl's cognitive functioning about $2\frac{2}{3}$ standard deviations below the mean, but so, too, were her language, motor, social emotional, and attention/executive functions. Overall, she was functioning at the developmental level in the 5-to-6-year-old range. Also, her academic skills were generally at the kindergarten level, with some at a beginning first-grade level, consistent with her developmental profile. Although she was slow to warm up and somewhat shy, she made good eye contact and became socially engaged with the assessment team, who did not observe at age 9 years diagnosable signs of autism.

In the feedback session with the mother, the team presented the results in developmental and instructional profiles, proposed that the prior and current assessments were more consistent with a diagnosis of pervasive developmental disability than intellectual disability, and recommended that she be taught at her overall developmental level with focus on both oral and written language instruction typical at that level. The mother cried and then thanked the team for being honest and admitted that she was looking for a diagnosis—she knew that something was different about her daughter. Using dynamic assessment, a psychologist on the team with prior teaching experience implemented oral language and reading instruction at the kindergarten level—the girl immediately became highly engaged in the activities and on RTI measures responded well to the instruction at her developmental level. Her mother and the teachers at school were thrilled by the turnaround of the girl from a disengaged to an engaged learner who experienced success in language learning when taught at her developmental and instructional levels.

Case 2

An 8-year-old third-grader was referred for reading fluency problems. He was not responding to multisensory, phonics, and repeated readings instruction. A careful developmental, medical, family, and educational history obtained through the parent interview revealed that this boy had had a stroke during birth related to a familial genetic disorder. Prior and current testing showed that his nonverbal cognitive development fell in the average-to-high-average range, but his verbal cognitive development fell in the low-average range, probably due to his overall language (not speech) development falling in the below-average range, even though he had no speech problems. Although his social and emotional development appeared to be age-appropriate, he showed signs of attention deficit, especially inattention and executive functions for self-regulating learning. He was especially impaired in word finding as well as syntax-level skills. In the feedback we explained to his mother that his problems in reading fluency were related to a specific developmental disability in oral language, which required specialized instruction in order to help him improve his reading fluency.

We recommended that the school provide specialized instruction in the general education program targeted to develop his oral word finding, vocabulary, and listening comprehension skills (e.g., Beck & McKeown, 2006; Beck, McKeown, & Kucan, 2008) and to monitor his progress through RTI with word-, syntax-, and text-level oral language tasks. Follow-up reports indicated that he responded to this oral language instruction that supplemented his reading instruction. When his oral language skills, initially at about a 6-year level, reached the 8-year level, his reading fluency—both his oral expression, reflecting smooth coordination of all the levels of language, and speed—improved markedly and became grade appropriate.

Case 3

A team of school professionals sought consultation about a sixth-grade boy who had received four years of special help with reading that emphasized phonological and phonics skills; his pseudoword decoding was grade appropriate, but he struggled greatly with reading real words and reading comprehension. (See the second case in Berninger and O'Malley-May, 2011, for results of a comprehensive assessment that identified his instructional needs in morphological and syntactic awareness and real word reading and reading comprehension and a description of the multicomponent language instruction that was provided during four weeks in the summer.) His reading comprehension improved substantially and feedback provided for his teachers for the coming school year emphasized strategies for improving his real word reading tied to vocabulary learning for specific content areas of the curriculum. This case illustrates the true value of curriculum-based assessment—a component for teaching language that had been missing in this boy's curriculum at school, but when added, he responded to instruction.

Case 4

A second-grade girl was adopted at age 2 years from Mexico. Little was known about the first two years of her life in a Spanish-speaking country, but she responded quickly to English immersion when she arrived in the United States. In fact, preschool and kindergarten teachers commented on her strengths in verbal skills. However, by first grade it became evident that despite her strengths in language by ear (listening) and by mouth (oral expression), she struggled in learning to associate sounds with letters and decode new, unfamiliar words. Comprehensive assessment documented significant problems in phonemic awareness, orthographic coding in working memory, rapid automatic naming, and reading pseudowords, but high-average verbal reasoning and a developmental profile well within the normal range across all five developmental domains. When providing feedback to the mother we explained that her daughter had a specific learning disability—dyslexia—that involved impairments in skills needed to learn word-level skills. The team recommended instructional resources for teaching phonemic awareness and the sound-spelling correspondences in alphabetic principle and their transfer to reading words in and out of context. They also emphasized the importance of beginning systematic spelling instruction because students with dyslexia can have as much difficulty learning to spell as decoding unknown words. This case illustrated that speaking a second language should not be an exclusionary criterion for specialized reading instruction. Even students who are English-language learners may show a hallmark instructional profile for dyslexia for which they need specialized instruction.

Case 5

A seventh-grade girl with an earlier history of dyslexia, which had been remediated, had significant academic problems when she made the transition from elementary to middle school. A comprehensive assessment showed that, although she had superior to very superior cognitive abilities, she had undiagnosed, untreated dysgraphia (impaired legible, automatic letter writing, serial finger organization, and spelling), which affected her completion of written work in both language arts and math (see Berninger, 2011b). Recommendations included the instructional intervention described in Berninger and O'Malley-May (2011) for the first case, which had been used successfully to help a boy of comparable age with dysgraphia. However, the team made recommendations on how to integrate this instruction in specific content areas of her general education program. For language arts, we recommended that she receive instruction and practice in (a) forming legible letters until she reached age-appropriate automaticity and speed for sustained writing; (b) self-monitoring the legibility of her letter writing in her own written work; (c) spelling using a systematic spelling program at her instructional level; (d) explicit self-regulation strategies for grade-appropriate composing tasks; and (e) frequent feedback when the quality of the content and organization of her compositions was grade appropriate so that she thinks of herself as a capable writer. (For lessons that can be used for teaching writing skills using these instructional approaches, see Berninger & Wolf, 2009b.)

For math, because of her extreme difficulty in writing numerals legibly and automatically alone, in multi-place numbers, and in written computations, we recommended instruction and practice in (a) forming the numerals; (b) writing numerals in multi-place numbers to express place value both to the right and left of decimal point; (c) counting along number line to model fast-forward adding (multiplication) or fast-backward subtracting (division) and then writing the math fact and graphing accuracy and time for progress monitoring; (d) self-monitoring strategies to pay attention to operation signs and check answers to written computations; and (e) strategies for writing math facts, computations, and equations in left-right and top-down/bottom-up orientation in space, and applying the sequential steps of computation algorithms in two-dimensional space. This girl struggled with the written expression of the language of math through the hand: numerals (subword level), place-value notation for whole and mixed numbers (word and syntax level), and written computations that require travel across horizontal and vertical planes of two-dimensional space (text level). Yet, she explained to the examiner the importance of taking into account time and space in solving science problems. Cognition and language by hand are not the same, but can be taught to work together for both math and written language learning.

REFERENCES

Abbott, R., Berninger, V., & Fayol, M. (2010). Longitudinal relationships of levels of language in writing and between writing and reading in grades 1 to 7. *Journal of Educational Psychology, 102*, 281–298.

Alston-Abel, N. (2009, May). Longitudinal trends in relationships among home literacy practices, children's self-regulation, and literacy achievement outcomes. Unpublished PhD dissertation, University of Washington.

Arfé, B., Dockrell, J., & Berninger, V. (Eds.). (in press). *Writing development and instruction in children with hearing, speech, and language disorders.* New York, NY: Oxford University Press.

Batshaw, M., Pellegrino, L., & Roizen, N. (2007). *Children with disabilities* (6th ed.). Baltimore, MD: Brookes.

Beck, I. L., & McKeown, M. G. (2006). *Improving comprehension with questioning the author: A fresh and enhanced view of a proven approach.* New York, NY: Scholastic.

Beck I. L., McKeown, M. G., & Kucan, L. (2008). *Creating robust vocabulary: Frequently asked questions and extended examples.* New York, NY: Guilford.

Berninger, V. (2007). *Process assessment of the learner* (2nd ed.). *Diagnostic for reading and writing (PAL-II RW) and user guide on CD with guidelines for Tier 1, 2, and 3 assessment-intervention.* San Antonio, TX: Psychological Corporation/Pearson.

Berninger, V. (2008). Defining and differentiating dyslexia, dysgraphia, and language learning disability within a working memory model. In E. Silliman & M. Mody (Eds.), *Language impairment and reading disability—Interactions among brain, behavior, and experience* (pp. 103–134). New York, NY: Guilford.

Berninger, V. (2009). Highlights of programmatic, interdisciplinary research on writing. *Learning Disabilities. Research and Practice, 24,* 68–79.

Berninger, V. (2010 –present). *Differential diagnoses and treatment for specific learning disabilities across development.* American Psychological Association Continuing Education. (Go to link on APA home page for Continuing Education. CE Credit available.).

Berninger, V. (2011a). Evidence-based differential diagnosis and treatment of reading disabilities with and without comorbidities in oral language, writing, and math for prevention, problem-solving consultation, and specialized instruction. In D. Flanagan & V. Alfonso (Eds.), *Essentials of specific learning disability identification* (pp. 203–232). New York, NY: Wiley.

Berninger, V. (2011b). Process assessment of the learner (2nd ed.): PAL II comprehensive assessment for evidence-based, treatment-relevant differential diagnosis of dysgraphia, dyslexia, oral and written language learning disability (OWL LD), and dyscalculia. In N. Mather & L. Fuchs (Eds.), *Comprehensive evaluations from experts in psychology and special education* (pp. 345–355). New York: Wiley.

Berninger, V. (2012, May-June). Strengthening the mind's eye: The case for continued handwriting instruction in the 21st century (pp. 28–31). *Principal.* National Association of Elementary School Principals. Retrieved from www.naesp.org

Berninger, V., & Abbott, D. (2010). Listening comprehension, oral expression, reading comprehension and written expression: Related yet unique language systems in grades 1, 3, 5, and 7. *Journal of Educational Psychology, 102,* 635–651.

Berninger, V., Abbott, R., Thomson, J., Wagner, R., Swanson, H. L., Wijsman, E., & Raskind, W. (2006). Modeling developmental phonological core deficits within a working-memory architecture in children and adults with developmental dyslexia. *Scientific Studies in Reading, 10,* 165–198.

Berninger, V., & Dunn, M. (2012). Brain and behavioral response to intervention for specific reading, writing, and math disabilities: What works for whom? In B. Wong & D. Butler (Eds.), *Learning about LD* (4th ed., pp. 59–89). San Diego, CA: Academic Press.

Berninger, V., & Miller, B. (2011). Adolescent specific learning disabilities (SLDs). In B. Brown & M. Prinstein (Eds.), *Encyclopedia of adolescence* (Vol. 3, Ch. 115, pp. 21–29). San Diego, CA: Academic Press.

Berninger, V., & O'Malley-May, M. (2011). Evidence-based diagnosis and treatment for specific learning disabilities involving impairments in written and/or oral language. *Journal of Learning Disabilities, 44,* 167–183.

Berninger, V., Raskind, W., Richards, T., Abbott, R., & Stock, P. (2008). A multi-disciplinary approach to understanding developmental dyslexia within working-memory architecture: Genotypes, phenotypes, brain, and instruction. *Developmental Neuropsychology, 33,* 707–744.

Berninger, V., & Richards, T. (2010). Inter-relationships among behavioral markers, genes, brain, and treatment in dyslexia and dysgraphia. *Future Neurology, 5,* 597–617. doi: 10.2217/fnl.10.22

Berninger, V., & Wolf, B. (2009a). *Teaching students with dyslexia and dysgraphia: Lessons from teaching and science.* Baltimore, MD: Brookes. Reviewed in NASP *Communiqué, 39*(83), November 2010, by Pam Abrams.

Berninger, V., & Wolf, B. (2009b). *Helping students with dyslexia and dysgraphia make connections: Differentiated instruction lesson plans in reading and writing.* Baltimore, MD: Brookes. [Spiral book with teaching plans from University of Washington Research Program].

Bishop, D. V. M., & Snowling, M. J. (2004). Developmental dyslexia and specific language impairment: Same or different? *Psychological Bulletin, 130,* 858–886.

Byrne, B., Coventry, W., Olson, R., Samuelsson, S., Corley, R., Willcutt, E. G., Wadsworth, S., & DeFries, J. C. (2009). Genetic and environmental influences on aspects of literacy and language in early childhood: Continuity and change from preschool to Grade 2. *Journal of Neurolinguistics, 22,* 219–236.

Cain, K., & Oakhill, J. (2007). *Children's comprehension problems in oral and written language. A cognitive perspective.* New York, NY: Guilford.

Carrow-Woolfolk, E. (2011), *Comprehensive Assessment of Spoken Language (CASL)—Second Edition.* Torrance, CA: Western Psychological Services.

Cassiday, L. (2009). *Mapping the epigenome: New tools chart chemical modifications of DNA and its packaging proteins,* pp. 11–16. Retrieved September 14, 2009, from www.gen.on-line.org

Catts, H. W., Hogan, T. P., & Adlof, S. M. (2005). Developmental changes in reading and reading disabilities. In H. W. Catts & A. G. Kamhi (Eds.), *The connections between language and reading disabilities* (pp. 25–40). Mahwah, NJ: Lawrence Erlbaum.

Catts, H. W., & Kamhi, A. G. (2005). *The connections between language and reading disabilities.* Mahwah, NJ: Erlbaum.

Connelly, V., Dockrell, J., & Barnett, A. (2012). Children challenged by writing due to language and motor difficulties. In V. W. Berninger (Ed.), *Past, present, and future contributions of cognitive writing research to cognitive psychology* (pp. 217–245). New York, NY: Psychology Press.

Denton, C., Vaughn, S., Wexler, J., Bryan, D., & Reed, D. (2012). *Effective instruction for middle school students with reading difficulties: The reading teacher's sourcebook.* Baltimore, MD: Brookes.

Fayol, M., Alamargot, D., & Berninger, V. (Eds.). (2012). *Translation of thought to written text while composing: Advancing theory, knowledge, methods, and applications.* New York, NY: Psychology Press/Taylor Francis Group.

Fletcher, J., Barth, A., & Stuebing, K. (2009). A response to intervention (RTI) approach. In D. Flanagan & V. Alfonso (Eds.), *Essentials of specific learning disability identification* (pp. 115–144). New York, NY: Wiley.

Fletcher, J., Stuebing, K., Barth, A., Denton, C., Cirino, P., Francis, D., & Vaughn, S. (2011). Cognitive correlates of inadequate response to reading intervention. *School Psychology Review, 40,* 3–22.

Goldblatt, J. (2011). *Oral and Written Language Scales (OWLS)—Second Edition.* Los Angeles, CA: Western Psychological Services.

Jarvis, S., Bestgen, Y., Crossley, S. A., Granger, S., Paquot, M., Thewissen, J., & McNamara, D. S. (2012). The comparative and combined contributions of n-grams, Coh-Metrix indices and error types in the L1 classification of learner texts. In S. Jarvis & S. A. Crossley (Eds.), *Approaching language transfer through text classification: Explorations in the detection-based approach.* (pp. 154–177). Bristol, UK: Multilingual Matters.

Kaufman, A., & Kaufman, N. (2004). *Kaufman Test of Educational Achievement—Second Edition (KTEA)* San Antonio, TX: Pearson.

Kovelman, J., Baker, S., & Petitto, L. (2008). Age of first bilingual exposure as a new window into bilingual reading development. *Bilingualism: Language and Cognition, 11,* 203–223.

Kratochwill, T., Hitchcock, J., Horner, R., Levin, J., Odom, S., Rindskopf, D. M., & Shadish, W. (2009). *Single-case intervention research design standards.* Findings of the National Singe-Case Design Panel based on the What Works Clearinghouse. Retrieved from http://ies.ed.gov/ncee/wwc/pdf/wwc_scd.pdf

Ladson-Billings, G. (2006). 2006 presidential address: From the achievement gap to the education debt: Understanding achievement in U. S. schools. *Educational Researcher, 35,* 3–12.

Liberman, A. (1999). The reading researcher and the reading teacher need the right theory of speech. *Scientific Studies of Reading, 3,* 95–111.

Liberman, L., Shankweiler, D., Fischer, F., & Carter, B. (1974). Explicit syllable and phoneme segmentation in the young child. *Journal of Experimental Child Psychology, 18*, 201–212.

Lyytinen, H., Aro, M., Elklund, K., Erskine, J., Guttorm, T., Laakso, M. L., . . . Torppa, M. (2004). The development of children at familial risk for dyslexia: Birth to early school age. *Annals of Dyslexia, 54*, 184–220.

McNamara, D.S., & CSEP Lab. (2005). *Coh-Metrix: Automated cohesion and coherence scores to predict text readability and facilitate comprehension.* Annual project report submitted to the Institute of Education Sciences (IES).

McNamara, D.S., & CSEP Lab. (2010). W-Pal: Writing Pal. Annual project report submitted to the Institute of Education Sciences (IES).

McNamara, D. S., & Graesser, A. C. (2012). Coh-Metrix: An automated tool for theoretical and applied natural language processing. In P.M. McCarthy & C. Boonthum-Denecke (Eds.), *Applied natural language processing and content analysis: Identification, investigation, and resolution* (pp. 188–205). Hershey, PA: IGI Global.

McNamara, D. S., Graesser, A. C., Cai, Z., & Kulikowich, J. M. (2011). Coh-Metrix easability components: Aligning text difficulty with theories of text comprehension. *Proceedings of the American Educational Research Association (AERA).*

Nation, K., & Snowling, M. J. (2004). Beyond phonological skills: Broader language skills contribute to the development of reading. *Journal of Research in Reading, 27*(4), 342–356.

Nelson, N., Bahr, C., & Van Meter, A. (2004). *The Writing Lab approach to language instruction and intervention.* Baltimore, MD: Brookes.

Nelson, N. W., Anderson, M. A., & Applegate, E. B. (2011, June). *Evidence for differential diagnosis of spoken and written language disorders based on a new Test of Integrated Language and Literacy Skills (TILLS).* Poster presented at the annual meeting of the International Academy for Research in Learning Disabilities, Padua, Italy.

Nelson, N. W., Helm-Estabrooks, N., Hotz, G., & Plante, E. (2011). *Test of Integrated Language and Literacy Skills* (TILLS; standardization version 2). Baltimore, MD: Brookes.

O'Connor, R., & Vadasy, P. (Eds.). (2011). *Handbook of reading interventions.* New York, NY: Guilford Press.

Olson, R., Byrne, B., & Samuelson, S. (2009). Reconciling strong genetic and strong environmental influences on individual differences and deficits in reading ability. In K. Pugh & P. McCardle (Eds.), *How children learn to read: Current issues and new directions in the integration of cognition neurobiology, and genetics of reading and dyslexia research and practice.* Hillsdale, NJ: Erlbaum/Taylor Francis.

Pennington, B. (2006). From single to multiple deficit models of developmental disorders. *Cognition, 101*, 385–413.

Pennington, B., McGrath, L., Rosenberg, J., Barnard, H., Smith, S., Willicut, E., . . . Olson, R. K. (2008). Gene × environment interactions in reading disability and attention-deficit/ hyperactivity disorder. *Development. Psychology, 45*, 77–89.

Petitto, L. (2009). New discoveries from the bilingual brain and mind across the life span: Implications for education. *Mind, Brain, and Education, 3*, 185–197.

Plomin, R., & Bergeman, C. (1991). The nature or nurture: Genetic influence on "environmental" measure. *Behavior Brain Science, 14*, 373–427.

Plomin, R., DeFries, J., McClearn, G., & McGuffin, P. (2008). *Behavioral genetics* (5th ed.). New York, NY: Worth.

Psychological Corporation. (2005). *Wechsler Individual Achievement Test–Second Edition.* San Antonio, TX: Psychological Corporation.

Pugh, K., & McCardle, P. (Eds.). (2009). *How children learn to read: Current issues and new directions in the integration of cognition neurobiology, and genetics of reading and dyslexia research and practice.* Hillsdale, NJ: Erlbaum/Taylor Francis.

Rice, M., & Warren, S. (2004). *Developmental language disorders: From phenotypes to etiologies.* Mahwah, NJ: Lawrence Erlbaum.

Riddihough, G., & Zahn, L. (2010). What is epigenetics? Introduction to special issue on epigenetics, *Science, 330,* 611.

Scarborough, H. S. (2005). Developmental relationships between language and reading: Reconciling a beautiful hypothesis with some ugly facts. In H. W. Catts & A. G. Kamhi (Eds.), *The connections between language and reading disabilities* (pp. 3–24). Mahwah, NJ: Lawrence Erlbaum.

Seml, E., Wiig, E., & Secord, W. (2004). *Clinical Evaluation of Language Fundamentals, Fourth Edition (CELF 4)* San Antonio, TX: Pearson.

Silliman, E. R., & Berninger, V. W. (2011). Cross-disciplinary dialogue about the nature of oral and written language problems in the context of developmental, academic, and phenotypic profiles. *Topics in Language Disorders, 31,* 6–23.

Silliman, E. R., & Mody, M. (2008). Individual differences in oral language and reading: It's a matter of individual differences. In M. Mody & E. R. Silliman (Eds.), *Brain, behavior, and learning in language and reading disorders* (pp. 349–386). New York, NY: Guilford Press.

Silliman, E. R., & Scott, C. M. (2009). Research-based oral language intervention routes to the academic language of literacy: Finding the right road. In S. Rosenfield & V. W. Berninger (Eds.), *Implementing evidence-based academic interventions in school settings* (pp. 107–145). New York, NY: Oxford University Press.

Slavin, R. (1987). Ability grouping and student achievement in elementary schools: A best-evidence synthesis. *Review of Educational Research, 57,* 293–336.

Snowling, M. J., & Hayiou-Thomas, M. E. (2006). The dyslexia spectrum: Continuities between reading, speech, and language impairments. *Topics in Language Disorders, 26*(2), 110–126.

Steubing, K., Fletcher, J., Marin, L., & Francis, D. (2012). Evaluation of the technical adequacy of three methods for identifying specific learning disabilities based on cognitive discrepancies. *School Psychology Review, 41,* 3–22.

Tomblin, J. B., Zhang, X., Weiss, A., Catts, H., & Ellis Weismer, S. (2004). Dimensions of individual differences in communication skills among primary grade children. In M. L. Rice & S. F. Warren (Eds.), *Developmental language disorders* (pp. 53–76). Mahwah, NJ: Erlbaum.

Troia, G. (Ed.). (2009). *Instruction and assessment for struggling writers. Evidence-based practices* (pp. 15–50). New York, NY: Guilford.

Troia, G. A. (2011). How might pragmatic language skills affect the written expression of students with language learning disabilities? *Topics in Language Disorders, 31*(1), 40–53.

Waesche, J. B., Schatschneider, C., Maner, J. K., Ahmed, Y., & Wagner, R. K. (2011). Examining agreement and longitudinal stability among traditional and RTI-based definitions of reading disability using the affected-status agreement statistic. *Journal of Learning Disabilities, 44,* 296–307.

Wagner, R. K., Torgesen, J. K., & Rashotte, C. A. (1999). *The Comprehensive Test of Phonological processing.* Austin, TX: Pro-Ed.

Washington, J., & Thomas-Tate, S. (2009). How research informs cultural-linguistic differences in the classroom: The bi-dialectical African American child. In S. Rosenfield & V. Berninger (Eds.), *Implementing evidence-based academic interventions in school settings* (pp. 147–163). New York. NY: Oxford University Press.

White, O. (2009). A focus on the individual: Single-subject evaluations of response to intervention. In S. Rosenfield & V. Berninger (Eds.), *Implementing evidence-based academic interventions in school settings* (pp. 531–558). New York, NY: Oxford University Press.

Widiger, T., & Trull, T. (2007). Plate tectonics in the classification of personality disorder: Shifting to a dimensional model. *American Psychologist, 62,* 71–83.

Wise, B., Rogan, L., & Sessions, L. (2009). Training teachers in evidence-based intervention: The story of linguistic remedies. In S. Rosenfield & V. Berninger V. (Eds.), *Handbook on implementing evidence based academic interventions* (pp. 443–447). New York, NY: Oxford University Press.

Woodcock, R., McGrew, K., & Mather, N. (2001). *Woodcock-Johnson Tests of Cognitive Abilities—Third Edition.* (Also, Woodcock Johns Tests of Academic Achievement). Itasca, IL: Riverside.

🐟 TEST YOURSELF 🐟

1. **Which of the following statements is true?**
   a. Language learning difficulty is a single disorder.
   b. Language learning difficulty should be a single category for qualifying students for special education services.
   c. Language learning difficulty can manifest in many ways and effective treatment depends on which aspect(s) of language is(are) impaired.
   d. None of the statements are true.
   e. All of the statement are true.

2. **Which skills should be assessed in identifying students with language learning difficulties?**
   a. Sensory and motor skills that are used for receiving or producing language, respectively
   b. Level of language impaired in a specific language system (by ear, by mouth, by eye, or by hand)
   c. Development in each of five domains—cognitive/memory, receptive and expressive language, sensory and motor, attention and executive functions, and social emotional
   d. All of the above

3. **Level of language refers to:**
   a. Size of the unit of language, for example, smaller than a word, word, multi-word within syntax, or multi-syntax
   b. Ears, eyes, mouth, and hand
   c. Both a and b
   d. Neither a nor b

4. **Which of the following statements is *not true*?**
   a. Children who struggle in learning to decode words but have normal speech processing and production are likely to have phonemic awareness problems.

b. Children who struggle in learning to decode words but have normal speech processing and production are likely to have phonetic awareness problems.

c. Children with speech sound disorder are likely to have phonetic problems.

d. Phonotactic knowledge of permissible sound patterns in spoken words contributes to learning both decoding in reading and encoding in spelling.

5. **Which of the following statements is *false*?**

a. Children who are late-talkers are at risk for written language problems during the school years.

b. Some students have difficulty in reading comprehension and written expression even though they have adequate decoding skills.

c. Students throughout schooling benefit from instruction in listening skills, initially to make connections between spoken and written language, and later in learning to take written notes in response to oral lectures.

d. Oral language instruction is not relevant in the school-age years.

6. **The most effective way to teach struggling readers and writers is:**

a. To provide instruction in a pull-out program with other students of varying instructional needs and levels

b. To teach students at their instructional level in reading and/or writing in small groups with peers at comparable instructional levels, either in the same classroom or in "walkabouts" involving one or two grade levels

c. Drill and skill on isolated skills

d. None of the above

7. **A student, who was a late-talker, continues to have listening comprehension, reading comprehension, and written expression problems during the school years. This student may have:**

a. Dysgraphia

b. Dyslexia

c. OWL LD (SLI)

d. Speech-sound disorder

8. **A student has trouble discriminating among words with all the same sounds except one and sometimes has slurred speech, but has normal silent reading comprehension. This student may have:**

a. Dysgraphia

b. Dyslexia

c. OWL LD (SLI)

d. Speech-sound disorder

9. **A student initially struggled to learn to decode unknown words while reading and then had persistent spelling problems, even though the student has normal silent reading comprehension. This student may have:**

a. Dysgraphia

b. Dyslexia

(continued)

(*continued*)

   c. OWL LD (SLI)

   d. Speech-sound disorder

10. **A student has grade-appropriate reading skills but has always struggled in writing letters legibly and automatically. This student may have:**

   a. Dysgraphia

   b. Dyslexia

   c. OWL LD (SLI)

   d. Speech-sound disorder

Answers: 1. c; 2. d; 3. a; 4. b; 5. d; 6. b; 7. c; 8. d; 9. b; 10. a

Part III

INTERVENTIONS FOR UNDERSERVED AND MIS-SERVED POPULATIONS

Nine

INTERVENTIONS FOR ENGLISH LEARNERS WITH LEARNING DIFFICULTIES

Julie Esparza Brown
Samuel O. Ortiz

INTRODUCTION

The growth in English Learner (EL) students in U.S. public schools continues to be unprecedented, with the majority of the change taking place in communities with little or no experience educating children not fluent in English. It is estimated that by 2030, ELs will comprise 40% of the school population (Maxwell & Shah, 2011). As a group, ELs are diverse and represent over 322 languages nationwide (Ballantyne, Sanderman, & Levy, 2008). The largest linguistic subgroup among all ELs (85%) speaks Spanish as their native language. The next most common native languages, in order, are Chinese (includes Mandarin and Cantonese), Vietnamese, Hmong, and Korean (Ballantyne et al., 2008). Due to the linguistic and cultural diversity within their homes, EL students often lack access to Standard English models and thereby face challenges learning in this setting. Consequently, ELs' academic achievement often trails behind children from English-only homes. The growth of ELs nationally and their historic underachievement has created significant interest in strategies and instruction that have demonstrated effectiveness in promoting greater academic success. This chapter provides a discussion of the factors that influence the academic development of ELs and offers guidance on how to deliver instruction and use strategies that promote the academic success of all ELs.

Current Achievement of ELs

Data from the National Assessment of Educational Progress (NAEP [National Center for Education Statistics (2011)]), known as the "Nation's Report Card," reports dismal achievement for ELs. NAEP reading scores for ELs indicated that 69% were below basic level and 31% at basic or above as compared to non-ELs where only 28% scored below basic and 72% at basic or above (National Center for Education Statistics, 2011). The fact that ELs are not meeting proficiency standards and scoring at levels substantially lower than English-only peers, has far-reaching societal consequences in the areas of employment, income, housing, crime rates, health, and other indicators of well-being. Although it is clearly in the nation's best interest to educate *all* students well, most teachers are not prepared to instruct ELs effectively. In 2002, the National Center for Educational Statistics found that among 41% of U.S. teachers with EL students, only 12.5% had received even one day of professional development in the instruction of ELs. To understand the unique learning needs of EL students, educators must be prepared.

A significant and pervasive impact of lack of teacher preparation is the misunder-standing and misdiagnosis of EL students' learning challenges. In a pivotal article, Dunn (1968) first raised the issue of disproportionate representation of minority students in some disability categories over 50 years ago. Disproportionality continues today and occurs when children from a particular group are placed in special education at higher or lower rates than expected based on the group's representation in the general population (Oswald, Coutinho, Best, & Singh, 1999). This phenom-enon is generally observed only in the categories of Specific Learning Disability (SLD), Emotional Disturbance (ED), and Intellectual Disability (ID), which, according to the Data Accountability Center (2010), accounts for 59% of all students in special education programs. These categories are sometimes called the "soft" or "high-incidence" categories because eligibility does not rest on a medical diagnosis, but rather professional judgment by eligibility teams who often have little training on assessing minority and EL students (Rhodes, Ochoa, & Ortiz, 2005). Thus, teams may confuse the academic lags that EL students exhibit when learning a new language, and learning new concepts in the new language, with an intrinsic disorder.

While most of us readily agree that minorities continue to be disproportionately represented in special education programs, where this agreement usually ends is on the question of how we determine who should be eligible for services. Despite the specific legal prohibitions against it, some remain convinced that if special education is the only available support, placement is beneficial. Others main-tain that *misplacement* into special edu-cation programs solely on the basis of perceived academic need in the absence of a disability not only violates

CAUTION

Nationally, ELs are overrepresented in three special education categories: (1) Specific Learning Disability, (2) Emo-tional Disturbance (ED), and (3) Intel-lectual Disability (ID).

the intent of federal special education law regarding educating children in the least restrictive environment and the protection of their civil rights, it also sends a potentially damaging message to the individuals that their difficulties are of their own doing because they are disabled (Klingner & Bianco, 2006). Whereas the intent in misplacing ELs in special education may have a benevolent basis, instruction in special education faces the very same difficulties that exist in general education and is unlikely to meet with any greater success than the failed efforts that prompted the referral in the first place (Rhodes et al., 2005). It is commonly said that there is nothing special about special education and whether an English learner is so identified; linguistically and culturally appropriate interventions will likely not occur in special education, either, if the instruction fails to consider developmental language issues. Indeed, the coupling of a disability with any of the various types of instructional programs commonly used with English learners creates a situation in which the learning needs will become greater and more complicated.

Although there are references throughout this chapter to ELs with disabilities, we wish to note that the instructional strategies, teaching techniques, and interventions discussed here may well be applicable to all ELs, irrespective of whether they have been identified as having a disability. The main difference between intervention efforts for each group is that possession of a disability creates an additional barrier to learning above and beyond that of linguistic comprehension and results in a significantly larger adverse effect on development and academic achievement as compared to those that are due to a linguistic difference alone (Rhodes et al., 2005). Moreover, although the intensity of need is clearly higher for the EL with a disability, its idiosyncratic manifestation with respect to the manner in which it impacts learning will also likely warrant more deliberate consideration of the specific type of instruction or intervention needed since, by definition, general strategies have already proven to be unsuccessful.

To assist educators in providing the most appropriate services to ELs, this chapter uses a three-tiered Response to Intervention (RTI) framework: (1) to outline the critical factors that tend to adversely impact the achievement of ELs; (2) provide examples of research-based instruction and intervention across the tiers; and (3) discuss culturally and linguistically appropriate special education programs and Individualized Education Plan (IEP) development for EL students who have been found eligible for special education through a least discriminatory evaluation process.

RTI and ELs

With the latest reauthorization of the Individuals with Disabilities Education Improvement Act (IDEIA, 2004), a new process was developed for determining

DON'T FORGET

....

At the first sign of difficulties, students can be provided appropriate instructional support rather than waiting for interventions via a lengthy referral process.

eligibility for special education as a student with a Specific Learning Disability (SLD) known as Response to Intervention (RTI). RTI focuses on early prevention of reading and other academic difficulties by providing targeted interventions of increasing intensity across multiple tiers and frequent progress monitoring. Thus, at the first sign of difficulties, students can be provided appropriate instructional support rather than waiting for interventions via a lengthy referral process.

An RTI model for ELs is outlined in Figure 9.1. The base of the triangle in darkest gray represents general education and demonstrates that approximately 80% of students should be meeting grade-level targets. The focus of intervention, then, is on the 20% who are not meeting these targets. Based on universal screening data, the 20% of students who are not meeting grade-level targets receive interventions that are selected to match their area of need (e.g., acquisition of basic reading skills). There are two key areas of clarification for systems in which ELs are served. First, 80% of *subgroups* (e.g., ELs, students receiving Title I free and reduced-cost lunch services) should be meeting targets and 20% of *each subgroup* may need intervention. If, instead, the 20% of struggling students are all ELs, then

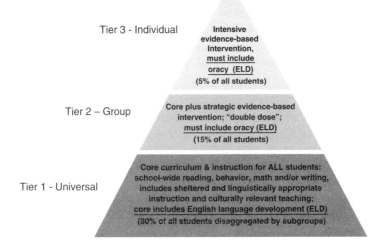

Tier 3 - Individual

Intensive evidence-based Intervention, must include oracy (ELD) (5% of all students)

Tier 2 – Group

Core plus strategic evidence-based intervention; "double dose"; must include oracy (ELD) (15% of all students)

Tier 1 - Universal

Core curriculum & instruction for ALL students: school-wide reading, behavior, math and/or writing, includes sheltered and linguistically appropriate instruction and culturally relevant teaching; core includes English language development (ELD) (80% of all students disaggregated by subgroups)

Figure 9.1. Typical Three-Tiered Response-to-Intervention Framework for English Learners

the focus should be on the core curriculum. Adjustments for ELs' proficiency in the instructional language and cultural differences are required to core instruction so that ELs benefit from instruction. Second, English Language Development (ELD) (also known as English as a Second Language) is *not* an intervention. For ELs, ELD services is part of the core curriculum. The literature with respect to the efficacy of various types of ELD programs implemented within an RTI framework is small but growing and shows promise (Vanderwood & Nam, 2008). However, all instruction and interventions must be tailored so that it is appropriate to each EL's level of proficiency in the instructional language. We discuss this in more detail in the following sections.

Interventions across the tiers differ in their focus and intensity. In Tier 1 (the light-gray section of the triangle), interventions should reinforce the core curriculum for those students who are close to grade level. In Tier 2 (the medium-gray section of the triangle), interventions are generally conceived of as a "double dose," meaning that students continue to receive core instruction in general education but need small-group interventions to reinforce classroom instruction. Tier 3 (the dark-gray section) is generally for students below grade level who need a separate curriculum because they are "severely below grade level" (Brown-Chidsey, Bronaugh, & McGraw, 2009, p. 28), and the most intensive support.

Each level of increasingly intense interventions must consider the language, cultural, and experiential needs of ELs. To do so requires an understanding of their unique characteristics as well as the potential challenges they may face. In what follows, we discuss critical information that should be gathered when an EL student struggles. These factors include first and second language acquisition, background experiences, education, culture, and family context.

Factors That Impact Academic Achievement
First and Second Language Acquisition

Prior to intervening with ELs it is important to understand their ability to use their first and second (or more) languages. As development of one's native language (L1) is a lifelong process, so is the development of the second language (L2). In the United States, ELs by definition come from homes where English is not the native language, and, as such, at some point along their development (usually when starting school) they were introduced to English. Such ELs are often referred to as "circumstantial bilinguals" and form the most common pattern of development in L1 and L2. In some family settings, ELs are exposed to their L1 and English from birth and are known as "simultaneous bilinguals" but this occurs much less frequently in the United States (Reyes, 2006). For families residing in the United

States, the home language will necessarily compete with the dominant language of the culture (i.e., English), which will in most cases be the instructional language upon entering school as well. When there is a significant differential in the status of languages (i.e., the extent to which either one is valued or utilized in society), English learners often abandon their L1 due to socialization pressures stemming from a desire for acceptance and a reluctance to be associated or identified with a lower-status language and culture (Cahnmann, 2003).

By itself, abandonment of L1 in favor of L2 is not an inherently problematic issue as it relates to notions regarding assimilation and is quite consistent with the "melting pot" mentality that has long been the root of an American identity. However, this is not to say that there are no negative effects on other aspects of functioning, including self-identity, when one chooses to use the new language. Because language is an integral part of and the most direct method for transmission of a culture from one generation to the next, it profoundly influences the development of all individuals and the way in which each person ultimately thinks, feels, acts, and believes. Unlike students, parents who have immigrated from other countries are less likely to summarily give up their lifelong cultural beliefs and native language in favor of the dominant ones and are more likely to continue to transmit to their children what they already know and believe in the language they already speak. When the language of instruction is not matched by the primary language spoken in the home, children will develop varying proficiencies in both languages, which may place them academically at risk (Goldenberg, 2008; Thomas & Collier, 2002; Rhodes et al., 2005).

For example, the age of exposure to the L2 appears to affect later proficiency in both L1 and L2. It has been suggested that "children who have significant input in two languages before the age of three seem to experience minimal interference between the languages and that those who are exposed to L1 during infancy and learn an L2 at a later time show greater diversity in rates and stages of acquisition" (Rosa-Lugo, Nutta, & Mihai, 2012, p. 120). Thus, whenever possible, it is beneficial for children to learn two languages early in their development. There is a significant difference, however, between "learning" a second language for the purpose of conversation and learning it to the degree required for academic success (Cummins, 1984). The type of language proficiency required in school continues to advance developmentally across the age and grade spectrum so that after about 5–7 (or more) years of formal education the necessary Cognitive-Academic Language Proficiency begins to emerge (CALP; Cummins, 1984). This level of proficiency is predicated upon a program of instruction that capitalizes on a pattern of linguistic development that occurs, for the most part, from birth. If a student's educational program (which usually begins in kindergarten at age 5) requires the learning of a new language for the purposes of receiving core instruction, the student will be at an artificial developmental language disadvantage as compared to native English speakers and will not develop CALP within the expected time frame and likely encounter significant academic difficulty (Goldenberg, 2008).

Language develops along a continuum beginning with a nonverbal stage and ending in full conversational proficiency as depicted in Rapid Reference 9.1. Typically, educators describe this continuum as occurring across five (or sometimes six depending on the instrument used for evaluation) proficiency levels. Because the labels for each level differ across the country, we identify them here simply as 1 through 5. Many factors, besides a language impairment (e.g., type of instructional program, parents' socioeconomic status, lack of acculturative learning experiences, limited opportunity to hear Standard English), impact second language development (Hammer, Miccio, & Rodriguez, 2004). In general, students progress at a rate of about one level per year but the situation is complicated when two languages are involved and when the instructional language does not match the home language. Kohnert and Pham (2010) summarized the literature on language acquisition to highlight three possibilities related to L1 and L2 development when L1 is not the language of instruction: (1) L1 continues to grow but at a slower pace than L2; (2) L1 plateaus at a lower level than L2; and (3) L1 skills regress while L2 skills increase. These paths, or profiles, should not be misconstrued as language disorders but rather language learning circumstances that create an environment where neither language is likely to reach age- or grade-based expectations of proficiency or development. "Persisting discrepancies in language performance between ELs and their English-only peers reflect fundamental differences in language experiences between these groups" (Kohnert & Pham, 2010, p. 54).

With respect to intervention and the provision of specially designed instruction for ELs with disabilities, the adverse effect on learning that occurs when the instructional program and language cannot be supported in the home must be well understood and acknowledged. No type of intervention or remedial strategy can compensate for learning problems that are the result of an ineffective instructional program as well as a disability. Whereas ELs can be provided with "better" and more appropriate instruction—instruction that will in fact improve academic

DON'T FORGET

It has been suggested that "children who have significant input in two languages before the age of three seem to experience minimal interference between the languages and that those who are exposed to L1 during infancy and learn an L2 at a later time show greater diversity in rates and stages of acquisition" (Rosa-Lugo, et al., 2012, p. 120). Thus, whenever possible, it is beneficial for children to learn two languages early in their development.

Rapid Reference 9.1 Language Proficiency Continuum

Level	English learner characteristics	How ELs gain language?	What ELs understand?	What can ELs do?
1	Can be silent for an initial period Recognizes basic vocabulary and high-frequency words May begin to speak with few words or imitate	Multiple repetitions of language Simple sentences Practice with partners Use visuals and realia Model, model, model Check for understanding Build on cultural and linguistic history	Instructions such as: Listen, Line up, Point to, List, Say, Repeat, Color, Tell, Touch, Circle, Draw, Match, Label	Use gestures Use other native speakers Use high-frequency phrases Use common nouns Communicate basic needs Use survival language (i.e., words and phrases needed for basic daily tasks and routines, e.g. *bathroom*, *no*, *yes*)
2	Understands phrases and short sentences Begins to use general vocabulary and everyday expressions Grammatical forms may include present, present progress, and imperative	Multiple repetitions of language Visual supports for vocabulary Pre-teach content vocabulary Link to prior knowledge	Present and past tense School-related topics Comparatives/superlatives Routine questions Imperative tense Simple sequence words	Routine expressions Simple phrases Subject–verb agreement Ask for help
3	Increased comprehension in context May sound proficient but has social, not academic, language Inconsistent use of standard grammatical structures	Multiple repetitions of language Use synonyms and antonyms Use word banks Demonstrate simple sentences Link to prior knowledge	Past progressive tense Contractions Auxiliary verbs/verb phrases Basic idioms General meaning Relationship between words	Formulate questions Compound sentences Use precise adjectives Use synonyms Expanded responses
4	Very good comprehension More complex speech and with fewer errors	Multiple repetitions of language	Present/perfect continuous General and implied meaning Varied sentences	Range of purposes Increased cultural competence (USA)

Engages in conversation on a variety of topics and skills Can manipulate language to represent his or her thinking but may have difficulty with abstract academic concepts Continues to need academic language development	Authentic practice opportunities to develop fluency and automaticity in communication Explicit instruction in the use of language Specific feedback Continued vocabulary development in all content areas	Figurative language Connecting ideas	Standard grammar Solicit information
5 Communicates effectively on a wide range of topics Participates fully in all content areas at grade level but may still require curricular adjustments Comprehends concrete and abstract concepts Produces extended interactions to a variety of audiences	May not be fully English proficient in all domains (i.e., reading, writing, speaking, listening) Has mastered formal and informal language conventions Multiple opportunities to practice complex grammatical forms Meaningful opportunities to engage in conversations Explicit instruction in the smaller details of English usage Focus on gaps or areas still needing instruction in English Focus on comprehension instruction in all language domains	Analyze, Defend, Debate, Predict, Evaluate, Justify, Hypothesize and Synthesize, Restate, Critique	May not yet be fully proficient across all domains Comprehends concrete and abstract topics Communicates effectively on a wide range of topics and purposes Produces extended interactions to a variety of audiences Participates fully in all content areas at grade level but may still require curricular modifications Increasing understanding of meaning, including figurative language Read grade-level text with academic language support Support their own point of view Use humor in native-like way

Source: Turner & Brown (2012).

achievement and learning—it cannot be expected to resolve issues that are either rooted in a true disability or more likely the direct result of educational programming (e.g., non-content-based ESL pull-out only) that has been demonstrated to have detrimental effects (Thomas & Collier, 1997, 2002). Whenever ELs are placed in circumstances that do not take advantage of their development in L1 (i.e., when instruction is provided only in L2), they will invariably lag behind their monolingual English-speaking peers throughout their school careers (Goldenberg, 2008; Thomas & Collier, 1997, 2002). Rather than fostering academic progress, the failure to utilize a student's early language development and to provide instruction in that language has the opposite effect because it places the average student at a disadvantage where he or she simply cannot catch up (Ortiz, 2012; Rhodes et al., 2005). As noted by Goldenberg (2008), "teaching students to read in their first language promotes higher levels of reading achievement in English" (p. 14). Such a statement appears rather counterintuitive on the surface, but reinforces the notion that there is no substitute for building on the language development that occurs in the home prior to when a student enters school.

Language Registers

In an effort to explain the relationship between the first and second language acquisition processes and their connection to academic achievement, Cummins (1984) outlined a "developmental interdependence" hypothesis that utilized a more nuanced definition of language proficiency. Rather than consider language proficiency as a continuum related to oral skills (i.e., speaking and listening), Cummins instead emphasized the functional aspect of language relative to educational demands. To this end he proposed two registers of language: a social register, commonly known as Basic Interpersonal Communication Skills (BICS); and a formal register, known as Cognitive Academic Language Proficiency (CALP; Cummins, 1984; 2000). Together, these registers make up a child's language reservoir that not only includes the full extent of all the languages they have learned but also the degree of language skill that he or she brings to the classroom to meet curricular demands.

Educators with limited experience with EL students often confuse the two language registers when trying to identify the root of the problem when an EL student struggles academically. Because it is the more obvious aspect of language (i.e., used for functional communication), BICS is often ascribed much more significance relative to educational attainment than it merits. Consider that BICS is often referred to as *playground language*, and develops readily over the course of one to three years. Under normal circumstances, even infants will have developed initial levels of BICS by age 3 and students about to enter kindergarten typically have no difficulty communicating with their teachers, assuming the teacher and student speak the same language. In contrast, CALP is more about *thinking* in a language rather than simply speaking it. Moreover, CALP is dependent on the provision of formal academic instruction and does not develop in the absence of education or in typical social situations. As such, it can take between 5 and 7 years or more for CALP to begin to emerge, depending on the language of instruction (Thomas & Collier, 2002). For all students, the emergence and continued development of CALP is necessary for access to grade-level texts and tests that continue to increase in both language and content demands in each successive grade. The value of understanding these two language registers lies in recognizing that although learning to speak and understand the language of instruction is an important foundational skill, it will not be sufficient to promote academic success beyond elementary school. If ELs are to reach levels of academic attainment that are comparable to their English-speaking peers, they will need to develop higher levels of proficiency in the language of instruction (i.e., English, typically). Effective intervention for ELs will thus require an assessment of both language registers to determine the degree and nature of remediation that will be necessary to meet any particular academic standard. See Rapid Reference 9.2 for a definition of language registers.

Generational Language Patterns

Valdes and Figueroa (1992) identified generational language patterns in ELs. First-generation (foreign-born) individuals have usually had the opportunity to be instructed and socialized in just one language—the language of their home country. In cases where there has been no interruption in language development or education, learning a second language (e.g., English) can occur readily since it will build upon a solid L1 foundation. However, because the process of learning a second language will have occurred after the natural physiologically based "critical"

≣ Rapid Reference 9.2   Language Registers

A student's total language reservoir may be defined as comprising two language registers:

1. The *social register*, or Basic Interpersonal Communication Skills (BICS), also called "playground language," which typically begins to emerge in 1 to 3 years
2. The *formal register*, or Cognitive Academic Language Proficiency (CALP), which begins to emerge after 5 to 7 years or more of formal instruction, depending on the language of instruction

period, the individual may exhibit an accent in pronunciation but will have no other limitations in its actual use and application. The second-generation individuals, who are the first to be born in the United States, tend to struggle more than the first generation if they are not accorded the opportunity to build a solid L1 language foundation as a part of their educational experiences and either before English is introduced or learned concurrently. Second-generation EL students are often the most at-risk academically as compared to prior and later generations (Rhodes et al., 2005). By the third generation, students may not have been taught and may not speak the native/heritage language much or at all, although there may be some retention of receptive abilities. These students are essentially native English speakers, are treated as such in the educational system, and yet may still have substantial experience with the heritage language and are less likely to hear the type of English at home that could support later schooling (i.e., advanced vocabulary, complex grammar, idiomatic expressions).

INSTRUCTIONAL INTERVENTIONS FOR ELs

The evidence on effective instruction and intervention for ELs builds on decades of work examining first and second language acquisition, achievement outcomes of bilingual program models, and the more recent evidence on the main pillars of reading (Artiles & Ortiz, 2002; August & Shanahan, 2006; Klingner, Artiles, & Barrera, 2006; Orosco & Klingner, 2010). Although this base certainly provides guidance to practitioners, it is in no way as robust as the research on English-only learners. Thus, the field must continue to build the empirical evidence on effective instruction for ELs. In addition, as noted previously, effective interventions and instructional strategies for ELs (with and without disabilities) continues to run up against the learning difficulties that are created as a function of instruction in English rather than in the native language. Consequently, even those interventions and strategies that have been empirically validated are not likely to result in dramatic gains or be successful enough to overcome other circumstantial obstacles to learning.

Language Instruction

Kohnert (2009) outlined a framework that identifies three general factors that interact to affect general language proficiency and first and second language acquisition. They are *means, opportunities*, and *motivation* (MOM). The notion of means examines the student's neurobiology to determine if their system is intact and they are able to learn language. If there is a disorder, language acquisition may be challenging. Along with means, the opportunity to learn language through multiple sources and contexts is imperative to successful development. And last, the student's own motivation to learn plays a key role in the process. Considerations of these factors can

CAUTION

"Low proficiency in only one language because of reduced opportunities or motivation is sometimes a natural consequence of evolving circumstances" (Kohnert & Pham, 2010, p. 53).

help identify the intensity of language instruction and support an EL may require. According to the authors, "When one or more aspects of MOM are weak, either language—or both—may be affected. Reduced proficiency in both languages because of developmental delays, sensory deficits, or injury is not typical and comes under the purview of special education. Low proficiency in only one language because of reduced opportunities or motivation is sometimes a natural consequence of evolving circumstances" (Kohnert & Pham, 2010, p. 53).

Every teacher who instructs ELs should know their students' current English language proficiency and, if possible, in L1 as well. This information is generally readily available in the various files collected by a school's English as a Second Language (ESL/ESOL) department, and is critical in guiding teachers in appropriately identifying the level of language the student can use and the type of language instruction necessary in the delivery of general instruction and intervention (see Table 1). In addition to language proficiency, a child's general developmental experiences, particularly those that are closely related to language (e.g., culture-specific content), must be considered—a student's total educational and experiential repertoire will have important ramifications for school-based learning.

Educational Experiences

Children's educational experiences can be as diverse as their own cultural and linguistic backgrounds. Consequently, educators may need to examine the extent of a student's formal educational experiences, if any, in their native country and in the United States. For example, children who come from a rural area in their native country may have a vastly different educational background than those who hail from urban settings. A good source of this information for educators may be found in the student's cumulative file where a list of the grades completed within and perhaps outside of the United States are noted. Even in cases where formal schooling experiences are listed, educators should not assume comparability to U.S. educational standards and will need to consider the quality and consistency of any prior education on an individual basis. In another scenario, if students were in bilingual programs in the United States, they may have received ESL support only, differing percentages of native language instruction, or a two-way dual-language program (Thomas & Collier, 2002). This information helps educators evaluate the EL students' current skills relative to their opportunity to learn and helps to sort out whether students' struggles are more likely to be rooted in intrinsic learning disorders or whether the student simply has not been taught the skills or given sufficient opportunity to acquire them. In addition to the child's literacy, their family's literacy can also be a support or a challenging factor for the student.

Family Context

While it is commonly understood that the formal educational experiences of parents and family have direct consequences on a child's academic achievement, it is less frequently acknowledged that EL students' experiential backgrounds are often rich with social language, cultural ties to their heritage, knowledge of the workings of the communities they come from, and strong oral traditions (Moll, Amanti, Neff, & Gonzalez, 1992). These experiences should be viewed as strengths or "funds of knowledge" (Moll et al., 1992). For far too long, educators have viewed diverse learners' backgrounds as deficits because their experiences usually differ from middle-class, mainstream American ones. Yet, learning different ways of viewing the world benefits all, particularly as the United States and its economic livelihood becomes increasingly more dependent on a global market. It is true, unfortunately, that these differing experiences may do little to prepare EL students for the expectations and demands of American classrooms. To bridge the differences, educators should strive to develop reciprocal relationships with families where parents can be taught how they can support their children's education and schools can embrace new cultures and new ways of viewing the world. Even when families have limited formal literacy, there are many ways schools and families can form reciprocal relationships so that we can build on the literacy practices found in the home (Gonzalez, Moll, & Amanti, 2005; Moll et al., 1992).

In sum, ELs enter school with differing levels of language proficiency in two or more languages, varying degrees of formal education, developmental experiences rooted in a wide range of cultures, and often limited experience with Standard English language and specific aspects of U.S. culture. Educators must delve into students' experiences and their developmental backgrounds to determine if the academic and language skills they demonstrate

DON'T FORGET

Even when families have limited formal literacy, there are many ways schools and families can form reciprocal relationships so that we can build on the literacy practices found in the home.

make sense within the context of their current educational placement and what the causes of limited academic skill development or knowledge acquisition might be. Once background information is gathered, appropriate support can be provided within a variety of intervention frameworks, including RTI, any of which will aid school-based intervention teams in making appropriate educational and remediation decisions, including whether students should be referred for special education evaluation. The following section focuses on appropriate literacy instruction and interventions for ELs based on what is known about their backgrounds.

Literacy Instruction
Explicit and Direct Instruction

The remainder of this chapter discusses explicit instruction of strategic skills and concepts. Use of explicit instruction, in particular, is often criticized for a perceived focus on rote learning and lack of connection to students' backgrounds. However, this approach is fundamental to quality instruction for ELs and was identified in an Institute of Education Sciences (IES) report as one of the five evidence-based recommendations to improve literacy levels for all students (Kamil et al., 2008). The three main components of *direct instruction* (Watkins & Slocum, 2008) are: (1) The program is designed so that main concepts are taught through using clear language, (2) instructional grouping, lesson sequence, and progress monitoring are organized so that each student receives appropriately intense instruction, and (3) students are actively engaged through frequent student–teacher interaction and work toward skill mastery. The point must be made that to be an independent reader and to engage fully in a curriculum that encourages higher-order thinking often depends on students' mastering basic skills. Although sometimes criticized, the structured nature of a direct instruction approach is appropriate for short, efficient skills development and would not occur during an entire literacy block. As with all instruction, students' language proficiency and background must be considered. A framework for enhancing lessons taught through a direct instruction approach will be presented later in this chapter. See Rapid Reference 9.3 for three main components of direct instruction.

The Big-Five Reading Pillars and ELs

In 2006, the National Literacy Panel on Language–Minority Children and Youth (August & Shanahan, 2006) found that while ELs need to learn the same five critical areas of reading as English-only students, instruction needs to be adjusted to ELs'

Rapid Reference 9.3 Three Main Components of Direct Instruction

The three main components of *direct instruction* (Watkins & Slocum, 2008) are:

1. The program is designed so that main concepts are taught through using clear language.
2. Instructional grouping, lesson sequence, and progress monitoring are organized so that each student receives appropriately intense instruction.
3. Students are actively engaged through frequent student–teacher interaction and work toward skill mastery.

---

proficiency level in the instructional language and their cultural knowledge. Specifically, the five critical components of reading that all students must learn are: (1) phonemic awareness, (2) phonics, (3) fluency, (4) vocabulary, and (5) comprehension. As noted, each skill must be tailored to the unique needs of ELs and the reader is referred to Rapid Reference 9.4 for a list of the recommended adjustments for teaching the five areas of reading to ELs. Two of these skills, *phonemic awareness* and *phonics*, together form an overarching area—the *alphabetic principle*. The alphabetic principle is the understanding that words are composed of letters and that there is a relationship between printed letters and spoken words. This principle is the foundation of any alphabet-based writing system. This principle is most easily applied to languages where there is a consistent one-to-one correspondence between a letter and sound. For example, Estonian, Finnish, Italian, Spanish, Polish, Hungarian, and Turkish are considered transparent languages because each letter makes only one sound as opposed to English (an opaque language) where consonant letters (e.g., *c*) are frequently pronounced in different ways (e.g., *c* as in "car" vs. *c* as in "cease") and there are numerous inconsistencies and a significant lack of correspondence between the sounds and their letter symbols (Geva, 2006). Direct instruction in phonemic awareness and phonics helps students learn the alphabetic principle. With this in

DON'T FORGET

ELs must be taught the same five critical areas of reading as English-only students, namely: (1) phonemic awareness, (2) phonics, (3) fluency, (4) vocabulary, and (5) comprehension.

DON'T FORGET

The alphabetic principle is the understanding that words are composed of letters and that there is a relationship between printed letters and spoken words.

≡ Rapid Reference 9.4 Tailoring Essential Reading Components for ELs

- Emphasize English-language phonemes that may not be available in the home language.
- Whenever possible, build on students' first language strengths.
- Teach word meanings clearly through a variety of techniques.
- Identify and clarify confusing reading passages.
- Provide many opportunities for students to practice oral language within the context of the curriculum.
- Provide ample practice reading words, sentences, and whole text.

mind, the five essential building blocks of reading are presented next, including discussion regarding the specific adjustments needed for EL students.

Phonemic Awareness

The ability to manipulate phonemes within words, known as *phonemic awareness* (PA), is one of the best predictors of future reading success (Adam, 1990; Griffith & Olson, 1992; Linan-Thompson & Vaughn, 2007; National Reading Panel, 2000; Shaywitz, 2003; Stanovich, 1990). However, Adam (1990) asserts that without direct instructional support, PA eludes about 25% of middle-class first-graders and a larger proportion of students from less language-rich backgrounds, such as ELs. Although precise pronunciation of phonemes is dependent on the age at which they are first heard, acquisition of the sounds of a language is not a function of age. For all students, explicit instruction in PA is critical and even students at the beginning stages of language acquisition can successfully acquire PA skills without much difficulty. Thus, English proficiency is not a necessary precursor to phonemic awareness instruction (Durgunoglu, Nagy, & Hancin-Bhatt, 1999; Geva, 2006), although the vocabulary used in PA activities must also be expressly taught to students.

CAUTION

Without direct instructional support, PA eludes about 25% of middle-class first-graders and a larger proportion of students from less language-rich backgrounds, such as ELs.

DON'T FORGET

When teaching phonemic awareness to ELs, be sure to use words that are familiar to them (or use pre-teaching to ensure familiarity prior to the lesson).

DON'T FORGET
....
Research is clear that PA is a transferable skill, meaning that when it is learned in L1, it can be used to learn to read in English or another language.

Research has also demonstrated that PA is a transferable skill, meaning that even when it is learned and developed within the context of L1, it can still be used to learn to read in English or another language (Durgunoglu, 2002). Skills are most readily transferable, of course, in languages that are similar and that share an alphabet, such as between Spanish and English. According to Peregoy and Boyle (2000), "at a more specific level, transfer of literacy ability from one language to another depends on the similarities and differences between their writing systems, including the unit of speech symbolized by each character" (p. 241).

For ELs, PA activities in English can be complicated by having to recognize sounds in English that do not exist in their L1. Instructionally, it is important for teachers to determine informally some of the similarities and differences between English and the students' native language to ensure that more instruction is placed on those sounds the student is unlikely to hear at home or with which he or she may have limited experience and opportunity to learn. For an example, the reader is referred to Rapid Reference 9.5 for a list of the English-language sounds that do not exist in Spanish. Teachers are strongly encouraged to develop a similar chart for the other native languages of their students, and such information may be found readily through a simple Web search. As is true with all aspects of reading instruction, the vocabulary and concepts of the curriculum must also make sense and be comprehensible to EL students. For example, nursery rhymes are commonly used to teach PA. Consider the following rhyme:

A cat came fiddling out of a barn,

With a pair of bagpipes under her arm.

She could sing nothing but fiddle-dee-dee,

The mouse has married the bumblebee.

Pipe, cat; dance, mouse;

We'll have a wedding at our good house.

Although nursery rhymes are meant to capture children's interest and imagination, nursery rhymes that have little cultural relevance to the student and that contain new and infrequent vocabulary (e.g., bagpipes) and concepts (e.g., the meaning of "fiddle-dee-dee") will likely prove less useful than rhymes that can be pantomimed and that use familiar vocabulary and common cultural concepts. For example, consider this well-known rhyme:

Humpty Dumpty sat on a wall,

Humpty Dumpty had a great fall.

All the king's horses and all the king's men

Couldn't put Humpty together again.

Apart from the potential debate regarding the abstract meaning to the rhyme, it can be taken literally and understood as such by ELs given the more common vocabulary and concrete concepts. Thus, "for ELs, as with all students, it is important that instruction have meaning, so that the words and sounds students are manipulating are familiar. It is therefore necessary for ELs to have knowledge of the English vocabulary within which they are to understand phonemes" (Antunez, 2002, p. 5).

≡ Rapid Reference 9.5 English Sounds That Do Not Exist in Spanish

Initial consonants of *g* as in "geode," *h* as in "happy," *j* as in "jump," *r* (if untrilled), and *v* (which is not distinguished from *b*)

Digraphs of *ch* as in "character," *dg* as in "fudge," *sh* as in "wash," *th* as in "the" or "fifth," and *wh* as in "who, what, when"

Letter combinations of -*ck*, -*ght*, -*nd*, -*ng*, -*nt*, *sc*-, *sch*-, *scr*-, *sk*-, *sl*-, *sm*-, *sp*-, *spl*-, *spr*-, *sq*-, *st*-, *str*-, *sw*-, -*tch*, *thr*-, *tw*-

Some long and some short vowel sounds: /a/ as in "ace" or "apple," /e/ as in "eek" or "early," /i/ as in "ice" and "in," /o/ as in "ok" and "on," /u/ as in "use" or "up"

Diphthongs: *au* as in "audio," *aw* as in "paw," *ew* as in "sew," *oi* as in "point," *ou* as in "you," *ow* as in "owl," *oy* as in "boy," *ue* as in "sue"

R-controlled vowels: /ar/ as in "park," /er/ as in "perk," /ir/ as in "quirk," /or/ as in "cork," /ur/ as in "turk"

Schwa (the unstressed central vowel) as in "again" or as beginning/ending sound in "around" or "camera," *e* as in "stolen" or as second *e* in "obedience," *o* as in "dragon," and *u* as in "suspect"

Silent letters: *gn*- as in "gnu," *kn*- as in "know," -*mb* as in "dumb," *wr*- as in "write"

Phonics

While phonemic awareness instruction helps children learn the sounds of a language and the sounds specific letters make, phonics instruction teaches them to apply this knowledge to sound out words as a beginning strategy for learning to read. Whereas PA is readily acquired, proficiency in phonics is more difficult for ELs, and yet remains essential to becoming a successful reader. Part of the reason for this limitation is that phonics must rely on developed vocabulary—that is, the student identifies and recognizes words that have been sounded out only to the extent that the word itself resides in the student's own vocabulary. Since ELs have typically had less opportunity for learning English, their English vocabularies are correspondingly smaller, thereby limiting the words available to them for decoding via a phonics approach (Bialystok, 2001). For this reason, "it generally is much more difficult for ELs to learn phonics in English when they have not already acquired this understanding in their first language. The process becomes much more abstract and less meaningful" (Hoover, Klingner, Baca, & Patton, 2008, p. 192). Therefore, a phonics program for ELs should include the following components: (a) follow a defined sequence; (b) explicitly teach skills; (c) teach sets of letter-sounds relationships; (d) teach linguistic patterns; (e) bring meaning to the vocabulary words used; (f) include books and stories with decodable text; and (g) provide opportunities for students to write their own stories using the letter-sound relationships they are learning (see Rapid Reference 9.6 for phonics programs for ELs).

One useful strategy to promote transfer of knowledge across two languages, when such knowledge is available, is to use a bilingual alphabet chart (Herrera, Perez, & Escamilla, 2010, p. 70). The chart lists the phonemes and corresponding letters that are the same in English and Spanish (or other language). Families could be asked to provide this information in their native language, although some families may need support from their community or teachers to complete this project. However, such a project helps create positive links between home and school and affirms children's backgrounds. As an extension, teachers could

≡ Rapid Reference 9.6 Phonics Programs for ELs

A phonics program for ELs should include the following components: (a) follow a defined sequence; (b) explicitly teach skills; (c) teach sets of letter-sounds relationships; (d) teach linguistic patterns; (e) bring meaning to the vocabulary words used; (f) include books and stories with decodable text; and (g) provide opportunities for students to write their own stories using the letter-sound relationships they are learning.

identify *cognates*, or words that sound similar in both languages and have the same meaning (e.g., "color" or "animal").

Fluency

Fluency is defined as reading quickly, accurately, and with expression. Fluency grows as students develop knowledge of phonics, expand their vocabulary, increase their ability to comprehend written text, and move toward development of orthographic processing skills (Richards & Leafstedt, 2010). Fluency represents the bridge between word recognition and facile comprehension. Research regarding the development of reading fluency appears to indicate that the most common fluency intervention strategies are repeated readings, passage preview, and phrase-drill error correction; however, the strongest reading gains occur when the intervention strategies are combined (Chard, Vaughn, & Tyler, 2002; Denton, Anthony, Parker, & Hasbrouck, 2004; Therrien, 2004). These strategies are described in the following.

> **DON'T FORGET**
> ....
> Fluency represents the bridge between word recognition and comprehension.

> **DON'T FORGET**
> ....
> Research regarding the development of reading fluency appears to indicate that the most common fluency intervention strategies are repeated readings, passage preview, and phrase-drill error correction; however, the strongest reading gains occurred when the intervention strategies were combined.

To apply a *repeated readings* strategy, choose an appropriate text and discuss such reading behaviors as phrasing, rate, and prosody. Have students practice reading the text several times until they can read it fluently. Although there is some obvious concern about the rote methodology, research suggests that "although the effect of text-reading fluency on comprehension was rather small, it was significant, suggesting that there is something special about rapid, automatic fluent reading of words in connected text that is not explained by other well-known predictors of reading comprehension" (Crosson & Lesaux, 2010, p. 489). Reading-connected discourse thus appears to produce better effects than word-level reading; however, it may be helpful to work at the word level as well. For example, EL students benefit from learning high-frequency words that can be taught individually and development of a large sight-word vocabulary will facilitate fluency.

Implementing a *passage preview* approach can be conducted with an individual student or via small group. The teacher and student together view one copy of a text or each can have their own text. The teacher reads a short passage of text for about a minute or two and asks the student to follow along. When finished, the student is asked to read the same passage out loud. In this strategy, students are told that they will be helped if they encounter an unknown word. The process is repeated to finish the selected passage or story.

In the *phrase-drill error correction* approach (Joseph, 2008), students are given a passage to read orally. The teacher makes note of any words that were read incorrectly. Feedback is then provided on the miscues and the teacher models the correct reading of the word. Students reread the *phrase* that contains the miscue three times. Finally, students read the entire passage once again.

As with any aspect of educational achievement, the language of instruction has an important impact relative to the native or heritage language. For example, oral reading fluency interventions in L1 were found to be highly predictive of reading fluency skills in English for Spanish speakers (Ramirez, 2001) and for native English speakers who were learning to read in Hebrew (Geva, Wade-Wooley, & Shany, 1997) and reinforces the significant benefits of native language instruction. Thus, for EL students with the most intensive needs, providing fluency interventions in their L1 and using research-based strategies in L1, such as those just described, will likely prove most effective for developing fluency in L2.

Vocabulary

One consequence of the difference in experience with and the opportunity to learn English between ELs and their native-English-speaking peers is a relative lack of breadth and depth of English vocabulary and general word knowledge. Because EL students' lives are distributed across two languages, so is their vocabulary knowledge (Bialystok, 2001; Lesaux, 2006). In the early elementary school grades, a low comparative vocabulary level in ELs is often a major limiting factor in the development of reading comprehension skills (Mancilla-Martinez & Lesaux, 2011). In fact, when not provided any native-language instruction, ELs do not generally reach age-level standards in vocabulary and comprehension as compared to monolingual English speakers (Mancilla-Martinez & Lesaux, 2011; Rhodes et al., 2005). Thus, vocabulary instruction must increase the store of words in the instructional language(s) through explicit instruction and through text-level reading. Unfortunately, due to the sheer number of vocabulary words in English as well as the need for considerably more exposure, repetition, and usage to aid in their acquisition, intervention efforts designed to expand reading vocabulary have proven more time consuming and significantly less amenable to amelioration as compared to other facets of language, such as phonological awareness (Ortiz, Ochoa, & Dynda, 2012). Because they are often behind their peers in English when they start school, the normal and expected rate and degree of vocabulary acquisition tied to grade level represent an enormous challenge for EL students, who often have the additional burden of living in households where the parents may have limited education themselves and

DON'T FORGET

As EL students' lives are distributed across two languages, so too is their knowledge of.

who may not speak English well or at all. The degree to which ELs can get behind in vocabulary development may be appreciated by recognizing the tremendous influence that living with parents who speak often versus seldom has on language development and educational attainment for native English speakers. Research by Hart and Risley (1995) suggested that native-English-speaking children in high-verbal families had heard an estimated 30-million more words than children in low-verbal families by age 3 years. Factor in the lack of opportunity for ELs to hear any English at all and it is easy to see why vocabulary can be a difficult area to remediate within the limitations of the typical classroom.

The plight of ELs in terms of vocabulary is further highlighted by research that estimates that the average student can only be explicitly taught about 400 words per school year (Beck, McKeown, & Kucan, 2002). Direct instruction will simply be insufficient for ELs. Therefore, apart from teaching words explicitly, students will need to increase their vocabulary through independent, engaged reading. The vocabulary found in books usually offers a depth and breadth not found in everyday conversational oral language. As identified previously, ELs who struggle with reading unfortunately tend to resist reading—a cycle that reinforces Stanovich's concept of the "Matthew Effect" (1986), which posits that those who read more, learn more, and by the same token, those who read less, benefit even less. Thus, in reading, as in many other areas, the rich get richer and the poor get poorer. For this reason, it is important to foster early success in reading, which will likely lead to a tendency to engage in more reading, and in turn more reading will translate into more learning. As noted previously, explicit teaching of reading skills can be highly effective but it is not possible to teach directly all the vocabulary words a student needs to learn to be able to read fluently. Therefore, two factors are critical when teaching ELs to read. Students must be taught strategies for learning new vocabulary and teachers must explicitly teach content area vocabulary to permit students to retain contact with the curriculum. See Rapid Reference 9.7 for effective methods of vocabulary instruction.

To help students expand their vocabulary and learn relationships between words, teaching *word families* is also useful. Another strategy to build word knowledge is to teach how *changing word endings* changes the form of a word (Chiappe-Collins & Scarcella, 2010).

≡ Rapid Reference 9.7 Five Effective Methods of Vocabulary Instruction

Five effective methods of vocabulary instruction were identified by the National Reading Panel (2000). They are:

Method	Example
1. Explicit Instruction	Providing definitions
2. Implicit Instruction	Exposure to words via wide reading of varied material
3. Using Multimedia	Graphic representations and hypertext
4. Capacity Methods	Emphasizing practice to gain automaticity
5. Association Methods	Drawing connections between known and unknown words

In addition to the recommendations of the National Reading Panel, another useful framework comes from Beck and colleagues (2002), who organize vocabulary around a word's usefulness and frequency in a three-tiered approach (not to be confused with RTI tiers). The first tier includes words that students are likely to already know; words in the second tier are those that students are likely to encounter frequently in text and reading material but whose meanings students may not know; and last, words in the third tier are usually content-area-specific and rarely appear in text but are such that when using context clues, students can usually establish their meaning. Calderón (2011) adapted the Beck and colleagues model for ELs. Rapid Reference 9.8 describes the tiers of the Calderón model. Tier 1 includes common words and cognates (words that look similar and have the same meaning in two languages). Research shows that up to 15,000 English words are actual Spanish-English cognates or have substantial equivalents (discussed ahead) (Heibert & Lubliner, 2008). Words in Tier 2 are those that should be taught explicitly because they are commonly found across content areas and students will likely encounter them frequently. Tier 3 words are specialized content-area words necessary for access to the curriculum and are taught as needed.

DON'T FORGET

Cognates are words that look similar and have similar meaning across two languages. Since English and Spanish have Latin roots, 30 to 40% of words in English have a Spanish cognate or a substantial equivalent. Cognates, then, can be an excellent bridge between the two languages.

≡ Rapid Reference 9.8 Vocabulary Tiers for ELs

Tier 1: Basic vocabulary and conversational words	Tier 2: High-frequency words found in texts	Tier 3: Specialized content-area vocabulary
Instruction: Some words cannot be demonstrated but must be taught (i.e., aunt). Direct instruction and demonstration is an effective strategy at all tiers. If students know a word in their L1, providing a simple explanation or quick English translation is also useful. Tier 2 words are the most important to be taught. (*Note:* Some words are high-frequency words in one language but low frequency in the other.)		
Everyday words that ELs typically know in their L1; words used frequently, such as happy, good, run	High-frequency, high-utility words that are important to comprehension, such as author, setting, character, plot	Complex, technical, and low-frequency words found in context books
Simple high-frequency words that are cognates, such as doctor/doctor, sofa/sofa	Words with multiple meanings used across domains	Vocabulary of a specific discipline
Simple false cognates, such as rope/ropa (clothing)	Idioms and common expressions Roots, prefixes, and suffixes Abstract concepts Words that have connections to other words and concepts, such as between, among, by	

Source: Calderón. © Solution Tree Press. Reprinted with permission.

Since English and Spanish have Latin roots, approximately 30 to 40% of words in English have an actual Spanish cognate or a substantially equivalent word. Cognates, then, can be an excellent bridge between the two languages but it will presume some degree of development and formal education (perhaps even up to the student's current grade) in the native language. One common misconception in the education of ELs is that language development and academic skills will naturally develop in the native language even when all instruction is provided in English only. Learning is heavily context dependent and if a student has not been educated in his or her native language, there can be no reasonable expectation of age- or grade-level development of linguistic or academic skills, particularly vocabulary. Thus, while using cognates is a powerful strategy, most students will need direct instruction in just learning to recognize and use cognates, assuming they are available in the student's vocabulary repertoire in the first place (Nagy, García, Durgunoglu, & Hancin, 1993). A graphic organizer with the following headings can be posted on classroom walls and, as cognates are encountered throughout the curriculum, new words can be added: (a) words spelled exactly the same (e.g., debate/debate), (b) words spelled similarly (e.g., pearl/perla), (c) words that are less similar but with the same root (e.g., past/pasado), and (d) words spelled differently but with similar sound and same meaning (e.g., peace/paz). A second graphic organizer can be created for two more word categories: (a) multiple-meaning words (e.g., rent/rentar), and (b) false cognates (e.g., exit/éxito).

Comprehension

Comprehension is the most difficult aspect of reading for most ELs. If instruction focuses more on word reading without linking to meaning, EL students may not understand that reading is intended to communicate meaning. For example, a teacher once noted anecdotally that at the beginning of a new school year she innocently asked her EL students to begin reading, and they in turn asked her, "How fast?" Another challenge is that comprehension is contingent upon extensive vocabulary knowledge and must continue to expand yearly. Teachers must ensure that EL students have adequate word and world knowledge (Vaughn, & Linan-Thompson, 2007) even in the face of experiences that have been limited with respect to exposure to and use of English. In other words, for EL students, instruction should build upon their prior knowledge (if available) as new concepts and vocabulary are taught and no assumptions can be made that ELs have adequate or sufficient grade-level word knowledge.

Initially, listening comprehension is often developed through "read-alouds." After hearing a story, children can be taught meaning-making strategies, such as creating mental images of the story. Through teacher-led "think-alouds," the process of learning how to clarify confusing parts of stories can be modeled so that students can learn to monitor their own reading (Francis, Rivera, Lesaux, Kieffer, & Rivera, 2006). Good readers must also learn to use metacognitive strategies (thinking about their own thinking) such as identifying the purpose for reading, monitoring their understanding throughout their reading, and checking for understanding.

One such meta-cognitive strategy is Collaborative Strategic Reading (CSR; Klingner & Vaughn, 1998). CSR explicitly teaches students to preview text, give ongoing feedback at the end of each paragraph using "click" (*I get it*) or "clunk" (*I don't get it*), "getting the gist" (understanding the most important parts of the

≡ Rapid Reference 9.9 Collaborative Strategic Reading (CSR)

CSR explicitly teaches students to preview text, give ongoing feedback at the end of each paragraph using "click" (*I get it*) or "clunk" (*I don't get it*), "getting the gist" (understanding the most important parts of the text), and "wrapping up" key ideas. Initially CSR is instructed to a whole group through modeling, think-alouds, and role playing.

text), and "wrapping up" key ideas. Initially CSR is instructed to a large group through modeling, think-alouds, and role playing. Then smaller, collaborative groups are formed where each student has a defined role in either modeling reading, providing feedback, gauging comprehension, or summarizing the text, as outlined in Rapid Reference 9.9.

Teaching summarization and how to ask questions also supports comprehension. To teach summarization, teachers should discuss the following questions: (a) What are the main ideas?, (b) What are the crucial details necessary for supporting the ideas?, and (c) What information is irrelevant or unnecessary? The answers are used to draft a text summary (see Rapid Reference 9.10). Another popular strategy for improving comprehension is the Question-Answer Relationship (QAR) strategy (Raphael, Highfield, & Au, 2006), which asks students to consider whether the text offers explicit or implicit information. Students answer four types of questions: (a) *right there*—questions that have a correct answer that can be found in one place in the text, (b) *think and search*—questions that are based on facts found in more than one place in text, (c) *author and you*—questions that require students to use their prior knowledge as well as what they have learned from text, and (d) *on your own*—questions based on prior knowledge. Through modeling and guided practice, students can learn how to use these and other strategies independently to facilitate comprehension.

≡ Rapid Reference 9.10 Summarization Strategies

To teach summarization, teachers should discuss the following questions:

a. What are the main ideas?

b. What are the crucial details necessary for supporting the ideas?

c. What information is irrelevant or unnecessary?

Currently, many systems use published, research-based interventions that have been demonstrated to be effective in developing reading skills in most English-only students. However, the vast majority of these programs have not been validated for use with ELs and do not provide adequate language support to enable EL students to

DON'T FORGET

Instruction and interventions for EL students must include all five components of reading (phonemic awareness, phonics, vocabulary, fluency, and comprehension), match student needs with instructional intensity, explicitly instruct unfamiliar vocabulary and language structures, and regularly monitor progress.

fully benefit from them. It is not that there is an expectation that such programs would not work with ELs but rather that the rate of progress or the appropriate level of skill attainment cannot be based on that used for native English speakers or it may prove discriminatory (Ortiz, 2008; Vanderwood & Nam, 2008). Therefore, to address concerns regarding equity and to provide a framework for enhancing intervention programs, the PLUSS model (Sanford, Brown, & Turner, 2012) was proposed recently and is discussed more fully in what follows. The *PLUSS* acronym stands for: *P*re-teach critical vocabulary, *L*anguage modeling and opportunities for using academic language, *U*se visual and graphic organizers, *S*ystematic and explicit instruction, and *S*trategic use of native language and teaching for transfer.

PLUSS Model

Much has been written about scripted reading intervention programs designed to systematically teach basic reading skills, such as *Reading Mastery* (Engelmann et al., 2002). Proponents emphasize the efficacy of scripted programs in boosting the skills of struggling readers (Adams & Engelmann, 1996; Borman, Hewes, Overman, & Brown, 2003; Hattie, 2009). Critics of scripted programs suggest that they reduce the skill required of teachers, fail to contextualize learning to students' histories, experiences, and communities, and ignore reading comprehension (Eppley, 2011; Lovett et al., 2008). As discussed previously, an understanding of ELs' developmental language proficiency necessitates that all instruction be connected to students' lives while at the same time providing rigorous instruction of critical skills. As indicated by NAEP scores reported earlier, most EL students are not achieving basic levels of academic proficiency. One reasonable conclusion is that much of their instruction is ineffective based on their unique linguistic needs and experiential backgrounds. Thus, when supporting students' reading achievement through either an RTI or pre-referral process, instruction must target academic skill gaps (e.g., phonological awareness, fluency) identified by assessments, emphasize that the purpose of reading is to understand, and be tailored to consider a student's current language proficiency level in the instructional language as well as his or her cultural/experiential background. While there are several existing instructional models such as the Sheltered Instruction Observation Protocol (SIOP; Echevarría, Vogt, & Short, 2008) or Guided Language Acquisition Design (GLAD; Brechtel & Haley, 1991) to help teachers tailor instruction when teaching content to EL students, there are currently no models to help teachers tailor academic interventions. The PLUSS model has been specifically developed as a framework to tailor interventions for ELs (Sanford et al., 2012).

DON'T FORGET

....

When supporting students' reading achievement through either an RTI or pre-referral process, instruction must target gaps identified by assessments, emphasize that the purpose of reading is to understand, and be tailored to consider a student's current language proficiency level in the instructional language as well as his or her cultural/experiential background.

The PLUSS framework addresses ELs' unique instructional needs at all tiers of instructional support, including special education, by overlaying instructional enhancements in language and background knowledge onto the core curriculum or interventions. See Rapid Reference 9.11 for the definitions of the key components of the PLUSS model and research that supports them. See Rapid Reference 9.12 for examples of strategies for each component of the model.

Pre-teach

The first component of the PLUSS model involves tasks that preview or pre-teach critical language and concepts within intervention programs appropriate to students' language proficiency levels. For example, to pre-teach critical vocabulary, strategies might include using realia (real objects), Word Splash (choose key words or concepts from a passage/chapter before reading and relate new words or concepts to main topic), and Four Corners Vocabulary (fold a blank paper into fourths, labeling each section with one of the following: word, picture, sentence, and definition; students then fold their paper so only the picture shows; peers guess at the definition, and with each incorrect guess another clue from the page is given).

DON'T FORGET

....

The PLUSS framework addresses ELs' unique instructional needs at all tiers of instructional support, including special education, by overlaying instructional enhancements in language and background knowledge onto the core curriculum and/or interventions.

≡ Rapid Reference 9.11 PLUSS Framework for Research-Based Instruction for ELs

PLUSS Framework	Definition	Evidence
Pre-teach critical vocabulary	Present critical vocabulary prior to lessons to ensure later comprehension using direct instruction, modeling, and connections to native language.	Beck et al. (2002); Heibert & Lubliner (2008); Mancilla-Martinez & Lesaux (2011); Nag et al. (1993)
Language modeling and opportunities for practice	Teacher models appropriate use of academic language, then provides structured opportunities for students to practice using the language in meaningful contexts.	Dutro & Moran (2003); Echevarria et al. (2008); Gibbons (2009); Linan-Thompson & Vaughn (2007); Scarcella (2003)
Use visuals and graphic organizers	Strategically use pictures, graphic organizers, gestures, realia, and other visual prompts to help make critical language, concepts, and strategies more comprehensible to learners.	Brechtal (2001); Echevarría & Graves (1998); Haager & Klingner (2005); Linan-Thompson & Vaughn (2007); O'Malley & Chamot (1990)
Systematic and explicit instruction	Explain, model, and provide guided practice with feedback, and opportunities for independent practice in content, strategies, and concepts.	Calderón (2007); Flagella-Luby & Deshler (2008); Gibbons (2009); Haager & Klingner (2005); Klingner & Vaughn (2000); Watkins & Slocum (2008)
Strategic use of native language and teaching for transfer	Identify concepts and content students already know in their native language and culture to explicitly explain, define, and help them understand new language and concepts in English.	Carlisle, Beeman, Davis, & Spharim (1999); Durgunoglu et al. (1993); Genesee, Geva, Dressler, & Kamil (2006); Odlin (1989); Schecter & Bayley (2002)

Source: © NCCRESt. Reprinted with permission.

≡ Rapid Reference 9.12 Examples of PLUSS Framework Applied in the Classroom

PLUSS Framework	Example
Pre-teach critical vocabulary	Select 3–5 high-utility vocabulary words crucial to understanding text (not necessarily content-specific words) and explicitly teach student-friendly definitions, model using the words, and provide students with repeated opportunities to use the words over time (Honig et al., 2008; Beck et al., 2002).
Language modeling and opportunities for practicing	Provide language frames and sentence starters to structure language interaction. For example, after having defined the word *preoccupied*, ask students to use the word *preoccupied* in a sentence, "Think of a time when you were preoccupied." (Pause to give time to think.) "Turn to your partners and share, starting your sentence with, 'I was preoccupied when . . . .' What will you start your sentence with?" (Have students repeat the sentence-starter before turning to their neighbor and sharing.)
Use visuals and graphic organizers	Consistently use a *Venn diagram* to teach concepts, such as compare-and-contrast, and use realia and pictures to support the teaching of concepts (Echevarría et al., 2008).
Systematic and explicit instruction	Teach strategies like summarization, monitoring, and clarifying, and decoding strategies through direct explanation, modeling, guided practice with feedback, and opportunities for application (Honig et al., 2008).
Strategic use of native language and teaching for transfer	Use native language to teach cognates (e.g., teach that *preoccupied* means the same thing as *preocupado* in Spanish) or explain/clarify a concept in the native language before or while teaching it in English.

Language Modeling

This is demonstrated effectively through the use of sentence frames. Sentence frames help to relieve students' linguistic load by providing a scaffold for oral and written responses at their proficiency level. For example, determining cause and effect is a common classroom task, but students may not know how to respond appropriately. The following sentence frames can be used:

Levels 1 and 2—The cause of _____ is _____ . The effect of _____ is_____.
Level 3—One effect of_____ _____was_____ .
Levels 4 and 5— _____happens because _____. Because _____ (happens), _____(happens). Several things caused _____to happen.
They were _____, _____, and _____.

After students complete their sentence frames, instruction should allow for "talk time" where they may engage in oral conversation and practice to reinforce the learning.

Use Visuals and Graphic Organizers

A *framed outline* is a very specific and structured graphic organizer where students place important information from a passage that they have listened to or read (or even a video they have watched) in the correct order. Signal words and pictures help students make connections from concrete to abstract concepts. As with all strategies, teachers should differentiate the outlines based on their students' proficiency levels. The following is an example of a framed outline where the focus skill is on -*ed*.

First, the tomatoes are ___ ed. When they are ripe, the tomatoes are ___ ed.
Then the tomatoes are_____ed. This means they are washed and sorted.
Next, the tomatoes are_____ed. This means they are put on a truck and taken to the store.
At the end the tomatoes are_____ ed.

Systematic and Explicit Instruction

In the PLUSS model this usually involves implementing an intervention program such as Rewards (Archer, Gleason, & Vachon, 2000), Reading Mastery (Engelmann et al., 2002), or another evidence-based intervention program.

One of the central tenets of RTI is that a research-based intervention be taught with fidelity to the program. In other words, teachers must adhere to the instructions or script provided by the intervention program. In the PLUSS model, the *P*, *L*, and *U* components are used to preview the language and concepts that may be difficult for EL students.

Strategic Use of Native Language and Teaching for Transfer

The final *S* reminds teachers to bridge concepts by using the native language whenever possible. Rapid Reference 9.13 provides examples of the PLUSS framework as applied in a classroom or intervention setting.

After providing research-based interventions that are adjusted for language proficiency, as well as experiential and cultural backgrounds, there will be some students whose progress is not commensurate with "true peers" (Brown and Doolittle, 2008). In other words, some students will not progress at similar rates as students with similar language proficiencies in English and native language, birth country, educational experience, and cultural background. In these cases, a referral for a special education evaluation may be appropriate. Because it is not the intent of this chapter to discuss nondiscriminatory assessment practices for ELs, we will briefly review the laws guiding the instruction of dual-identified students (students in both EL and special education programs), culturally and linguistically appropriate IEP development, and service delivery.

> ## CAUTION
>
> Some students will not progress at similar rates as students with similar language proficiencies in English and native language, birth country, educational experience, and cultural background. In these cases, a referral for a special education evaluation may be appropriate.

Instruction of ELs in Special Education

Intersecting Laws

English learners who have not been redesignated as *fully English proficient* (FEP) and have not been exited from ESL/ESOL services prior to placement into special education programs continue to qualify for and remain fully entitled to receive those same services. According to the Individuals with Disabilities Education Improvement Act (IDEIA, 2004), students with disabilities are entitled to receive a free appropriate public education (FAPE) as specified in an individualized educational program (IEP) delivered in the least-restrictive environment (LRE). In addition, they remain entitled to receive any service or program that is ordinarily available to students without disabilities, including ESL/ESOL services. To deny ESL/ESOL services merely upon entry into special education has been cited by the Office of Civil Rights as a discriminatory act prohibited by IDEIA and a clear violation of the student's and his or her parents' rights. Other legislation, such as Titles I and III of the Elementary and Secondary Education Act (now known as No Child Left Behind), govern English language acquisition programs for ELs and ensure that they receive a systematic program of ELD to promote

> ## DON'T FORGET
>
> ELs who have not been redesignated as *fully English proficient* (FEP) and who have not been exited from ESL/ESOL services prior to placement into special education programs continue to qualify for and remain fully entitled to such services.

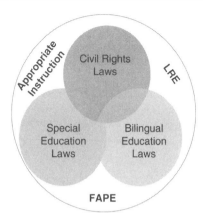

Figure 9.2. Laws and Entitlements Governing EL Students in Special Education Program

Source: Serpa (2011). © Gaston Institute. Reprinted with permission.

annual progress toward full English proficiency. And finally, other civil rights legislation, such as Section 504 of the Vocational and Rehabilitation Act of 1974, (1) prohibits discrimination against students on the basis of national origin, (2) prohibits exclusion of students from effective participation in general education simply because they do not speak, read, or understand English, and (3) prevents students from being placed into special education programs simply because of their language differences. Figure 9.2 highlights the three areas of law applicable to EL students in special education and these entitlements based on the laws. The last entitlement on Figure 9.2 to discuss is appropriate instruction, which, as noted, remains an important and necessary consideration regardless of whether the student has been identified as having a disability or is being provided special education services.

DON'T FORGET

Appropriate instruction for EL students in special education programs should consider three areas: (1) language learning needs (in L1 and L2), (2) disability needs/special learning needs, and (3) cultural and experiential backgrounds.

Instruction for ELs in Special Education Programs

Appropriate instruction for EL students in special education programs should consider three areas: (1) language learning needs (in L1 and L2), (2) disability needs/special learning needs, and (3) cultural and experiential backgrounds. Figure 9.3 provides a model for planning and adapting instruction in ways

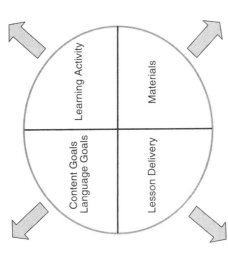

Skills and concepts to teach based on standards

Consideration: Will student's instructional target be based on grade level standards or their present skill?

Instructional activities students engage in to work towards goals

Consideration: What vocabulary and/or language structures need to be taught and practiced prior, during or after main lesson? Students must practice and apply their learning while integrating speaking, listening, reading, and writing skills in English.

The language the teachers use for giving directions, teaching routines and procedures, lesson scripts

Consideration: What vocabulary and/or language structures used in teacher's instruction need to be taught prior to main lesson?

Materials used to teach skills, concepts and language

Consideration: What adaptations or alternative to lesson materials are needed based on student's individual learning and language needs and cultural experiences?

Content Goals
Language Goals

Learning Activity

Lesson Delivery

Materials

Brown, E. (2011). *Working with English language learners with differences and disorders. Modules Addressing Special Education and Teacher Education (MAST).* Greenville, NC: East Carolina University. Available from http://mast.ecu.edu/modules/psell

Figure 9.3. Adapting Instruction for ELs with Special Needs

Source: Brown (2011). © Reprinted with permission.

that consider the areas noted previously. Four components of instruction are addressed: (1) content and language goals, (2) lesson delivery, (3) learning activities, and (4) materials. Each of these components will be expanded upon ahead, within our discussion of how IEP goals can target both learning and language needs.

When ELs are placed into special education programs, careful consideration must be given regarding the exact manner in which students will continue to receive services from the ESL program and special education services. Best practice generally recommends a collaborative, transdisciplinary model of instruction rather than the more typical pull-out type of programs for several reasons (Ortiz, 2012). First, a transdisciplinary approach makes more effective use of limited resources. Second, such collaboration helps to reinforce the notion that the student's needs may well be spread across different programs and personnel who might not ordinarily engage in cooperative service delivery. And last, such an approach ensures that individuals with the most expertise and knowledge in serving the language needs of the students are utilized in a manner that keeps them in a position to either directly provide necessary instruction or engage in consultative services to assist others who may do so.

Content and Language IEP Goals
To provide special education services to ELs, Individual Education Plan (IEP) goals and objectives must be written to include academic skills and the language they will need to learn to achieve the skill. This intent is made clear in IDEIA (2004), which states: "In the case of a child with limited English proficiency, consider the language needs of the child as those needs relate to the child's IEP" [34 CFR § 300.324(a)(2)(ii)]. Consequently, considerations must include grade-level standards, state-approved English Language Proficiency (ELP) standards, and the student's present level of English proficiency. Learning the language of school, or *academic language*, is crucial for ELs' success in school as language barriers are often the primary source of difficulty for them across the grade levels.

Language Functions and Forms
One helpful model to assist educators in determining the appropriate language focus is the work of Dutro and Moran (2003), who separate academic language into three categories: *function, form,* and *fluency*. Function is the purpose for the language being used. Form includes both grammar and vocabulary. Academic language (forms and functions) is learned through multiple practice opportunities and results

DON'T FORGET

"In the case of a child with limited English proficiency, consider the language needs of the child as those needs relate to the child's IEP" [34 CFR § 300.324(a)(2)(ii)].

in language fluency. Rapid Reference 9.13 provides examples of forms and functions.

Consideration of these two aspects of language will set the stage for EL students to learn the language necessary to advance academically. As stated earlier, function is the purpose for speaking or writing, such as to compare and contrast, or to describe a process. Valdez Pierce and O'Malley (1992) found the following language functions to be characteristic of classroom discourse: (1) seeking information, (2) informing, (3) justifying, (4) persuading, (5) analyzing, (6) solving problems, (7) comparing, (8) synthesizing, (9) classifying, (10) evaluating, (11) predicting, and (12) hypothesizing. The functions listed by Valdez Pierce and O'Malley (1992) align with those identified by Dutro and Moran (2003). Form, as stated earlier, is the grammatical feature or the tools needed for discourse and engagement in cognitive processes. Rapid Reference 9.14 provides an example of the language forms needed to perform a particular function, in no particular order.

≡ Rapid Reference 9.13 Language Functions and Forms

Language Functions	Form
Expressing needs and likes	Indirect/direct object Subject/verb agreement Pronouns
Describing people, places, and things	Nouns Pronouns Adjectives
Describing spatial and temporal relations	Prepositional phrases
Describing actions	Present progressive Adverbs
Retelling/relating past events	Past tense verbs Perfect aspect (present and past)
Making predictions	Verbs: future tense, conditional mode
Asking informational questions	Verbs and verb phrases in question
Asking clarifying questions	Questions with increasing specificity
Expressing and supporting opinions	Sentence structure
Comparing	Adjectives and conjunctions Comparatives Superlatives Adverbs

(continued)

(continued)

Contrasting	Comparative adjectives
Summarizing	Increasingly complex sentences with increasingly specific vocabulary
Persuading	Verb forms
Literary analysis	Sentence structure
	Specific vocabulary
Cause and effect	Verb forms
Drawing conclusions	Comparative adjective
Defining	Nouns, pronouns and adjectives
Explaining	Verb forms
	Declarative sentences
	Complex sentences
	Adverbs of manner
Generalizing	Abstract nouns
	Verb forms
	Nominalizations
Evaluating	Complex sentences
	Increasing specificity of nouns, verbs, and adjectives
Interpreting	Language of propaganda
	Complex sentences
	Nominalizations
Sequencing	Adverbs of time
	Relative clauses
	Subordinate conjunctions
Hypothesizing and speculating	Modals (would, could, might)
	Compound tenses (would have been)

Source: Oregon DOE; Dutro & Moran (2003).

Goal Development

To illustrate IEP goal development for an EL student, we will consider Liana, a third-grade student with a visual impairment. The Common Core State Standard for Grade 3, Reading for Informational Text: Integration of Knowledge and Ideas #9 says, "Compare and contrast the most important points and key details presented in two texts on the same topic." Since Liana is an English learner, we also consider her English proficiency level. Records indicate that Liana is at level 3 (where 1 is a beginner and 5 is highly fluent) on the language proficiency continuum, so we know that while she may sound fairly fluent in English, she continues to need language instruction and support to acquire academic language. To help in developing appropriate goals, it may be useful to consider the English Language Proficiency standards, as specified either by tests or tools used to evaluate the initial need for ESL services upon enrollment or by other instruments that might serve a monitoring or exiting function (e.g., state-developed language proficiency tests, individually administered proficiency tests, teacher observations, and evaluation).

Referring back to Figure 9.3, to determine appropriate instruction, it can be seen that the first consideration involves *Content and Language Goals* and must address the question: "Will Liana's instructional target be based on grade-level standards or her present skill level?" Liana's present levels of performance indicate that, although she is below grade level, she is close to grade-level range. Thus, we choose the grade-level standard.

The next consideration centers on the *Learning Activity* and identification of the language structures needed for Liana to perform the skills of comparing and contrasting (see Figure 9.3). If we refer back to Rapid Reference 9.13 and find the functions "comparing" and "contrasting" in the left-hand column, it can be seen in the right-hand column that several language forms are listed that might be helpful when engaging in these types of tasks. For example, we may choose to focus on the adjectives *similar* and *different*. The next area to consider depicted in Figure 9.3 is *Lesson Delivery*, which focuses on teacher language or directions that a student may need help understanding. The final component illustrated in Figure 9.3, *Materials*, reminds us to consider how Liana will access instruction. In this case, she will need a magnifier to read the material. The goal might look something like this:

> By December 2, 2013, when given a written prompt, using a magnifier Liana will compare information from several sources using "similar to" and "different from" in a complete sentence in four out of five opportunities as measured by teacher observation and tracking sheet.

In this way, we are ensuring that Liana will have the necessary assistive technology, and will be taught the language she likely does not yet know but that is needed to be able to compare and contrast, and that is standards based.

SUMMARY AND CONCLUSION

Klingner and Bianco (2006) once asked the question, "What makes bilingual special education 'special'?" They answered their own question by indicating that: (1) The learning environment must be supportive, culturally responsive, and include validated instructional practices; and (2) there is a heightened instructional focus on *language* and *culture*. In consideration of their question and response, this type of instruction is sorely needed by all EL students and all educators must expand their toolkit to facilitate such instruction. There is no question that educators need guidance on providing instruction to ELs that is appropriate and effective. The rapidly changing ethnic demographics in many states and the unabating increase in students entering school who come from diverse cultural and ethnic backgrounds is creating something of a panic situation for many districts that until recently felt no significant impact regarding a diverse community or student body. The issues and strategies outlined in this chapter are in line with this need and are intended to offer guidance as we continue to develop multi-tiered systems of support effective for *all* students. However, it should be understood that no type or amount of intervention or instruction can truly replace the effectiveness and success offered by the delivery of native-language instruction. The type of circumstantial "delays" that occur in cognitive and academic development that stem from the rejection of the native language in favor of another language (usually English) for the purposes of instruction are significant and not redressed by any particular teaching technique (Ortiz, 2008, 2011; Rhodes et al., 2005). Nevertheless, given appropriate types of instruction that have been demonstrated to be effective (as those described in this chapter), ELs can be expected to achieve far better than they have historically and are likely to benefit far more from schooling than they would otherwise.

Design and implementation of instruction and interventions must attend to the unique developmental issues characteristic of students whose backgrounds include more than one language and culture. When provided with high-quality instruction appropriate to the student's developmental language proficiency in the language of instruction, and that is consonant with the principles of learning unique to ELs, solid academic success becomes a reasonable and attainable goal.

REFERENCES

Adam, M. J. (1990). *Beginning to read: Thinking and learning about print*. Cambridge, MA: Massachusetts Institute of Technology.

Adams, G. L., & Engelmann, S. (1996). *Research on Direct Instruction: 25 years beyond DISTAR*. Seattle, WA: Educational Achievement Systems.

Antunez, B. (2002). Implementing reading first with English language learners. *Directions in Language and Education*, *15*, 1–12.

Archer, A., Gleason, M. M., & Vachon, V. (2000). *REWARDS*. Frederick, CO: Sopris.

Artiles, A. J., & Ortiz, A. (Eds.). (2002). *English language learners with special education needs*. Washington, DC: Center for Applied Linguistics.

August, D. L., & Shanahan, T. (2006). Introduction and methodology. In D. L. August and T. Shanahan (Eds.), *Developing literacy in a second language: Report of the National Literacy Panel*. Mahwah, NJ: Lawrence Erlbaum.

Ballantyne, K. G., Sanderman, A. R., & Levy, J. (2008). *Educating English language learners: Building teacher capacity*. Washington, DC: National Clearinghouse for English Language Acquisition. Available at http://www.ncela.gwu.edu/practice/mainstream_teachers.htm

Beck, I. L., McKeown, M. G., & Kucan, L. (2002). *Bringing words to life: Robust vocabulary instruction*. New York, NY: Guilford Press.

Bialystok, E. (2001). *Bilingualism in development: Language, literacy, and cognition*. New York, NY: Cambridge University Press.

Borman, G. D., Hewes, G. M., Overman, L. T., & Brown, S. (2003). Comprehensive school reform and achievement: A meta-analysis. *Review of Educational Research, 73*(2), 125–230.

Brechtal, M. (2001). *Bringing it all together: Language and literacy in the multilingual classroom*. Carlsbad, CA: Dominie Press.

Brechtel, M., & Haley, L. (1991). *Project GLAD: Guided language acquisition design*. Fountain Valley, CA: Fountain Valley School District.

Brown, E. (2011) *Working with English language learners with differences and disorders. Modules Addressing Special Education and Teacher Education (MAST)*. Greenville, NC: East Carolina University. Retrieved from http://mast.ecu.edu/modules/psell.

Brown, J. E., & Doolittle, J. (2008). *A cultural, linguistic, and ecological framework for response to intervention with English language learners*. Tempe, AZ: National Center for Culturally Responsive Educational Systems. Retrieved from http://www.nccrest.org/Briefs/Framework_for_RTI.pdf.

Brown-Chidsey, R., Bronaugh, L., & McGraw, K. (2009). *RTI in the classroom: Guidelines and recipes for success*. New York, NY: Guilford Press.

Cahnmann, M. (2003). To correct or not to correct bilingual students' errors is a question of continuing reimagination. In N. H. Hornberger (Ed.), *Continua of biliteracy* (pp. 187–204). Clevedon, England: Multilingual Matter Ltd.

Calderón, M. (2007). *Teaching reading to English language learners: Grades 6-12*. Thousand Oaks, CA: Corwin Press.

Calderón, M. (2011). *Teaching reading & comprehension to English learners, K–5*. Bloomington, IN: Solution Tree.

Carlisle, J. F., Beeman, M., Davis, L. J., & Spharim, G. (1999). Relationship of metalinguistic capabilities and reading achievement for children who are becoming bilingual. *Applied Psycholinguistics, 20,* 459–478.

Chard, D. J., Vaughn, S., & Tyler, B. J. (2002). A synthesis of research on effective interventions for building reading fluency with elementary students with learning disabilities. *Journal of Learning Disabilities, 35,* 386–406.

Chiappe-Collins, P., & Scarcella, R. (2010, November). *Recommendations from the IES practice guide: Effective literacy and language instruction for English learners in the elementary grades*. Seattle, WA: Presentation.

Crosson, A. C., & Lesaux, N. K. (2010). Revisiting assumptions about the relationship of fluent reading to comprehension: Spanish-speakers text-reading fluency in English. *Reading and Writing: An Interdisciplinary Journal, 23,* 475–494.

Cummins, J. (1984) *Bilingual Education and Special Education: Issues in Assessment and Pedagogy*. San Diego: College Hill.

Cummins, J. (2000). *Language, power and pedagogy: Bilingual children in the crossfire*. Clevedon, England: Multilingual Matters.

Data Accountability Center. (2010). Retrieved July 6, 2012, from https://www.ideadata.org/arctoc9.asp#partbCC.

Denton, C. A., Anthony, J. L., Parker, R., & Hasbrouck, J. E. (2004). Effects of two tutoring programs on the English reading development of Spanish-English bilingual students. *The Elementary School Journal, 104*(4), 289–305.

Dunn, L.M. (1968). Special education for the mildly retarded—Is much of it justifiable? *Exceptional Children, 23,* 5–21.

Durgunoglu, A.Y. (2002). Cross-linguistic transfer in literacy development and implications for language. *Annals of Dyslexia, 52*, 189–204.

Durgunoglu, A., Nagy, W., & Hancin-Bhatt, J. (1993). Cross—language transfer of phonological awareness. *Journal of Educational Psychology, 85*, 453–465.

Dutro, S., & Moran, C. (2003). Rethinking English language instruction: An architectural approach. In G. García (Ed.), *English learners: Reaching the highest level of English literacy* (pp. 227–258) Newark, DE: International Reading Association.

Echevarría, J., & Graves, A. (1998). *Sheltered content instruction: Teaching English-language learners with diverse abilities.* Des Moines, IA: Allyn & Bacon.

Echevarría, J., Vogt, M. E., & Short, D. (2008). *Making content comprehensible for English language learners: The SIOP model* (3rd ed.). Boston, MA: Pearson/Allyn & Bacon.

Egbert, J. L., & Ernst-Slavit, G. (2010). *Access to academics: Planning instruction for K–12 classrooms with ELLs.* Boston, MA: Allyn & Bacon.

Engelmann, S., Arbogast, A., Bruner, E., Lou David, K., Engelmann, O., Hanner, S. et al. (2002). *SRA reading mastery.* DeSoto, TX: SRA/McGraw-Hill.

Eppley, K. (2011). Reading Mastery as pedagogy of erasure. *Journal of Research in Rural Education, 26*(13), 1–5.

Flagella-Luby, M.N., & Deshler, D.D. (2008). Reading comprehension in adolescents with LD: What we know; what we need to learn. *Learning Disabilities Research and Practice, 23*(2), 70–78.

Francis, D., Rivera, M., Lesaux, N., Kieffer, M., & Rivera, H. (2006). *Practical guidelines for the education of English language learners: Research-based recommendations for instruction and academic interventions.* Portsmouth, NH: RMC Research Corporation, Center on Instruction. Retrieved August 27, 2012, from http://www.centeroninstruction.org/files/ELL1-Interventions.pdf.

Genesee, F., Geva, E., Dressler, C., & Kamil, M. L. (2006). Synthesis: Cross-linguistic relationships. In D. August and T. Shanahan (Eds.), *Developing literacy in second-language learners: Report of the National Literacy Panel on language-minority children and youth* (pp. 153–174). Mahwah, NJ: Erlbaum.

Geva, E. (2006). Learning to read in a second language: Research, implications, and recommendations for services. In R. E. Tremblay, R. G. Barr, & R. Peters (Eds.), *Encyclopedia on early childhood development.* Montreal, Quebec: Centre of Excellence for Early Childhood Development.

Geva, E., Wade-Wooley, L., & Shany, M. (1997). The development of reading efficiency in first and second language. *Scientific Studies in Reading, 1*, 119–144.

Gibbons, P. (2009). *English learners, academic literacy, and thinking: Learning in the challenge zone.* Portsmouth, NH: Heinemann.

Goldenberg, C. (2008). Teaching English language learners: What the research does and does not say. *American Educator*, 8–44.

Gonzalez, N., Moll, L., & Amanti, C. (2005). *Funds of knowledge: Theorizing practices in households, communities and classrooms.* London, UK: Lawrence Erlbaum.

Griffith, P. L., & Olson, M. W. (1992). Phonemic awareness helps beginning readers break the code. *The Reading Teacher, 45*(7), 516–23.

Haager, D., & Klingner, J. (2005). *Differentiating instruction in inclusive classrooms: The special educator's guide.* Boston, MA: Pearson Education.

Hammer, C. S., Miccio, A. W., & Rodriguez, B. L. (2004). Bilingual language acquisition and the child socialization process. In B. A. Goldstein (Ed.), *Bilingual language development and disorders in Spanish-English speakers* (pp. 21–50). Baltimore, MD: Brookes.

Hart, B., & Risley, T. R. (1995). *Meaningful differences in the everyday experience of young American children.* Baltimore, MD: Brookes.

Hattie, J. (2009). *Visible learning: A synthesis of over 800 meta-analyses relating to achievement.* London, UK and New York, NY: Routledge.

Heibert, E. H., & Lubliner, S. (2008). The nature, learning, and instruction of general academic vocabulary. In A. E. Farstrup & S. J. Samuels (Eds.), *What research has to say about vocabulary instruction* (pp. 106–129). Newark, DE: International Reading Association.

Herrera, S. G., Perez, D. R., & Escamilla, K. (2010). *Teaching reading to English language learners: Differentiated literacies.* New York, NY: Allyn & Bacon.

Honig, B., Diamond, L., & Gutlohn, L. (2008). *Teaching reading sourcebook* (2nd ed.). Novato, CA: Arena Press.

Hoover, J., Klingner, J. K., Baca, L., & Patton, J. (2008). *Methods for teaching culturally and linguistically diverse exceptional learners.* Upper Saddle River, NJ: Prentice Hall.

Individuals with Disabilities Education Improvement Act of 2004. Pub. L. 108–446 (2004).

Joseph, L. M. (2008). Best practices in interventions for students with reading problems. In A. Thomas & J. Grimes (Eds.), *Best practices in school psychology, 72*(4), 1163–1180.

Kamil, M. L., Borman, G. D., Dole, J., Kral, C. C., Salinger, T., & Torgesen, J. (2008). *Improving adolescent literacy: Effective classroom and intervention practices: A practical guide* (NCEE #2008-4027). Washington, DC: National Center for Education Evaluation and Regional Assistance, Institute of Education Sciences, U.S. Department of Education. Retrieved from http://ies.ed.gov/ncee/wwc.

Klingner, J., & Bianco, M. (2006). What is special about special education for culturally and linguistically diverse students with disabilities? In B. Cook & B. Schirmer (Eds.), *What is special about special education?* (pp. 37–53). Austin, TX: PRO-ED.

Klingner, J. K., Artiles, A. J., & Barrera, L. M. (2006). English language learners who struggle with reading: Language acquisition or LD? *Journal of Learning Disabilities, 39* (2), 108–128.

Klingner, J. K., & Vaughn, S. (1998). Using collaborative strategic reading. *Teaching Exceptional Children, 30*(6), 32–37. Retrieved from http://www.ldonline.org/ld_indepth/teaching_ techniques/collab_reading.html.

Klingner, J. K., & Vaughn, S. (2000). The helping behaviors of fifth-graders while using Collaborative strategic reading (CSR) during ESL content classes. *TESOL Quarterly, 34*, 69–98.

Kohnert, K. (2009). Cross-language generalization following treatment in bilingual speakers with aphasia: A review. *Seminars in Speech and Language, 30*, 174–186.

Kohnert, K., & Pham, G. (2010). Sentence interpretation by typically developing Vietnamese-English bilingual children. *Applied Psycholinguistics, 31*(3), 507–529.

Lesaux, N. K. (2006). Development of literacy of language minority learners. In D. L. August & T. Shanahan (Eds.), *Developing literacy in a second language: Report of the National Literacy Panel.* Mahwah, NJ: Lawrence Erlbaum.

Linan-Thompson, S., & Vaughn, S. (2007). *Research-based methods of reading instruction for English language learners: Grades K–4.* Alexandria, VA: Association for Supervision and Curriculum Development.

Lovett, M. W., De Palma, M., Frijters, J., Steinbach, K., Temple, M., Benson, N., & Lacerenza, L. (2008). Interventions for reading difficulties: A comparison of response to intervention by ELL and EFL struggling readers. *Journal of Learning Disabilities, 41*(4), 333–352.

Mancilla-Martinez, J., & Lesaux, N.K. (2011). The gap between Spanish-Speakers' word reading and word knowledge: A longitudinal study. *Child Development. 82*, 1544–1560.

Maxwell, L. A., & Shah, N. (2011). NAEP test-taking pool grows more inclusive. *Education Week, 31*(12), 14–15.

Moll, L. C., Amanti, C., Neff, D., & Gonzalez, N. (1992). Funds of knowledge for teaching: Using a qualitative approach to connect homes and classrooms. *Theory into Practice*, *31*(2), 132–141.

Nagy, W. E., García, G. E., Durgunoglu, A., & Hancin, B. (1993). Spanish-English bilingual children's use and recognition of cognates in English reading. *Journal of Reading Behavior*, *25*(3), 241–259.

National Center for Education Statistics (2011). The Nation's Report Card: Reading 2011 (NCES 2012-457). National Center for Education Statistics, Institute of Education Sciences, U.S. Department of Education, Washington, DC.

National Reading Panel. (2000). *Report of the National Reading Panel: Teaching children to read*. Washington, DC: National Institute of Child Health and Human Development.

Odlin, T. (1989). *Language transfer: Cross-linguistic influence in language learning*. Cambridge, England: Cambridge University Press.

O'Malley, J. M., & Chamot, A. U. (1990). *Learning strategies in second language acquisition*. Cambridge, England: Cambridge University Press.

Orosco, M. J., & Klingner, J. K. (2010). One school's implementation of RTI with English language learners: "Reforming into RTI." *Journal of Learning Disabilities*, *43*(3), 29–288.

Ortiz, S. O. (2008). Best practices in nondiscriminatory assessment. In A. Thomas & J. Grimes (Eds.), *Best practices in school psychology V* (pp. 661–678). Washington, DC: National Association of School Psychologists.

Ortiz, S. O. (2011). Separating cultural and linguistic difference (CLD) from specific learning disability (SLD) in the evaluation of diverse students. In D. P. Flanagan & V. C. Alfonso (Eds.), *Essentials of specific learning disability identification* (pp. 299–326). Hoboken, NJ: Wiley.

Ortiz, S. O. (2012). Multicultural issues in school mental health: Responsive intervention in the educational setting. In R. B. Menutti, A. Freeman, & R. W. Christner (Eds.), *Cognitive behavioral interventions in educational settings: A handbook for practice* (2nd ed., pp. 53–80). New York, NY: Brunner-Routledge.

Ortiz, S. O., Ochoa, H. S., & Dynda, A. M. (2012). Testing with culturally and linguistically diverse populations: Moving beyond the verbal-performance dichotomy into evidence-based practice. In D. P. Flanagan & P. L. Harrison (Eds.), *Contemporary intellectual assessment* (3rd ed., pp. 526–552). New York, NY: Guilford Press.

Oswald, D. P., Coutinho, M. J., Best, A. M., & Singh, N. N. (1999). Ethnic representation in special education: The role of school related economic and demographic variables. *Journal of Special Education*, *32*, 194–206.

Peregoy, S. F., & Boyle, O.F. (2000). English learners reading English: What we know, what we need to know. *Theory into Practice*, *39*(4), 237–247.

Ramírez, M. C. (2001). An investigation of English language learners and reading skills on reading comprehension for Spanish-speaking English language learners. *Dissertation Abstracts International*, *62*, 2716.

Raphael, T. E., Highfield, K., & Au, K. H. (2006). *QAR now: A powerful and practical framework that develops comprehension and higher-level thinking in all students*. New York, NY: Scholastic.

Reyes, I. (2006). Exploring connections between emergent biliteracy and bilingualism. *Journal of Early Childhood Literacy*, *6*(3), 267–292.

Rhodes, R., Ochoa, S. H., & Ortiz, S. O. (2005). *Assessment of culturally and linguistically diverse students: A practical guide*. New York, NY: Guilford Press.

Richards, C., & Leafstedt, J. (2010). *Early reading interventions: Strategies and methods for struggling readers*. Boston, MA: Pearson Allyn & Bacon.

Rosa-Lugo, L. I., Nutta, J., & Mihai, F. (2012). *Language and literacy development: An interdisciplinary focus on English learners with communication disorders.* San Diego, CA: Plural Publishing.

Sanford, A., Brown, J. E., & Turner, M. (2012). Enhancing instruction for English learners in response to intervention systems: The PLUSS model. *Multiple Voices, 13*(1), 56–70.

Scarcella, R. (2003) Academic English: A conceptual framework. *Linguistic Minority Research Institute Newsletter.* Santa Barbara, CA: University of California, Santa Barbara.

Schecter, S. R., & Bayley, R. (2002). *Language as cultural practice: Mexicanos en el Norte.* Mahwah, NJ: Erlbaum.

Serpa, M. B. (2011). *An imperative for change: Bridging special and language learning education to ensure a free and appropriate education in the least restrictive environment for ELLs with disabilities in Massachusetts.* Boston, MA: Mauricio Gastón Institute for Latino Community Development and Public Policy, University of Massachusetts.

Shaywitz, S. (2003). *Overcoming dyslexia: A new and complete science-based program for reading problems at any level.* New York, NY: Knopf.

Stanovich, K. E. (1986). Matthew effects in reading: Some consequences of individual differences in the acquisition of literacy. *Reading Research Quarterly, 21,* 36–407.

Stanovich, K. E. (1990). Concepts in developmental theories of reading skill: Cognitive resources, automaticity, and modularity. *Developmental Review, 10,* 72–100.

Therrien, W. J. (2004). Fluency and comprehension gains as a result of repeated reading: A meta-analysis. *Remedial and Special Education, 25,* 252–261.

Thomas, W. P., & Collier, V. P. (1997). *School effectiveness for language minority students.* Washington, DC: National Clearinghouse for Bilingual Education.

Thomas, W. P., & Collier, V. P. (2002). *A national study of school effectiveness for language minority students' long-term academic achievement.* Santa Cruz, CA: Center for Research on Education, Diversity, & Excellence.

Turner, M., & Brown, J. E. (2012). Unpublished manuscript.

Valdes, G., & Figueroa, R. (1992). *Bilingualism and testing: A special case of bias.* Norwood, NJ: Ablex.

Valdez Pierce, L., & O'Malley, J. M. (1992). *Performance and portfolio assessment for language minority students.* Washington, DC: National Clearinghouse for Bilingual Education.

Vanderwood, M. L., & Nam, J. (2008). Best practices in using a response to intervention model with English language learners. In A. Thomas & J. Grimes (Eds.), *Best practices in school psychology V.* Bethesda, MD: National Association of School Psychologists.

Vaughn, S., & Linan-Thompson, S. (2007). *Research-based methods of reading instruction for English language learners, Grades K–4.* Alexandria, VA: Association for Supervision and Curriculum Development.

Watkins, C. L., & Slocum, T. A. (2008). The components of direct instruction. *Journal of Direct Instruction, 3*(2), 75–100.

🔆 TEST YOURSELF 🔆

1. **The largest linguistic subgroup of English learners speak**

   a. Mandarin

   b. Vietnamese

(continued)

(*continued*)

    c. Cantonese

    d. Spanish

2. **English learners are disproportionately represented in three special education categories. They are:**

    a. Communication Disorder (CD), Emotional Disturbance (ED), and Intellectual Disability (ID)

    b. Specific Learning Disability (SLD), Communication Disorder (CD), and Intellectual Disability (ID)

    c. Other Health Impaired (OHI), Communication Disorder (CD), Specific Learning Disability (SLD)

    d. Specific Learning Disability (SLD), Emotional Disturbance (ED), and Intellectual Disability (ID)

3. *True or False?:* **Placing English learners without a disability but who are struggling academically into special education programs is advisable.**

    a. True

    b. False

4. **If the 20% lowest achieving students in a class are from one subgroup, the cause may be**

    a. Students' lack of English proficiency

    b. Inappropriate core instruction

    c. Lack of student motivation

    d. High mobility

5. *True or False?:* **Second-generation ELs tend to struggle academically more than either first- or third-generation students.**

    a. True

    b. False

6. **The National Literacy Panel identified five components of an effective reading program for ELs. They are:**

    a. Phonemic awareness, the alphabetic principle, phonics, fluency, and vocabulary

    b. Phonemic awareness, phonics, fluency, vocabulary, and accuracy

    c. Phonemic awareness, comprehension, phonics, fluency, and vocabulary

    d. Phonemic awareness, phonics, fluency, cognates, and vocabulary

7. **Experts report that English-only students must learn how many words per year?**

    a. 5,000–6,000

    b. 1,000–2,000

    c. 7,000–8,000

    d. 3,000–4,000

8. **The term *true peers* means students with similar**

    a. Language proficiencies in L1 and L2, birth country, education, and cultural background

b. Birth country, family constellation, height, and weight

c. Achievement scores, language proficiency scores, and grades

d. Language, culture, and hobbies

9. **Which three areas of law guide provision of services to EL students in special education programs?**

a. Titles I, II, and X

b. Immigration and Titles I and X

c. NCLB, Immigration, and IDEA

d. IDEA, Titles I and II, and civil rights

10. **Which four areas should be considered when planning instruction for an EL in special education?**

a. Content goals, learning activity, lesson delivery, and materials

b. Content and language goals, curriculum, assessment, and lesson delivery

c. Content and language goals, learning activity, lesson delivery, and materials

d. Language goals, curriculum, assessment, and lesson delivery

Answers: 1. d; 2. d; 3. b; 4. b; 5. a; 6. c; 7. d; 8. a; 9. d; 10. c

Ten

INTERVENTIONS FOR STUDENTS WITH EXECUTIVE SKILLS AND EXECUTIVE FUNCTIONS DIFFICULTIES

George McCloskey
Caitlin Gilmartin
Betti Stanco Vitanza

To discuss interventions that address executive skills and executive functions difficulties, it is necessary to have a definition of executive functions as a starting point. The definition of executive functions provided here is a widely inclusive multidimensional theoretical model referred to as the *Holarchical Model of Executive Functions* (HMEF; McCloskey & Perkins, 2012; McCloskey, Perkins, & VanDivner, 2009).

Consistent with the common thread throughout the defining literature, the term *executive functions* can be viewed as an overarching developmental cognitive neuropsychological construct that is used to represent a set of neural mechanisms that are responsible for *cueing, directing,* and *coordinating* multiple aspects of perception, emotion, cognition, and action (Gioia, Isquith, Guy, & Kenworthy, 1996; McCloskey et al., 2009; Stuss & Alexander, 2000). The HMEF, which anchors the discussion of executive functions in this chapter, is depicted visually in Figure 10.1. The HMEF is not discussed in detail here, but is elaborated fully in other sources (McCloskey & Perkins, 2012; McCloskey et al., 2009).

The nature and expression of executive functions is highly diverse. The HMEF proposes a set of executive capacities that are structured in the form of five holarchically organized tiers representing different levels of specificity of executive control. At the most basic level, that of self-regulation, multiple executive functions cue and direct functioning differentially across four general *domains*

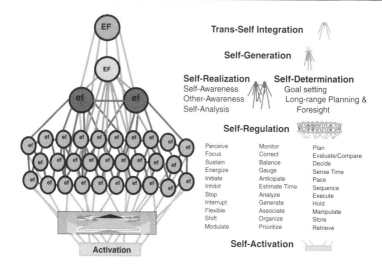

Figure 10.1. Holarchical Model of Executive Functions

Source: Copyright © 2012 George McCloskey.

(Perception, Emotion, Thought, and Action) within four *arenas of involvement* (Intrapersonal, Interpersonal, Environment, and Symbol System).

The HMEF specifies 33 separate self-regulation executive functions that can be grouped within 7 overarching clusters. Rapid Reference 10.1 shows problem behaviors likely to be exhibited in school settings by students experiencing difficulties with self-regulation executive capacities. Executive difficulties with the greatest impact in early elementary school years are represented in the Attention, Engagement, Optimization, and Efficiency clusters. The impact of executive difficulties with the Inquiry, Solution, and Memory clusters becomes much more prominent in late elementary and middle and high school years as the complexity and level of abstraction of learning and production increase.

DON'T FORGET

Executive functions difficulties with the greatest impact in early elementary school years are represented in the Attention, Engagement, Optimization, and Efficiency clusters. The impact of executive functions difficulties with the Inquiry, Solution, and Memory clusters becomes much more prominent in late elementary and middle and high school years as the complexity and level of abstraction of learning and production increase.

≡ Rapid Reference 10.1 Ineffective Behaviors Likely to Be Exhibited in School Settings by Students Experiencing Self-Regulation Executive Functions Difficulties

Self-Regulation Executive Function	Observed Behaviors Related to Inefficient Use of Executive Skills and/or Executive Functions
Attention Cluster	
Perceive Cue	Does not see signs, directions, etc.; does not hear directions; does not touch or handle materials; seems unaware of own thoughts and actions
Focus/Select	Does not attend to information being presented
Sustain	Has difficulty working on tasks for extended periods of time
Engagement Cluster	
Effort	Puts little energy or effort into work on school tasks
Initiate	Slow to get started with tasks; long pauses occur before a response is offered
Inhibit	Blurts out comments in class; acts impulsively; can't wait for turn
Stop	Continues even after being told to stop
Interrupt/Pause	Does not return to work on a task after a brief interruption
Flexible	Resists the idea of doing things a different way or feeling or thinking a different way; insists on doing things the same way
Shift	Has difficulty going from one activity to another or moving from one thought or feeling to another
Optimization Cluster	
Monitor	Doesn't check work for errors; has difficulty realizing when he/she has made a mistake; has a hard time identifying inaccurate thoughts or feelings
Modulate	Has difficulty adjusting activity level; is overactive or underactive; gets overstimulated or understimulated; overreacts or underreacts to situations
Balance	Has difficulty finding the balance between extremes (speed vs. accuracy, quality vs. quantity; general vs. specific statements; depth vs. breadth; talking vs. listening, sharing too much vs. sharing too little; being humorous vs. being serious)
Correct	Has trouble correcting mistakes or apologizing for inappropriate behavior
Efficiency Cluster	
Sense Time	Seems unaware of the passage of time; does not know how long he/she was working on a task or thinking about something

(continued)

(*continued*)

Pace	Has difficulty changing pace to go slower or go faster as conditions dictate
Sequence	Has difficulty getting the steps of a routine in the right order; performs sequenced tasks out of order
Execute	Has trouble effectively using routines that most children the same age have automated; lacks follow-through on tasks even when interested and attending
Memory Cluster	
Hold	Has difficulty holding onto information for more than a few seconds
Manipulate	Has difficulty actively working with information that is being held in mind
Store	Has difficulty with storing information so it will be available for later use
Retrieve	Has difficulty retrieving stored information when needed
Inquiry Cluster	
Gauge	Has difficulty "sizing up" what is needed to complete a task; under- or overestimates the difficulty of tasks
Anticipate	Has difficulty looking ahead or anticipating what will be next; difficulty considering the consequences of his or her actions before acting
Estimate Time	Is very poor at estimating the time or estimating how long it takes to do things
Analyze	Has difficulty with examining things in more detail to understand them better
Compare/Evaluate	Has difficulty evaluating the quality of his or her work or thinking; difficulty comparing one thing with another on various dimensions
Solution Cluster	
Generate	Has difficulty coming up with a new idea or finding a novel solution to a problem
Associate	Has difficulty understanding or seeing how two or more things or ideas are similar
Organize	Has difficulty with arranging things or thoughts in an orderly manner
Plan	Has difficulty working out in advance a way of doing things or thinking about things
Decide	Has difficulty choosing among options; can't choose how to think, feel, or act
Prioritize	Has difficulty assigning an order of importance to things or activities

Source: Copyright © 2012 George McCloskey.

DISTINGUISHING BETWEEN EXECUTIVE SKILLS AND EXECUTIVE FUNCTIONS

Note that the definition of executive functions provided earlier indicates that executive functions cue and direct perceptions, feelings, thoughts, and actions. Executive functions, therefore, are strictly *directive* in nature; they are not the mental mechanisms used to express the perceptions, feelings, thoughts, and actions that are being cued. For example, executive functions are involved in the creation of plans, but their role is limited as they represent only a portion of the neural network, the portion that is housed in the frontal lobes of the brain. This part of the neural network is involved in the act of planning only by cueing and directing other segments of a neural network that is routed through the frontal lobes and various other cortical and subcortical regions of the brain. The parts of the neural network that are responsible for actually creating the plan are referred to collectively here as an *executive skill*. Executive skills, therefore, are the mental capacities that are cued and directed by executive functions when some form of self-regulation is required. The executive skills drive the perceptions, feelings, thoughts, and actions that are deemed necessary by the executive functions.

The distinction between executive functions and executive skills is a critical one. Because executive functions refer only to the part of the neural network responsible for cueing and directing and not for the part of the neural network responsible for carrying out the directives, it is really not appropriate to use the term *executive functions* to designate the entire self-control neural network. The terms *executive* or *executive capacity*, therefore, will be used when reference is being made to the combination of executive functions and executive skills that together represent executive control.

Each executive capacity listed in Rapid Reference 10.1 therefore represents an executive skill and an executive function. The executive function is responsible for

DON'T FORGET

Executive functions are strictly directive in nature; they are not the mental mechanisms used to express the perceptions, feelings, thoughts, and actions that are being cued.

Executive skills are the mental capacities that are cued and directed by executive functions when some form of self-regulation is required. The executive skills drive the perceptions, feelings, thoughts, and actions that are deemed necessary by the executive functions.

cueing and directing the executive skill (for example, the Focus executive function recognizes the need to focus attention and cues the executive skill network responsible for focusing attention). The distinction is important as it is necessary to determine the nature of the executive difficulty associated with the problem when planning and implementing interventions. An executive skill difficulty involves either a lack of knowledge of how to perform an executive skill or a lack of practice with performing the executive skill. An executive function difficulty involves either a lack of awareness of when to use an executive function or a lack of awareness of how to engage the executive function to respond effectively under conditions of external demand.

> **CAUTION**
> ••
> The distinction between executive functions and executive skills is a critical one. Because executive functions refer only to the part of the neural network responsible for cueing and directing and not for the part of the neural network responsible for carrying out the directives, it is really not appropriate to use the term *executive functions* to designate the entire self-control neural network. The terms *executive* or *executive capacity*, therefore, will be used when reference is being made to the combination of executive functions and executive skills that together represent executive control.

Difficulties related to the executive capacities of all seven clusters may involve a lack of practice of executive skills or a lack of awareness of when and how to direct the executive skills. The executive skills of the Attention, Engagement, Optimization, and Efficiency clusters typically do not need to be taught as they have been developing and in use to varying degrees from near-birth. The executive capacities of the Inquiry, Solution, and Memory clusters, on the other hand, are more likely to require teaching of the skill or further refinement of the expression of the skill to meet increased demands for cueing and directing of perceptions, feelings, thoughts, and actions at a higher level of conceptual abstraction. For example, although a rudimentary form of planning can be cued

> **DON'T FORGET**
> ••
> The executive skills of the Attention, Engagement, Optimization, and Efficiency clusters typically do not need to be taught as they have been developing and in use to varying degrees from near-birth. The executive capacities of the Inquiry, Solution, and Memory clusters, on the other hand, are more likely to require teaching of the skill or further refinement of the expression of the skill to meet increased demands for cueing and directing of perceptions, feelings, thoughts, and actions at a higher level of conceptual abstraction.

and performed by a 4-year-old child, the more complex forms of abstract planning that are available to a 14-year-old may require formal instruction to refine the skill and instruction to recognize when and how to effectively direct the newly refined planning skills.

CAUTION

For the purpose of determining whether executive difficulties are impacting academic learning and production, careful observation of the child's behavior during the performance of academic tasks is critical.

EXECUTIVE DIFFICULTIES AND ACADEMIC PRODUCTION

It is usually beneficial to identify ahead of time the specific executive capacities that are related to the behaviors of concern in order to plan an intervention. In the case of classroom production related to the use of specific academic skills, however, it is often much more difficult to identify the specific executive capacities that are not being engaged effectively. This is partly due to the fact that (1) any academic task involves multiple executive capacities, any number of which may be engaged ineffectively, and (2) any academic task requires the use of multiple process, abilities, skills, and lexicons. A central focus of executive capacities, therefore, becomes the coordination of the multiple processes, abilities, skills, and lexicons and the multiple executive functions required to perform the task. The topic of executive capacity involvement in academic production is discussed in detail in other sources (McCloskey & Perkins, 2012; McCloskey et al., 2009). For the purpose of determining whether executive difficulties are impacting academic learning and production, careful observation of the child's behavior during the performance of academic tasks is critical. Rapid References 10.2, 10.3, and 10.4 provide lists of behaviors likely to be indicative of executive difficulties when performing reading, writing, or math tasks, respectively.

ASSESSMENT OF EXECUTIVE DIFFICULTIES

Prior to intervention efforts, an assessment must be conducted to determine whether executive difficulties are playing a role in the observed problems. If executive difficulties are implicated, the assessment also should identify the nature of the difficulty (an executive skills problem and/or an executive functions problem) and identify any executive capacity strengths that could be used to support intervention efforts. There are multiple methods that can be employed to help identify executive capacity strengths and weaknesses as outlined in Rapid Reference 10.5. A detailed discussion of the various methods is beyond

≡ Rapid Reference 10.2 Reading Task Behaviors Likely to Be Indicative of a Lack of Effective Use of Executive Capacities (EC)

Executive Capacity Involvement in Reading	Self-Regulation Executive Capacities Likely to Be Involved	Process-Oriented Observations of Reading Behavior Indicative of a Lack of Use of ECs
1. Cueing/directing/coordinating immediate and sustained attention to orthography for accurate letter/word perception and discrimination.	1. Perceive, Focus, Monitor, Correct	1. Quick but inaccurate offerings for individual words with no recognition of the errors being made; words offered are highly similar in visual configuration to the correct word or start with the same letter or letter combination as the correct word or the nonsense word when performing decoding tests.
2. Cueing/directing/coordinating the use of phonological and orthographic knowledge and oral motor functioning for accurate sight-word retrieval and pronunciation.	2. Retrieve, Inhibit, Execute, Monitor, Correct	2. Mispronunciation of words that previously have been recognized by sight and correctly pronounced.
3. Cueing/directing/coordinating the use of phonological and orthographic knowledge, decoding skills, and oral motor functioning to sound out and match unknown words with known pronunciations of words.	3. Monitor, Inhibit, Interrupt, Shift, Retrieve, Execute, Sequence, Correct	3. Lack of application of decoding skills when reading sentences and passages for words that have been decoded correctly during skill drills and/or substitutes similarly configured sight-words for nonsense words instead of applying decoding skills.
4. Cueing/directing/coordinating speeded oral motor production for fluent word reading and/or fluent word decoding.	4. Execute, Pace, Balance, Monitor, Correct, Sustain	4. Word reading rate is not consistent with rate demonstrated during fluency instruction.
5. Cueing/directing/coordinating speeded oral motor production and prosody for fluent sentence and passage reading.	5. Execute, Pace, Balance, Monitor, Correct, Sustain	5. Sentence or passage reading rate is not consistent with rate demonstrated during fluency instruction.

(continued)

(continued)

6. Cueing/directing/coordinating the retrieval of word meanings.

6. Monitor, Retrieve, Correct

6. Despite demonstrating knowledge of a word in the past, student indicates he or she doesn't know the meaning of that word when reading.

7. Cueing/directing/coordinating the use of abilities and the retrieval of phrase meanings and topic knowledge from lexicons to comprehend the meaning of sentences and passages.

7. Monitor, Anticipate, Gauge, Analyze, Generate, Associate, Evaluate/Compare, Choose/Decide, Retrieve, Correct

7. Despite demonstrating knowledge about a topic, student does not make the connection between what they know and what they are reading.

8. Cueing/directing/coordinating the use of working memory resources while reading words, sentences and passages and constructing meaning from text.

8. Hold, Manipulate

8. When asked questions about what was just read, student must go back and reread in order to answer the question unless reminded ahead of time that he or she will need to answer questions after reading.

9. Cueing/directing/coordinating the use of strategies for reading words, sentences, and passages and constructing meaning from text.

9. Monitor, Retrieve, Correct

9. Despite demonstrating knowledge of reading comprehension strategies, student does not apply known strategies when reading for meaning.

10. Cueing/directing/coordinating the oral expression of meaning derived from text comprehension.

10. Hold, Manipulate, Balance, Gauge, Sequence, Execute

10. Despite demonstrating effective oral expression, student is not able to orally communicate the meaning of what was read.

11. Cueing/directing/coordinating the integration of all facets of the act of reading.

11. Energize, Initiate, Interrupt, Flexible, Shift, Sense Time, Pace, Execute, Hold, Store, Manipulate, Retrieve, Monitor, Correct, Sustain

11. Difficulty getting started with reading, zoning out while reading, unable to sustain interest and effort for reading passages; inadequate use of acquired reading skills (inconsistent sight-word recognition, inconsistent use of decoding skills, inconsistent reading rate and/or poor comprehension despite good reasoning and language abilities and good word reading skills).

≡ Rapid Reference 10.3 Writing Task Behaviors Likely to Be Indicative of a Lack of Effective Use of Executive Capacities (EC)

Executive Capacity Involvement in Written Expression	Self-Regulation Executive Capacities Likely to Be Involved	Process-Oriented Observations of Reading Behavior Indicative of a Lack of Use of ECs
1. Cueing/directing/coordinating the generation of a topic and/or ideas, or the acceptance of a topic and/or ideas provided by an outside source.	1. Energize, Focus, Initiate, Sustain, Gauge, Flexible, Generate, Associate, Choose/Decide, Monitor, Correct, Balance	1. Resistance to topic/idea generation or resistance to accepting the topic/ ideas of an outside source.
2. Cueing/directing/coordinating the use of working memory resources while generating a topic and/or ideas or considering a topic and/or ideas from the outside source.	2. Hold, Manipulate, Sustain	2. Generated ideas are quickly forgotten.
3. Cueing/directing/coordinating the generation of language to represent the topic/ideas.	3. Energize, Focus, Initiate, Sustain, Generate, Associate, Balance, Monitor, Correct	3. Ideas are poorly articulated; paucity of language production.
4. Cueing/directing/coordinating the accessing of word and phrase knowledge and specific content knowledge lexicons to generate and enhance the language used to represent the topic/ideas.	4. Retrieve	4. Written text is overly simplistic and minimal compared to good knowledge store and good oral expression of knowledge.
5. Cueing/directing/coordinating the use of reasoning and/or visuospatial abilities to guide selection and modification of language to construct rational arguments or trigger visuospatial representations in the reader's mind.	5. Energize, Focus, Initiate, Gauge, Anticipate, Generate, Associate, Analyze, Evaluate/Compare, Plan, Organize, Choose/ Decide, Monitor, Correct, Balance, Sustain	5. Arguments lack coherence of reason or do not create a visual image despite adequately developed reasoning, language, and/or visuospatial abilities.
6. Cueing/directing/coordinating the use of working memory to hold and manipulate the language	6. Hold, Manipulate, Sustain	6. Good initial use of reasoning or visuospatial abilities deteriorates as writing progresses.

(continued)

(continued)
generated to represent
the topic/ideas.

7. Cueing/directing/coordi-
nating text generation,
which will vary depending
on skill:

   a. Skilled handwriting/
   assistive technology
   use: cueing/directing/
   coordinating
   automated routines
   for generating written
   text by hand using
   pen, pencil, keyboard,
   text keys, etc.

   b. Unskilled handwriting:
   cueing/directing/coor-
   dinating the accessing
   of orthographic, pho-
   nologic, and grapho-
   motor lexicons and
   the use of orthographic
   and phonologic proc-
   essing and graphomo-
   tor functioning to
   produce individual letters and words by hand
   using pen, pencil, keyboard, text keys, etc.

8. Cueing/directing/coordi-
nating the use of working
memory to hold and
manipulate the language
generated to represent
the topic/ideas while performing text transcription
to achieve text generation.

9. Cueing/directing/coordi-
nating the accessing of, or
generation of, correct
spellings of words used
in text generation.

10. Cueing/directing/coordi-
nating the reviewing and
revising of generated
text.

11. Cueing/directing/coordi-
nating the use of working
memory to hold and

7.

   a. Energize, Perceive,
   Focus, Initiate,
   Retrieve, Execute,
   Sequence, Pace,
   Balance, Monitor,
   Correct, Sustain

   b. Energize, Perceive,
   Focus, Initiate,
   Retrieve, Execute,
   Sequence, Pace,
   Balance, Monitor,
   Correct, Sustain

8. Hold, Manipulate,
Sustain

9. Retrieve, Execute,
Sequence, Monitor,
Correct

10. Energize, Focus, Initiate,
Gauge, Anticipate, Gen-
erate, Associate, Analyze,
Evaluate/Compare, Plan,
Organize, Choose/
Decide, Monitor,
Correct, Balance, Sustain

11. Hold, Manipulate,
Sustain

7.

   a. Amount of written
   production is limited
   or writing is avoided
   despite adequate
   ideas and language
   representation.

   b. Use of pencil is
   resisted; pencil grasp is
   awkward and/or
   overly fatiguing;
   complaints are
   vocalized about the
   need to write.
   Letters and words are
   poorly formed, overall
   legibility is poor.
   Pace slows noticeably
   with passage of time.

8. Child indicates that ideas
are lost once text tran-
scription is started.

9. Long pauses needed to
access correct spellings
or words usually spelled
correctly on tests are
spelled incorrectly in
written products.

10. Inaccuracies, poor word-
ing, poor punctuation,
and misspellings are not
checked and/or not cor-
rected.

11. Child indicates they know
what they want to say in
revision but ideas are lost

(continued)
manipulate language while reviewing and revising generated text.

12. Cueing/directing/coordinating the entire act of written expression.

12. Energize, Focus, Initiate, Sense Time, Gauge, Anticipate, Plan, Organize, Pace, Sequence, Execute, Balance, Hold, Manipulate, Monitor, Correct, Sustain

(continued)
once text revision is started.

12. Inability to get energized for, initiate, and remain engaged with the act of writing; difficulties with planning and organizing thoughts about what to write; difficulties with judging the adequacy of a written product and/or recognizing when text needs to be revised.

≡ Rapid Reference 10.4 Mathematics Task Behaviors Likely to Be Indicative of a Lack of Effective Use of Executive Capacities (EC)

Executive Capacity Involvement in Mathematics	Self-Regulation Executive Capacities Likely to Be Involved	Process-Oriented Observations of Reading Behavior Indicative of a Lack of Use of ECs
1. Cueing/directing/coordinating all facets of the act of reading to obtain information about the problem to be solved.	1. Reading EF cues listed in Rapid Reference 10.2	1. Reading difficulties listed in Rapid Reference 10.2.
2. Cueing/directing/coordinating the use of quantification and reasoning abilities and/or retrieval of number concepts and applications knowledge to identify a solution to the problem.	2. Focus, Monitor, Inhibit, Anticipate, Gauge, Analyze, Generate, Associate, Evaluate/Compare, Choose/Decide, Retrieve, Correct, Sustain	2. Despite demonstrated knowledge of math concepts and adequate quantification and reasoning abilities, student is unable to identify solutions to math problems.
3. Cueing/directing/coordinating the retrieval of procedural knowledge needed to carry out the steps in the identified solution.	3. Monitor, Retrieve, Correct	3. Algorithms or procedures that have been used correctly in past situations are not retrieved; student "draws a blank" on how to solve problem.

(continued)

(continued)

4. Cueing/directing/coordinating the use of number and notation transcription skills to write out the steps in the problem solution.	4. Perceive, Focus, Execute, Pace, Balance, Monitor, Correct, Sustain	4. Numbers are reversed or incorrectly sequenced; signs are substituted (e.g., use of a – sign for a - sign or a divide sign); steps are left out; writing is illegible or so poorly organized that student cannot read own handwriting or find place in the problem-solving process.
5. Cueing/directing/coordinating retrieval of basic math facts as needed for the steps in the problem solution.	5. Monitor, Retrieve, Execute, Correct	5. Basic facts are calculated rather than retrieved automatically; long pauses are needed to recall basic facts; facts are recalled incorrectly despite prior demonstration of accurate storage and retrieval.
6. Cueing/directing/coordinating the retrieval and use of automated calculation routines or the application of math computation skills to complete the steps and identify the final solution.	6. Monitor, Retrieve, Execute, Pace, Balance, Correct	6. Well-known calculation routines are applied incorrectly (e.g., steps are applied out of sequence; basic calculation errors occur; transferred numbers are recorded incorrectly.
7. Cueing/directing/coordinating the use of working memory resources while working on the math problem.	7. Hold, Manipulate, Sustain	7. Adequate working memory capacity is not effectively applied during problem-solving as errors reflecting lapses in working memory are evident.
8. Cueing/directing/coordinating the integration of all facets of the act of math problem solving.	8. Energize, Initiate, Interrupt, Flexible, Shift, Sense Time, Pace, Execute, Hold, Store, Manipulate, Retrieve, Monitor, Correct, Sustain	8. Difficulty getting started with math problem-solving, zoning out while working, unable to sustain interest and effort for doing math; inadequate use of acquired math skills (inconsistent fact retrieval, inconsistent attention to calculation signs, inconsistent application of algorithms and problem-solving strategies despite prior effective use of these capacities).

⟹ Rapid Reference 10.5 Executive Functions Assessment Methods

	Assessment Technique	
Assessment Approach	**Formal** Tests and rating scales that make use of standards established through normative comparisons	**Informal** Interviews, records reviews, and observation and interpretation methods that do not make use of standards established through normative comparisons
Direct Collecting information through direct interactions with, or through direct observations of, the client while performing tasks that might involve the use of executive functions	Individually administered standardized tests (e.g., Delis-Kaplan Executive Function System, NEPSY-II, Wisconsin Card Sorting Test, Behavior Assessment of the Dysexecutive Syndrome, Behavior Assessment of the Dysexecutive Syndrome–Children)	Process-oriented interpretation of standardized test administrations and classroom work samples completed during direct observation of the client Systematic and nonsystematic behavioral observations
Indirect Collecting information in a manner that does not involve direct observation of the client while performing tasks that might involve the use of executive functions	Behavior rating scales Parent rating scales Teacher rating scales Self-report scales (e.g., Behavior Rating Inventory of Executive Functions: parent, teacher, and self-rating forms)	Interviews of client, parents, teachers, adult informants Process-oriented Interpretation of behavior rating scale responses Records review

the scope of this chapter, but is provided in *Essentials of Executive Functions Assessment* (McCloskey & Perkins, 2012). While each of the methods listed in Rapid Reference 10.5 has limitations, clinical interviewing of parents, teachers, and the child teamed with process-oriented observations of performance (see Rapid References 10.2, 10.3, and 10.4) is the combination most likely to provide clinicians with the greatest amount of relevant information for designing an effective intervention tailored to meet the needs of a specific child.

CONCEPTUAL BASIS FOR EXECUTIVE CAPACITY INTERVENTIONS

Intervention for executive difficulties depends on effective assessment and conceptualization of the child's capabilities. Case conceptualization involves a thorough appreciation of the nature and impact that executive difficulties are having on the child's learning and production. Effective case conceptualization is grounded in six key concepts related to the nature of executive function difficulties. These key concepts are described in Rapid Reference 10.6.

≣ *Rapid Reference 10.6 Key Concepts for Guiding Case Conceptualization When Executive Capacity Difficulties Have Been Identified*

••

1. *Executive difficulties are associated with suboptimal brain function.* While it might appear to be the case that the child is consciously choosing how to perceive, feel, think, and act when a lack of production is observed, proper conceptualization of executive difficulties requires an acknowledgment that the observed problems most likely are the result of less-than-optimal nonconscious brain function rather than consciously choosing to act in a contrary manner. Parents, teachers, and others involved with a child with executive difficulties must be careful not to attribute the particular production deficits they observe to character flaws or consciously chosen states of mind, such as laziness, lack of motivation, apathy, irresponsibility, or stubbornness. It also must be understood that immediately changing that current state of brain function most likely is not within the nonconsciously or consciously controlled skill set of the child.

2. *Brain function can be altered through intervention.* While it is certainly true that, in cases of more severe brain damage, neural networks have been altered or damaged to the point where little change in the current level of executive function capacity is likely, these cases are much more the exception than the rule. In the absence of clear evidence that the child was born with severe brain damage or has suffered a severe traumatic brain injury, it is best to assume that a child possesses the neural capacity to alter their current state of brain function. The important assumption here is that internal change that would enable the child to demonstrate the desired self-regulation capacities is possible. This optimistic stance enables the clinician to develop an intervention plan with the goal of positive change rather than the goal of simply managing a suboptimal state of functioning. A lack of progress over time toward positive goals, however, may necessitate the inclusion of behavior management strategies to deal with a child's current lack of executive control.

(continued)

(*continued*)

3. *Interventions can activate the use of intact brain function.* If the observed executive difficulties are the result of disuse of intact neural capacities, then an intervention plan focused on positive behavior change goals will focus on teaching the child how to activate the existing executive skills neural networks through practice to achieve positive behavioral goals. In this situation, the amount and rate of progress toward positive behavior goals will be constrained only by other contextual factors such as the level of functioning of other cognitive capacities (e.g., the child's capacity to benefit from language-based learning).

4. *Maturational delays in the development of executive capacities will slow the rate of progress during intervention efforts.* When the child is experiencing delays in the development of one or more executive capacities, progress toward positive goals is likely to be slower and less consistent than might be expected even when other contextual factors are not creating any conditions that might constrain progress. In some cases the presence of developmental delays can be established at the outset. In other cases, if intervention attempts progress over time with less than the desired results, even after modifications in the strategies used to obtain results, the presence of developmental delays is the most likely source of the lack of progress. The presence of developmental delays, however, does not indicate that the child will never further develop these executive capacities; it will just take them longer to develop these capacities. Appreciating the nature of developmental delays enables all involved in intervention efforts to maintain hope for future results and offers the encouragement needed to maintain patience with the slow rate of progress that might be occurring. Although as time progresses, the lack of progress might suggest to some that the child is not capable of developing the executive capacities they lack, in the absence of clear physical evidence of severe neural dysfunction, the best course of action is to maintain a positive outlook and continue to assist the child in their efforts to improve these executive capacities.

5. *Most executive difficulties reflect an inability to respond effectively to external demands for the use of executive capacities.* One of the most difficult paradoxes to reconcile in the minds of the parents and teachers of a child experiencing executive functions difficulties is why the child seems so capable of using executive skills when engaged with activities that they enjoy, and yet seems so inept at engaging these same executive skills when requested to do so for tasks the child finds uninteresting or difficult. It would seem that the ineptness is a matter of choice and reflects an apathetic or oppositional stance by the child. In actuality, the paradox reflects the difference between executive capacity engagement by internal command and engagement by external demand. Under conditions of internal demand, when the child is motivated to perform a task, the synchronization of reward centers of the brain and executive capacities happens non-consciously and enables a natural flow of perceptions, feelings, thoughts, and actions consistent with the desired outcomes. Conversely, under conditions of external demand, when the child is being commanded by others to perform a task, the child must first disengage from the natural internal connection between reward centers and executive capacities, flexibly consider the external request being made, determine what it will take in the way of perception, feeling, thought, and action to comply with the request, engage the needed executive capacities to

cue and direct the perceptions, feelings, thoughts, and actions needed to fulfill the request, monitor the adequacy of performance, and correct any errors that might be made. Moving from the natural state of responding to internal command to the unnatural state of responding to external demand is a skill that eludes many children who experience difficulties with the use of executive functions. For these children, their difficulties with responding on external command are as mystifying to the child as they are to the parents and teachers who impose the demands. Because the child does not understand what is happening with their brain and cannot explain to themselves or others, typical reactions to external demands can range from simply ignoring the request to explosive episodes of frustration and anger during which many things may be said that do not accurately reflect what is happening with the child.

6. *Executive difficulties are reflected in producing difficulties much more than learning difficulties.* Understanding how executive functions are involved in learning and in demonstrating what has been learned is critical to planning and implementing appropriate interventions. Self-regulation executive function capacities play a critical role in the learning process as they are used to effectively coordinate the interplay of various cognitive capacities. Children who exhibit executive function difficulties require much more input from other sources to assist them in the learning process. When good classroom instruction practices are used, students with executive function difficulties are able to make more efficient use of other adequately developed cognitive capacities.

It is critical to note, however, that addressing executive functions difficulties during instruction does not guarantee that adequate production will be obtained from those with executive functions difficulties when new learning is assessed. When executive capacity difficulties are exhibited, inefficiencies in the learning process are manifested in inadequate forms of production (for example, inadequate responses to questions during instruction, failed tests, poorly completed or undone assignments and projects). If the individual learner has not been taught how to overcome their executive capacity difficulties, these difficulties are likely to impact efforts at demonstrating what is learned even though learning did take place. Because learning is judged, not on the process of learning, but rather on the product of that learning, students who demonstrate executive functions difficulties can easily be mislabeled as having a learning disability when in fact they have what is more appropriately termed a *producing disability*.

CAUTION

Because learning is judged, not on the process of learning, but rather on the product of that learning, students who demonstrate executive functions difficulties can easily be mislabeled as having a learning disability when in fact, they have what is more appropriately termed a *producing disability*.

In other words, producing disabilities (or in their milder form, producing difficulties) are not the same thing as learning disabilities (or in their milder form, learning difficulties). This distinction is critical to understanding the nature of the problem and how to address it. Learning disabilities involve the disruption of basic processes such that initial perceptions are not adequately prepared for mental representation. When learning disabilities are exhibited, a person is much less capable of learning new skills and building skill-based lexicons. Although demonstration of what has been learned will be poor for these individuals, the source of their poor production is the learning disability, not a producing disability.

The situation is different, however, for the child who does not have a learning disability but who does have executive functions difficulties. In the absence of a learning disability, the person will be able to learn effectively as long as the executive functions difficulties are being addressed effectively during instruction and/or during periods of study. When assessment of what has been learned involves a degree of self-regulation beyond the person's existing capacities and no support is offered during the assessment, the person is at risk of not being able to demonstrate what they have learned (i.e., a producing disability).

Students whose executive functions development is lagging in one or more areas often have difficulty consistently producing at levels that effectively demonstrate what they have learned, especially during the initial period of a transition to the next level of schooling. Such "surprise" nosedives in academic production often occur during three specific education-level transitions: from elementary to middle or junior high school; from middle or junior high school to senior high school; and from high school to a post-secondary setting such as a college or technical school. There are many possible reasons for the sudden appearance of executive functions difficulties during educational transitions. Abrupt shifts in teaching style; an increase in the number of teachers and teaching styles; increased complexity of learning and production demands and increased expectations for

---

CAUTION

Students whose executive functions development is lagging in one or more areas often have difficulty consistently producing at levels that effectively demonstrate what they have learned, especially during the initial period of a transition to the next level of schooling. Such "surprise" nosedives in academic production often occur during three specific education-level transitions: from elementary to middle or junior high school; from middle or junior high school to senior high school; and from high school to a post-secondary setting such as a college or technical school.

DON'T FORGET

....

There are many possible reasons for the sudden appearance of executive functions difficulties during educational transitions. Abrupt shifts in teaching style; an increase in the number of teachers and teaching styles; increased complexity of learning and production demands and increased expectations for self-direction of learning and producing all can have a negative impact on students who do not possess the executive functions capacities needed to handle the changed conditions.

self-direction of learning and producing all can have a negative impact on students who do not possess the executive functions capacities needed to handle the changed conditions.

ADDITIONAL ISSUES RELATED TO INTERVENTION CONCEPTUALIZATION

Along with the six basic principles discussed in the previous rapid reference, several other issues must be considered and addressed when planning and implementing interventions. These issues are discussed in Rapid Reference 10.7.

≣ Rapid Reference 10.7 Additional Issues Related to Conceptualizing Executive Capacity Interventions

....

1. *Balancing the teaching of internal control with requirements for external control.* Although the goal of any intervention should be to increase the child's capacity for internally directed self-regulation, many interventions are likely to involve one or more external control strategies in the initial stages to begin the process of modifying the impact of executive difficulties. Effective interventions, therefore, often will involve finding the proper balance between teaching the child strategies and techniques that will affect internal change for improving self-regulation, while simultaneously supplying the requisite external controls that might be needed to support the child and manage behavior as long as severe self-regulation difficulties are being manifested. As a child learns to increase the use of existing executive capacities, or experiences developmental shifts that increase the engagement of executive capacities, the external controls can be lessened gradually with the goal of eventually being eliminated altogether. Careful monitoring of progress during the intervention period is required to enable the clinician and the child's parents to make the necessary decisions about the timing and extent of alterations made to external control contingencies.

2. *The executive environment in which interventions will be implemented.* The effectiveness of any intervention attempt will depend greatly on the executive capacities of the clinician and of those most closely associated with the child—family, friends, teachers, administrators, and so on. A caring environment populated with individuals who exhibit at least average levels of executive development and use can help the child in many ways. Such individuals are more likely to model effective use of executive capacities and help with the implementation of a consistent intervention plan and are more likely to be counted on to react appropriately to the executive miscues of the child. For the clinician, there are few situations more challenging than being faced with planning an intervention for a child whose parents are experiencing as many, or even more executive difficulties than the child.

3. *The use of rewards and punishment during intervention.* The effectiveness of the use of rewards and punishments in interventions depends on the nature of the executive difficulties. If the child's difficulties are related only to disuse due to a lack of awareness of the need to engage executive functions or a lack of desire to do so, rewards and punishments may provide the impetus needed to change externally demanded conditions into internally commanded conditions, thereby increasing the likelihood of effective use of the needed executive functions. In the case of a child with more severe executive skills and/or executive functions deficits or maturational delays, however, the difficulties they experience with external demand conditions cannot be overcome simply with a shift to an internally commanded context. As a result, rewards will never be obtained and/or punishment will always be delivered, likely resulting in anger, frustration, and withdrawal or refusal. The lack of production evidenced in these cases typically is not the result of a lack of motivation to engage but rather a lack of capacity for doing so. A lack of effectiveness of a behavior management plan that emphasizes reward or punishment signals the need to incorporate a teaching component as part of the intervention in order to build the capacity to respond effectively. Even when rewards and punishment produce the desired results, it should be realized that programs that rely strictly on rewards and punishment to produce the desired results are only external forms of control. They do not teach a child to become consciously aware of, reflect on, and internalize the regulation of behavior; they simply reward the presence of the behavior and/or punish its absence.

4. *Maturation of frontal lobe neural circuits.* Given that executive capacities follow a developmental progression dependent on the maturation of the neural circuitry of the frontal lobes, perhaps the most powerful intervention tool is time itself. Over time, most children and adolescents gradually improve their capacities for self-activation, self-regulation, self-realization, and self-determination. Problems arise when cultural expectations impose arbitrary timelines on brain function development. For children faced with overly aggressive expectations for brain maturation, a little time may be all that is needed to achieve the desired levels of executive capacity. For others with more substantial developmental delays, the ultimate solution to the executive difficulties may simply be more time to allow for greater development. One of the goals of working with a child experiencing executive difficulties should be to help family members develop a perspective

(continued)

(*continued*)
that engenders hope for the future. Discussing the developmental nature of most executive difficulties offers the clinician an opportunity to help the family reframe the issues in a more positive way and maintain hope for future improvement. While maturation is likely the single most significant factor in determining the ultimate resolution of executive difficulties, this does not mean that clinicians and family members should adopt a wait-and-see approach to dealing with current problems. Energy and effort should be put into developing and implementing interventions in the present that attempt to produce positive behavior changes in current areas of difficulty. Appreciating the likelihood of a slow trajectory of neural development for the child, however, provides the impetus for professionals and parents to persist with intervention efforts, remain patient, and maintain hope for improved functioning in the future despite less-than-optimal results in the present.

SUGGESTED GENERAL GUIDELINES FOR PLANNING AND IMPLEMENTING INTERVENTIONS

In light of the discussions of the six basic principles of case conceptualization and four related issues, Rapid Reference 10.8 offers a set of general guidelines for planning and implementing interventions for children exhibiting executive difficulties.

≡ Rapid Reference 10.8 General Guidelines for Planning and Implementing Interventions for Children Exhibiting Executive Difficulties

1. Conduct a broad-based assessment to determine the extent to which self-regulation executive difficulties are the source of the referral problem.
2. When self-regulation executive difficulties are implicated, it is necessary to
   a. Identify the specific executive capacities that are likely to be at the root of the problem.
   b. Identify the severity of the problem in terms of frequency (how often does it occur) and/or duration (how long do incidents involving the difficulties last)?
   c. Determine the nature of the problem; does the problem involve:
      i. A lack of knowledge of how to perform one or more executive skills
      ii. A lack of practice with performing one or more executive skills
      iii. A lack of awareness of when to engage one or more executive functions
      iv. A lack of awareness of how to engage one or more executive functions to respond effectively under conditions of external demand

3. Draw on general intervention strategies to tailor a specific intervention. Intervention efforts should be focused on developing the child's executive capacities to increase the occurrence of desired behaviors.

4. Interventions may need to start with external control strategies, but they should always be designed so that the use of external control strategies is reduced over time and the use of internal control strategies is increased.

5. All intervention efforts should start with collaboratively establishing the desired outcomes (the perceptions, feelings, thoughts, or actions that are to be self-regulated) and helping the child to become aware of the specific executive capacities that are needed to achieve the desired outcomes.

6. Provide the child with as rich an "executive environment" as possible; whenever possible, engage the assistance of family members and others who have frequent contact with the child who are capable of modeling effective executive capacity use and capable of encouraging the development of similar capacities in the child.

7. Monitor the use of the interventions closely to determine when to begin the gradual or complete withdrawal of external control in order to allow for the demonstration of the use of newly developed internally driven executive capacities.

8. Maintain and model attitudes of hope, perseverance, and patience with intervention efforts, realizing that in many cases, gains may be minimal and may require prolonged periods of time to achieve.

9. Maintain, and foster in others, reasonable expectations for behavior change and sensible and reasonable consequences for any unacceptable behaviors that stem from the child's executive difficulties.

GENERAL INTERVENTION STRATEGIES FOR IMPROVING THE USE OF EXECUTIVE CAPACITIES

A set of general intervention strategies that have been most effective in producing positive behavior change and academic production and improving the use of self-regulation capacities is presented in Rapid Reference 10.9. This list was developed from a broad-based review of the intervention literature

≡ Rapid Reference 10.9 General Strategies for Improving Executive Functions

Orienting Strategies
Establishing intervention goals—At the outset of the intervention, specific goals should be established collaboratively with the child. Each goal should represent specific actions, thought patterns, emotional states, or modes of perception. Each goal should be demonstrated or modeled in a concrete way so that the child has an experiential template that can be used to visualize and guide growth toward the
(continued)

(*continued*)
goal. During interventions, goals should be revisited and demonstrated again to keep them fresh in the child's mind. Progress toward the goals should be documented so the child can see the growth over time.

Increasing awareness of executive capacities—In tandem with the setting of goals for intervention efforts, the clinician will want to discuss the nature of the executive capacities that are required to achieve the intervention goals. Explain in basic terms what executive skills do and how we can become aware of when we need to use them, and how we can accomplish more things or change how we see (or hear) things, how we feel, how we think, and how we act by using executive capacities to cue and direct our perceptions, feelings, thoughts, and actions.

Increasing awareness of personal executive strengths and weaknesses—Also in tandem with the discussion of goals and how executive capacities work, discuss specific executive capacities that may be viewed as strengths of the child and discuss executive difficulties that lead to perceptions, feelings, thoughts, and actions that are at the root of the problems that the child is experiencing. Shift the focus as quickly as possible to the kinds of perceptions, feeling, thoughts, and actions that would be positive alternatives to the problems that have been identified, noting that these positive ways of perceiving, feeling, thinking, and acting will be the focus of the things that the clinician will be doing with the child.

External Control Strategies

Structuring the environment—Structuring the environment is a strategy that can be used to reduce executive capacity demands on a child that has not yet learned how to effectively use executive skills or how and when to use executive functions to cue and direct the use of these skills. Additionally, for some children with executive difficulties, the problems they encounter relate more to an inability to handle the number and frequency of the demands for the use of executive capacities than to the engagement of individual executive capacities per se. Modifying the executive demands by structuring the environment and implementing consistent behavior management plans can greatly reduce the number of executive-related problems these children exhibit.

Structuring time—As is the case with structuring the environment, providing aids for time management can greatly aid students who have difficulties self-regulating the use of the executive capacities of Sense Time, Estimate Time, and Pace. Strategies include maintaining and posting consistent schedules for activities, using clocks and timers, and building time-monitoring into activities.

Providing prompts—External prompting for, or direct delivery of, self-regulation cues is perhaps the most widely used strategy for external control of executive function difficulties. Much of what is considered good teaching practice involves a great deal of prompting for and/or delivery of self-regulation cues. In some cases, the prompting process needs to be made a more concrete part of the child's environment in order to encourage performance of actions in the proper sequence for adequate work production. Such concrete prompts include making lists of the steps to be completed for a task, and the specific order of completion of the steps, posting to-do lists where they are sure to be seen, or providing and checking homework assignment books.

Providing rewards or administering punishments—Although the use of externally administered rewards or punishments can increase the likelihood of obtaining desired executive control outcomes, the use of rewards and punishments should be carefully planned and monitored for the reasons discussed in this chapter.

Pharmacological treatment—Psycho-stimulant medication use is a common form of external control intervention for ADHD symptomatology. Although the use of medication enables many children to demonstrate increased use of some self-regulation skills, it is likely a gross oversimplification to suggest that the medication is directly acting on the frontal lobe, executive components of the activated neural networks. In fact, some research suggests that psycho-stimulant medications are primarily acting on portions of the activated neural network located in other parts of the cerebral cortex and/or subcortical regions (Hoeppner et al., 1997; Hale et al., 1998; Hale, Fiorello, & Brown, 2005). Whatever the specific brain mechanisms at work, the observable effect for children who benefit from the use of these medications very often is improved use of some self-regulation capacities, especially the Focus/Select, Sustain, Inhibit, and Modulate capacities.

Bridging Strategies

Reflective questioning—Teachers, parents, and clinicians (referred to here as *mediators*) can encourage children to engage executive capacities through the use of reflective questioning. A child who asks others for assistance rather than trying to figure out the answer to their question on their own or who is unaware of the need to ask questions to be an active learner and producer is not engaging the executive capacities needed for self-reflection. In situations where the child asks a question, reflective questioning involves the mediator repeating the question back to the child instead of providing an answer. In situations where the child seems unaware of the need to be asking questions for adequate engagement, reflective questioning involves the mediator asking the child a question that is intended to make the child aware of the need to engage executive capacities and to subsequently engage them. In either case, the child is being prompted in a more general way to try to identify and engage executive capacities to the extent possible in order to respond to the question that was posed to them. The responses provided by the child offer the mediator great insight into the effectiveness of the child's executive capacities once they are cued for activation in a nonspecific manner. After receiving a response from the child, the mediator should engage in the next strategy described here—providing feedback about the adequacy of the child's response.

Providing feedback about the accuracy of performance—Feedback should be provided in as many situations as possible when a child attempts to engage executive capacities or in all situations when a child responds to questions designed to cue engagement of executive capacities. Providing immediate and frequent feedback about the effectiveness of performance, or feedback about the adequacy of responses to questions about performance, is perhaps the most effective means of increasing the likelihood of effective engagement of self-regulation capacities as well as a means for helping with the transition from external to internal control.

(continued)

(continued)

Modeling appropriate use of executive functions—Social modeling strategies are an effective means of helping children consciously or nonconsciously engage executive capacities to self-direct functioning.

Teaching specific executive skill routines—Although applied primarily in cognitive strategy training approaches focusing on improvement of academic functioning, these techniques can be adapted to address executive difficulties in the intrapersonal, interpersonal, and environment arenas as well. As in the academic arena where the task is dismantled into its component pieces and the child is given explicit self-direction cues (i.e., a plan of attack or action), to complete or accomplish the task, this same scaffolding can be provided for a child's interactions with others, awareness of self, or navigation of the environment.

Using verbal mediation—The capacity for generating internalized language is an extremely effective tool for improving self-regulation capacities. Cognitive Behavior Therapy (CBT) approaches are particularly effective examples of the use of self-talk to increase self-control. Social-story techniques also make great use of mediated language to generate changes in behavior.

Using verbal or nonverbal labeling—This strategy involves the development of a common vocabulary or set of metaphors or a common set of nonverbal symbols or images representing cues for the engagement of executive capacities or for describing internal experiences. One of the significant strengths of many CBT-oriented approaches such as Ross Greene's collaborative problem-solving approach (Greene, 2001, 2009; Greene & Albon, 2006) and Myrna Shure's *I can problem solve* (Shure, 1992, 2005) methods is the emphasis on developing a common vocabulary that can be used to describe the child's internal experiencing of perceptions, feelings, and thoughts and linking these mental experiences to routines for behavior control. In the case of children who are more visually oriented in their thinking and/or who have significant language impairments, nonverbal labels can serve a similar function (e.g., mentally picturing the image of a Stop sign to represent the inhibit cue).

Practice and rehearsal—The cognitive psychology literature on the development of expertise has made it clear that practice is the single best strategy for increasing proficiency. A child with executive difficulties will need to practice the use of the deficient executive capacities in order to become more effective in their application in a self-regulated manner. Practice also is the strategy most likely to accelerate neural growth, thereby helping to close the gap produced by maturational delays. Additionally, routines and the conditions in which they would be used can be rehearsed ahead of time to increase the likelihood that executive capacities will be used effectively in situations where they are required.

Aligning external demands with internal desires—For many children with executive difficulties, directing externally demanded production is much more difficult to accomplish than directing internally commanded production. This observed fact can be capitalized on in situations where flexibility can be exercised with external demands. When possible, making externally demanded production requirements match internally commanded desires for production will increase the likelihood of the child's effective use of self-regulation capacities to achieve the desired outcomes.

Teaching internal control strategies—Preparing the child to become self-regulated through the use of internal control requires the teaching of specific internal control strategies. These include ways to provide self-feedback (internal feedback), ways to select and self-administer rewards, and ways to self-monitor effectiveness and efficiency of executive capacity use. Some children with executive difficulties need assistance with learning how to generate and/or cue the use of internal perceptions, feelings, or thoughts or images of action to provide themselves with feedback about their perceptions, feelings, thoughts, or actions. Although many intervention approaches including CBT rely heavily on self-talk as a source for internal feedback, such feedback can come in the form of nonverbal processing of mental imagery.

Internal Control Strategies

Internal feedback—Once learned, knowing how and when to talk to oneself or when and how to engage internal imagery to guide perceptions, feelings, thoughts, and actions enables full internal control of self-regulation executive capacities and greater access to and control of other higher level executive capacities that are developing.

Self-administered rewards—Self-administered rewards are an effective way of self-aligning external demands with internal desires. Once learned and internally regulated, self-reward routines can be generated and used by the child to overcome resistance to, and to comply with, external demands for production and also to meet self-determined long-term goals.

Self-monitoring—Self-directed monitoring of perceptions, feelings, thoughts, and actions can ensure adequate production without any cueing or prompting from external sources. Once self-monitoring strategies have been learned and internalized, the self-regulated learner is able to recognize situations in which self-monitoring could be used and is able to cue and direct the effective use of self-monitoring strategies.

(McCloskey et al., 2009). The strategies discussed in this section are organized into four general categories:

1. *Orienting strategies*—These strategies are designed to increase the child's awareness of executive capacities and awareness of the executive difficulties that the child may be experiencing, and to set goals for behavior change through increased use of executive capacities.

2. *External control strategies*—These strategies are designed to manage executive difficulties; they involve things that others will do to have an immediate impact on the child's perceptions, feelings, thoughts, and actions to ameliorate problems.

3. *Bridging strategies*—These strategies are used to teach executive skills, to help the child engage existing executive skills that are not being used, to help the child practice underutilized executive skills, to increase the

child's awareness of when to engage one or more executive functions, or to increase awareness of how to engage one or more executive functions to respond effectively under conditions of external demand.

4. *Internal control strategies*—These strategies are used to help the child improve the capacity for internal self-regulation of executive capacities without input from others.

All of the strategies described in Rapid Reference 10.9, with the exception of pharmacology, are applicable to efforts to improve the use of the full spectrum of executive capacities used to direct perceptions, feelings, thoughts, and actions within the intrapersonal, interpersonal, environment, and symbol system arenas of involvement and in multiple settings within each arena (e.g., home, school, community). When tailoring an intervention for a specific child or a group of children, the orienting strategies listed should always be used. Beyond the orienting strategies, interventions will need to be tailored to fit the specifics of the case. External, Bridging, and Internal strategies represent a layered continuum of intervention options as shown in Figure 10.2.

The number and type of strategies employed will depend on the specific executive strengths of the client and the severity of the executive difficulties that are being exhibited. The more severe the executive difficulties the more likely it will be that multiple strategies will need to be used from the External Control category, and the more likely that these strategies will need to be employed for prolonged periods of time. Over time, the External Control strategies would

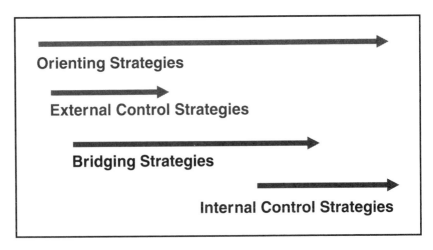

Figure 10.2. Layered Continuum of Executive Control Intervention Options

gradually be supplemented with Bridging strategies. As Bridging strategies increase in effectiveness, External Control strategies are faded out. Ideally, over time, Internal Control strategies would be introduced to supplement the Bridging strategies, eventually allowing for the fading out of the Bridging strategies and exclusive reliance on self-regulated Internal Control strategies. Children with milder executive difficulties and multiple executive strengths may move directly from Orienting strategies to Bridging strategies and make rapid progress toward the introduction of Internal Control strategies. A child (usually self-referred and older) presenting with only minor executive difficulties and many executive strengths may move directly from Orienting strategies to Internal Control strategies.

The CD that accompanies this book contains a case study describing the development and implementation of an intervention involving many of the strategies listed in Rapid Reference 10.9 to address the executive functions difficulties of a student with reading and writing disabilities.

INTERVENTIONS FOR EXECUTIVE DIFFICULTIES IMPACTING ACADEMIC SKILL PRODUCTION

Problems with reading, writing, and math that are typically associated with executive difficulties are listed in Rapid References 10.2, 10.3, and 10.4. This section discusses the application of the general intervention strategies listed in Rapid Reference 10.9 to address executive difficulties that significantly impact academic skill production in reading, writing, and math. Each of these general strategies can be adapted and tailored to the reading, writing, and math difficulties of any student regardless of the specific programs or techniques that are being used for academic skill instruction.

Rapid Reference 10.10 provides a general blueprint for the application of the general intervention strategies to improve executive capacities that significantly impact academic skill production. Note that the type and number of strategies used with a child will depend on the specific skill problems being exhibited and the specific executive capacities likely to be underlying the problem as well as the nature of the child's executive skills and executive functions strengths and weaknesses. The academic case study included on the CD accompanying this book provides an example of what a tailored intervention would look like for a child with executive difficulties impacting the use of specific academic skills.

Although Rapid References 10.2, 10.3, and 10.4 show the link between executive capacities and the performance of academic skills, clinicians may find

☰ Rapid Reference 10.10 Applying Strategies for Improving the Use of Executive Capacities When Reading, Writing, or Doing Math

Intervention Strategy (Type of Strategy)	Application of the Strategy to Academic Skills
Increasing Awareness of Executive Capacities (Orienting) **Using Verbal Mediation (Bridging)** **Establishing Intervention Goals (Orienting)** **Using Verbal or Nonverbal Labeling (Bridging)**	Engage in a direct discussion with the child to increase awareness of the specific problems that the child is having with academic skill production (e.g., not paying enough attention to each word when reading).
	Explain how executive capacities direct what we do even though we usually are not aware of them doing so, and how sometimes they do not work as well as they need to in order for us to do things well (e.g., the problem is not that the child cannot pay attention; the problem is that the child is not always directing their attention to make sure that they are paying close attention to every word).
	Explain how executive capacities can be improved so that we can see improvements in how we do things and that you are going to help him or her improve their executive capacities so that they can improve their specific reading, writing, or math difficulties.
	Explain that at first you will be providing lots of help with knowing when to use executive capacities and how to use them, but that, eventually, you want them to be able to tell himself or herself when and how to use them.
	Develop and share with the child (or more preferably include the child in the development of) goals for increased use of executive capacities while performing the targeted academic skills.
	Use metaphors and analogies to increase the child's understanding of the executive capacities that are used when performing the targeted academic skills.

Modeling Appropriate Use of Executive Capacities (Bridging)

Model effective use of executive capacities by performing the targeted academic skills. Explain how, even though you were not specifically thinking about them, your executive capacities were directing what you did. Explain that if you wanted to, you could have thought about how to direct what you were doing, and model a "think-aloud" to demonstrate.

Demonstrate use of the targeted skills and explain how the mistakes you made were the result of poor use of executive capacities to direct performance, then model a "think-aloud" about how to improve performance by using the needed executive capacities and demonstrate through improved performance.

Using Reflective Questioning (Bridging)

If the child asks questions about how to apply strategies that are being taught, reflect the question and have the child provide their thoughts on how to do what they are asking.

Prior to introducing a task, ask the child to tell you what they are thinking about how they are going to perform the task (e.g., What skills will you need to do this task? What questions will you need to be asking yourself as you do this task to make sure you do it correctly or effectively?).

Providing Feedback (Bridging)

Give feedback about the accuracy or adequacy of the child's responses.

Teaching Executive Skills Routines (Bridging)

Teach the student(s) how to engage in self-regulation routines for effectively performing the targeted academic skills.

Create a list of the cues (specifically the ones that the child frequently does not use) that can be consciously activated and practice the use of these routines.

(continued)

(*continued*)

Practice and Rehearsal (Bridging)

Providing Feedback (Bridging)

Discuss when in the performance of the targeted skills these routines would need to be activated for effective use.

Discuss ways to self-cue the recognition of the need to use the routines and ways to cue the engagement of the routines.

Rehearse and practice the use of taught routines.

Provide feedback about the child's efforts to self-regulate the use of executive capacities when performing the targeted academic skills.

Provide feedback about the effectiveness of the child's efforts to respond to external cues when performing the targeted academic skills.

Structuring the Environment (External Control)

During skill instruction, place on the child's desk a list of the steps of the strategy you want them to use during the lesson and prompt them to refer to the list as needed.

Providing Prompts (External Control)

While presenting a skill lesson, monitor the child's performance and offer prompts for engagement of the needed executive capacities. For example, for specific reading skills these would include prompts such as: "Look carefully at every letter of that word; now try to sound it out." "Stay focused on what you are reading." "Read each word as I point to it and keep pace with the movement of my finger." "Are you remembering to apply the comprehension strategy you learned?"

Structuring Time (External Control)

Help the student(s) improve awareness of the amount of time it takes them to perform tasks involving the targeted academic skills.

Provide time guidelines and prompts to monitor the length of time it takes to perform a task involving the targeted academic skills.

Providing Prompts (External Control)

Set time limits for specific tasks and provide time-related prompts to help students maintain awareness of the passage of time.

Providing Rewards (External Control)	Provide positive reinforcement and rewards for the effective self-regulation of the use of executive capacities when performing the targeted academic tasks. Use carefully selected rewards and establish reinforcement contingencies that are obtainable and realistic.
Aligning External Demands with Internal Desires (External Control)	Provide opportunities for the child to engage in activities of their own choosing, for example, reading books of their own choosing or writing on a topic of great interest to them. As much as possible, build lesson plans around topics that are of greatest interest to the child.
Teach the Use of Internal Feedback and Self-Monitoring (Bridging)	Teach the child how to use self-talk and self-monitoring routines to become aware of when to use specific executive capacities during task performance and to be aware of when they are using, or not using, the needed cues.
Teach the Use of Self-Administered Rewards (Bridging)	Help the child to develop internal sources of motivation for wanting to improve their performance of the targeted academic skills. Find ways to help the child realize the connection between the skills they need to improve and the activities for which they have the greatest interest. Help the child select rewards that can be self-administered and learn how to self-reward for effective performance of the targeted academic skill.

it difficult to sort out the role that each of the specific executive capacities plays in guiding academic production. While knowing exactly how each executive capacity impacts skill performance and which ones are not working effectively would undoubtedly increase the efficiency of intervention efforts, such definitive knowledge is not a necessary prerequisite for planning and implementing an effective intervention to improve the use of the deficient executive capacities.

Clinicians are encouraged to apply a collaborative problem-solving approach as elaborated by Greene (2009) when designing and implementing interventions intended to address executive difficulties. Such an approach relies more on the dialogue between the clinician and child to clearly identify the problem resulting from inadequate use of executive capacities and to determine the language or nonverbal images and metaphors that will enable the child to grasp the nature of the executive involvement in the problem and to tailor an intervention approach rather than on an understanding of the specifics of the neural mechanisms that are likely to be involved in the problem and the intervention. The goal of the collaborative process would be to identify language that can be used to describe the role of all of the executive capacities likely to be involved in effective production.

INTERVENTIONS FOR EXECUTIVE DIFFICULTIES IMPACTING READING

Even the best teachers using the best programs for teaching word recognition and decoding skills are sometimes mystified by students' inaccurate applications of the skills they have learned. When reading connected text, some of these students may inaccurately pronounce words that have been established as part of their sight-word recognition lexicon or fail to decode words that they have correctly decoded in the past. It is most likely that these students are not effectively using one or more self-regulation executive functions such as the Perceive, Focus, Monitor, Inhibit, Interrupt, Shift, Retrieve, Execute, Sequence, or Correct cues to process effectively the orthography of the words on the page. Intervention efforts to correct these word-reading difficulties should focus explicitly on improving the use of the executive capacities necessary for effective performance of these skills.

Children who exhibit poor use of the Pace cue when attempting to read words quickly often show a curious pattern of performance. These students read slowly, but increase their rate when the teacher uses prompting strategies to guide them, and then return to their slow pace when the external guidance is removed. Reading programs that focus on improving reading rate for these students employ various strategies, including guided repeated oral reading, paired reading, speeded word reading training, and the neural impress method. All of these techniques begin by externalizing the Pace cue by having someone or something other than the student set the pace for word reading rate. Gradually, through hundreds of practice trials, these students learn to adjust their internal Pace cueing to match the rate established by the use of the external Pace cues. Over time, the external Pace cues are faded and finally removed when the student has internalized a Pace cue setting more consistent with the average of age- or grade-level peers, and is able to maintain growth in adjusting that setting consistent with the growth experienced by same-age or same-grade peers.

DON'T FORGET
Multidimensional cognitive strategy instruction techniques and specific self-monitoring routines have been shown to be effective means of helping students develop a greater facility in using executive capacities during reading comprehension.

The complex nature of reading comprehension produces numerous ways for executive functions difficulties to impact students' reading production. Multidimensional cognitive strategy instruction techniques (Collins Block & Parris, 2008; Pressley et al., 1992; Pressley & Woloshyn, 1995) and specific self-monitoring routines (Borkowski & Muthukrishna, 1992; Case, Pericola, & Karen, 1992; Gerstein, Fuchs, Williams, & Baker, 2001; Jitendra, Hoppes, & Xin, 2000; Rosenshein & Meister, 1997) have been shown to be effective means of helping students develop a greater facility in using executive capacities during reading comprehension.

INTERVENTIONS FOR EXECUTIVE FUNCTION DIFFICULTIES IMPACTING WRITTEN EXPRESSION

The gateway skill for written production using pen/pencil and paper is the skill of handwriting. Developing the handwriting skill of young children presents a tremendous challenge to kindergarten and first-grade teachers charged with this task. Helping young children with relatively poor executive capacities automate the complex process of handling a writing implement and staying focused while retrieving recently stored kinetic melodies is no small feat. Not surprisingly, programs designed to help students develop automatic handwriting skills focus on creating in the student a conscious awareness of the motor processes involved in forming letters (Levine Rubbell, 1999; Olsen, 2008). Knowing the requirements of the task makes it much more likely that a young child will know what executive capacities need to be used and when they need to be used when attempting to produce printed letters. Of course, even knowing this does not necessarily guarantee success for children who are far behind their peers in executive control of attention and effort, motor memory, and motor production. For these students, intervention strategies will be almost exclusively focused on the use of external control substitutes during closely supervised guided practice sessions. In this area more than any other, recognizing the constraining effects of maturation on skill development is necessary, not just when working with young children, but also when working with late-elementary, middle, junior, and senior high school and college-age students.

Patience with slower rates of development and less-than-expected production is necessary to help students remain engaged with efforts to improve production with this very difficult skill. While it is critical to develop the capacity to communicate language through the motor systems that control the hands, it is essential to keep in mind that manipulating pens or pencils is not the only source of production of printed material. Although the belief is strong that handwriting strengthens the capacity for depth of processing of language when writing (Berninger & Richards, 2002), it is unclear whether this supposed advantage holds for children whose brains, from near-birth on, are continually exposed to the use of keyboards as a form of written language communication. What is certainly clear, however, is that the use of keyboarding skills, besides being the most viable alternative to handwriting, also happens to be the written production method for which mastery is almost universally demanded in the world of work.

Whether or not students learn to communicate their thoughts through printed and/or cursive handwritten script in early elementary school, there is no doubt that from junior high school age on they will be required to communicate those thoughts by keyboarding text. Recognition of this fact should inform decisions about what text production skills students are taught to automate and at what age they are taught to automate them, especially in the case of a student who consistently struggles with text production using pencils and pens despite adequate instruction to improve these skills.

Beyond the development of text transcription skills, a central technique of programs designed to help students improve written expression skills is the provision of highly structured, explicit strategies for generating, editing, and revising text. These programs make use of externally cued structures to scaffold the writing process in the absence of more internally directed cueing capacities. These scaffolds include strategy routines for idea generation, pre-planning and organi-zation of ideas, generation of text, monitoring text production for accuracy, and reviewing and revising produced text. The Self-Regulated Strategy Development (SRSD) model of Graham and Harris (2005) exemplifies this type of scaffolded strategy instruction approach. The model (Graham, Harris, & Troia, 2000) includes: planning by delineating what is required for the writing process (engaging the Gauge, Modulate, Plan, Organize, and Retrieve cues); conferencing on goals and strategies (activating the Initiate, Gauge, Modulate, Generate, Associate, Plan, Organize, and Retrieve cues); modeling the strategy; putting the strategies to be employed in memory by use of mnemonics (engaging the Store cue and developing a knowledge base to be accessed later by the Retrieve and

Execute cues); actual employment of the strategies (engaging the Retrieve, Execute, Monitor, and Correct cues in conjunction with the Hold, Manipulate, Generate, and Associate cues); and, finally, independent practice with the goal of skill generalization (self-regulation of all of the executive capacities). The efficacy of the SRSD approach is well-documented (Graham & Harris, 2005; De La Paz & Graham, 2002; Graham et al., 2000; Troia & Graham, 2002); its efficacy is likely due not only to the fact that automatization of these individual components is emphasized, but also to the fact that the skills learned model the use of the executive capacities required to direct the writing process. Additional study by De La Paz et al., (1998) also noted the efficacy of a structured and routinized approach that externally cues the process of reviewing and revising text. Graham (1997) highlighted the degree to which the subskills used in the revising process needed to be identified before students could develop real improvement in their ability to revise what they had written. Ferretti, MacArthur, and Dowdy (2000) also contributed to the findings relative to the efficacy of explicit planning and goal-setting along with instruction in cognitive and self-regulated strategies for persuasive writing.

The acquisition of handwriting, spelling, and composition (idea generation, text generation, revising, editing) skills involves a complex developmental progression. The acquisition of sufficient writing skills over the grades requires the coordination of multiple executive capacities to oversee the multitasking of cognitive skills used in the production of written material. Interventions for individuals with written expression weaknesses need to address the underlying skill deficits that contribute to the poor task attainment. For those with executive deficits, achieving fluency in the lower-level skills of handwriting and spelling allow for greater attention to the more complex processes involved in composition. At this more complex level, interventions need to help students learn how to self-regulate—through scaffolding routines and modeling—the coordination of the cognitive skills required for planning, organizing, generating, editing, and revising a written product.

INTERVENTIONS FOR EXECUTIVE FUNCTIONS DIFFICULTIES IMPACTING MATH

As was the case with handwriting, automaticity of graphomotor production of numbers and mathematics symbols is critical to the effective development of computation skills (Berninger & Richards, 2002). Students exhibiting executive difficulties with control of the production of numbers and symbols will require intervention efforts similar to those provided for handwriting. Students who make computation errors such as misreading operation signs or transposing numbers are experiencing difficulties with the Perceive, Inhibit, and/or Focus cues in a manner similar to students who have difficulty attending to orthography when reading, and would benefit from the use of strategies similar to those recommended for readers with such difficulties.

Helping students improve the use of executive capacities for efficient production with procedural routines for computation and problem solving is analogous to the situation encountered in helping students be more productive writers. Similar to the cognitive strategy interventions that attempt to enable students to self-regulate the complex processes involved in writing, interventions for improved math computation and problem-solving production focus on cognitive strategy instruction routines (Jitendra & Hoff, 1996; Kelly & Carnine, 1996) designed to increase the self-cueing capacities of the student.

INTERVENTION FOR EXECUTIVE-RELATED ACADEMIC PRODUCTION DIFFICULTIES IN THE UPPER GRADES

Clinicians who develop an understanding of executive functions and how they impact behavior and academic production can apply this knowledge to help parents, teachers, administrators, and other school staff in understanding the increased demands the upper grades place on students. Rapid Reference 10.11 provides a list of ways that instruction can be tailored to help students adjust more effectively to these increased demands.

≡ Rapid Reference 10.11 Tailoring Instruction in Upper Grades to Address Executive Difficulties

1. Orientation sessions and extended orientation periods to help students become aware of, and adjust to, the increased executive demands of new settings.
2. Availability of, or mandatory scheduling of, study skills courses to help students become more consciously aware of the kinds of executive capacities that will be required for success in the new setting and to help them develop skill-based routines and cognitive strategies that they can apply when studying.
3. Demonstration, usually embedded in content area courses, of the steps in planning and organizing long-term projects, and guided practice through the steps before assignment of large-scale, independent projects.
4. Direct instruction in test-taking skills.
5. Direct instruction in note-taking skills.

6. Peer tutoring programs that offer assistance with homework, studying for tests, and planning and organization of large-scale projects.

7. Provision of systems to improve home–school communication, such as homework hotlines and posting homework assignments and grades online at a school website.

8. Practice of good classroom test construction principles by teachers, such as avoiding "executive traps" on tests, and realizing the effects of format on performance.

9. Thoughtful use of reward/punishment systems as incentive to complete homework, for example, providing extra points for on-time completion of homework rather than loss of points for not completing homework on time.

PROGRESS MONITORING

The ultimate test of an intervention is whether we can see progress toward the goals we have established. Progress monitoring therefore is critical. Patience, however, is required. Not all interventions work quickly, especially if the child's difficulties are related to maturational delays. Practice is the critical element. Clinicians sometimes eschew the use of cognitively loaded orienting and bridging strategies, preferring to stick with more behaviorally oriented external control strategies. One advantage of external control strategy use is that these strategies are easier to monitor and progress is more likely to be seen since the external manipulations serve to compensate for the lack of adequate development in the child's brain. If the interventionist has a well-developed set of executive functions, gains can be immediate. The danger in exclusively using external control strategies, however, is that the child usually is not made consciously aware of what is happening and does not take an active role in the strategies. External control strategies do not teach the child how to take greater control of perceptions, feelings, thoughts, or actions; rather they manipulate the child into a circumstance where greater control of perceptions, feelings, thoughts, and actions occurs.

In situations where immediate progress is paramount, there will be a great deal of pressure on clinicians to rely solely on external control strategies because they are the most likely to produce immediate results and continue to produce consistent results over time. The clinician must have a plan for moving from external control strategies to bridging strategies and eventually to internal control strategies in order for the ultimate goal of effective self-regulated production to be realized.

In the case of academic interventions, external control likely will produce results only while the clinician is directly involved with the child's efforts to produce. Beyond the use of some individually administered assessment formats, however, progress in the use of executive capacities to improve academic production typically is measured through the use of assessment formats that require greater levels of self-regulation of learned strategies. As a result, progress monitoring is not likely to produce the desired results unless bridging strategies leading to greater self-regulated internal control have been implemented and are taking hold.

SUMMARY

Appropriate assessment and intervention of executive difficulties begins with a definition and understanding of how executive skills and executive functions interact. This complex neural network drives the perceptions, feelings, thoughts, and actions that are deemed necessary by the executive functions. The nature and expression of executive functions is highly diverse. In the case of academic performance, it is often difficult to identify the specific executive capacities that are not being engaged efficiently since academic tasks may involve multiple executive capacities and require the use of multiple processes, abilities, skills, and lexicons. If executive difficulties are implicated, assessment also should utilize direct and/or indirect measures to identify the nature of the difficulty, along with the identification of executive capacity strengths that could be used to support intervention efforts.

Effective assessment and conceptualization of the child's capabilities plays an important role in the development of an appropriate intervention plan. General guidelines for planning and implementing interventions for children exhibiting executive difficulties include broad-based assessment, an understanding of the frequency and nature of the problem, and frequent progress monitoring to determine when a shift from externally controlled to internally driven strategies is appropriate. Orienting strategies, external control strategies, bridging strategies, and internal control strategies provide a comprehensive model for intervening in ways appropriate to student developmental level and environment, and these general

---

DON'T FORGET

If executive difficulties are implicated, assessment also should utilize direct and/or indirect measures to identify the nature of the difficulty, along with the identification of executive capacity strengths that could be used to support intervention efforts.

strategies can be applied to academic and behavioral need areas across grade levels. Finally, as the ultimate goal of the practitioner/interventionist is to facilitate change in the student, practitioners must remain committed to progress monitoring of all strategies utilized. Such monitoring can ensure that executive needs are being addressed and interventions are tailored appropriately on an ongoing basis to match the student's current strengths and weaknesses.

REFERENCES

Berninger, V. W., & Richards, T. L. (2002). *Brain literacy for educators and psychologists.* New York, NY: Academic Press.

Borkowski, J. G., & Muthukrishna, N. (1992). Moving metacognition into the classroom: "Working models" and effective strategy teaching. In M. Pressley, K. R. Harris, & J. T. Guthrie (Eds.), *Promoting academic competence and literacy in school* (pp. 477–501). San Diego, CA: Academic Press.

Case, L., Pericola, H., & Karen, R. (1992). Improving the mathematical problem-solving skills of students with learning disabilities: Self-regulated strategy development. *Journal of Special Education, 26,* 1–14.

Collins Block, C., & Parris, S.E. (2008). *Comprehension instruction* (2nd ed.): *Research-based best practices.* New York, NY: Guilford Press.

De La Paz, S., & Graham, S. (2002). Explicitly teaching strategies, skills, and knowledge: Writing instruction in middle school classrooms. *Journal of Educational Psychology, 94,* 687–698.

De La Paz, S., Swanson, P. N., & Graham, S. (1998). The contribution of executive control to the revising by students with writing and learning difficulties. *Journal of Educational Psychology, 90,* 448–460.

Ferretti, R. P., MacArthur, C. A., & Dowdy, N. S. (2000). The effects of an elaborated goal on the persuasive writing of students with learning disabilities and their normally achieving peers. *Journal of Educational Psychology, 92,* 694–702.

Gerstein, R., Fuchs, L. S., Williams, J. P., & Baker, S. (2001). Teaching reading comprehension strategies to students with learning disabilities: A review of research. *Review of Educational Research, 71*(2), 279–320.

Gioia, G. A., Isquith, P. K., Guy, S. C., & Kenworthy, L. (1996). *Behavior rating inventory of executive function: Professional manual.* Lutz, FL: Psychological Assessment Resources.

Graham, S. (1997). Executive control in the revising of students with learning and writing difficulties. *Journal of Educational Psychology, 89,* 223–234.

Graham, S., & Harris, K. R. (2005). Improving the writing performance of young struggling writers: Theoretical and programmatic research from the Center of Accelerating Student Learning. *Journal of Special Education, 39,* 19–34.

Graham, S., Harris, K. R., & Troia, G. A. (2000). Self-regulated strategy development revisited: Teaching writing strategies to struggling writers. *Topics in Language Disorders, 20,* 1–15.

Graham, S., MacArthur, C.A., & Fitzgerald, J. (Eds.). (2007). *Best practices in writing instruction.* New York, NY: Guilford Press.

Greene, R. W. (2001). *The explosive child: A new approach for understanding and parenting easily frustrated, chronically inflexible children.* New York, NY: Perennial.

Greene, R. W. (2009). *Lost at school: Why our kids with behavioral challenges are falling through the cracks and how we can help them.* New York, NY: Scribner.

Greene, R. W., & Albon, J. S. (2006). *Treating explosive kids: The collaborative problem-solving approach.* New York, NY: Guilford Press.

Hale, J. B., Fiorello, C. A., & Brown, L. (2005). Determining medication treatment effects using teacher ratings and classroom observations of children with ADHD: Does neuropsychological impairment matter? *Educational and Child Psychology, 22*, 39–61.

Hale, J. B., Hoeppner, J. B., DeWitt, M. B., Coury, D. L., Ritacco, D. G., & Trommer, B. (1998). Evaluating medication response in ADHD: Cognitive, behavioral, and single-subject methodology. *Journal of Learning Disabilities, 31*(6), 595–607.

Hoeppner, J. B., Hale, J. B., Bradley, A. M., Byrnes, M., Coury, D. L., Lennie, L., & Trommer, B. L. (1997). A clinical protocol for determining methylphenidate dosage levels in ADHD. *Journal of Attention Disorders, 2*(1), 19–30.

Jitendra, A. K., & Hoff, K. (1996). The effects of schema-based instruction on the mathematical word-problem-solving performance of students with learning disabilities. *Journal of Learning Disabilities, 29*(4), 422–431.

Jitendra, A. K., Hoppes, M. K., & Xin, Y. P. (2000). Enhancing main idea comprehension for students with learning problems: The role of summarization strategy and self-monitoring instruction. *Journal of Special Education, 34*(3), 127–139.

Kelly, B., & Carnine, D. (1996). *Teaching problem-solving strategies for word problems to students with learning disabilities.* Unpublished manuscript. Retrieved from http://www.cldinternational.org/PDF/Initiatives/MathSeries/kelly.pdf.

Levine Rubell, B. (1999). *Big strokes for little folks.* San Antonio, TX: Psychological Corporation.

McCloskey, G., & Perkins, L. A. (2012). *Essentials of executive functions assessment.* New York, NY: Wiley.

McCloskey, G., Perkins, L. A., & VanDivner, B. (2009). *Assessment and intervention for executive function difficulties.* New York, NY: Routledge Press.

Olsen, J.Z. (2008). Handwriting Without Tears research review. *Handwriting Without Tears.* Retrieved January 28, 2013, from http://www.hwtears.com/hwt/why-it-works/research.

Pressley, M., El-Dinary, P., Gaskins, I., Schuder, T., Bergman, J., Almasi, J., & Brown, R. (1992). Beyond direct explanation: Transactional instruction of reading comprehension strategies. *Elementary School Journal, 92*(5), 513–555.

Pressley, M., & Woloshyn, V. (Eds.). (1995). *Cognitive strategy instruction that really improves children's academic performance.* Cambridge, MA: Brookline Books.

Rosenshine, B., & Meister, C. (1997). Cognitive strategy instruction in reading. In S. A. Stahl & D. A. Hayes (Eds.), *Instructional models in reading* (pp. 85–107). Hillsdale, NJ: Lawrence Erlbaum Associates.

Shure, M. B. (1992). *Cognitive problem solving program.* Champaign, IL: Research Press.

Shure, M. B. (2005). *Thinking parent, thinking child.* Champaign, IL: Research Press.

Stuss, D. T., & Alexander, M. P. (2000). Executive functions and the frontal lobes: A conceptual view. *Psychological Research, 63*(3–4), 289–298.

Troia, G. A., & Graham, S. (2002). The effectiveness of a highly explicit, teacher-directed strategy instruction routine: Changing the writing performance of students with learning disabilities. *Journal of Learning Disabilities, 35*, 290–306.

 **TEST YOURSELF**

1. **A holoarchical model of executive functions is based on the concept of:**

   a. External locus of control

   b. Multiple levels of executive control

   c. Singular executive control center

   d. Holographic model of executive control

2. **All of the following reflect ineffective use of self-regulation executive capacities *except*:**

   a. Inability to focus attention

   b. Failure to correct errors

   c. Falling asleep in class

   d. Inability to inhibit impulsive responding

3. **The relationship between executive functions and executive skills is most like the relationship between:**

   a. Senator and citizen

   b. Orchestra conductor and section leader

   c. Coach and athlete

   d. Sister and brother

4. **Executive functions difficulties in the classroom are most likely to be described by classroom teachers as:**

   a. Problems with effective production

   b. Problems with effective learning

   c. Problems with parenting

   d. Problems with early development

5. **All of the following statements describe keys to accurate conceptualization of executive capacity difficulties *except*:**

   a. Executive difficulties are associated with suboptimal brain function.

   b. Brain function associated with executive functions can be altered through intervention.

   c. Maturational delays in the development of executive capacities will slow the rate of progress during intervention efforts.

   d. Executive difficulties are the result of a lack of motivation to perform well.

6. **A problem with overreliance on rewards and punishments to improve a student's classroom production is that rewards and punishments:**

   a. Don't work

   b. Don't teach students how to improve their use of executive capacities

   c. Require too much time and effort on the part of the teacher

   d. Require participation of the parents as well as the teacher

   (continued)

(continued)

7. Any executive capacity intervention efforts should always start with a(n)

a. Orienting strategy

b. External control strategy

c. Bridging strategy

d. Internal control strategy

8. An intervention that teaches a student how to improve the use of executive capacities is referred to as a(n)

a. Orienting strategy

b. External control strategy

c. Bridging strategy

d. Internal control strategy

9. Self-monitoring is an example of a(n)

a. Orienting strategy

b. External control strategy

c. Bridging strategy

d. Internal control strategy

10. Asking students questions that require them to use executive capacities in order to provide an answer is an example of a(n)

a. Orienting strategy

b. External control strategy

c. Bridging strategy

d. Internal control strategy

Answers: 1. b; 2. c; 3. c; 4. a; 5. d; 6. b; 7. a; 8. c; 9. d; 10. c

Eleven

INTERVENTIONS FOR STUDENTS WITH MEMORY DIFFICULTIES

Milton J. Dehn

S tudents with memory difficulties are an under-identified and underserved population. Alloway and Gathercole (2006), who have investigated the prevalence of childhood memory difficulties in the United Kingdom (UK), reported that 10% of children have working memory deficits. In another UK study by Temple and Richardson (2006), approximately 6% of students without disabilities were found to have long-term memory difficulties. Most children with memory impairments remain unidentified, primarily because in-depth memory testing is seldom conducted during cognitive assessment and because memory impairments are not recognized as a type of educational disability. Despite the absence of data on how many children and adolescents with memory difficulties (identified or unidentified) receive school-based interventions specifically for memory difficulties, it can be safely assumed that the majority do not.

The strong connection between memory and learning is evident in students with specific learning disabilities (SLD). In a study by Gathercole and Pickering (2001), the working memory performance of 4-year-olds was an accurate predictor of who would need special education in early elementary school. Alloway (2011) contends that working memory is the best predictor of academic learning, even better than IQ. Dehn (2010) estimates that approximately half of students with SLD have a memory impairment. Given that academic learning and performance depend heavily on working memory and that the acquisition of knowledge depends on long-term memory, it is alarming that students with memory impairments are under-identified and underserved.

A COMPREHENSIVE ASSESSMENT

Once it is hypothesized that memory is a weakness for a student, an assessment that reliably and validly samples all of the major memory systems and processes is essential for planning, selecting, and tailoring effective memory interventions. The auditory or verbal and visual-spatial dimensions of all three major memory systems—working memory, short-term memory, and long-term memory—should be tested (see Rapid Reference 11.1). Each of the components listed in Rapid Reference 11.1 are defined later in this chapter. In addition, the executive aspects of working memory need to be considered, along with metamemory development and the use of memory strategies (Dehn, 2008). Attempts should also be made to differentiate functioning of the long-term memory processes of encoding, consolidation, storage, and retrieval (Dehn, 2010).

To keep such a comprehensive assessment time-efficient, a selective, cross-battery testing approach should be used. Cross-battery assessment of memory is essentially a neuropsychological approach in which more than one assessment instrument is used. Cross-battery testing is necessary because a single instrument (even one designed for memory assessment) seldom includes measures of all the fundamental memory components. To apply the cross-battery testing model, practitioners should begin with the most comprehensive memory battery available, and then supplement it with additional scales until all of the essential memory

≡ Rapid Reference 11.1 Memory Components and Processes to Assess When Designing Memory Interventions

- Phonological short-term memory
- Visual-spatial short-term memory
- Verbal working memory
- Visual-spatial working memory
- Executive working memory
- Verbal long-term memory
- Visual-spatial long-term memory
- Encoding
- Consolidation
- Storage
- Retrieval
- Metamemory
- Memory strategy use

functions have been sampled (see Flanagan, Ortiz, & Alfonso, 2007, 2013). For the sake of efficiency, redundancy should be avoided. After a memory component has been adequately sampled with two subtests, there's no need to administer additional subtests from other batteries. For example, when there are verbal working memory scores available from previous cognitive testing, there is no need to administer additional verbal working memory subtests when a memory scale is used to supplement the cognitive scale. Examiners can also be efficient by being cognizant of subtests that measure certain memory dimensions, but are not officially labeled or classified as doing so. For example, the Woodcock-Johnson® III Tests of Achievement's (WJ III ACH) *Understanding Directions* test (Woodcock, McGrew, & Mather, 2001) is an appropriate measure of executive working memory, even though the WJ III ACH lists it as a measure of oral language. (Selective testing tables for working memory can be found in Dehn, 2008, and similar tables for long-term memory in Dehn, 2010.) Once selective, cross-battery testing is complete, the examinee's memory strengths, weaknesses, and deficits can be identified by using a cross-battery analysis procedure (Dehn, 2008, 2010; see the "Analysis of Test Results" section later in this chapter).

Cross-battery testing of working memory can be illustrated with the use of the Wechsler Intelligence Scale–Fourth Edition (WISC-IV; Wechsler, 2003) and the processing supplement to the WISC-IV, known as the WISC-IV–Integrated (Kaplan, Fein, Kramer, Delis, & Morris, 2004). First, verbal working memory could be assessed with the WISC-IV's Letter-Number Sequencing and Digit Span Backward. Then, the WISC-IV–Integrated could be employed to measure visual-spatial working memory only (ignoring its verbal working memory subtests), using Spatial Span Backward. Similarly, after testing verbal long-term memory with the Test of Memory and Learning–Second Edition (TOMAL2; Reynolds & Voress, 2007), an additional memory battery will be necessary in order to cover visual-spatial long-term memory (which the TOMAL2 does not measure). In this instance, the Children's Memory Scale (CMS; Cohen, 1997) could be utilized to assess visual-spatial long-term memory without administering any of the CMS's verbal long-term memory subtests.

Health and Developmental History

The collection of a thorough health and developmental history is a crucial component of any memory assessment because there are numerous health conditions and developmental disorders that predispose children to memory impairments. For example, childhood diabetes puts children at risk for memory problems. Rapid Reference 11.2 summarizes the research on many of these conditions by identifying the memory components and processes that are most commonly affected by the health condition or related to the developmental disorder. For example, research indicates that childhood diabetes will affect both verbal and visual-spatial long-term memory, as well as short-term memory and metamemory. The informed examiner will also need to be aware of the variables that increase the risk of memory impairments. For childhood diabetes, early onset and poor management of the disease increase the risk of cumulative damage to the hippocampus (Hershey, Lillie, Sadler, & White, 2003). Certain disabilities and disorders, such as *attention-deficit/hyperactivity disorder* (ADHD) and *post-traumatic stress disorder* (PTSD), also tend to have comorbid memory impairments. See Dehn (2010) for a more detailed discussion on how these and other health conditions and disorders impact memory components and processes.

Metamemory Development and Strategy Use

Metamemory development and strategy use are executive function dimensions that impact working memory performance and long-term retention of information. Metamemory involves knowledge and understanding of human memory functions, such as understanding the difference between short- and long-term memory (Schneider, 2010). Metamemory also includes self-awareness of one's memory strengths and weaknesses, for instance, knowing that one has stronger visual-spatial than verbal memory. Finally, metamemory includes self-regulation of memory functions, such as making a conscious effort to retrieve information. Poor metamemory development is associated with limited use of memory strategies because the individual does not understand why, how, and when to use strategies.

As metamemory develops there is a corresponding increase in memory strategies and their application (Harris, 1996). Increased strategy use also is correlated with academic learning demands (Ornstein, Grammer, & Coffman, 2010). Strategy development progresses from simple rehearsal in the preschool years to more complex mnemonics, such as the use of acronyms and semantic clustering of items. Students with specific learning disabilities and memory impairments tend to be less strategic, even when they are aware of strategies. One reason that these students employ strategies infrequently is that strategy learning and use add to cognitive load. As cognitive load increases, less information is retained in short-term and working memory (Barrouillet, Portrat, & Camos, 2011). As a result, students with working memory weaknesses become frustrated

Rapid Reference 11.2 Types of Memory Significantly Affected by Specific Health and Developmental Risk Factors

Risk Factor	Verbal	Visual-Spatial	Short-Term	Working	Long-Term	Encoding	Retrieval	Metamemory
ADHD				X				X
Asthma medication	X							X
Autism	X	X	X					X
Childhood diabetes	X	X	X					X
Childhood stroke			X		X		X	
Congenital hypothyroidism			X		X	X	X	
Depression	X	X	X	X		X		X
Developmental amnesia					X		X	
Down syndrome	X	X	X				X	
Epilepsy	X	X	X				X	
Excess bilirubin levels			X					
Frontal lobe lesions					X	X	X	X
Graves' disease			X	X				X
Learning disabilities	X			X		X	X	X
Medulloblastoma	X	X				X	X	X
Obsessive-compulsive disorder	X	X	X	X		X	X	X
Pediatric bipolar disorder	X	X		X	X			X

(continued)

Risk Factor	Verbal	Visual-Spatial	Short-Term	Working	Long-Term	Encoding	Retrieval	Metamemory
Perinatal asphyxia	X	X			X			
Prematurity	X				X			
Prenatal alcohol exposure	X	X	X	X		X	X	
Prenatal cocaine exposure	X	X	X	X				
PTSD, abuse, chronic stress	X		X			X	X	
Reye's syndrome	X	X		X	X	X		X
Sleep apnea	X		X	X		X	X	X
Specific language impairment	X					X		
TBI	X	X	X	X	X	X	X	X
Williams syndrome	X	X		X				X

with trying to apply a new memory strategy. Consequently, they abandon the new strategy.

Although most working memory impairments are related to diminished capacity (Swanson, 2000) and most long-term memory impairments result from hippocampal damage (Dehn, 2010), recall of information depends

DON'T FORGET

....

Examinees with memory problems should be carefully questioned about their use of memory strategies in order to informally appraise how much of their poor memory performance can be attributed to limited use of strategies, rather than neurologically based memory impairments.

heavily on strategic behavior. For instance, Schneider (2010) reported a very strong correlation of .81 between strategy use and recall. Thus, practitioners should interview examinees about metamemory development and strategy use in order to appraise the influence that these factors have on the examinee's memory performance. Interview items should address the examinee's beliefs about human memory limitations, understanding of individual memory strengths and weaknesses, use of strategies, and knowledge about the applications of strategies (see Rapid Reference 11.3 for examples of metamemory interview items). For example, an adolescent who believes that all memory strategies are ineffective is unlikely to invest much time in attempting to memorize information. Another informal procedure is to assess the examinee's "judgments of learning" by having the examinee estimate how well he or she will recall information that is studied (Koriat, 2008). Unrealistically high judgments of learning recall are indications of immature memory development (Son, 2005).

≋ Rapid Reference 11.3 Examples of Metamemory Interview Items

....

1. What are the different kinds of memory that you have?
2. What kinds of information are easier for you to remember?
3. How long does short-term memory last?
4. Why do people forget things?
5. What do you do when you really want to remember something?
6. Do you have any control over how well you remember?

Classroom Environment and Academic Performance

The examinee's teacher can have a strong influence on the examinee's memory-dependent classroom performance and long-term recall. As such, an instructional observation is important when assessing memory functioning and identifying targets for memory interventions. Practitioners should observe for teacher behaviors that increase the learner's *cognitive load* (Kirschner, 2002), such as verbosity and disorganized presentations (see Rapid Reference 11.4), and that result in an *overloaded* working memory that is unable to complete a cognitive task or effectively encode new learning into long-term memory (de Jong, 2010). Practitioners also should appraise the instructor's *mnemonic style*. That is, does the teacher encourage and support the use of strategic behavior? For example, a mnemonic teacher will remind students to frequently review information and give them the opportunity to do so. Also, teachers should be interviewed to evaluate their understanding of the student's difficulties as they relate to memory functioning. For example, a naïve teacher will frequently attribute poor working memory ability to attention deficits and poor long-term recall to a lack of motivation for studying.

A classroom observation should also note student behaviors that are indicative of memory difficulties (see Rapid References 11.5 and 11.6). Of course, there are often several potential problems that can underlie poor performance associated with memory. For example, not completing multistep directions could be due to memory limitations but could also occur because of such factors as inattentiveness

---

≡ Rapid Reference 11.4 Teacher Behaviors That Increase the Learner's Cognitive Load, Making It Difficult for the Learner to Encode Information Into Long-Term Memory

- Long, complex, and inconsistent verbalizations
- Disorganized presentations and lessons
- Not allowing enough time for learners to process information
- Requiring students to multitask
- Not allowing students to use memory aids
- Allowing a noisy learning environment
- Excessively long lessons
- Introducing procedural steps before they are needed

≡ Rapid Reference 11.5 Examples of Student Behaviors Indicative of Working Memory Deficits

- Forgets what he or she was going to say when called on in class
- Forgets some of the steps when given multistep directions
- Requires frequent repetition and reminders
- Forgets what he or she was doing
- Has trouble remembering information for just a few seconds
- Has difficulty thinking about and retaining information at the same time
- Forgets the necessary information before completing a mental task
- Has difficulty repeating what was just said to him or her
- Has difficulty listening and taking notes at the same time
- Has difficulty remembering what he or she just saw
- Loses place when counting
- Has difficulty organizing information when writing
- In the middle of an activity, forgets how to continue or finish it
- Has difficulty multitasking without forgetting information
- Has difficulty with mental arithmetic

Source: Dehn (2012), with permission from Schoolhouse Educational Services.

≡ Rapid Reference 11.6 Examples of Student Behaviors Indicative of Long-Term Memory Impairments

- Is slow to recall names of people, objects, or events
- Has difficulty memorizing and retaining new facts
- Has difficulty remembering step-by-step procedures
- Has difficulty remembering details
- Has difficulty recalling information during tests
- Has difficulty remembering nursery rhymes or stories
- Has difficulty rapidly naming well-known objects
- Needs prompts and cues to recall what he or she knows
- Has difficulty remembering the sequence of events
- Has difficulty remembering information presented in class

Source: Dehn (2012), with permission from Schoolhouse Educational Services.

or lack of interest. Consequently, multiple behaviors that can be associated with memory difficulties should be evident before any conclusions regarding memory deficits are drawn. Data on the student's classroom examination performance should also be gathered during a comprehensive long-term memory assessment. The memory demands of the examinations on which the student struggles should be noted. For example, a science exam that requires the recall of many new facts, science terms, and equations will place higher demands on long-term memory than a language arts quiz on a recently read chapter from a novel. An attempt should be made to correlate test scores with study time and use of strategies by questioning the student in depth about study habits and strategies. For instance, a memory problem is indicated when a student with average intelligence performs poorly on an exam after spending hours preparing for an exam while utilizing appropriate memory strategies. When scholastic data and standardized test results are inconsistent, the specific reasons for the inconsistency should be investigated. Students with significant memory difficulties in a busy classroom will sometimes perform better on a standardized memory battery because the testing protocol provides structure and allows the student to focus.

Analysis of Test Results

After all the assessment data have been gathered, the test scores should be analyzed with the goal of identifying the individual's memory strengths and weaknesses. When there has been selective, cross-battery testing, all of the subtest scores should be analyzed together (see Dehn, 2010, for a cross-battery analysis worksheet). Either a global ability score (e.g., the examinee's IQ) or the mean of the subtest scores from the different batteries can be used to predict subtest and cluster scores. Scores that are 12 or more standard score points (using a mean of 100 and standard deviation of 15) discrepant from the prediction can be considered intra-individual (ipsative) strengths or weaknesses. Memory components that are ipsative weaknesses and also below average (relative to most people) are associated with more serious learning and memory problems than ipsative weaknesses that are within the average range. When a score is both below average (below a standard score of 90) and an ipsative weakness, it should be considered a *deficit* (Dehn, 2006). Deficits are rare and are indicative of underlying neurological problems.

The next step is to compare pairs of scores for relative strengths and weaknesses. For this procedure, the difference should be at least 15 points.

Memory components that should be paired for comparison are opposites, such as verbal and visual-spatial memory, and components that should be similar, such as phonological short-term memory and verbal working memory. Pairwise comparisons will be particularly helpful when designing interventions. The final

DON'T FORGET
....
Further assessment may be necessary when inconsistencies between test scores and informal assessment data cannot be explained.

step is to review informal assessment data and determine how well it corroborates the strengths and weaknesses indicated by the analysis of test scores. When there is an inconsistency, the practitioner should develop hypotheses to account for it or pursue more assessment to determine the actual functioning level of the memory component.

DESIGNING AN INTERVENTION

The memory weaknesses identified through assessment can be improved through evidence-based interventions (see Dehn, 2008, 2010, for reviews of the research). Strategies that improve long-term recall have been studied for more than 50 years, whereas most of the research on exercises that can boost short-term and working memory capacity has occurred within the last 15 years (e.g., Holmes, Gathercole, & Dunning, 2009). Only recently has there been consistent evidence that working memory exercises can strengthen working memory functions. For instance, Tageuchi et al. (2010) discovered measureable growth in the brain's white matter along with improved working memory performance following working memory training.

Given recent evidence of the brain's plasticity in regard to working memory, interventions for working memory deficits should include procedures designed to strengthen working memory rather than just providing accommodations or teaching the learner to compensate for the deficit. In contrast, there are no evidence-based exercises that "strengthen" or "remediate" long-term memory impairments (Wilson, 2009). The approach with long-term memory problems is to employ strategies that enhance memory performance through more effective utilization of the individual's weak memory functions. Some of these strategies might be thought of as *compensatory*, such as visual recoding of verbal information when verbal memory is weaker than visual memory, but they all serve the same purpose of enhancing recall. Ideally, an intervention should be designed to capitalize on the individual's strengths

368 ESSENTIALS OF INTERVENTIONS FOR UNIQUE LERNERS

while simultaneously trying to strengthen the weaknesses (Rankin & Hood, 2005). Accommodations should also be included, especially when the impairment is severe.

Selecting Exercises and Strategies

Given the sizable menu of exercises and strategies from which to draw, the challenge is to select options that best meet the learner's needs, without overly relying on trial-and-error. Rapid References 11.7 and 11.8 list recommendations for specific memory weaknesses. The strategies listed in these rapid references are explained later in this chapter. A single exercise or strategy will seldom be sufficient. For successful working memory training, several exercises may be necessary. Likewise, several long-term memory strategies may be necessary to address the different types of materials and situations the learner may encounter. However, once a successful set of methods has been established, the trainer and trainee should hone in on these; it is not necessary to learn every available strategy.

In making the initial selection, the trainer should consider:

1. *The learner's current needs, goals, and priorities.* For example, a student who must learn a second language will find the keyword mnemonic (keyword procedures are described under the "Visual Mnemonics" section later in this chapter) helpful but would otherwise have little use for it.
2. *Related cognitive processing weaknesses.* For instance, a student with poorly developed executive functions may find complex strategies too difficult.
3. *The severity of any working memory deficits.* Learning and applying a new strategy increases the cognitive load that working memory must cope with. In such instances, the cognitive load will further reduce the amount of information that can be retained. In these situations, the best options are simple strategies or complex strategies that can be practiced one step at a time. For students with low working memory ability, memory aids, such as visual aids and lists of strategy steps, will also minimize the additional load created during strategy learning.
4. *How well the strategy generalizes.* Some strategies, such as keyword, which is designed for learning new vocabulary, apply only to certain types of materials.

≡ *Rapid Reference 11.7 Exercises and Strategies for Specific Short-Term Memory (STM) and Working Memory (WM) Deficits*

Memory Deficit	Rehearsal	N-Back	Counting Span	Arithmetic Flash Cards	Visual-Spatial Recall	Following Directions
Phonological STM	X					X
Visual-spatial STM	X				X	
Verbal WM				X		X
Visual-spatial WM		X	X		X	
Executive WM		X	X	X		X

Rapid Reference 11.8 Strategies for Specific Long-Term Memory Deficits

Memory Deficit	Semantic Clustering	Elaboration	Rehearsal	Dual Encoding	Self-Testing	Visual Mnemonics
Verbal	X	X		X	X	X
Visual			X	X		
Encoding	X	X		X	X	X
Retrieval	X	X		X	X	X
Metamemory	X	X		X	X	

5. *The extent of practice required to obtain fluency with the strategy.* Time constraints and the motivation of the learner need to be considered.

6. *The learner's age, cognitive ability, and extent of meta-memory awareness.* The methods selected need to be appropriate for the trainee's developmental level.

> **CAUTION**
>
> For a student with below-average working memory capacity, avoid overloading the student's working memory during strategy training. Begin with simple strategies and introduce and practice complex strategies one step at a time.

Monitoring Progress and Modifying the Intervention

As with any problem-solving approach, progress should be constantly monitored, and modifications to the intervention should be made whenever an exercise or strategy is not working for the individual. Data should constantly be collected during practice and should also be gathered on tasks, such as improved ability to study independently, that have been identified as needing improvement. Working memory exercises (brain-based training) take time (a minimum of several weeks) before measurable improvement in memory span or academic performance may occur. However, improved performance on the exercises themselves, such as increasing a span from three to four items, should be noticeable from the beginning. During training in long-term memory strategies, students should almost immediately demonstrate higher recall with a new strategy as compared to the old strategy they have been using. Improved performance on relevant tasks, such as classroom exams, should occur within a few weeks. When progress is less than expected, an exercise or strategy does not necessarily need to be abandoned. Rather, modifying the strategy may be all that is necessary. For example, extra steps may be added, retrieval cues may be provided, or two strategies may be combined.

Trainer Requirements

Psychologists, school psychologists, educators, and related professionals who design memory interventions and provide training to groups or individuals should be familiar with recent research on working memory development and training, as well as the neuropsychology of long-term memory functions. For example, awareness of the neuroscience research on long-term consolidation (Dudai,

<table>
<tr><td>

CAUTION

•••

Any modifications made to evidence-based memory strategies need to be consistent with *why* the strategy works.

</td></tr>
</table>

2004) would be important. Sources that can provide updates on memory research include Baddeley, Eysenck, and Anderson (2009) and Dehn (2008, 2010). Trainers especially need to understand why, from a neurological perspective, each memory strategy works. For example, testing and self-testing are effective strategies because they force the learner to actually retrieve the information instead of just rehearsing it. Neurologically, retrieval, especially effortful retrieval, strengthens the connections among neural networks more effectively than rehearsal (Roediger & Karpicke, 2006). Such expertise will allow trainers to effectively modify interventions and adapt strategies to best meet the trainee's needs. Trainers may also be more effective by using a detailed training guide such as Dehn (2011).

Trainers also should know how to effectively teach strategies. General strategy training procedures include: (a) informing the learner of the purpose and rationale for each strategy; (b) modeling all of the steps of a strategy while thinking aloud; (c) demonstrating the strategy's effectiveness; (d) providing prompts and cues when the student first practices the strategy; (e) focusing on the aspects of the strategy that are not well understood or are difficult to perform; (f) encouraging the student to think aloud during initial practice; (g) providing corrective feedback on proper strategy use; (h) reinforcing the learner for applying the new strategy; (i) encouraging the learner to attribute improved performance to strategy use; and (j) discussing applications of the strategy to promote generalization.

DEVELOPMENT OF METAMEMORY

Regardless of the trainee's age, metamemory development should be emphasized during any intervention for memory difficulties. The trainee is less likely to maintain and generalize the newly acquired strategies when this critical dimension is omitted from the intervention. The primary objective during metamemory training is to help the learner realize that the new strategies are effective. This is mainly accomplished by constantly showing the student the data, not just data demonstrating improved performance on memory tasks but also data that documents the higher level of recall resulting from the use of a new strategy.

Following are the essential steps for development of metamemory. Additional procedures for enhancing metamemory can be found in Dehn (2011).

1. In an age-appropriate manner, educate the learner about human memory functions, including the typical limitations. For example, it's important for the learner to realize that the retention interval for short-term and working memory is typically only a few seconds long.
2. Review the learner's memory strengths and weaknesses that have been identified through assessment.
3. If not discussed previously, query the learner about his or her use of memory strategies and his or her beliefs regarding the efficacy of those strategies.
4. Make sure that the learner understands the rationale for each strategy that is taught. That is, the trainee needs to understand *why* and *how* the strategy works from the perspective of human memory functioning (Lange & Pierce, 1992). For example, self-testing is effective because it requires the individual to actually retrieve information, and retrieval strengthens the neural pathways.
5. Help the student recognize when and how to use a specific strategy. For example, it's important to know which strategy is effective for a particular type of material.
6. Emphasize improved performance, such as higher scores on classroom examinations following application of a new memorization strategy, and attribute the improved performance to the use of the new strategy.

WORKING MEMORY EXERCISES

Within the past decade, several studies (reviewed by Morrison and Chein, 2011) have reported significant improvements in working memory performance following repetitive training exercises. The observable changes seem to be the result of increased working memory capacity. The neural correlates of the improved performance recently have been measured. For example, Tageuchi et al. (2010) discovered measurable growth in the brain's white matter that was correlated with the extent of training and the amount of improved performance. Some of these training programs are Internet-based and have a game-like format, whereas others utilize more traditional procedures, such as *n*-back tasks (Jaeggi, Buschkuehl, Jonides, & Perrig, 2008), which are described in what follows. The gains have not been limited to measures of working memory; there have been several instances of transfer. Some studies have found growth in related cognitive functions, such as fluid reasoning (Jaeggi et al., 2008). Holmes et al. (2009) reported improved performance in mathematics reasoning and students' ability to follow classroom instructions. Maintenance of the gains also has been documented over intervals up to 18 months (Dahlin, Nyberg, Backman, & Neely, 2008). Not just any brain training exercise will result in working memory growth. What sets the exercises evaluated in the professional literature apart is that they adhere to training regimens that consistently demand high cognitive workloads (Morrison & Chein, 2011). For a working memory exercise to be effective, it must require simultaneous processing and storage, constantly adapt the level so that the task remains challenging, and be motivating enough for the trainee to practice on a regular basis. Exercises that challenge executive working memory, especially those that require the integration of visual and verbal information or those that require inhibition of irrelevant information (see Rapid Reference 11.7), have the greatest chance of increasing working memory capacity and performance.

The following working memory exercises (also described in Dehn, 2011) are recommended for use with children and adolescents.

N-Back

N-back requires the individual to remember an item that was presented a certain number of items previously. For example, with 2-back, the trainer might display and remove a series of letters one at a time. If the letters are *b-q-f-j-r*, then the student would say "*b*" when the *f* is displayed, "*q*" when the *j* is displayed, and "*f*" when the *r* is displayed. One application of this method is to use a deck of regular playing cards and follow these guidelines: (1) Display each card for 1–2 seconds; (2) have the trainee name the appropriate *n*-back card when it is time to do so; (3) start the process over whenever the trainee makes an error; (4) increase the *n*-back by 1 when the trainee successfully completes a sequence of 10 cards three times in a row.

Counting Span

In this activity the trainee counts the number of items on a series of cards displayed and removed one at a time, and then must recall the count for each card in the correct sequence. For materials, cards with dots or stars on them would be appropriate. If the first card has 7 items, the second has 4 items, and the third has 9 items, the student would say "7, 4, 9" after the last card has been counted and removed. Each time the student successfully completes three series, another card should be added to the sequence.

Arithmetic Flashcards

For this exercise only arithmetic facts that the student has mastered or nearly mastered should be used. For example, multiplication flashcards could be used with a student who knows mul-

CAUTION

For exercises to be effective they must tax working memory to its limits over a sustained period of time.

tiplication tables. The procedure is similar to that for counting span. The student computes and says the answer for each card as it is displayed, and then must recall the answers in the correct sequence after all the cards have been presented. Incorrect calculations should be accepted, provided the trainee says the same number when recalling the sequence.

Visual-Spatial Recall

The materials for this activity are a sheet or board with grids, such as a "4 × 4," and tokens, such as chips. For each trial, the trainer should display a set number of tokens on random squares for up to five seconds, then remove the chips, and then rotate the board 90 degrees. The student must then correctly place the tokens on the squares where they were originally placed.

Following Directions

For this exercise, complex scenes containing several items should be used. For example, a picture of a school playground with children would be appropriate. The trainer states a series of items that the student must point to after the directions are complete. For example, the trainer might say, "Point to the swing, then the teacher, and then the bush next to the building."

REHEARSAL

Although rehearsal benefits all types of memory, it is not the most effective approach for strengthening long-term recall (Glisky & Glisky, 2002). Thus, it should be used only for short-term memory deficits, working memory deficits, or with young children (under 10 years of age) who have long-term memory difficulties. Most children independently learn to repeat information to themselves, but not all of them do it in a systematic or effective manner. Rehearsal training is fairly straightforward. The key is to teach students to overtly repeat sequences of words, adding new words in a cumulative fashion. For example, if a student needs to remember a sequence of steps, such as "draw, fold, cut, staple, paste," the student would repeat these words several times in order. After students have mastered the approach, they are directed to whisper during rehearsal, and then finally to subvocalize. One advantage of rehearsal is that the procedure does not add substantially to working memory load.

LONG-TERM MEMORY STRATEGIES

The strategies described ahead are a sample of the numerous strategies for long-term memory problems that have been evaluated empirically. For more strategies and details see Dehn (2011).

Semantic Clustering

Cognitive psychologists have long promoted a memory model that emphasizes the inherent organization of memory. Similarly, neuroscientific research has documented that related pieces of information are more closely linked. Accordingly, the encoding of organized information produces improved retention and recall. The best example of an organizational strategy for memory is semantic clustering, a robust method of memorization that consists of recognizing and grouping information according to meaningful categories. The neurological explanation for enhanced recall with semantic clustering is that more information can always be recalled through recognition than through uncued or minimally cued retrieval. That is, the learner may recall additional items by "recognizing" items while mentally running through exemplars of the category.

To train learners on the use of this strategy, present a list of words that can be grouped into a few semantic categories such as animals, tools, or clothing. First, have the trainee group the words by category. Then have the trainee rehearse the information, with an emphasis on memorizing the names of the groups, the number of groups, and the number of items in each group, rather than trying to memorize individual items. Finally, teach the trainee to follow the same sequence during retrieval. First, the trainee should recall the number of categories, the name of each category, and the number of items in each category. Then, the trainee should recall as many items under each category as possible. To retrieve missing items, teach the trainee to mentally run through exemplars of the semantic category in an effort to recognize missing items.

Elaboration

Elaboration is the effortful process of associating new information with related prior knowledge. The elaboration strategy is based on the principle that information that is associated with related knowledge is more memorable, whereas unassociated information is forgotten more quickly. The student should be taught to stop and think about how new information is connected with related prior knowledge. This step activates relevant prior knowledge (related neural networks) and ensures that the new information will be associated or closely connected with related information, thereby facilitating retrieval. That is, information that "fires together" is "wired together." An application of the elaboration strategy that is easy for students to adopt is known as the *interrogative approach* (Pressley, 1982). With this approach, when a student encounters new information, the student should ask and answer the question, "Why does this new fact make sense?"

Self-Testing

Another prominent memory principle is that retrieval pathways are strengthened each time a memory is retrieved. Consequently, actually retrieving information is much more effective than just repeating it. Moreover, retrieval has an even greater impact when it takes effort to retrieve the desired information because it has been partially forgotten. A straightforward approach to ensuring that retrieval occurs is self-testing. Study cards may be used to teach the trainee proper self-testing procedures, the essence of which is to make an effort to retrieve the information before checking to see if the response is correct.

Dual Encoding

Dual encoding consists of encoding information both visually and verbally. The rationale for this strategy is that the probability of recalling information is increased when the information is encoded in more than one way. Also, learners with specific memory deficits in either the verbal or visual-spatial domain tend not to consciously encode information both ways, missing an opportunity to capitalize on their stronger memory domain. When verbal information, such as new vocabulary, needs to be memorized, trainees should be taught to visualize the information. When visual-spatial information needs to be retained, such as a route to follow, trainees should be taught to recode the information verbally.

Visual Mnemonics

Visual mnemonics are specialized memory techniques that enhance encoding, retention, and retrieval. They are based on the principle that the effectiveness of encoding determines the success of retrieval. Whereas visual mnemonics and memory strategies both involve manipulation and transformation of information, visual mnemonics are distinct in that they usually involve memory representations that bear little or no relation to the conceptual content of the material being committed to memory. Visual mnemonics create unique cueing structures, usually in the form of visual images. During retrieval the cue is accessed first, and this in turn leads to recall of the desired information. Visual mnemonics are most effective when the images are created by the learner. Also, images are easier to recall when they are funny, interactive, and idiosyncratic. Another reason visual mnemonics are effective is because the new information is associated with something the learner already knows and will not forget. Loci (see below) is a prime example of a visual mnemonic that incorporates unrelated knowledge that will almost never be forgotten.

Keyword

The process of forming and retrieving a keyword mnemonic consists of several stages: The first stage is the acoustical link stage, in which the learner thinks of a word (the keyword) that sounds like the target word; in the second stage the learner creates an image with the keyword that makes the meaning of the target word apparent; and in the final stage the learner first retrieves the keyword and then recalls the image with the keyword, which leads to the correct response. For example, if a student wants to remember that the Spanish word *pato* means "duck," the student might first think that *pato* sounds like "pot" and then create an image connecting a pot and a duck, such as a duck splashing in a pot of water.

Loci

Loci involves associating items with a sequence of familiar objects or locations. For instance, a student might associate information to be learned with furniture and objects in his or her room. The room's objects are a fixed arrangement of elements that the student already knows and won't forget. To remember new information, the student creates an image in which each item to be remembered is associated with a different object or location. For example, when a student needs to memorize that the Spaniards, French, and English were the main European nations to explore North America, the student might create an image of each group associated with each of the three objects in his or her bedroom. The first image might consist of an armored Spaniard on a horse standing on the student's bed. During retrieval, the student pictures each bedroom object, recalls the associative images, and recognizes the responses.

RECOMMENDATIONS FOR CLASSROOM INSTRUCTION

Interventions for students with identified memory impairments should include consultation with the students' teachers. Instructors can help students with working memory difficulties by reducing the cognitive load in the classroom (de Jong, 2010). Minimizing the processing demands in the learning environment will help impaired students overcome the working memory limitations that are impacting their learning and performance (Elliott, Gathercole, Alloway, Holmes, & Kirkwood, 2010). The higher the cognitive load, the less information the learner can maintain in working memory, resulting in less information encoded into long-term memory. Some examples of what teachers can do to reduce cognitive load include: (a) maintaining a quiet learning environment; (b) differentiating instruction such that the processing demands are appropriately matched to the individual learner's working memory capacity; (c) utilizing structured teaching approaches, such as *direct instruction* (Swanson, 1999), that have built-in repetition so that the learner can focus more on the processing dimension and less on retaining information; (d) avoiding presentation of nonessential or confusing information; (e) not presenting procedural steps until they are actually needed; and (f) requiring only one process at a time.

In addition to minimizing cognitive load to support encoding, teachers can enhance long-term retention and retrieval of information by such practices as: (a) reminding students to use memory strategies during learning activities; (b) modeling the use of memory strategies; (c) reinforcing the use of memory strategies; (d) explicitly linking new information to the student's prior knowledge; (e) presenting information in an organized manner; (f) providing information in both verbal and visual formats; (g) providing prompts and cues to support retrieval; (h) structuring content in a manner that facilitates strategy use; (i) conducting periodic reviews; and (j) using quizzes as a method of strengthening retention and recall.

> ## DON'T FORGET
> The greater the mental processing demands in the classroom, the less information the student will be able to retain in working memory, leading to difficulty completing tasks and less information being encoded into long-term memory.

EDUCATIONAL ACCOMMODATIONS

Interventions for memory deficits should also include written recommendations or a plan that specifies appropriate accommodations. Accommodations might include:

(a) informing the student and parents of test dates well in advance; (b) extended testing time; (c) reference materials, such as a list of procedures (Rankin & Hood, 2005); (d) not requiring the student to take notes; (e) recognition testing, such as providing a word bank from which to choose answers; (f) providing review sheets in the same format as the test; (g) and (in severe cases) the use of a "memory book" (Wilson, 2009).

CASE STUDY

When "Jason" was 16 years old he underwent brain surgery to remove a cancerous tumor, and he completed a course of chemotherapy to shrink another brain tumor. As a result, his memory functions were affected in much the same manner as if he had suffered a traumatic brain injury (TBI). His working memory and long-term memory were impaired in both the verbal and visual-spatial domains. Prior to the brain trauma Jason had been an "A" student. After the trauma, his grades dropped significantly but he was able to graduate from high school and gain admission to a junior college.

Jason and his parents came seeking assistance for his memory problems when his junior college placed him on academic probation at the end of his first semester. Even with 504 accommodations, Jason had struggled to pass his classes. Three years had passed since the surgery and chemotherapy. During that interval Jason's memory functions had recovered to a certain extent, but it was evident to Jason and his parents that his memory difficulties persisted in the home and school environments. The problem was that they didn't know what to do about it. Their goal was for Jason to remember information well enough to continue in college.

The assessment prior to beginning the intervention consisted of in-depth interviewing of Jason and his parents and a careful review of his records. Jason had completed three rounds of formal memory testing with a neuropsychologist and was unwilling to be tested again. The most recent test results indicated that Jason's working memory was average, but that he continued to have deficits in verbal and visual-spatial long-term memory. These deficits not only made academic learning very difficult, but everyday memory problems, such as losing items and forgetting to complete tasks, were also a concern.

Tailoring the Intervention

The intervention began with Jason setting goals for memory improvement, with the central goal focusing on remembering academic information well enough to pass course examinations. Accordingly, the tracking of Jason's test scores during the upcoming semester was part of monitoring his progress. Jason's other main goal was to reduce his forgetfulness in the home environment. As Jason lived with his parents, they were enlisted to report on his functioning at home. (One or both of Jason's parents sat in on his memory training sessions so that they knew what he was working on and could provide reminders as needed.)

In Jason's case, his clear-cut goals and the need to survive academically would primarily determine the training methods and memory strategies selected for his intervention. For example, effective encoding strategies that would enhance retrieval were a must. In addition to selecting strategies that would make learning more memorable, Jason's memory weaknesses influenced the approach that would be taken with him. Dual encoding would be an important strategy to begin with because both his verbal and visual-spatial memory were deficient. Thankfully, Jason's working memory was strong, opening the door for the learning and application of complex memory strategies. As always, trial-and-error would be involved, with the final selection of strategies for Jason's "memory plan" based on which ones had proved to be the most effective for him. Finally, adjustments and additions were made as Jason implemented his memory plan. For example, at one point he needed to be taught to take frequent study breaks to reduce interference. Another time, later in the intervention, he was taught cueing and retrieval strategies to use while taking exams (something that was not originally planned but incorporated after Jason reported that he was struggling with retrieval during exams).

Metamemory Development

Despite the fact that three years had elapsed since the onset of his memory problems, Jason's study behaviors and memorization strategies had remained unchanged, except that Jason spent more time studying than he had prior to the brain trauma. More concerning was that Jason's metamemory had not grown in response to his memory challenges. Thus, the development of his metamemory was emphasized throughout the intervention. Fortunately, Jason had an interest in psychology and was keen to fully understand his memory functions and challenges. The metamemory training began with teaching Jason how human memory works, followed by helping him understand his current memory strengths and weaknesses. An important aspect of the metamemory training consisted of demonstrating the efficacy of the new memory strategies by monitoring his college test scores and by comparing recall with and without each new strategy during the training sessions. Each time a new strategy was taught, the trainer explained why Jason needed the strategy and why the strategy worked from a brain-based perspective. The goal was to help Jason develop his metamemory to the point where he would maintain and generalize the new skills he was learning. When questioned about the rationale for each strategy, Jason's responses were always accurate. The final test of Jason's advanced metamemory was to ask him to adapt and combine memory strategies to meet a particular need. He passed this test with flying colors.

Memory Strategies to Enhance Learning and Recall

Although structured visual mnemonics were not used with Jason (because of their limited generalizability), he was taught the importance of visualizing verbal information. For example, he learned to picture the items or concepts when he studied new vocabulary. He was also taught a more advanced form of visualization to utilize while reading. For example, as he read about an event in the history of psychology he was instructed to pause and visualize that event, and then place himself in the scene as an observer. The other side of this dual encoding approach was to verbalize visual-spatial information, such as telling himself where he had placed an object or describing a travel route that he needed to know.

Organizing information while studying was another important part of the intervention. Jason discovered that organized or clustered information was more memorable than discrete, isolated, or random pieces of information. An application of this memory principle involved reorganizing class notes prior to reviewing them (Jason had a note-taker in class but also took some notes on his own). Notes were reorganized in a manner such that information was regrouped by specific topic.

The success of this intervention ultimately depended on Jason's ability to retain and recall information that he needed to independently acquire from textbooks. A modified *PQRST* (*P*review, *Q*uestion, *R*ead, *S*tudy, *T*est) approach that included self-elaboration was implemented. This strategy included: (a) previewing the text prior to reading (to activate relevant background knowledge); (b) selecting and highlighting one important piece of information from each paragraph; (c) asking and answering the question, "Why does this piece of information make sense?" (this was the elaboration component); (d) reviewing the highlighted information on a periodic basis (at least three times prior to a test); and (e) self-testing with flashcards that were created during one of the reviews.

The steps for each of the methods (there were more than those described here) were written out in Jason's digital memory book, which was also part of the intervention. The memory book also included a calendar to track appointments, assignments, and plans; a list of important people and their contact information; the locations of important objects; and reminders of general memory tips, such as taking "interference" breaks and getting enough sleep. Learning to constantly carry and consult the memory book was perhaps the most challenging behavior change for Jason.

Jason seriously applied all of the memory strategies taught during his intervention. His feedback during the intervention allowed the tweaking of some strategies and the addition of an unplanned strategy. During that semester of college Jason's test scores and grades improved (a GPA of 2.835) and he was removed from academic probation. At the end of his junior college program he had a cumulative GPA of 3.5. However, his coping with everyday memory challenges was less consistent and he continued living with his parents.

REFERENCES

Alloway, T. P. (2011). *Improving working memory: Supporting students' learning*. London, UK: Sage.

Alloway, T. P., & Gathercole, S. E. (Eds.). (2006). *Working memory and neurodevelopmental disorders*. New York, NY: Psychology Press.

Baddeley, A. D., Eysenck, M. W., & Anderson, M. C. (2009). *Memory*. New York, NY: Psychology Press.

Barrouillet, P., Portrat, S., & Camos, V. (2011). On the law relating processing to storage in working memory. *Psychological Review, 118,* 175–192.

Cohen, J. (1997). *Children's memory scale*. San Antonio, TX: Psychological Corporation.

Dahlin, E., Nyberg, L., Backman, L., & Neely, A. S. (2008). Plasticity of executive functioning in young and older adults: Immediate training gains, transfer, and long-term maintenance. *Psychology and Aging, 23,* 720–730.

Dehn, M. J. (2006). *Essentials of processing assessment*. Hoboken, NJ: Wiley.

Dehn, M. J. (2008). *Working memory and academic learning: Assessment and intervention*. Hoboken, NJ: Wiley.

Dehn, M. J. (2010). *Long-term memory problems in children and adolescents: Assessment, intervention, and effective instruction*. Hoboken, NJ: Wiley.

Dehn, M. J. (2011). *Helping students remember: Exercises and strategies to strengthen memory*. Hoboken, NJ: Wiley.

Dehn, M. J. (2012). *Children's psychological processes scale*. Onalaska, WI: Schoolhouse Educational Services.

de Jong, T. (2010). Cognitive load theory, educational research, and instructional design: Some food for thought. *Instructional Science, 38,* 105–134.

Dudai, Y. (2004). The neurobiology of consolidations, or, how stable is the engram? *Review of Psychology, 55,* 51–86.

Elliott, J. G., Gathercole, S. E., Alloway, T. P., Holmes, J., & Kirkwood, H. (2010). An evaluation of a classroom-based intervention to help overcome working memory difficulties and improve long-term academic achievement. *Journal of Cognitive Education and Psychology, 9*, 227–250.

Flanagan, D. P., Ortiz, S. O., & Alfonso, V. C. (2007). *Essentials of cross-battery assessment* (2nd ed.). Hoboken, NJ: Wiley.

Flanagan, D. P., Ortiz, S. O., & Alfonso, V. C. (2013). *Essentials of cross-battery assessment* (3rd ed.). Hoboken, NJ: Wiley.

Gathercole, S. E., & Pickering, S. J. (2001). Working memory deficits in children with special educational needs. *British Journal of Special Education, 28*, 89–97.

Glisky, E. L., & Glisky, M. L. (2002). Learning and memory impairments. In P. J. Eslinger (Ed.), *Neuropsychological interventions: Clinical research and practice* (pp. 137–162). New York, NY: Guilford.

Harris, J. R. (1996). Verbal rehearsal and memory in children with closed head injury: A quantitative and qualitative analysis. *Journal of Communication Disorders, 29*, 79–93.

Hershey, T., Lillie, R., Sadler, M., & White, N. H. (2003). Severe hypoglycemia and long-term spatial memory in children with type 1 diabetes mellitus: A retrospective study. *Journal of the International Neuropsychological Society, 9*, 740–750.

Holmes, J., Gathercole, S. E., & Dunning, D. L. (2009). Adaptive training leads to sustained enhancement of poor working memory in children. *Developmental Science, 12*, F9–F15.

Jaeggi, S. M., Buschkuehl, M., Jonides, J., & Perrig, W. J. (2008). Improved fluid intelligence with training on working memory. *Proceedings of the National Academy of Sciences of the United States of America.* doi: 10.1073/pnas.0801268105

Kaplan, E., Fein, D., Kramer, J., Delis, D., & Morris, R. (2004). *Wechsler Intelligence Scale for Children–Fourth Edition–Integrated.* San Antonio, TX: PsychCorp.

Kirschner, P. A. (2002). Cognitive load theory: Implications of cognitive load theory on the design of learning. *Learning and Instruction, 12*, 1–10.

Koriat, A. (2008). Easy comes, easy goes? The link between learning and remembering and its exploitation in metacognition. *Memory and Cognition, 36*, 416–428.

Lange, G., & Pierce, S. H. (1992). Memory-strategy learning and maintenance in preschool children. *Developmental Psychology, 28*, 453–462.

Morrison, A. B., & Chein, J. M. (2011). Does working memory training work? The promise and challenges of enhancing cognition by training working memory. *Psychonomic Bulletin Review, 18*, 46–60.

Ornstein, P. A., Grammer, J. K., & Coffman, J. L. (2010). Teachers' "mnemonic style" and the development of skilled memory. In H. S. Waters & W. Schneider (Eds.), *Metacognition, strategy use, and instruction* (pp. 23–53). New York, NY: Guilford.

Pressley, M. (1982). Elaboration and memory development. *Child Development, 53*, 296–309.

Rankin, P. M., & Hood, J. (2005). Designing clinical interventions for children with specific memory disorders. *Pediatric Rehabilitation, 8*, 283–297.

Reynolds, C. R., & Voress, J. K. (2007). *Test of Memory and Learning–Second Edition.* Austin, TX: PRO-ED.

Roediger, H. L., & Karpicke, J. D. (2006). Test-enhanced learning: Taking memory tests improves long-term retention. *Psychological Science, 17*, 249–255.

Schneider, W. (2010). Metacognition and memory development in childhood and adolescence. In H. S. Waters & W. Schneider (Eds.), *Metacognition, strategy use, and instruction* (pp. 54–84). New York, NY: Guilford Press.

Son, L. K. (2005). Metacognitive control: Children's short-term versus long-term study strategies. *Journal of General Psychology, 132*, 347–363.

Swanson, H. L. (1999). Instructional components that predict treatment outcomes for students with learning disabilities: Support for a combined strategy and direct instruction model. *Learning Disabilities Research, 14*, 129–140.

Swanson, H. L. (2000). Are working memory deficits in readers with learning disabilities hard to change? *Journal of Learning Disabilities, 33*, 551–566.

Tageuchi, H., Sekiguchi, A., Taki, Y., Yokoyama, S., Yomogida, Y., Komuro, N., & Kawashima, R. (2010). Training of working memory impacts structural connectivity. *Journal of Neuroscience, 30*, 3297–3303.

Temple, C. M., & Richardson, P. (2006). Developmental amnesia: Fractionation of developing memory systems. *Cognitive Neuropsychology, 23*, 762–788.

Wechsler, D. (2003). *Wechsler Intelligence Scale for Children—Fourth Edition.* San Antonio, TX: Psychological Corporation.

Wilson, B. A. (2009). *Memory rehabilitation: Integrating theory and practice.* New York, NY: Guilford Press.

Woodcock, R. W., McGrew, K. S., & Mather, N. (2001). *Woodcock-Johnson III Tests of Achievement.* Itasca, IL: Riverside.

🔖 TEST YOURSELF 🔖

1. **Which of these options should be used to predict memory scores when analyzing scores from a cross-battery assessment?**

   a. Grade point average

   b. Ipsative strengths

   c. Strategy use

   d. Full scale IQ

2. **Metamemory includes all of the following *except* _____ .**

   a. Understanding human memory functions

   b. Inhibiting irrelevant information

   c. Conscious regulation of memory functions

   d. Knowledge of one's memory strengths and weaknesses

3. **Most long-term memory impairments are the result of _____.**

   a. A diminished working memory capacity

   b. Learning disabilities

   c. Limited strategy use

   d. Damage to the hippocampus

4. **Learners with a working memory deficit might find using a memory strategy frustrating when _____.**

   a. The strategy adds to their cognitive load

   b. They don't believe in the efficacy of strategies

   c. Their metamemory development is delayed

   d. They have a comorbid learning disability

(continued)

(continued)

5. In order to be effective, working memory exercises must _____.
a. Be verbal and visual
b. Include executive functions
c. Be challenging
d. Include rehearsal

6. Which strategy is least effective at enhancing long-term memory recall?
a. Rehearsal
b. Elaboration
c. Keyword
d. Dual encoding

7. Visual mnemonics work best when _____.
a. The trainer creates the images
b. The images are very objective
c. They are supported by verbal mnemonics
d. They are interactive and funny

8. The least helpful data for evaluating the success of a memory intervention is
a. Classroom test scores
b. Recall during practice
c. Standardized test scores
d. Performance on exercises

Answers: 1. d; 2. b; 3. b; 4. a; 5. c; 6. a; 7. d; 8. c

Twelve

INTERVENTIONS FOR STUDENTS WITH LECTURE NOTE–TAKING DIFFICULTIES

Stephen T. Peverly
Gardith Marcelin
Michael Kern

After elementary school, the amount of information students are required to understand increases dramatically (Thomas, Iventosch, & Rohwer, 1987) and most information is presented in forms students find difficult to process: lecture (Piolat, Olive, & Kellogg, 2005; Putnam, Deshler, & Schumaker, 1993) and expository texts (Mulcahy-Ernt & Caverly, 2009; Snow, 2002). Thus, as adolescent and young adult learners progress through school, they increasingly take notes (Thomas et al., 1987), a cryptic written record of important information presented in lecture or text (Piolat et al.), to help them encode and subsequently more thoroughly process and remember important information. Most college students, for example, rate lecture note–taking as an important educational activity (Dunkel & Davy, 1989) and most take notes in classes (approximately 98%; Palmatier & Bennett, 1974; an ongoing survey of college undergraduates in our lab indicates that 100% take lecture notes at least some of the time). In addition, research supports the efforts students expend in taking notes. Students who take and/or review lecture notes (Armbruster, 2009; Fisher & Harris, 1973; Kiewra & Benton, 1988; Kiewra, Benton, & Lewis, 1987; Kiewra, DuBois, Christian, McShane, Meyerhoffer, & Roskelley, 1991; Peverly et al., 2007; Titsworth & Kiewra, 2004) or text notes (Bretzing & Kulhavy, 1981; Peverly, Brobst, Graham, & Shaw, 2003; Peverly & Sumowski, 2011; Rickards & Friedman, 1978; Slotte & Lonka, 1999) typically do better on tests than those who do not.

The purpose of this chapter is to review research on the predominant type of note-taking, lecture notes, for the purposes of helping educators and students improve their note-taking. Toward that end, we review research on: (a) the relative importance of the two primary functions of note-taking, *encoding* and *review*, (b) the cognitive processes and other variables that seem to be related to individual differences in note-taking, and (c) how note-taking can be improved.

THE FUNCTIONS OF NOTE-TAKING: ENCODING AND REVIEW

In a now-classic study that spawned years of research on the functions of note-taking, DiVesta and Gray (1972) postulated that note-taking consists of two activities: encoding and external storage. In the former, note-takers transcribe whatever is perceived to be important, which can include students' impressions and/or inferences about the material. In the latter (external storage), notes are available for later review and further processing. To test their assumption and to evaluate the importance of each function and their combination to test performance, DiVesta and Gray had college undergraduates listen to a lecture in one of three conditions: listening only (no notes), encoding only (note-taking), and encoding plus review (note-taking plus review of notes). In general, the results indicated that those who took notes did better than those who did not, and those who were allowed to review their notes did better than those who were not allowed to review. Dozens of subsequent experiments comparing various combinations of listening only, note-taking only, review only (e.g., notes handed out by the professor or notes taken by other students; a review-only group was not included in DiVesta & Gray, 1972), and note-taking plus review found that note-taking plus review is superior to the other conditions (see Armbruster, 2009, Kiewra 1985, 1991, for reviews).

In a relatively recent set of meta-analyses, Kobayashi (2005, 2006) calculated the effect size of the functions of note-taking on test performance. Comparisons of students who were allowed to take notes to those who were not (listening only) yielded a moderate effect size (.26) in support of note-taking (Kobayashi, 2005). Comparisons of groups who took and reviewed their notes to listening/read-only groups (i.e., no notes and no review) and/or listening/read-only groups who were allowed to mentally review (without notes), yielded a substantially larger effect size (.75) in favor of note-taking and review (Kobayashi, 2006). In addition, Kobayashi (2006) evaluated differences in test performance between studies that included interventions meant to facilitate note-taking and/or review and those that did not include interventions (e.g., templates provided by teachers to facilitate note-taking). He found a moderate effect size (.36) in favor of interventions. Finally, he

≋ Rapid Reference 12.1 Summary of Findings on Note-Taking

1. Students should take and review their notes.
2. Reviewing notes is more important to test outcomes than taking notes.
3. Teachers should provide support for note-taking (e.g., skeletal or guided notes) and review (e.g., matrixes to help students reorganize and better conceptualize their notes).
4. Less-capable students profit more from interventions than more-capable students. (We return to all of these issues in the section "How to Improve Note-Taking," later in this chapter.)

used a multiple regression analysis to isolate variables related to the effectiveness of interventions. He found that providing a framework for note-taking and/or review was superior to other interventions (e.g., verbal instructions on how to take notes) and that lower-academic-ability participants benefited more from interventions than higher-academic-ability participants (see also Boyle & Rivera, 2012). See Rapid Reference 12.1 for a summary of findings on note-taking.

INDIVIDUAL DIFFERENCES IN NOTE-TAKING AND THEIR RELATIONSHIP TO TEST PERFORMANCE

Historically, the focus of research on studying has been the relative efficacy of the components of a method (encoding vs. review in note-taking), as discussed previously, or of different methods (e.g., underlining versus outlining or summarizing; Anderson & Armbruster, 1984). Individual differences have rarely been considered. However, there are data on individual differences associated with the encoding component of note-taking. Although students do not typically take very complete notes, usually recording between 20 and 40% of the information contained in lecture (Armbruster, 2009; Kiewra, 1985), individual differences in the completeness of notes, the amount of information presented in lecture contained in notes, are positively related to test performance (Armbruster, 2009; Peverly et al., 2007). The question is: What are the cognitive characteristics associated with completeness?

Although there has been very little research on the cognitive characteristics of good note-takers, there is no shortage of speculation on what these characteristics might be. Ours and others' analyses of note-taking (Kiewra & Benton, 1988; Kiewra et al., 1987; Kobayashi, 2005; Peverly, 2006; Piolat et al., 2005) suggest

> ## DON'T FORGET
> ....
> Expertise in note-taking may be related to several variables: transcription fluency, working memory, verbal ability, background knowledge, and the ability to attend, among others.

that it is a difficult and cognitively demanding skill—students must hold lecture information in verbal working memory, use higher-level cognitive resources such as verbal ability and/or background knowledge to select, construct, and/or transform important thematic units before the information in working memory is forgotten, quickly transcribe (via writing or typing) the information held in working memory, again before the information is forgotten, and attend to the lecture over long periods of time. Thus, expertise in note-taking may be related to several variables: transcription fluency, working memory, verbal ability, background knowledge, and the ability to attend, among others. Hypothetically, inadequate lecture notes could result from a breakdown in any one of these variables. For example, because of the substantial cognitive load typically present during lecture (Piolat et al., 2005), slow transcription speed could strain the capacity limitations of working memory and cause students to forget some of the information in working memory (through decay or interference) and lose continuity of the lecture (Suritsky, 1992).

Research on the cognitive and demographic characteristics of good lecture note-takers has found a few variables that are positively and significantly related to lecture notes: transcription (writing) speed (Gleason, 2012; Peverly et al., 2007; Peverly et al., in preparation; Peverly et al., under review), verbal ability (Gleason, 2012; Peverly et al., under review; Reddington, 2011; Vekaria, 2011), sustained attention (Gleason, 2012; Vekaria, 2011; Peverly, Garner, & Vekaria, in preparation), and gender (Cohn, Cohn, & Bradley, 1995; Reddington, 2011). Relative to the latter, females have been found to be better note-takers than males.[1] Similar results

---

1. Reddington (2011) was the first to evaluate systematically differences in note-taking between men and women undergraduates. Specifically, she evaluated the relationship of transcription fluency, working memory, verbal ability, conscientiousness, goal orientation, and gender to skill in note-taking, and of all of these variables, including notes, to written recall. She found that (a) women had significantly higher scores on all of the independent and dependent variables, with the exception of goal orientation, than men, and (b) gender, verbal ability, and the gender × verbal ability interaction were significant predictors of notes' quality. Relative to the latter, there were significant differences in note-taking in favor of women at higher levels of verbal ability but not at lower levels. In a follow-up regression that included women only, working memory and verbal ability significantly predicted notes' quality.

have been found in research on text note-taking. Peverly and Sumowski (2011) found variations in the quality of text notes were related to transcription speed and verbal ability. Collectively, these data suggest that students who write faster, have higher levels of verbal skill and sustained attention, and are female take better notes.

The reader should note that several studies have evaluated the relationship of working memory to notes. We did not include working memory in our list of variables related to note-taking because the research on its relationship to notes is mixed. Some studies found a significant positive relationship between working memory and note quality (Kiewra & Benton, 1988; Kiewra et al., 1987; McIntyre, 1992) and others did not (Cohn et al., 1995; Hadwin et al., 1999; Peverly et al., 2007; Peverly & Sumowski, 2011). The inconsistency may be due to the variety of measures used to assess working memory (Peverly et al.). Investigations that used more generally accepted measures of working memory did not find a significant relationship with quality of notes (Cohn et al., 1995; Hadwin et al., 1999; Peverly et al., 2007; Peverly & Sumowski, 2011).

Regarding test performance, although decades of research on note-taking indicate that taking and reviewing notes is significantly related to students' performance on tests (Kobayashi, 2005, 2006), any of a number of cognitive variables may influence test performance, either alone or in addition to notes. Indeed, it is possible that the relationship between notes and test outcomes could be eliminated once the cognitive characteristics of learners are measured and included in analyses along with measures of the completeness of notes (i.e., quantity and quality). Also, the influence of these variables may vary by test type (e.g., essay, multiple choice) or what the test is measuring (memory, under-standing). Although a variety of different test types has been used in note-taking research (recall, multiple choice, fact recognition, transfer, synthesis, etc.), they typically measure either (a) memory for information stated directly in text, or (b) the ability to infer or to go beyond the text to understand concepts and relationships not explicitly stated in text. According to Kintsch (1998), tests such as written recall and multiple-choice items that assess information stated directly in text measure the *textbase*, a

CAUTION

Regarding test performance, although decades of research on note-taking indicate that taking and reviewing notes is significantly related to students' performance on tests, any of a number of cognitive variables may influence test performance, either alone or in addition to notes. The relationship between notes and test outcomes could be eliminated once the cognitive characteristics of learners are measured and included in analyses along with measures of the completeness of notes (i.e., quantity and quality).

mental representation of the propositions derived from text (or lecture) and their interrelationships, which have not necessarily been elaborated upon by students' knowledge and experiences. In his view, measures of the textbase are measures of memory but not necessarily understanding, since they have not explicitly assessed understanding. Tests that measure inferences, however, are measures of the *situation model*, a textbase that has been more deeply processed and enriched by readers' or listeners' general and domain-specific knowledge, experiences, and so on. In Kintsch's view, tests that measure students' situation models of lectures and text measure understanding.

In what follows we consider the research of Peverly and his colleagues primarily. Very little research other than theirs has measured the cognitive characteristics of students in investigations on note-taking, which allow us to estimate the extent to which notes are related to outcomes once the cognitive characteristics of the learner are taken into account. Prediction patterns in the studies by Peverly and colleagues suggest that notes are consistently related to tests of memory (textbase), but not understanding (situation model). Several studies found a positive, significant relationship between notes and written recall (Peverly et al., 2007; Peverly & Sumowski, 2011; Vekaria, 2011) and multiple-choice items that measure information stated directly in text or lecture (Peverly & Sumowski, 2011; Gleason, 2012). Multiple-choice questions that measured understanding (via inferences) were not significantly related to notes. Only background knowledge was related to inference items in Peverly and Sumowski and verbal ability was the only variable related to inference items in Gleason (2012; a measure of background knowledge was not included in Gleason's investigation). Findings from other studies that evaluated the relationship of notes to test performance, but did not measure the cognitive characteristics of learners largely agree with our conclusions with the caveat that note-taking interventions that produced more elaborated notes, such as outlines or matrixes, are sometimes related to performance on tests based on inferences (Kiewra, Benton, Kim, Risch, & Christensen, 1995; Kiewra, DuBois, Christensen, Kim, & Lindberg, 1989; Kiewra et al., 1991).

Intuitively these findings make sense. The rapidity of most lectures and the demands note-taking (lecture or text; Piolat et al., 2005) can place on cognitive processing may inhibit the deeper levels of processing required to answer inferences unless students are given notes or required to generate notes with more elaborated relationships among important information. A very tentative model of the relationships among the cognitive variables related to note- and test-taking, based on the research of Peverly and colleagues, is presented in Figure 12.1.

It is important for educators to note that the development of the ability to take notes, from a general cognitive perspective, is no different from the development

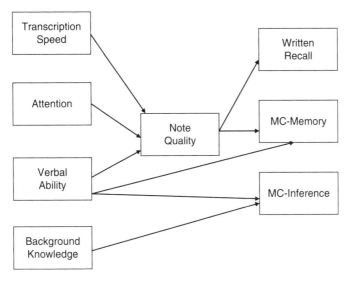

Figure 12.1. Hypothesized Relationships Among Cognitive Processes, Notes, and Test Performance

of other academic skills. For example, theories of performance in academic skills such as reading (Rayner, Foorman, Perfetti, Pesetsky, & Seidenberg, 2001; Vellutino, Fletcher, Snowling, & Scanlon, 2004), writing (Berninger, 2012; Berninger et al., 2006; McCutchen, 1996), and mathematics (Geary, 1994) all recognize that (a) competence in academic skills requires the parallel execution of domain-specific basic and higher-level processes within a limited-capacity working memory; (b) domain-specific basic skills must be executed automatically/fluently so that limited working memory resources can be directed toward the application of higher-level cognitive skills, and (c) once basic skills are sufficiently automatic or fluent, competence in a skill is largely determined by the quality of higher-level skills. In skilled reading, for example, Perfetti's (1985, 2007) Verbal Efficiency Theory suggests that reading comprehension requires the parallel execution of word recognition and the higher-level cognitive processes needed to interpret text, such as language ability (see also Hulme & Snowling, 2011). Since comprehension occurs in a limited-capacity working memory, word recognition must be automatized if language ability and the other higher-level cognitive processes related to comprehension are to be applied effectively. Similarly, in note-taking, research suggests that transcription must be fluent so that attention can be directed to the application of verbal ability and background knowledge to comprehend lectures. This means that instruction in academic skills must emphasize basic skills in the early elementary grades, transcription speed in the case of note-taking, and higher-order skills once basic skills begin to become fluent.

Now that we have established that note-taking is important and we have addressed some of the reasons why some students are better note-takers than others, we turn to ways to improve students' note-taking.

HOW TO IMPROVE NOTE-TAKING

As discussed previously, lecture note-taking is a very cognitively demanding strategy (Peverly et al., 2007; Piolat et al., 2005). To help students adapt to the cognitive demands of recording and reviewing important information from lecture, researchers have focused on a number of strategies. Predominant among these are methods that change (a) the presentation of the lecture (e.g., the rate of lectures), (b) how students take notes, and (c) how students review notes. We also argue that there may be a fourth way to improve students' note-taking and review: developing the cognitive processes that underlie them.

Changes in Lecture

In our ongoing survey of note-taking among college undergraduates, mentioned earlier, the second most frequent response to the question on the conditions under which they would take better notes was "if the instructor talked more slowly" (48.5%). Thus, it is not surprising that most of the research on lecture modifications has focused on helping students compensate for rate of the lecture, either by repeating the lecture, slowing the rate via pauses, or providing cues to help students process lecture content more efficiently (see Rapid Reference 12.2 for ways to help students compensate for speed of lectures or slow transcription speed).

≡ Rapid Reference 12.2 Compensating for Speed of Lectures or Slow Transcription Speed

Help students compensate for the speed of lectures, and possibly their slow transcription speed, by:

1. Recording lectures so that students can view them again if they wish
2. Including pauses in lectures for questions and student collaboration
3. Using cues to highlight the organization and important themes in lectures

Lecture Repetition

Kiewra and Mayer (1997) and Kiewra, Mayer, Christensen, Kim, and Risch (1991) had college participants listen to a lecture one, two, or three times and take notes. In these studies, the number of presentations affected the number of idea units recorded in notes, with significant increases from one presentation to two and from two presentations to three. Kiewra et al. also analyzed whether the number of presentations had a differential effect on the proportion of idea units recorded by level, from the most important (Level 1) to the least important (Level 3). Although students' notes were strongly biased toward Level 1 information, no levels effect was found. That is, there were no significant changes in the number of idea units recorded in notes within levels, across presentations. Regarding performance, Kiewra and Mayer found that the number of presentations did not affect recall but did affect performance on a fact recognition test. Students who saw the presentation two or three times performed better than students who saw it once. In Kiewra et al. there were significant increases in total recall and in recall at each level of importance with each presentation. As with notes, students' recall was strongly biased toward important information.

Although it would be impractical for instructors to repeat lectures in real-time classrooms, these data suggest that students should review lectures more than once if they have been recorded (e.g., online courses). Repeated listening can provide students with the opportunity to note missing information, make corrections, and so forth.

Pauses

In a series of four studies, Kathy Ruhl and colleagues measured the effect of a pause procedure during lecture on test outcomes (Ruhl, 1996; Ruhl, Hughes, & Gajar, 1990; Ruhl, Hughes, & Schloss, 1987; Ruhl & Suritsky, 1995) and note-taking (Ruhl et al., 1987; Ruhl & Suritsky, 1995). The pause procedure involved stopping a lecture three times for a period of two minutes each time. During pauses students discussed the lecture content with peers for corrections, elaborations, clarifications, and so forth.

Before discussing the results, there were several variations in design across studies that deserve mention. Although all of the studies used undergraduates as participants, two used participants who were diagnosed with a learning disability (Ruhl, 1996; Ruhl, & Suritsky, 1995), one used participants who were not diagnosed with a learning disability (Ruhl et al., 1987), and the last included both populations (Ruhl et al., 1990). Also, all but one (Ruhl, 1996) compared a pause to a no-pause group (in Ruhl, 1996, students were matched with a peer or told to work privately, reflect on the lecture, and make changes to notes) and two used trained peer confederates (Ruhl, 1996; Ruhl & Suritsky). Confederates were given complete notes to facilitate discussion among peers during pauses. Further, two studies required note-taking. Ruhl and Suritsky compared a Pause group to an Outline group (a lecturer-generated skeletal outline) and a combined group, Pause plus Outline. All three groups were required to take notes. The students in Ruhl (1996) also took notes. Finally, there was a fair amount of variation across studies in dependent measures, although most used free recall and multiple-choice exams.

Across studies, results indicated that the pause procedure facilitated test performance, for students with and without disabilities (there were no differences between groups), although there was some variation across outcome measures. Additional findings were: (a) no significant differences between private reflection and peer collaboration on test performance in Ruhl (1996), although more research is needed to determine if the pause procedure is effective in the absence of peer collaboration, and (b) a small positive effect for the presence of a peer on note-taking in Ruhl. Although there were no differences between groups on the total number of complete idea units included in notes, the peer discussion group included more incomplete idea units.

Thus, the research by Ruhl and colleagues suggests that rate of a lecture can have an untoward effect on students' test performance and possibly on note-taking. One effective way of compensating for rate is to use short pauses during lecture to allow students time to consult with their peers or instructors to update their notes, check understanding, and so on.

Verbal Lecture Cues

In a series of three studies, Titsworth (2001, 2004; Titsworth & Kiewra, 2004) evaluated the effects of organizational cues provided in lecture on note-taking and/ or test performance. All three studies used the same lecture, which covered four theories of communication and, within each theory, four subthemes. Lectures with organizational cues provided explicit statements that a theory or sub-theme of the theory was about to be discussed ("First we are going to discuss [name of theory or sub-theme]"). The comparison group, sometimes described as a "no cues" group and at other times as a "minimal cues" group, heard the same lecture but without cues as explicit as those in the organizational group ("Another [name of theory or sub-theme] we are going to discuss"). The primary difference between groups seemed to be the use of a number in the cues group to tell students which theory/sub-theme they were covering.

Two other variables were included in some of the experiments: teacher immediacy (high or low) and note-taking (note-taking vs. no note-taking). Teacher immediacy was defined as verbal and nonverbal behaviors related to perceptions of closeness with students, such as eye contact, hand gestures, facial expressions, movement around the classroom, use of humor, and so on. The high-immediacy conditions had more actions hypothesized to be related to closeness than low-immediacy conditions. Titsworth (2001) evaluated the effects of teacher immediacy, organizational cues, and note-taking on test performance, Titsworth (2004) evaluated the effects of the first two variables on note-taking, and Titsworth and Kiewra (2004) evaluated the effects of the same two variables on test performance and note-taking.

Results indicated that organizational cues and note-taking were significantly related to test performance (Titsworth, 2001; Titsworth & Kiewra, 2004) and organizational cues were related to notes (Titsworth, 2004; Titsworth & Kiewra, 2004). Immediacy was rarely related to outcomes. These data provide support for the value of note-taking discussed previously and also suggest that the beneficial effects provided by verbal organizational cues in lecture are comparable to those provided by cues (headings and subheadings) in linear and matrix notes, which were alluded to previously and are discussed more thoroughly in the next section.

Changes in Note-Taking

Again, referring to our survey, students' most frequent response to the question under what conditions they would take better notes was "if I was better at figuring out what was important" (62.9%). Thus, it is not surprising that the primary technique used by researchers to improve note-taking is to provide students with handouts that help them focus on main ideas and their interrelationships (see Rapid Reference 12.3). The most typical handouts are (a) skeletal (linear) notes, which contain headings and subheadings related to main ideas with spaces for students to record information related to them, (b) guided notes, which are

≡ Rapid Reference 12.3 Self-Generated versus Other-Notes

Data on note-taking handouts and review of self-generated versus other-notes strongly suggest that instructors should:

1. Provide students with linear (skeletal) outlines, matrixes, or some other comparable support to facilitate note-taking and test performance.
2. Give them a complete set of notes and encourage students to use them along with their own notes when studying.
3. Include the cues given in note-taking handouts in their lectures to make the organizational structure of the lecture more obvious.

very similar to skeletal notes but also provide students with numbers or other cues to indicate how many ideas should be recorded, (c) matrixes, which require students to record notes in cells created by the intersection of headings and subheadings, and (d) complete notes. Typically, handout groups are compared to listening-only and/or conventional note-taking groups who are not given a handout.

Overall, results indicated that handouts facilitated note-taking compared to listening or conventional notes, and lower-ability students benefited more from handouts than higher-ability students (Austin, Lee, & Carr, 2004; Benton, Kiewra, Whitfill, & Dennison, 1993; Boyle & Rivera, 2012; Cohn et al., 1995; Gleason, 2012; Grabe, Christopherson, & Douglas, 2004–2005; Kiewra et al., 1995; Kiewra, DuBois, Christensen, Kim, & Lindberg, 1989; Kiewra et al., 1991; Morgan, Lilly, & Boreham, 1988; Neef, McCord, & Ferreri, 2006; Ruhl & Suritsky, 1995). The reader should note that it is difficult to determine whether one type of handout is better than another given the diversity in handouts, materials, students, length of lecture, outcome measures, and time between lecture and test, among other variables across studies. However, in an early review of seven studies on the relative efficacy of students taking and reviewing their own notes and/or instructor's notes, Kiewra (1985) concluded that due to the incompleteness of students' notes, students generally performed better on tests if they reviewed instructor's notes rather than their own notes but that students who reviewed both performed the best of all. He also noted that students recalled proportionally more from their own notes than instructor's notes. Thus, he concluded that students should be given and should be encouraged to use both.

Changes in Review

As noted by Kobayashi (2005, 2006), reviewing notes contributes more to test performance than taking notes. Logically, this makes perfect sense. The rapid pace of most lectures and the cognitive complexity of note-taking make it difficult enough for students to record (typically only 20–40% of the important information contained in lectures is recorded in notes) let alone engage the strategies needed to conceptualize fully and remember important information. It is during review that students have time to conceptualize and remember.

Improving Notes for Review
One way to improve review is to improve the quality of the notes students have for review. Kiewra, DuBois Christian, and McShane (1988) evaluated the effects of different types of notes provided for review on college students' test performance

(students did not take notes). Specifically, students watched a lecture without taking notes and were randomly assigned a week later to one of four review groups: matrix notes, linear outline notes, a complete text of the lecture, and a control group (no notes; mental review only). After review, students took three tests: factual recognition, cued recall, and transfer. Given the importance of review, Kiewra et al. (1988) hypothesized that all three review groups would perform better than the control group on all of the tests. They also hypothesized that the outline and matrix groups would perform better than the complete text group on the cued recall and transfer tests, because performance on those tests was more dependent on the interrelationships among ideas in memory made clear in the outlines and matrixes. Given the greater clarity among ideas in the matrix group as compared to the outline group and the greater clarity of understanding demanded by transfer tests, they hypothesized that students in the matrix group would perform best on the transfer test. Finally, they predicted that there would be no differences between groups on the factual recognition test because memory for isolated facts is not dependent on interrelationships. All of their hypotheses were confirmed. These data suggest that review, especially review that promotes deeper, more integrative processing of new information, leads to better test performance in most situations.

Because of the pressures and complexities of note-taking, students do not have time to take notes that completely and thoroughly express all of the interrelations among ideas, like the notes given to students in Kiewra et al. (1988). Most of the integration, reconceptualization, and memorization needed for examinations must be done by the learner when reviewing his or her notes after class. Thus, in contrast to the students in Kiewra et al. (1988), some of whom were given more complete or integrated notes, most students produce them on their own. We now turn to other literatures that can inform educators on how to help students with the processes of review.

Semantic Maps

As stated earlier, under most circumstances, students do not have time to create notes that adequately express all of the relationships among ideas presented in lecture. Thus, while reviewing their notes, students should rewrite their notes to create those relationships, which in turn can lead to richer mental representations of the important information presented in lecture and better test performance. What follows is a review of the evidence on the efficacy of a nonlinear form of note-taking (e.g., outlines) called *semantic maps*. Because creating a semantic map can be very effortful and time consuming, semantic mapping techniques have been applied primarily to text note-taking, which is not as time-limited as lecture note-taking. Ultimately, we will recommend that students use semantic maps to rewrite the (linear) notes they typically create during lecture.

Semantic maps are visual-spatial representations of the conceptual organization of written text, which usually include arrows and/or verbal phrases such as "leads to" or "is similar to." Although there are subtle differences among the following, semantics maps can include concept maps (Novak & Gowin, 1984), knowledge maps (Dansereau & Simpson, 2009; O'Donnell, Dansereau, & Hall, 2002), and graphic organizers (Katayama & Robinson, 2000). Research on the application of semantic maps has focused on maps as a study or review tool, constructed either by the student, teacher, or textbook author (see Nesbit & Adesope, 2006, for review), as an explicit note-taking strategy, either during a lesson or in a group activity following a lesson (DiCecco & Gleason, 2002; Horton et al., 1993; Novak & Gowin, 1984), and as an adjunct tool to facilitate comprehension while reading text (Stull & Mayer, 2007; Weinstein & Mayer, 1986).

An early meta-analysis by Moore and Readance (1984) found semantic maps were more effective as a post-lesson review activity (effect size = .57) than as a pre-reading advanced organizer (effect size = .27). Subsequent studies of the effects of maps on learning outcomes continued to find that using maps for review fosters greater memory for information than do linearly structured notes such as outlines (Bahr & Dansereau, 2001, 2005; O'Donnell et al., 2002). For instance, Bahr and Dansereau (2001, 2005) found that students learned significantly more foreign (German) vocabulary words using maps than lists of translation equivalents. On a number of recall and/or transfer tasks, those who used maps, as compared to other forms of study or review formats such as outlines, generally demonstrated better performance (Chmielewski & Dansereau, 1998; Patterson, Dansereau, & Newbern, 1992; Stull & Mayer, 2007). Not only do map learners recall information better overall, those who use semantic maps to study also tend to generate a better understanding of concept relationships and the texts' or lectures' most important ideas (Robinson, 1998).

Unlike research on the encoding and review functions of note-taking, research on semantic maps has often focused on students who struggle academically. The results indicate that semantic maps are especially helpful to struggling learners of different ages and difficulties: middle school and high school learning-disabled and remedial students (DiCecco & Gleason, 2002; Horton, Lovitt, & Bergerud, 1990), students with low verbal ability (Chmie-lewski & Dansereau, 1998; O'Donnell et al., 2002; Patterson, Dansereau, & Wiegmann, 1993; Wiegmann, Dansereau, McCagg, Rewey, & Pitre, 1992), bilingual students (Amer, 1994), and the deaf and hard of hearing (O'Donnell & Adenwalla, 1991). For example, Chmielewski and Dansereau conducted a study where college students with low verbal ability were randomly assigned to a semantic maps or outlines group. After training they were asked to study two text passages. Five days later they were given a free-recall test on both passages. Results showed that low-verbal-ability students trained with maps recalled more important information from both passages than the outline group. There were no significant differences between groups on less important information. Additional findings from research on semantic maps are that semantic maps seem to apply equally well to different content areas (e.g., science and social studies; Horton et al., 1990), and that teaching students, especially struggling learners, how to use or generate maps is essential (e.g., Chmielewski & Dansereau; DiCecco & Gleason, 2002; Stull & Mayer, 2007).

Data reviewed in previous sections suggest that review is the most important function of note-taking and review of notes that are more complete and elaborated leads to better test performance. In this section we reviewed research on semantic maps for the purpose of arguing that semantic mapping methods can be used to generate more complete and elaborated notes for review. However, our take-home message is this: Regardless of the technique, students should rewrite their notes, not only to improve their understanding of the information presented in lecture but to improve their understanding of all of the content presented in the course. In other words, when rewriting their notes, students should incorporate into them lecture-related information from course readings (e.g., textbooks; course-related articles) and other materials.

Improving Recall of Notes via Repeated Retrieval

Students take notes during lecture for a reason—to help them prepare for examinations. For example, 95.4% of the respondents to our survey indicated that they studied their notes either "often" or "always" before tests. However, once you have rewritten your notes, are some ways of studying your notes better than others? In what follows, we will argue that students should engage in the often ignored and sometimes maligned act of repeated retrieval.

The strategy of retrieval is the poor cousin of memory strategy research. Research on memory strategies has focused more on encoding (e.g., rehearsal and organization) than retrieval (e.g., Bjorklund, Dukes, & Brown, 2009), college undergraduates do not often rate retrieval as a viable study strategy (Karpicke, Butler, & Roediger, 2009), and students' judgments

> **DON'T FORGET**
> When rewriting their notes, students should incorporate into them lecture-related information from course readings (e.g., textbooks; course-related articles) and other materials.

of learning and later test performance after repeated retrieval are surprisingly low and inaccurate (Roediger & Karpicke, 2006b).

Despite the relatively low status of retrieval, repeated retrieval (dubbed the *testing effect*) has consistently been shown to reliably enhance long-term memory more than repeated study (Roediger & Karpicke, 2006a). In what has become a classic demonstration of the testing effect, Roediger and Karpike (2006b, Experiment 2) conducted a two-phase, between-subjects experiment to evaluate the relative efficacy of studying a passage versus testing oneself on the content of the passage via written recall (without reference to the passage) on long-term memory. In the first phase, participants learned one prose passage in one of three conditions: four consecutive study periods (SSSS), three consecutive study periods and one testing period (SSST), or one study period and three testing periods (STTT). Each study period lasted 5 minutes and each test period lasted 10 minutes. Students did not have access to the passage during the test periods. At the end of phase one, participants were given a questionnaire and asked to predict how well they would remember the material in a week (1 = *not very well*; 7 = *very well*). In phase two of the experiment, all participants were asked to write down as much of the passage they could recall, without reference to the passage, either five minutes or one week after the end of phase one.

Results from the questionnaire indicated that participants in the SSSS condition were significantly more confident that they would recall the passage in a week than participants in either of the other two conditions. Results from phase two conformed to the classic pattern found in the literature on the testing effect. On the immediate (five-minute) test, participants in the SSSS condition recalled more (83%) than the participants in the SSST (78%) condition, who recalled more information than those in the STTT condition (71%). All differences were significant. On the delayed (one-week) condition the pattern was the opposite. Despite participants' prediction on the questionnaire, participants in the STTT group recalled more (61%) than those in the SSST (56%) group, who recalled more than participants in the SSSS condition (40%). Although the difference between the first two conditions was not significant, despite the fact that the SSST group studied the passage three times longer than the STTT group, both groups recalled significantly more than the SSSS condition. Thus, the testing effect (repeated retrieval) had a substantially positive effect on long-term retention.

The testing effect has been replicated many times with different materials and in different settings. In the laboratory these findings have been replicated with paired associates, short prose and fiction passages (Butler, Marsh, Goode, &

Roediger, 2006), and journal articles (Kang, McDermott, & Roediger, 2007). They have also been replicated with different types of intermittent and final tests, including multiple choice (McDaniel, Anderson, Derbish, & Morrisette, 2007), fact lists (Bouwmeester & Verkoeijen, 2011; Kang et al., 2007), cued and free recall (Carpenter &

> **DON'T FORGET**
> ....
> Despite the relatively low status of retrieval, repeated retrieval (dubbed the *testing effect*) has consistently been shown to enhance long-term memory more than repeated study.

DeLosh, 2006; Pyc & Rawson, 2010), and tests of the ability to infer relationships (Butler, 2010; Karpicke & Blunt, 2011). In actual classrooms the testing effect has been demonstrated with elementary school (Gates, 1917; Spitzer, 1939), middle school (Glover, 1989; McDaniel, Agarwal, Huelser, McDermott, & Roediger, 2011; Roediger, Agarwal, McDaniel, & McDermott, 2011), and college students (McDaniel et al., 2011).

The implications of the testing effect for note-taking are clear and straightforward. Once students have ensured that their notes adequately and thoroughly reflect the content of the lecture, and have studied them, they should repeatedly attempt to recall their notes (when they are not visually present), subsequently rechecking their notes to ensure accurate recall, while preparing for exams or subsequent classes. In addition to using repeated retrieval while studying notes and related materials for exams, individuals should engage in the following research-supported activities: (a) Avoid massed review and recall—distributing studying over days (e.g., one hour a day for 5 days) usually results in substantially better test performance than studying five hours the day before the test; Dempster, 1988); (b) generate questions—try to anticipate test questions and answer them (Rosenshine, Meister, & Chapman, 1996; Weinstein, McDermott, & Roediger, 2010); and (c) answer practice questions provided by the instructor or the questions provided in text, especially those that are inserted in margins of texts to check understanding as students read or those placed at the end of chapters to check understanding after reading, see Rapid Reference 12.4 for recommendations on reviewing notes (Hamaker, 1986; Peverly & Wood, 2001; Rothkopf, 1996; Weinstein et al., 2010).

Individual Differences in Note-Taking

Earlier we suggested that three cognitive variables may be related to skill in note-taking: transcription speed, verbal ability, and sustained attention. Although we do not know of research-supported interventions on improving these

≡ *Rapid Reference 12.4 Reviewing Notes*

Review is the most important function of note-taking. Thus, we recommend that students do the following:

1. Since the notes they take in lecture are often linear, incomplete, and lacking in organization and elaboration, students should rewrite their notes, not only to improve their understanding of the information presented in lecture but to improve their understanding of all of the content presented in the course. In other words, when rewriting their notes, students should incorporate into them lecture-related information from course readings (e.g., textbooks; course-related articles) and other materials.
2. Engage in repeated retrieval of their notes.
3. Emphasize distributed rather than massed review.
4. Generate and answer questions.
5. Answer practice questions provided by the instructor or in course materials (e.g., textbooks).

skills and evaluating the relationship between improved performance on them and performance in note-taking, we have general educational suggestions for each.

Regarding transcription, schools should not abandon handwriting instruction in the early elementary grades. All but five states have adopted the Common Core State Standards (In the States, 2011), which recommends instruction in printing in the first grade and no longer recommends instruction in cursive, despite the fact that the corticospinal pathways related to writing continue to develop until approximately age 10 (Conti, 2012). Moreover, handwriting speed, which is facilitated by instruction, is related to writing outcomes in children (Graham, & Santangelo, 2012; McCutchen, 2012) and adults (Peverly, 2006). Also, unlike keyboarding, handwriting seems to be related to the development of letter recognition skills in children (James, 2012; James & Gauthier, 2006), which facilitates the development of spelling and word recognition. In addition to instruction in handwriting, students should receive instruction in keyboarding to ensure that it is fluent and efficient (Berninger, Abbott, Augsburger, & Garcia, 2009; MacArthur, 2009).

Verbal ability is strongly related to the comprehension of spoken and written discourse (Kintsch, 1998; Perfetti, 2007), including the identification of important information in lecture (Gleason, 2012; Peverly et al., 2007; Peverly et al., under review). Schools can promote the development of verbal ability by using research-supported instruction to teach students to read well. Good readers tend to read more and thus have greater exposure to and learn more new vocabulary and complex grammatical forms than poor readers (semantics or vocabulary and grammar are the primary components of skill in language; Perfetti, 1986; Stanovich, 1986). Conversely, students who do not learn to read words well, read less and over time show declines in verbal skills relative to their peers who are good readers (Stanovich, 1986). Also, good reading comprehension programs in the primary and secondary grades place a strong emphasis on skills related to good lecture note-taking, such as the identification of main ideas (Gersten, Fuchs, Williams, & Baker, 2001). It is not a coincidence, then, that reading comprehension correlates very strongly with listening comprehension among college adults (approximately .8 to .9; Gernsbacher, Varner, & Faust, 1990), which suggests that reading comprehension is a proxy for verbal ability in that population (Perfetti, 1986).

Finally, if students do not attend to instruction, they cannot learn from instruction. We have two general recommendations to improve attention. First, teach attentional control. The procedures developed by Lovass (1977) for students with autism, for example, how to sit and attend to teachers and educational materials and behave in classrooms, are also effective in general education classrooms (Greer & Ross, 2008). Second, motivation goal structures seem to be related to behavioral engagement and control (Dweck, 2002). In goal orientation theory, mastery goals are related to learning and improving one's skills and abilities through effort (e.g., Is your skill in multiplication better today than it was three weeks ago?) while performance goals focus on demonstrations of academic competence compared to one's peers (e.g., Is your grade on a test of multiplication skills better than your peers' test grades?). Evidence suggests that students in classrooms with more of an emphasis on mastery show higher levels of behavioral engagement (Hughes, Wu, & West, 2011).

SUMMARY

Note-taking is an extraordinarily popular and pervasive strategy, especially among high school and college students, for recording important information presented in lecture. Also, notes are related to good test performance. Taking notes, and especially reviewing notes, are related to better test outcomes. Research indicates that there are several interventions that can assist students in taking better notes (see Rapid Reference 12.5).

≡ *Rapid Reference 12.5 Note-Taking Interventions*

Research indicates that there are several interventions that can assist students in taking better notes. They are:

1. Pace your lectures. Do not speak too rapidly and use pauses and/or frequent opportunities for questions to give students the opportunity to complete and/or correct their notes.

2. If possible, record your lectures to provide students with the opportunity to view them more than once.

3. Provide students with an outline of the major points in the lecture, to promote more thorough and conceptually accurate and complete note-taking. Also, provide cues within the lecture that match the major points in the outline.

4. Provide students with a complete copy of your notes. (The first author provides these to students in his classes a week before each examination.)

5. Encourage students to rewrite their notes after each class. Rewriting will help students to conceptually integrate concepts (techniques such as semantic mapping or matrix notes can be very helpful here) as well as to highlight what they have and have not understood, which in turn will help them ask more thoughtful questions in class and provide better notes for studying.

6. Encourage spaced (rather than massed) review and repeated retrieval (testing effect).

7. Encourage students to answer questions provided by the instructor or contained within lecture-related materials (e.g., textbooks) and to generate and answer questions they think the instructor might ask on an examination.

8. Teach students how to take notes, create semantic maps, review, engage in repeated retrieval, and so on. For example, research indicates that SQ3R, one of the most frequently recommended study skills techniques, does not typically help students study better than they would have without SQ3R, primarily because it is a difficult strategy to execute and students are not typically given instruction in how to use it. Teaching is especially critical for weaker students.

9. More generally, thoroughly teach transcription by hand and computer, provide systematic and extensive instruction in reading words and in comprehension (to facilitate growth in students' verbal skills), train attention, and emphasize effort and mastery goals in classrooms.

REFERENCES

Amer, A. A. (1994). The effect of knowledge-map and underlining training on the reading comprehension of scientific texts. *English for Specific Purposes, 13*, 35–45.

Anderson, T. H., & Anderson, B. B. (1984). Studying. In P. D. Pearson (Ed.), *Handbook of reading research* (pp. 657–679). New York, NY: Longman.

Anderson, T. H., & Armbruster, B. B. (1984). Content area textbooks. In R. C. Anderson, J. Osborn, & R. J. Tierney (Eds.), *Learning to read in American schools* (pp. 193–224). Hillsdale, NJ: Erlbaum.

Armbruster, B. (2009). Notetaking from lectures. In R. F. Flippo & D. C. Caverly (Eds.), *Handbook of college reading and study strategy research* (2nd ed., pp. 220–248). New York, NY: Routledge.

Austin, J., Lee, M., & Carr, J. (2004). The effects of guided notes on undergraduate students' recording of lecture content. *Journal of Instructional Psychology, 31*, 314–320.

Bahr, G. S., & Dansereau, D. F. (2001). Bilingual knowledge maps (BiK-maps) in second-language vocabulary learning. *Journal of Experimental Education, 70*, 5–24.

Bahr, G. S., & Dansereau, D. F. (2005). Bilingual knowledge maps (BiK-maps) as a presentation format: Delayed recall and training effects. *Journal of Experimental Education, 73*, 101–118.

Benton, S. L., Kiewra, K. A., Whitfill, J. M., & Dennison, R. (1993). Encoding and external-storage effects on writing processes. *Journal of Educational Psychology, 85*, 267–280.

Berninger, V. (2012). *Past, present, and future contributions of cognitive writing research to cognitive psychology.* New York, NY: Psychology Press.

Berninger, V., Abbott, R., Augsburger, A., & Garcia, N. (2009). Comparison of pen and keyboard transcription modes in children with and without learning disabilities. *Learning Disability Quarterly, 32*, 123–141.

Berninger, V. W., Abbott, R. D., Jones, J., Wolf, B. J., Gould, L., Anderson-Youngstrom, M., & Apel, K. (2006). Early development of language by hand: Composing-, reading-, listening-, and speaking-connections, three letter writing modes, and fast mapping in spelling. *Developmental Neuropsychology, 29*, 61–92.

Bjorklund, D. F., Dukes, C., & Brown, R. D. (2009). The development of memory strategies. In M. L. Courage & N. Cowan (Eds.), *The development of memory in infancy and childhood* (pp. 145–175). New York, NY: Psychology Press.

Bouwmeester, S., & Verkoeijen, P. P. J. L. (2011). Why do some children benefit more from testing than others? Gist trace processing to explain the testing effect. *Journal of Memory and Language, 65*(1), 32–41. Elsevier. doi: 10.1016/j.jml.2011.02.005

Boyle, J. R., & Rivera, T. Z. (2012). Note-taking techniques for students with disabilities: A systematic review of the research. *Learning Disabilities Quarterly, 35*, 131–143. doi: 10.1177/0731948711435794

Bretzing, B. H., & Kulhavy, R. W. (1981). Notetaking and passage style. *Journal of Educational Psychology, 73*, 242–250.

Butler, A. C. (2010). Repeated testing produces superior transfer of learning relative to repeated studying. *Journal of Experimental Psychology: Learning, Memory, and Cognition, 36*(5), 1118–33. doi: 10.1037/a0019902

Butler, A. C., Marsh, E. J., Goode, M. K., & Roediger, H. L. (2006). When additional multiple-choice lures aid versus hinder later memory. *Applied Cognitive Psychology, 20*(7), 941–956. doi: 10.1002/acp.1239

Carpenter, S. K., & DeLosh, E. L. (2006). Impoverished cue support enhances subsequent retention: Support for the elaborative retrieval explanation of the testing effect. *Memory & Cognition, 34*, 268–276.

Chmielewski, T. L., & Dansereau, D. F. (1998). Enhancing the recall of text: Knowledge mapping training promotes implicit transfer. *Journal of Educational Psychology, 90*, 407–413.

Cohn, E., Cohn, S., & Bradley, J. (1995). Notetaking, working memory, and learning in principles of economics. *Research in Economic Education, 26*, 291–307.

Conti, G. (2012, January). *Handwriting characteristics and the prediction of illegibility in third and fifth grade students.* Presented at Handwriting in the 21st Century?: An Educational Summit, Washington, DC.

Dansereau, D. F., & Simpson, D. D. (2009). A picture is worth a thousand words: The case for graphic representations. *Professional Psychology: Research and Practice, 40*, 104–110.

Dempster, F. N. (1988). The spacing effect: A case study in the failure to apply the results of psychological research. *American Psychologist, 43,* 627–634.

DiCecco, V. M., & Gleason, M. M. (2002). Using graphic organizers to attain relational knowledge from expository text. *Journal of Learning Disabilities, 35,* 306–320.

DiVesta, F. J., & Gray, G. S. (1972). Listening and note taking. *Journal of Educational Psychology, 64,* 321–325.

Dunkel, P., & Davy, S. (1989). The heuristic of lecture notetaking: Perceptions of American and international students regarding the value and practice of notetaking. *English for Specific Purposes, 8,* 33–50.

Dweck, C.S. (2002). The development of ability conceptions. In A. Wigfield & J. S. Eccles (Eds.), *Development of achievement motivation* (Vol. XVII, pp. 57–88). San Diego, CA: Academic Press.

Fisher, J. L., & Harris, M. B. (1973). Effect of note-taking and review on recall. *Journal of Educational Psychology, 65,* 321–325.

Gates, A. I. (1917). *Recitation as a factor in memorizing. Archives of Psychology* (40th ed., pp. 1–104). New York, NY: Science Press. Retrieved from http://books.google.com/books/download/Recitation_as_a_factor_in_memorizing.pdf?id=YinQhb3ZS8YC&output=pdf&sig=ACfU3U0dCJ-oJYvoQ6ESH62kUpQQVGL2vQ.

Geary, D. C. (1994). *Children's mathematical development: Research and practical applications.* Washington, DC: American Psychological Association.

Gernsbacher, M. A., Varner, K. R., & Faust, M. E. (1990). Investigating differences in general comprehension skill. *Journal of Experimental Psychology: Learning, Memory, and Cognition, 16,* 430–445.

Gersten, R., Fuchs, L. S., Williams, J., & Baker, S. (2001). Teaching reading comprehension strategies to students with learning disabilities: A review of the research. *Review of Educational Research, 71,* 279–320.

Gleason, J. (2012). *An investigation of the lecture note-taking skills of adolescents with and without attention deficit/hyperactivity disorder: An extension of previous research.* New York, NY: Columbia University Teachers College.

Glover, J. A. (1989). The "testing" phenomenon: Not gone but nearly forgotten. *Journal of Educational Psychology, 81*(3), 392–399. doi: 10.1037//0022-0663.81.3.392

Grabe, M., Christopherson, K., & Douglas, J. (2004–2005). Providing introductory psychology students access to on-line notes: The relationship of note use to performance and class attendance. *Journal of Educational Technology Systems, 33,* 295–308.

Graham, S., & Santangelo, T. (2012, January). *A meta-analysis of the effectiveness of teaching handwriting.* Presented at Handwriting in the 21st Century: An Educational Summit, Washington, DC.

Greer, R. D., & Ross, D. E. (2008). *Verbal behavior analysis.* Boston, MA: Pearson.

Hadwin, A. F., Kirby, J. R., & Woodhouse, R. A. (1999). Individual differences in notetaking, summarization, and learning from lectures. *Alberta Journal of Educational Research, 45,* 1–17.

Hamaker, C. (1986). The effects of adjunct questions on prose learning. *Review of Educational Research, 56,* 212–242.

Horton, S. V., Lovitt, T. C., & Bergerud, D. (1990). The effectiveness of graphic organizers for three classifications of secondary students in content area classes. *Journal of Learning Disabilities, 23,* 12–22.

Horton, P. B., McConney, A. A., Gallo, M., Woods, A. L., Senn, G. J., & Hamelin, D. (1993). An investigation of the effectiveness of concept mapping as an instructional tool. *Science Education, 77*(1), 95–111.

Hughes, J. N., Wu, W., & West, S. G. (2011) Teacher performance goal practices and elementary students' behavioral engagement: A developmental perspective. *Journal of School Psychology, 49*, 1–23.

Hulme, C., & Snowling, M. J. (2011). Children's reading comprehension difficulties: Nature, causes, and treatments. *Current Directions in Psychological Science, 20*, 139–142.

In the, States. , (2011). *Common Core State Standards Initiative*. Retrieved from http://www.corestandards.org/in-the-states.

James, K. H. (2012, January). *How printing practice affects letter perception: An educational cognitive neuroscience perspective*. Presented at Handwriting in the 21st Century?: An Educational Summit, Washington, DC.

James, K. H., & Gauthier, I. (2006). Letter processing automatically recruits a sensory-motor brain network. *Neuropsychologia, 44*, 2937–2949.

Kang, S. H. K., McDermott, K. B., & Roediger, H. L. (2007). Test format and corrective feedback modify the effect of testing on long-term retention. *European Journal of Cognitive Psychology, 19*(4–5), 528–558. doi: 10.1080/09541440601056620

Karpicke, J. D., & Blunt, J. R. (2011). Retrieval practice produces more learning than elaborative studying with concept mapping. *Science (New York, NY), 331*(6018), 772–775. doi: 10.1126/science.1199327

Karpicke, J. D., Butler, A. C., & Roediger, H. L. (2009). Metacognitive strategies in student learning: Do students practise retrieval when they study on their own? *Memory (Hove, England), 17*(4), 471–479. doi: 10.1080/09658210802647009

Katayama, A. D., & Robinson. D. R. (2000). Getting students "partially" involved in note-taking using graphic organizers. *Journal of Experimental Education, 68*, 119–133.

Kiewra, K. A. (1985). Investigating note-taking and review: A depth of processing alternative. *Educational Psychologist, 20*, 23–32.

Kiewra, K. A. (1991). Aids to lecture learning. *Educational Psychologist, 26*, 37–53.

Kiewra, K. A., & Benton, S. L. (1988). The relationship between information processing ability and notetaking. *Contemporary Educational Psychology, 13*, 33–44.

Kiewra, K. A., Benton, S. L., Kim, S-I., Risch, N., & Christensen, M. (1995). Effects of note-taking format and study technique on recall and relational performance. *Contemporary Educational Psychology, 13*, 33–44.

Kiewra, K. A., Benton, S. L., & Lewis, L. B. (1987). Qualitative aspects of notetaking and their relationship with information-processing ability and academic achievement. *Journal of Instructional Psychology, 14*, 110–117.

Kiewra, K. A., DuBois, N. F., Christensen, M., Kim, S-I., & Lindberg, N. (1989). A more equitable account of the note-taking functions in learning from lecture and from text. *Instructional Sciences, 18*, 217–232.

Kiewra, K. A., DuBois, N. F., Christian, D., & McShane, A. (1988). Providing study notes: Comparison of three types of notes for review. *Journal of Educational Psychology, 80*, 595–597.

Kiewra, K. A., DuBois, N. F., Christian, D., McShane, A., Meyerhoffer, M., & Roskelley, D. (1991). Note-taking functions and techniques. *Journal of Educational Psychology, 83*, 240–245.

Kiewra, K. A., & Mayer, R. E. (1997). Effects of advanced organizers and repeated presentations on students' learning. *Journal of Experimental Education, 65*, 147–159.

Kiewra, K. A., Mayer, R. E., Christensen, M., Kim, S., & Risch, N. (1991). Effects of repetition on recall and note-taking: Strategies for learning from lectures. *Journal of Educational Psychology, 83*, 120–123.

Kintsch, W. (1998). *Comprehension: A paradigm for cognition*. Cambridge: Cambridge University Press.

Kobayashi, K. (2005). What limit the encoding effect of note-taking? A meta-analytic examination. *Contemporary Educational Psychology*, *30*, 242–262.

Kobayashi, K. (2006). Combined effects of note-taking/-reviewing on learning and the enhancement through interventions: A meta-analytic review. *Contemporary Educational Psychology*, *26*, 459–477.

Lovaas, O. I. (1977). *The autistic child: Language development through behavior modification*. New York, NY: Irvington.

MacArthur, C. A. (2009). Reflections on research on writing and technology for struggling writers. *Learning Disabilities Research & Practice*, *24*, 93–103.

McCutchen, D. (1996). A capacity theory of writing: Working memory in composition. *Educational Psychology Review*, *8*, 299–325.

McCutchen, D. (2012). Phonological, orthographic, and morphological word-level skills supporting multiple levels of the writing process. In V. Berninger (Ed.), *Past, present, and future contributions of cognitive writing research to cognitive psychology*. New York, NY: Psychology Press.

McDaniel, M. A., Agarwal, P. K., Huelser, B. J., McDermott, K. B., & Roediger, H. L. (2011). Test-enhanced learning in a middle school science classroom: The effects of quiz frequency and placement. *Journal of Educational Psychology*, *103*(2), 399–414. doi: 10.1037/a0021782

McDaniel, M. A., Anderson, J. L., Derbish, M. H., & Morrisette, N. (2007). Testing the testing effect in the classroom. *European Journal of Cognitive Psychology*, *19*(4–5), 494–513. doi: 10.1080/09541440701326154

McIntyre, S. (1992). Lecture notetaking, information processing, and academic achievement. *Journal of College Reading and Learning*, *25*, 7–17.

Moore, D. W., & Readance, J. E. (1984). A quantitative and qualitative review of graphic organizer research. *Journal of Educational Research*, *78*, 11–17.

Morgan, C. H., Lilly, J. D., & Boreham, N. C. (1988). Learning from lectures: The effect of varying detail in lecture handouts to note-taking and recall. *Applied Cognitive Psychology*, *2*, 115–122.

Mulcahy-Ernt, P. I., & Caverly, D. C. (2009). Strategic study-reading. In R. F. Flippo & D. C. Caverly (Eds.), *Handbook of college reading and study strategy research* (2nd ed., pp. 177–198). New York, NY: Routledge.

Neef, N. A., McCord, B. E., & Ferreri, S. J. (2006). Effects of guided notes versus completed notes during lectures on college students' quiz performance. *Journal of Applied Behavior Analysis*, *39*, 123–130.

Nesbit, J. C., & Adesope, O. O. (2006). Learning with concept and knowledge maps: A meta-analysis. *Review of Educational Research*, *76*, 413–448.

Novak, J. D., & Gowin, D. B. (1984). *Learning how to learn*. New York, NY: Cambridge University Press.

O'Donnell, A. M., & Adenwalla, D. (1991). Using cooperative learning and concept maps with deaf college students. In D. S. Martin (Ed.), *Advances in cognition, learning, and deafness* (pp. 348–355). Washington, DC: Gallaudet University Press.

O'Donnell, A. M., Dansereau, D. F., & Hall, R. H. (2002). Knowledge maps as scaffolds for cognitive processing. *Educational Psychology Review*, *14*, 71–86.

Palmatier, R. A., & Bennett, J. M. (1974). Notetaking habits of college students. *Journal of Reading*, *18*, 215–218.

Patterson, M. E., Dansereau, D. F., & Newbern, D. (1992). Effectiveness of communication aids and strategies on cooperative teaching. *Journal of Educational Psychology*, *84*(4), 453–461.

Patterson, M. E., Dansereau, D. F., & Wiegmann, D. A. (1993). Receiving information during a cooperative learning episode: Effects of communication aids and verbal ability. *Learning and Individual Differences 5*, 1–11.

Perfetti, C. A. (1985). *Reading ability*. New York, NY: Oxford University Press.

Perfetti, C. A. (1986). Cognitive and linguistic components of reading ability. In B. Foorman & A. W. Siegel (Eds.), *Acquisition of reading skills: Cultural constraints and cognitive universals* (pp. 11–40). Hillsdale, NJ: Lawrence Erlbaum Associates.

Perfetti, C. A. (2007). Reading ability: Lexical quality to comprehension. *Scientific Studies of Reading, 11*, 357–383.

Peverly, S. T. (2006). The importance of handwriting speed in adult writing. *Developmental Neuropsychology, 29*, 197–216.

Peverly, S. T., Brobst, K., Graham, M., & Shaw, R. (2003). College adults are not good at self-regulation: A study on the relationship of self-regulation, note-taking, and test-taking. *Journal of Educational Psychology, 95*, 335–346.

Peverly, S. T., Garner, J., & Vekaria, P. C. (in preparation). The complementary roles of transcription fluency and attention in lecture note-taking.

Peverly, S. T., Ramaswamy, V., Brown, C., Sumowski, J., Alidoost, M., & Garner, J. (2007). What predicts skill in lecture note taking? *Journal of Educational Psychology, 99*, 167–180.

Peverly, S. T., & Sumowski, J. F. (2011). What variables predict quality of text notes and are text notes related to performance on different types of tests? *Applied Cognitive Psychology*. doi: 10.1002/acp.1802.

Peverly, S. T., Vekaria, P. C., Reddington, L. A., Sumowski, J. F., Johnson, K. R., & Ramsay, C. (under review). There is more to skill in lecture note-taking than transcription fluency. *Applied Cognitive Psychology*.

Peverly, S. T., & Wood, R. (2001). The effects of adjunct questions and feedback on improving the reading comprehension skills of learning-disabled adolescents. *Contemporary Educational Psychology, 26*, 25–43.

Piolat, A., Olive, T., & Kellogg, R. T. (2005). Cognitive effort during note taking. *Applied Cognitive Psychology, 19*, 291–312.

Putnam, M. L., Deshler, D. D., & Schumaker, J. B. (1993). The investigation of setting demands: A missing link in strategy instruction. In L. S. Meltzer (Ed.), *Strategy assessment and instruction for students with learning disabilities* (pp. 325–354). Austin, TX: PRO-ED.

Pyc, M. A., & Rawson, K. A. (2010). Why testing improves memory: Mediator effectiveness hypothesis. *Science (New York, NY), 330*(6002), 335. doi: 10.1126/science.1191465

Rayner, K., Foorman, B. R., Perfetti, C. A., Pesetsky, D., & Seidenberg, M. S. (2001). How psychological science informs the teaching of reading. *Psychological Science in the Public Interest, 2*, 31–74.

Reddingtion, L. (2011). *Gender difference variables predicting expertise in lecture note-taking*. Available from Proquest Dissertations and Theses Database (UMI No. 2348429071).

Rickards, J. P., & Friedman, F. (1978). The encoding versus the external storage hypothesis in note taking. *Contemporary Educational Psychology, 3*, 136–143.

Robinson, D. H. (1998). Graphic organizers as aids to text learning. *Reading Research and Instruction, 37*, 85–105.

Roediger, H. L., Agarwal, P. K., McDaniel, M. A., & McDermott, K. B. (2011). Test-enhanced learning in the classroom: Long-term improvements from quizzing. *Journal of Experimental Psychology: Applied, 17*(4), 382–395. doi: 10.1037/a0026252

Roediger, H. L., & Karpicke, J. D. (2006a). The power of testing memory. *Perspectives on Psychological Science, 1*(3), 181–210. doi: 10.1111/j.1745-6916.2006.00012.x

Roediger, H. L., & Karpicke, J. D. (2006b). Test-enhanced learning: Taking memory tests improves long-term retention. *Psychological Science, 17*(3), 249–255. doi: 10.1111/j.1467-9280.2006.01693.x

Rosenshine, B., Meister, C., & Chapman, S. (1996). Teaching students to generate questions: A review of the intervention studies. *Review of Educational Research, 66*, 181–221.

Rothkopf, E. Z. (1996). Control of mathemagenic activities. In D. H. Jonassen (Ed.), *Handbook of research for educational communications and technology* (pp. 879–896). New York, NY: Simon & Schuster/Macmillan.

Ruhl, K. L. (1996). Does nature of student activity during lecture pauses affect notes and immediate recall of college students with learning disabilities? *Journal of Postsecondary Education and Disability, 12*, 16–27.

Ruhl, K. L., Hughes, C. A., & Gajar, A. H. (1990). Efficacy of the pause procedure for enhancing learning disabled and nondisabled college students' long- and short-term recall of facts presented through lecture. *Learning Disability Quarterly, 13*, 55–64.

Ruhl, K. L., Hughes, C. A., & Schloss, P. J. (1987). Using the pause procedure to enhance lecture recall. *Teacher Education and Special Education, 10*, 14–18.

Ruhl, K. L., & Suritsky, S. (1995). The pause procedure and/or an outline: Effect on Immediate free recall and lecture notes taken by college students with disabilities. *Learning Disability Quarterly, 18*, 2–11.

Slotte, V., & Lonka, K. (1999). Review and process effects of spontaneous note-taking on text comprehension. *Contemporary Educational Psychology, 24*, 1–20.

Snow, C. (2002). (Ed.). *Reading for understanding: Toward an R&D program in reading comprehension.* Santa Monica, CA: Rand.

Spitzer, H. F. (1939). Studies in retention. *Journal of Educational Psychology, 30*, 641–656.

Stanovich, K. E. (1986). Matthew effects in reading: Some consequences of individual differences in the acquisition of literacy. *Reading Research Quarterly, 21*, 360–407.

Stull, A. T., & Mayer, R. E. (2007). Learning by doing versus learning by viewing: Three experimental comparisons of learner-generated versus author-provided graphic organizers. *Journal of Educational Psychology, 99*, 808–820.

Suritsky, S. K. (1992). Notetaking difficulties and approaches reported by university students with learning disabilities. *Journal of Postsecondary Education and Disability, 10*, 3–10.

Thomas, J. W., Iventosch, L., & Rohwer, W. D. (1987). Relationships among student characteristics, study activities, and achievement as a function of course characteristics. *Contemporary Educational Psychology, 12*, 344–364.

Titsworth, B. S. (2001). The effects of teacher immediacy, use of organizational lecture cues, and students' notetaking on cognitive learning. *Communication Education, 50*, 283–297.

Titsworth, B. S. (2004). Students' notetaking: The effects of teacher immediacy and clarity. *Communication Education, 53*, 305–320.

Titsworth, B. S., & Kiewra, K. A. (2004). Spoken organizational lecture cures and student notetaking as facilitators of student learning. *Contemporary Educational Psychology, 29*, 447–461.

Vekaria, P. C. (2011). *Lecture note-taking in postsecondary students with self-reported attention-deficit/hyperactivity disorder.* New York, NY: Columbia University Teachers College.

Vellutino, F. R., Fletcher, J. M., Snowling, M. J., & Scanlon, D. M. (2004). Specific reading disability (dyslexia): What have we learned in the past four decades? *Journal of Child Psychology and Psychiatry, 45*, 2–40.

Weinstein, C. E., & Mayer, R. E. (1986). The teaching of learning strategies. In M. C. Wittrock (Ed.), *Handbook on research in teaching* (3rd ed., pp. 315–327). New York, NY: Macmillan.

Weinstein, Y., McDermott, K. B., & Roediger, H. L. (2010). A comparison of study strategies for passages: Rereading, answering questions, and generating questions. *Journal of Experimental Psychology: Applied, 16*(3), 308–316. doi: 10.1037/a0020992

Wiegmann, D. A., Dansereau, D. F., McCagg, E. C., Rewey, K. L., & Pitre, U. (1992). Effects of knowledge map characteristics on information processing. *Contemporary Educational Psychology, 17*, 136–155.

🪶 TEST YOURSELF 🪶

1. **Which of the following typically leads to better test outcomes for students?**
   a. Taking notes
   b. Taking and reviewing ones' own notes
   c. Taking and reviewing ones' own notes and the instructor's notes
   d. Reviewing the instructor's notes

2. **Which of the following three variables seem to be related to skill in note-taking?**
   a. Transcription fluency, verbal ability, and selective attention
   b. Transcription fluency, working memory, and selective attention
   c. Working memory, selective attention, and verbal ability
   d. Verbal ability, executive attention, and working memory

3. **Note-taking seems to be most strongly related to which of the following?**
   a. Tests of memory
   b. Tests of understanding
   c. Tests of both memory and understanding

4. **Research on how changes in lecture affect note-taking indicates that __ is not typically related to better note-taking or test performance**
   a. Using cues in lecture to signal main ideas
   b. Making lectures available for repeated reviewing
   c. Pausing occasionally for questions
   d. Increasing teacher immediacy to increase students' feelings of closeness to the teacher

5. **Research on changes in students' note-taking suggests that.**
   a. Students take good, complete notes. Changes are not needed
   b. Students should be provided with handouts
   c. Matrix notes are better than skeletal notes
   d. Guided notes are better than matrix notes

6. **Which of the following statements most accurately characterizes the process of reviewing notes?**
   a. Reviewing notes is not nearly as important as taking notes.
   b. Students should reread their notes repeatedly.
   c. Students should rewrite their notes before review.
   d. Notes should only be reviewed immediately before the test.

7. **_____ benefit the most from note-taking interventions.**
   a. Weaker students
   b. Stronger students
   c. All students

(continued)

(*continued*)

8. **If a student sets aside 1 hour a day for 4 consecutive days to prepare for an examination, which of the following schedules would you recommend to the student if there will be 10 hours between his/her last preparation period and the test? RR = rereading notes; T = self-testing without looking at your notes.**

   a. RR, RR, RR, RR

   b. RR, RR, RR, T

   c. T, RR, RR, RR

   d. RR, T, RR, T

9. **A student sets aside 4 hours to study for a test. If there will be 10 hours between his/her last preparation period and the test, which of the following study schedules would you recommend?**

   a. Study for 4 hours the night before the test.

   b. Study for 2 hours each day for 2 days.

10. **What would your response be to a school superintendent who asks for advice about eliminating the elementary school's block and cursive handwriting program, currently taught in grades 1 through 3?**

   a. It is definitely a good idea. The time would be better spent on instruction in reading, writing, and mathematics.

   b. It is definitely a very bad idea. Keep the handwriting curriculum and expand it to include instruction in keyboarding.

   c. Reduce the number of years spent on instruction in handwriting from 3 to 1.

   d. Eliminate the handwriting curriculum and substitute a keyboarding curriculum.

Answers: 1. c; 2. a; 3. a; 4. d; 5. b; 6. c; 7. a; 8. d; 9. b; 10. b

Thirteen

INTERVENTIONS FOR STUDENTS FROM LOW RESOURCE ENVIRONMENTS: THE ABECEDARIAN APPROACH

Craig T. Ramey
Joseph J. Sparling
Sharon L. Ramey

C hildren from poor and undereducated families are at high risk for developmental delay and lack of school readiness. This delay begins in early childhood and is routinely detectable by the second year of life (Martin, Ramey, & Ramey, 1990). Left unaddressed, the prognosis for normal development is bleak. To date we know of no school system in the United States that has reported data that show that these delays, frequently first detected in kindergarten, are routinely being eradicated in the early years of K–12 public education. By *routinely treatable*, we mean that the academic performance of such delayed development can be overcome so that high-risk children become indistinguishable in academic accomplishment from the typical U.S. student population. We hope that this bold statement will be contradicted by a slew of citations to the contrary. We have made this assertion in learned company before, however, without having our poor scholarship revealed.

If K–12 public education as practiced in the United States is

> **DON'T FORGET**
> ....
> Children from poor and undereducated families are at high risk for developmental delay and lack of school readiness. This delay begins in early childhood and is routinely detectable by the second year of life.

not equipped for this heavy lifting to counteract social and economic disadvantage, then what are the alternatives? Several possibilities come to mind:

1. Accept the status quo and live with the accompanying cascade of school failure, quitting school early, and the resulting sociodemographic and personal woes.
2. Pursue child-neglect legislation to prevent predicted harm through adoption.
3. Increase the school day and year so that children from low-resource families who are delayed get more effective and tailored instruction. This is often referred to as *tiered instruction* or *response-to-intervention*.
4. Pursue early childhood educational programs to prevent developmental delay by providing high-quality preschool programs that begin before delayed development occurs.

We and our colleagues have chosen to pursue the fourth option. Since 1972, we have been conducting a series of randomized controlled trials to test the proposition that systematic, individualized instruction beginning at birth can be a powerful tool to prevent intellectual delays and disabilities. In this chapter we present our educational model for the first three years of life and review our data relevant to the issue of the efficacy of preventive education.

The word *protocol* is used in this chapter to indicate that these Abecedarian concepts and procedures have been used as a tool in a series of scientific studies. The procedures collectively can be thought of as the "experimental treatment." In that sense, the *Abecedarian Protocol* (Table 13.1) is a set of standards, curriculum resources, and practices that were used in the interventions. *Abecedarian Approach* is the educational program and includes the four major *educational* elements of the intervention.

The major issue that drove the creation of the Abecedarian Project and its replication was whether the provision of theory-based, active learning delivered via early childhood education could produce preventive benefits in cognitive and social performance in children from highly impoverished, multi-risk families. Therefore, control groups of children who did not receive the Abecedarian Approach received the same levels of support as the educationally treated children for additional health care, free and unlimited nutritional supports, and active social work services to the families, as well as timely referrals when any problems were detected or suspected. Because the control groups received these multiple supports, the research findings provide a strong basis for concluding that it was the educational features of the Abecedarian Approach that produced the documented differences between the children in the experimental groups and the comparison groups to be summarized later in this chapter.

Table 13.1   Three Longitudinal Applications of the Abecedarian Protocol

	The Abecedarian Project	Project CARE	Infant Health & Development Program (IHDP)
Criteria for inclusion in the sample	Multicomponent socioeconomic risk (High Risk Score >11)[a]	Multicomponent socioeconomic risk (High Risk Score >11)	Low birthweight (< 2,500 g) and premature (< 37 weeks gestational age)
Duration of the child development center program	Age 6 weeks to age 5 years	Age 6 weeks to age 5 years	Birth to 3 years corrected age
Amount of child development center program offered	Full day,[b] 5 days/ week, 50 weeks/year	Full day, 5 days/ week, 50 weeks/ year	Full day, 5 days/week, 50 weeks/year
Visits in homes	As needed, for social support	Weekly educational visits (*LearningGames*®, 1979, 1984)	Weekly educational visits (*LearningGames*®, 1979, 1984, and *Partners for Learning*, 1984, 1995)
Health care	Onsite with nurses and MDs	Onsite with nurses and MDs	By family's own provider and with onsite pediatrician
Transportation to center	Provided by program	Provided by program	Provided by program
Parent-education group sessions	Several per year	Several per year	Every other month
Educational program	Abecedarian Approach	Abecedarian Approach	Abecedarian Approach

[a]The High-Risk Index for the Abecedarian Project and Project CARE.
[b]Children received approximately 8 hours/day, 5 days/week, and 50 weeks/year.

HISTORY OF IMPLEMENTING THE ABECEDARIAN APPROACH

The innovation of the Abecedarian Approach was to bring together for the first time the emerging scientific knowledge about how infants and young children learn and to incorporate these scientific principles into systematic playful learning activities and common caregiving routines. The steps in creating and implementing the Abecedarian Approach were sequential but overlapping. The following sections document a brief history of the Abecedarian Approach.

IDENTIFYING THE TARGET POPULATIONS TO RECEIVE THE PROGRAM

For the Abecedarian Project, and its first replication, *Project CARE*, a catchment area was identified and all providers of health care and social services to families were contacted about the project. Initially, the service providers identified women they thought were likely to be eligible based on their knowledge of the variables in the *High Risk Index* (see Table 13.2).

Table 13.2 High Risk Index for the Abecedarian Project and Project CARE

Mother's Educational Level (Highest Grade of School Completed)	Weights	Father's Educational Level (Highest Grade of School Completed)	Weights	Total Annual Family Income ($)	Weights
6th grade	8	6th grade	8	≤1,000	8
7th grade	7	7th grade	7	1,001–2,000	7
8th grade	6	8th grade	6	2,001–3,000	6
9th grade	3	9th grade	3	3,001–4,000	5
10th grade	2	10th grade	2	4,001–5,000	4
11th grade	1	11th grade	1	5,001–6,000	0
12th grade	0	12th grade	0		

Other Indications of High Risk and Point Values
Pts. (Weights)

3   Father absent from child's life for reasons other than health/death.

3   Absence of maternal adult relatives in local area (i.e., no parents, grandparents, or brothers or sisters of majority age).

3   Siblings of school age who were one or more grades behind age-appropriate grade, or who scored equivalently low on school-administered achievement tests.

3   Payments received from public assistance or welfare agencies within the past three years.

3   Record of father's work indicated unstable and unskilled or semiskilled labor.

3   Record of mother's or father's IQ score of 90 or below.

3   Records of one or more siblings with IQ scores of 90 or below.

3   Relevant social agencies in the community indicate that the family is in need of assistance currently.

1   One or more members of the family has sought mental health counseling or professional help in the past three years.

1   Special circumstances not included in any of the above that are likely contributors to cultural or social disadvantage.

Criterion for inclusion in high-risk sample is a score greater than or equal to 11.

Source: Ramey, C.T., & Smith, B. (1977).

Initial recruitment occurred when mothers were pregnant. The final screening to determine eligibility occurred after birth, with structured interviews, standardized assessments, and an intelligence test. Mothers with a High Risk Index score of 11 or higher were told about the project, the services that everyone would receive (nutritional, health, and social services), and the fact that half of them would be selected randomly (a process described as being like flipping a coin) to have their baby attend the child development center starting as early as 6 weeks of age and continuing until the child entered kindergarten.

CREATING THE CHILD DEVELOPMENT CENTER

The Abecedarian Project was implemented in a newly constructed *child development center*. The physical space for the child development program included rooms designed for infant care (until babies were walking, usually about 1 year of age) and large open spaces that were configured to serve separate groups of children of different preschool ages. The flexible and open space provided an easy way for the child development center staff and the leaders of the program to observe the teaching staff as they cared for children and implemented the curriculum. The classroom areas were approximately 1,000 square feet each, divided by low walls of bookcases or furniture. The physical space in each classroom was organized using the following principles (Harms & Cross, 1977), specifying that *nurturant care* environments for children should be:

- *Predictable* and promote self-help
- *Supportive* and facilitate social-emotional adjustment
- *Reflective* of the child's age, ability, and interests
- *Varied* in activities

We used child-sized furniture and stored toys and materials on low, open shelves to promote easy access by young children. Pictures, symbols, and/or word labels of the toys and materials designated the space these items occupied on a shelf or in an area. Through the use of pictorial labeling, even very young children were able to function somewhat independently in a print- and symbol-rich environment (see Rapid Reference 13.1 for principles of nurturant care environments).

We also felt that in a child development center, where children are part of a group, children might want to have privacy once in a while. In each classroom,

≡ Rapid Reference 13.1   Nurturant Care Environments

Nurturant care environments for children should be:

- *Predictable* and promote self-help
- *Supportive* and facilitate social-emotional adjustment
- *Reflective* of the child's age, ability, and interests
- *Varied* in activities

DON'T FORGET

The use of pictorial labeling, even with very young children, can enable them to function somewhat independently in a print- and symbol-rich environment.

---

a slightly separated space was created for the child who wanted to get away from the group and be alone. In addition, each classroom had a warm, cozy area with a rug and pillows where children could sit or lie down. Children's work was displayed throughout the room, on cabinets, walls, doors, windows, and shelves, and changed frequently as children created new "products" reflecting their learning, interests, and creative expression. Each classroom had a dining space where teachers ate meals and snacks family-style with the children daily, as part of the structured program. Mealtimes were intentional learning periods with interesting table conversation to make mealtime a pleasant and educationally stimulating experience. Field trips brought variety into the program. Children explored and learned through trips to various community settings. Teachers typically planned with children, preparing them for the trip, and carried out systematic follow-up activities on returning to the center. The outdoor equipment for the Abecedarian Approach included a sand area, climbing equipment, and a paved track for wheeled toys. Outdoor activities were considered as educationally valuable as indoor experiences.

DON'T FORGET

Mealtimes with children can be used as intentional learning periods through the use of interesting table conversation. Such intentional conversation can make mealtime not only a pleasant experience, but an educationally stimulating one as well.

The nursery for children under 1 year of age was the only space that was not defined through the use of low bookcases and storage units. The nursery was a series of interconnected rooms. These provided differentiated space for sleeping and play.

≡ Rapid Reference 13.2 Organized Spaces

Organized spaces can help children:

- Feel comfortable.
- Find things easily.
- Use things frequently.
- Understand, in a very natural way, the similarities and differences among things that get stored together or not, and why.

We considered the organization of space and materials to be important mainly to help both the adults and children be comfortable, find things easily, and use them frequently (see Rapid Reference 13.2). We concluded that an organized child development center setting also would help children understand, in a very natural way, the similarities and differences among things that get stored together or not, and why.

The Abecedarian child development center teaching staff was comprised of a lead teacher and one or more assistant teachers in each child group. Our staff/child ratios ranged from 1:3 for infants and toddlers to 1:6 for 3-year-olds. We did not keep the ratios and age groups completely consistent at all times. Rather, the ratios shifted slightly from time to time as we sometimes staggered the dates at which individual children graduated from one group to the next.

A full-time *education director* based at the child development center provided administration and daily supervision of the child development teaching staff. The education director was an experienced, master's degree–professional who played a pivotal role in the child development center's delivery of effective services.

Perhaps because we were embarking on a concerted effort to create an innovative program that would be measured frequently, a strong team spirit grew within the staff. This was helped along by staff meetings and in-service training sessions. In these sessions the curriculum development staff met weekly or biweekly with the child development center staff, usually while the children were napping. (Volunteers from outside the child development center provided child coverage.) The meetings focused specifically on teaching, curriculum, and children's development. These sessions were substantive and strongly interactive. Administrative details were kept out of the meetings as much as possible.

HEALTH AND FAMILY SUPPORT SERVICES

The Abecedarian Approach focused strong attention on innovative early childhood education with the purpose of producing educational results. But it was not possible to set one's sights on child education without also paying attention to other areas of prime concern to vulnerable families: health, nutrition, social services, and transportation.

CAUTION

It is important to remember when planning early education interventions for children of vulnerable families that other variables, including family health, nutrition, need for social services, and transportation, may be equally important areas to attend to.

Health Services

The initial Abecedarian families were living in extreme economic poverty, and their health care was far from stable or of high quality. Therefore, we provided onsite child health care in the original Abecedarian Protocol and Project CARE. A *family nurse practitioner* (FNP) was onsite full-time and worked under the supervision of a pediatrician, who was on the faculty and a co-investigator. The FNP was a new health-profession role in the early 1970s and this proved to be an effective way to provide quality health care at a moderate cost in the child development center setting. (See, for example, Collier & Ramey, 1976, for a fuller description of the health-care issues.)

Nutrition

The research design of the Abecedarian Project specified that iron-fortified formula should be given to all children to reduce the possibility of early nutritional disparity between the educationally treated and untreated groups. (*Note*: Despite encouragement, no mothers elected to breastfeed their babies.) Families could pick up the free formula at the center. When the children were at the center, they received nutritious and attractive meals and snacks, always served with adults present as part of the educational protocol.

A registered dietitian planned the meals and snacks, which were prepared onsite in the Abecedarian Project, CARE, and four of the eight Infant Health and Development (IHDP) sites. The other four IHDP sites contracted food preparation from a local school or hospital foodservice.

Family Partnership and Family Support Social Services

Many of the low-income Abecedarian families had needs that resulted in seeking out the social services available in the community. Since the families were likely to continue to have these needs while enrolled in our program, we responded to these needs in the Abecedarian Approach through a combination of home visits, parent group meetings, and individual sessions with parents.

In the Abecedarian Approach, parent groups served several functions. They made it possible for parents to share information and concerns on childrearing. Being part of such a group allowed the parents to see that they were not alone in many of their concerns. Groups provided contacts among families that sometimes helped build social networks that were a source of support during the life of the program and sometimes lasted well beyond. Parent groups also provided information or access to resources in the community that may not have been otherwise available. For example, we often asked a person from the community to talk to the parent group about topics of interest or to describe programs that might be beneficial. See Rapid Reference 13.3 for a summary of the benefits of parent groups.

Home visiting was an integral part of the Abecedarian Project and its replications. Over time, our Abecedarian Approach used two different home visit strategies: (1) The original Abecedarian Project employed as-needed social work home visits made at least monthly, and (2) the CARE and IHDP Abecedarian replications employed regular parent–child educational home visits (with referrals for social work and health issues).

In the original Abecedarian Project, a staff member filled a supportive social work role, meeting with individual families (in both the experimental and the

≡ Rapid Reference 13.3 Benefits of Parent Groups

Providing a mechanism for parents to partake in parent groups (e.g., through access to community agencies that sponsor such groups) may prove important for intervention planning. Similar to the experiences of parents participating in the Abecedarian Project, such groups may:

- Enable parents to share information and concerns on childrearing.
- Help the parents to see that they are not alone in many of their concerns.
- Provide contacts among families that can help build social networks as a longtime source of support.
- Provide information regarding access to available community resources.

≡ *Rapid Reference 13.4 Planning Interventions for Vulnerable Families*

Target goals when planning interventions for vulnerable families may include:
- Providing information on child development
- Providing health-care information and encouraging parents to use community resources as needed to maintain their children's health
- Providing emotional support to parents during stressful times
- Helping parents enhance their children's intellectual, physical, and social development
- Encouraging effective problem-solving
- Helping parents learn ways to positively interact with their children

control groups) in response to family needs or issues (see Rapid Reference 13.4 for points about planning interventions for vulnerable families). These were the issues that we found ourselves responding to:

- Health counseling and encouragement for healthy lifestyles
- Educational counseling and encouragement for mothers to continue their education
- Employment counseling and encouragement
- Lifestyle counseling and encouragement
- Crisis intervention
- Benefits counseling
- Transportation
- Cash assistance
- Neglect and abuse surveillance
- Home and neighborhood safety issues

In the CARE and IHDP replications, rather than making as-needed visits, teachers and/or visitors made weekly home visits on a regular basis and followed an agenda that was specifically focused on child and family education. In these educational visits, the home visitors were guided by the following goals:

- To provide information on child development
- To provide health-care information and encourage parents to use community resources as needed to maintain their children's health

- To provide emotional support to parents during stressful times
- To help parents enhance their children's intellectual, physical, and social development
- To encourage effective problem-solving
- To help parents with positive ways of interacting with their children

The Abecedarian Approach also included a toy-lending library as well as a book-lending library as a method of supplementing the educational resources in the home.

Transportation

Transportation was provided to and from the child development center on an as-needed basis to facilitate high attendance rates, which were in fact achieved. This was included because we felt that it otherwise would affect the participation rates of highly vulnerable families. Today it seems obvious that, to achieve the intended effect, a high level of participation in an intervention program is necessary. But the link between participation and outcome was not documented in the early 1970s. So, in the IHDP Abecedarian replication, we specifically studied child outcome as a function of participation in the first three years of the program.

DON'T FORGET

A high level of participation in an intervention program is necessary to achieve intended effects.

COMMITMENT TO HIGH QUALITY IN THE ABECEDARIAN APPROACH

In the Abecedarian Approach, there were four functional areas that were considered absolutely essential to help children grow and thrive. These areas were monitored through a variety of observational procedures, including video-taped time samples of classroom activities. These areas recently have been incorporated into an observational system known as the *Four Diamond Model of High Quality Early Care and Education* (Ramey, Ramey, & Sonnier-Netto, 2008, 2012; S. L. Ramey & Ramey, 2005; Table 13.3).

1. *Health and safety practices:* behaviors that seek to prevent all major problems and promote physical and mental health and safety, consistently implemented at all times.

Table 13.3 Four Diamonds Checklist

√ = YES
X = NO
N = NOT SCORED

Adult IDs

A$_1$	A$_2$	A$_3$	A$_4$

WARM AND RESPONSIVE CAREGIVING

1. Adults* use children's names often with real warmth.

2. Adults show joy, liking, and care for children.

3. Adults often chat back and forth with children.

4. Adults prompt children to explore and try new things.

5. Adults answer children's questions and help them when needed.

6. Adults care and teach about feelings and good ways to share them.

7. Adults encourage and help children to play and get along with others.

8. Adults watch children so they can adjust activities for each child.

9. Adults make sure no child is teased or bullied. If so, they act quickly.

10. For a child with special needs, adults learn ways to meet their needs.

LANGUAGE AND LEARNING ACTIVITIES

1. Adults* help children be curious and eager about learning.

2. Adults teach children lots of new words and phrases.

3. Adults arrange toys and books so they are easy for children to use.

4. Adults teach early literacy skills throughout the day.

5. Adults teach early math skills throughout the day.

6. Adults teach children a lot about "the big world."

7. Adults use daily routines and in-between times to teach.

8. Adults notice and show they care about what each child learns.

9. Adults help children to plan and think about what they are learning.

10. Adults keep records about each child's language and learning.

Time Observed _____ Date _____ Place _____

HEALTH AND SAFETY PRACTICES

1. Adults* always practice good hygiene.

2. Indoor and outdoor areas are safe and healthy.

3. Children and adults are physically active throughout the day.

4. Adults use safe practices when children behave badly.

5. Adults offer nap and quiet time throughout the day, but never harshly.

6. All adults look for and report possible abuse and neglect.

7. Adults use safe practices for napping, feeding, and going places.

8. Adults limit use of TV, video, and screen time.

9. Adults make sure almost all food and drinks are healthy.

10. Adults can use first aid and take care of problems.

FAMILY CONNECTIONS

1. Adults* ask parents to drop by, share ideas, and keep in touch.

2. Adults show warmth to parents and know their names.

3. Adults share with parents what children are learning and ways to practice.

4. Adults keep up-to-date about each child's family and home life.

5. Adults and parents meet often to talk about the child's growth.

6. Adults and parents talk about and try to fix problems.

7. Adults and parents help a child get ready for big changes.

8. Adults show caring and respect for all families.

9. Adults help parents learn about the rules in their setting.

10. Adults help parents protect children from harsh treatment and neglect.

Total √s

*Adult means any person who cares for a child on a regular basis.
© 2008, 2012 by Sharon Landesman Ramey, Craig T. Ramey, & Libbie Sonnier-Netto.

2. *Adult–child interactions:* behaviors that are frequent, warm, and responsive to the individual child.
3. *Language and learning activities:* adapted for the child's age and developmental level to maintain high interest and motivation.
4. *Caregiver–family relationships:* behaviors that are characterized as respectful, supportive, and informative; frequent communication between adults in the program and parents and other family members.

DON'T FORGET

Four areas that promote child development and are important to evaluate in intervention planning include:

1. The provision of consistent health and safety practices aimed at preventing health problems and promoting physical and mental health
2. Frequent, warm, and responsive adult–child interactions
3. Developmentally appropriate and interesting language and learning activities
4. Respectful and supportive caregiver–family or home–school relationships that are characterized by frequent communication

---

EDUCATION CURRICULUM

Children are learning all the time—put briefly, this was the explicit assumption based on research evidence and cognitive developmental theory. Therefore, the overall program and the educational curriculum were designed to be highly engaging, fun, and active—with learning occurring throughout the day in all activities (including daily caregiving, transitions, and physical play and exploration, as well as more structured learning activities). Activities included many adult–child individualized interactions as well as small-group activities, particularly as babies became older.

The systematic curriculum known as *LearningGames*® (Sparling & Lewis, 1979; Sparling and Lewis, 1984) was based on the identification of multiple types of learning processes in infants, toddlers, and young children—and was

DON'T FORGET

Intervention programs for children should be designed to be highly engaging, fun, and active—with learning occurring throughout the day and involved in a variety of activities (including daily caregiving, transitions, and physical play and exploration, as well as more structured learning activities).

paced to be appropriate for a child's developmental stage and to continuously provide challenges that were individualized for each child (Ramey, Yeates, & Short, 1984; Ramey, Breitmayer, Goldman, & Wakeley, 1996). The Abecedarian Approach strongly acknowledged the centrality of communication to the development of intelligence (McGinness & Ramey, 1981; Ramey, McGinness, Cross, Collier, & Barrie-Blackley, 1981). Thus, the planned "learning games" activities included many ways to use signs, symbols, sounds, words, sentences, stories, and interactive conversations—starting in the first year of life. Even conversational reading and play began in infancy with specially written picture/ word books. Adults used varied, complex, and informative language throughout the day and the use of Standard English in the child development center was emphasized.

SUPERVISION FOR THE CHILD DEVELOPMENT PROGRAM

The Abecedarian Approach included supervision focused specifically on the main educational features of the program. The education director was the primary supervisor and mentor, supplemented occasionally by the curriculum development staff and the program leaders. In the Abecedarian Approach we recognized the central issues of the attitudes, knowledge, and skills of the adults who cared for and taught the children. Our goal was to have teachers/caregivers who would:

- Show positive attitudes about promoting the language and learning of children from birth.
- Believe that their own actions make a big difference and that their interactions in language and learning will have a major influence on how a child progresses.
- Know that very early learning opportunities and language stimulation are essential parts of their responsibility, and if they fulfill their responsibility they will help children get ready to succeed in school.
- Display frequent smiles, use positive words and tones of voices, display pleasant and encouraging actions toward all children, no matter what the time of day or how tired they may feel.

RATIONALE FOR THE EDUCATIONAL ELEMENTS OF THE ABECEDARIAN APPROACH

The Abecedarian Approach had an educational emphasis with multiple parts, including: (1) learning games, (2) conversational reading, (3) language priority, and (4) enriched caregiving. These were implemented in close coordination with a comprehensive curriculum framework described by Ramey et al. (1976). We provide a rationale for each of these elements in the following.

Learning Games

The Abecedarian Approach has an explicit developmental focus with game-like activities at its core. The central conceptual rationale for learning games derives from insights first presented by J. McVicker Hunt (1961) and elaborated educationally within Vygotskian theory (Vygotsky, 1978, 1986) and undergirded by the insights of Piaget and Inhelder (2000) and Bijou and Baer (1965), among others. In this view the fundamental ways in which a child's higher mental functions are formed are through mediated activities shared with an adult or more competent peer. Each of the learning game activities is one of these mediated activities. Vygotsky proposed that educational activities should be in a "Zone of Proximal Development"; that is, the activity should be one that the child can do with a little help. This concept is similar to what J. McVicker Hunt (1961) earlier called the *problem of the match*. So we consistently documented what the level of challenge to the child was and sought what was just the right amount of developmental challenge, at the right time. We believe that if instruction is too simple, not much new learning occurs; if it is too advanced, children are likely to experience frustration and failure and withdraw from the activity.

> **CAUTION**
> ....
> If instruction is too simple, not much new learning occurs; if it is too advanced, children are likely to experience frustration and failure and withdraw from the activity.

The curriculum development process for the LearningGames consisted of three steps: (1) Objectives were synthesized or selected, (2) curriculum products were developed, and (3) the curriculum products were evaluated. This work was mainly accomplished in a pilot phase of the Abecedarian Project with other children.

Our system for synthesizing curriculum goals has its origins in the theoretical position presented by Ralph Tyler (1950). Within this framework, curriculum objectives are seen as the product of the interaction of a number of sources or factors. Our formulation identifies the interacting sources as (1) consumer opinions, (2) developmental theory, (3) developmental facts, (4) adaptive sets, and (5) high-risk indicators.

The five sources from which the LearningGames were synthesized are pictured in Figure 13.1. The first source of curriculum goals is *consumer opinions*. Very

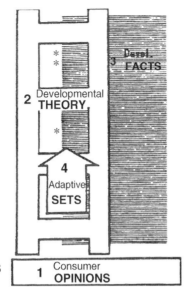

Figure 13.1. Five Sources for Synthesizing Curriculum Objectives

young children are, of course, the consumers of the infant curriculum. Through interviews, the hopes and aspirations parents have for their children were determined. Without this knowledge a project might proceed down a blind alley, producing a program that would in the end be rejected by the public it seeks to serve. It turns out that, in our experience, poor parents have remarkably similar hopes and dreams for their young children as do more affluent and educated parents. But they do tend to describe them using a somewhat different vocabulary.

> **DON'T FORGET**
> ....
> Poor parents have remarkably similar hopes and dreams for their young children as do more affluent and educated parents. But they tend to describe them using a somewhat different vocabulary.

The second source for deriving curriculum goals is *developmental theory*, largely that of Jean Piaget. The theory can be pictured as a ladder. On any rung of a ladder, one can look backward to see how the current status was arrived at or forward to see which steps are next.

The third source, *developmental facts*, acts as a background against which the developmental theory is viewed. Developmental facts provide a great amount of detail with which to supplement the theory. In this project, facts were gleaned from 30 sources, including Nancy Bayley, Charlotte Buhler, Arnold Gesell, Erik

Lenneberg, Dorothea McCarthy, Mary Margaret Shirley, and others. The facts were arranged in developmental sequence in four broad but overlapping developmental domains: language, motor, social/emotional, and cognitive/perceptive. Of all the sources of educational objectives, the most important may be what we call *adaptive sets*. This is especially true for LearningGames because it was created with the explicit purpose of changing or enhancing the positive adaptive sets of the infant and young child. The child with strong adaptive sets has the tendency to move forward (for example, to explore rather than withdraw, to persist rather than give up easily). Therefore, adaptive sets can be thought of as that class of behaviors that predictably generate age-appropriate success. More simply, adaptive sets are "winning strategies" and are shown as an arrow moving up the ladder. The process of selecting statements of adaptive sets for this project, it should be clear, relies on professionally informed value judgments as well as relying on research findings. Because value judgments exist in *any* process of selection of educational objectives, LearningGames attempts to identify this potential bias by making it overt and subject to examination. For example, the following are among the statements of adaptive sets in the Abecedarian Approach. All of these behaviors can be thought of as being exhibited to an age-appropriate degree with extensive use desired by age 36 months:

1. Uses adults as resources
2. Controls his or her immediate environment
3. Uses both expressive and receptive language extensively
4. Detaches self from mothering adult and explores independently
5. Exhibits high-attention behavior
6. Responds frequently with positive approach to new object or person
7. Easily adapts to changes in environment
8. Executes multistep activities
9. Anticipates consequences
10. Explores extensively with the distance receptors (the eyes and ears)
11. Uses cooperative behavior
12. Uses basic sharing behavior (showing, giving, pointing)
13. Generates specific instances of a behavior by guidance of a general rule
14. Relates positively to the family

The final source of educational objectives was an awareness of *high-risk indicators* coupled with an effort to eliminate these in the child's repertoire. The indicators are seen in Figure 13.1 as asterisks or "warning signs" along the developmental continuum. To a substantial degree the high-risk indicator behaviors are the mirror image of the adaptive set behaviors. That is, the class of behaviors called high-risk indicators could be thought of as maladaptive sets, or perhaps "losing strategies." Because this curriculum was designed especially for children who are at a high risk of developmental delay and because research is beginning to document some of the behavioral deficits that high-risk children consistently develop, it is hoped that these deficits (here called high-risk indicators) can be anticipated through educational objectives that are basically preventive. A more detailed description of the development and evaluation of the LearningGames curriculum can be found in Ramey, Sparling, and Ramey (2012).

Conversational Reading

Conversational reading is the second aspect of the Abecedarian Approach. The conversational reading technique was partially developed and used in pre-publication form during our first two intervention studies (the Abecedarian Project and Project CARE). Its first published edition appeared in 1984, just in time for use in the IHDP eight-site Abecedarian replication. Significantly, conversational reading is modeled on the way parents and children typically read together rather than the way reading typically occurs in the classroom. Thus, our conversational reading approach goes back and forth, between adult and child, like a conversation. It would not be until the late 1980s that targeted experimental studies would support this interactive reading strategy, including the expanded technique developed and coined as "Dialogic reading" by Whitehurst (Whitehurst et al., 1988, 1994).

The key element of conversational reading was a questioning or prompting technique that was designed to elicit responses from children on three increasing levels of difficulty (see Rapid Reference 13.5). Some of these levels were easy enough for babies to participate in and some were challenging enough for older preschoolers. The technique invited children to see, show, and say something about the book and became known as the *3S Strategy*.

≡ *Rapid Reference 13.5 Conversational Reading*

The key element of conversational reading is a questioning or prompting technique that is designed to elicit responses from children on three increasing levels of difficulty. The technique, known as the *3S Strategy*, invites children to see, show, and say something about the book being read.

CAUTION

Observational research has documented that high-resource families versus low-resource families show large and significant differences in adult language input and resultant child language, including child vocabulary and syntactic skill. As such, it is important for practitioners working with vulnerable families to integrate language activities wherever possible in intervention planning.

Language Priority

Giving priority to language means consistently weaving language stimulation into all parts of the day. This whole-day strategy was chosen because we thought language was likely to be the most important single pathway for the school success of children from poverty backgrounds, the group served exclusively in the first two Abecedarian studies. Since that time, careful observational research has documented that high-resource families versus low-resource families show large and significant differences in adult language input and resultant child language, including child vocabulary and syntactic skill (Ramey & Campbell, 1984; Hart & Risley, 1995; Huttenlocher, 1998).

Also since the 1970s when we developed our approach, other researchers have looked into homes and classrooms to discover and describe early language practices that are correlated with children's later success in school, especially in reading. Their analysis revealed three dimensions of children's experiences at home and in classrooms during the preschool and kindergarten years that are related to later literacy success: (1) exposure to varied vocabulary, (2) opportunities to be a part of conversations that use extended discourse, and (3) home and classroom environments that are cognitively and linguistically stimulating (Bradley et al., 1989; Dickinson & Tabors, 2001; Snow & Dickinson, 1991; see Rapid Reference 13.6). These documented practices have a lot in common with some of the assumptions we had made and the main language aspects featured in the Abecedarian Approach that we had adopted more than two decades earlier.

The language priority strategy we developed for the Abecedarian Project rested on several assumptions:

1. Gaining communicative competence is a primary goal.
2. Communicative competence is multifaceted, implying skills in at least three interrelated dimensions:
   a. Social (pragmatic) competence (language use).
   b. Representational competence (level of abstraction).
   c. Linguistic competence (language structure–syntax/semantics).

3. The child acquires effective communication skills mainly through exercising these skills with adults who are effective communicators and particularly in situations in which the child is able and motivated to engage intentionally in an interaction with the adult (McGinness & Ramey, 1981).

DON'T FORGET

....

Communicative competence is multifaceted, and includes skills in at least three interrelated dimensions:

1. Social (pragmatic) competence (language use)
2. Representational competence (level of abstraction)
3. Linguistic competence (language structure–syntax/semantics)

Enriched Caregiving

Certain actions and ways of interacting with children transcend the formal and explicit instructional curriculum. These actions comprise a *style* of education or intervention, and they are as important as other program elements. The Abecedarian Approach affirms that in the early years of life, education and caregiving cannot and should not be thought of as distinctly different activities.

The phrase *enriched caregiving* is intended to remind all of us (researchers, parents, caregivers, teachers, and program administrators) who care for an infant or young child that we can and should do several things at once. Care can meet the vital needs that support life and stimulate growth while also being responsive to the individual child's own preferences, abilities, and life situation. Further, care frequently can be enriched with educational content and individual flair. By highlighting the pivotal role of enriched caregiving in the education of young children, the Abecedarian Approach imbues all of the child's day with educational potential and meaning.

Enriched and responsive caregiving with protective and stable relationships is desirable and appropriate because it fits the contemporary notion of a humanistic

≡ Rapid Reference 13.6 Dimensions of Children's Home and Classroom Experiences

....

Three dimensions of children's experiences at home and in classrooms during the preschool and kindergarten years that have been found to relate to later literacy success include: (1) exposure to varied vocabulary, (2) opportunities to be a part of conversations that use extended discourse, and (3) home and classroom environments that are cognitively and linguistically stimulating.

CAUTION

Facts About Stress, Cortisol, and Development:

1. Research has shown that brain development is negatively affected by higher levels of stress early in life.

2. Scientists have also found, studying both center-based and family-based child-care settings, that preschoolers have larger rises in cortisol (a stress-sensitive hormone) over the day if the site had lower quality of interaction between caregivers and children.

3. Other studies with young children have shown that levels of cortisol are related to memory, attention, and emotion in children.

approach to childrearing. But what is being learned about stress and brain development provides another strong reason for ensuring all children receive responsive care. Through animal research, it is known that brain development is negatively affected by higher levels of stress early in life (Sapolsky, 1996). Scientists have also found, studying both center-based and family-based child-care settings, that preschoolers have larger rises in cortisol (a stress-sensitive hormone) over the day if the site had lower quality of interaction between caregivers and children (Tout, de Haan, Kipp-Campbell, & Gunnar, 1998). Other studies with young children have shown that levels of cortisol are related to memory, attention, and emotion in children (Gunnar, 1998). Although we do not yet know conclusively whether early experiences of mild repeated neuroendocrine stress have long-term influences on the developing brain, researchers still conclude that "Taken together, these data strongly suggest that sensitive, responsive, secure caretaking plays an important role in buffering or blocking elevations in cortisol for infants and young children" (Gunnar, 1998, p. 210).

Responsive caregiving has continued to be documented and shown to relate to and stimulate basic areas of child development vital for school success. Using the longitudinal data set from the National Institute for Child Health and Human Development (NICHD) Study of Early Child Care and Youth Development in 10 sites, researchers asked how changes in the sensitivity of both mothers and caregivers from 6 months to 6 years relates to language and academic outcomes at the start of formal schooling. They found that sensitive and responsive caregiving is positively associated with better cognitive and language outcomes for children (Hirsh-Pasek & Burchinal, 2006). This longitudinal study also

DON'T FORGET

Sensitive and responsive caregiving is positively associated with better cognitive and language outcomes for children. As such, practitioners planning interventions for children of vulnerable families should assess caregiver styles and provide caregiving support, where feasible, via connecting families with community resources, providing parents with informational handouts, encouraging participation in parent groups, and so forth.

Table 13.4 Seven Essentials of Enhanced Caregiving

1. **Encourage**
   Encourage exploration with all the senses, in familiar and new places, with others and alone, safely and with joy.

2. **Mentor**
   Mentor in basic skills, showing the *what*s and *when*s, the *in*s and *out*s of how things and people work.

3. **Celebrate**
   Celebrate developmental advances, for learning new skills, little and big, and for becoming a unique individual.

4. **Rehearse**
   Rehearse and extend new skills, showing a baby how to practice again and again, in the same and different ways, with new people and new things.

5. **Protect**
   Protect from inappropriate disapproval, teasing, neglect, or punishment.

6. **Communicate**
   Communicate richly and responsively with sounds, songs, gestures, and words; bring the baby into the wonderful world of language and its many uses.

7. **Guide**
   Guide and limit behavior to keep the child safe and to teach what's acceptable, and what's not—the rules of being a cooperative, responsive, and caring person.

found a variety of positive effects at age 15 years for children who had been in higher-quality and more responsive care in the early years (Vandell, Belsky, Burchinal, Steinberg, & Vandergrift, 2010).

In the Abecedarian Approach we have summarized our enriched caregiving into seven classes of adult behavior, presented in Table 13.4 from Ramey and Ramey (1999).

SUMMARY OF FINDINGS

It is beyond the scope of this chapter to provide a detailed presentation of results that have been published in scientific journals. Rather we want to summarize two aspects of our findings to date: (1) the primary evidence relevant to consistency of findings across the three educational experiments and (2) the evidence concerning variations in curriculum participation patterns and child development outcomes.

Figure 13.2 displays the cognitive performance of the Abecedarian and CARE participants at 12, 24, and 36 months as a function of treatment and control groups. Analyses of demographic data showed high similarity of families and

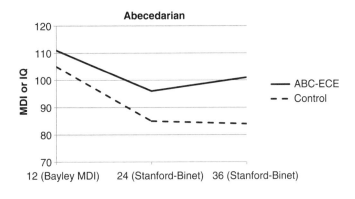

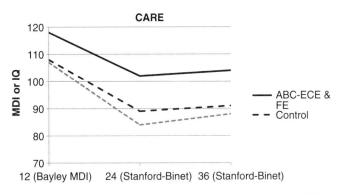

Figure 13.2. Cognitive Performance of the Abecedarian and CARE Participants at 12, 24, and 36 Months

children at program entry (Burchinal, Campbell, Bryant, Wasik, & Ramey, 1997). On standardized measures of cognitive performance at 12 months there was a 6-point difference favoring the Abecedarian–Early Childhood Education (ECE) group and a 10-point benefit in the CARE–ECE group over controls. The difference between the Abecedarian–Family Education (FE) and control groups was not statistically significant at 12 months or any subsequent measurement occasion.

In both the Abecedarian and CARE experiments the cognitive differences between the Abecedarian Approach group and the control groups grew over time such that by 36 months the Stanford-Binet IQ difference was approximately 17 points for the Abecedarian–ECE group and approximately 13 points in project CARE (see Ramey, Yeates, Short, 1984; and Ramey, Bryant, Sparling, & Wasik, 1985 for a more detailed presentation of these findings for the two studies respectively).

Based on the results from these two experiments, my colleagues and I were offered the opportunity to test whether similar cognitive benefits might be obtained in a multisite randomized controlled trial. After much discussion about what was needed to move the field of early intervention forward, we decided to extend the test to a population that shared varying degrees of biological risk and varying degrees of socioeconomic risk. This was accomplished by competitively selecting eight sites to implement the first multisite controlled intervention trial for a randomly selected cohort of low-birthweight (LBW) (< 2,500 grams) and premature infants (< 37 weeks gestation). Because LBW and premature infants come from all socioeconomic strata, it afforded us the opportunity to examine the joint consequences of biological and social risk factors and to examine whether the Abecedarian Approach to Early Childhood Education would be differentially efficacious for particular subgroups of participating infants and their families. We separated the selection of LBW and premature infants into two groups: (1) children < 2,000 grams and (2) children between 2,001 and 2,500 grams. We selected $\frac{2}{3}$ from the lighter LBW group and $\frac{1}{3}$ from the heavier LBW group. A group at Stanford University was responsible for data collection and analyses and my colleagues and I, then at the University of North Carolina, Chapel Hill, assumed responsibility for oversight of the program implementation. The program, called the *Infant Health and Development Program* (IHDP), is described in detail in an article by Ramey et al. (1992). The measurement strategy for the cognitive performance for the children followed the form established in the Abecedarian and CARE projects to provide a direct comparison.

The cognitive performance data at 12, 24, and 36 months for the 2,001-to-2,500-gram group for each of the eight sites are presented in Figure 13.3.

At each of the eight sites the treatment and control groups were quite similar in Bayley Mental Development Index performance at 12 months but diverged in performance over the next two years. Analyses of each site indicated all eight sites differed significantly at 36 months with a mean difference slightly greater than 13 IQ points.

Figure 13.4 presents similar graphs for the < 2,000-gram infants. Individual comparisons revealed that 7 of the 8 comparisons were statistically significant at age 3 and at one site the scores at 36 months were almost identical. In addition, the magnitude of the differences was somewhat smaller at slightly greater than 6 IQ points when averaged across the eight sites. Because the Abecedarian and CARE samples were in the predicated direction at 36 months of age and significantly different across treatment and control comparisons, and because 15 of the 16 comparisons were as predicated in the IHDP, we can use the sign test to compare the results from the overall pattern of 17 positive signs for the treatment group

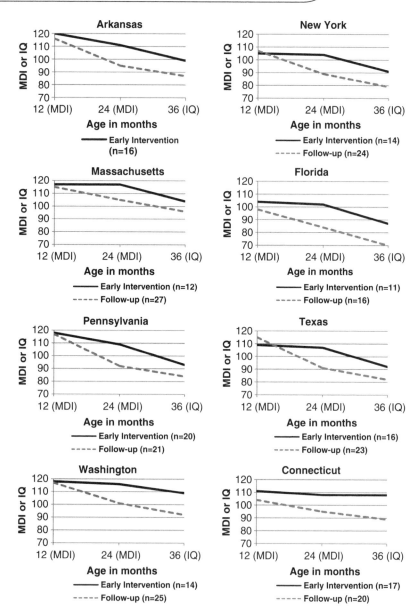

Figure 13.3. Cognitive Scores for Participants in the IHDP by Site for Infants 2,001–2,500 Grams at Birth

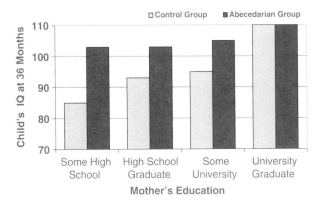

Figure 13.4. Child's Age-36-Months Stanford-Binet IQ by Mother's Education

over the comparison group (the tie score in the $< 2{,}000$-gram group in Massachusetts being eliminated); we calculate the likely result of this positive pattern as being $p < .001$ as a consequence of chance using the sign test (Siegel, 1956).

To address the issue of differential risk and differential response to intervention, we examined the Stanford-Binet IQ scores at 36 months as a function of the different educational backgrounds of the mothers of the low-birthweight infants. We grouped the educational backgrounds into four groups:

1. Less than high school graduate
2. High school graduate
3. Some university
4. University graduate

Results from this analysis are displayed in Figure 13.4.

The performance of the children in the control group shows a stair-step pattern with respect to maternal education. Children whose mothers had only some high school scored at approximately 85 on the Stanford-Binet IQ test at 36 months. Children whose mothers had a college degree scored at approximately 110. In the treatment group, all four of the maternal education groups had children who scored between 105 and 110. Thus, the effects of the Abecedarian Early Childhood Education program were to provide the greatest relative benefits to the children from the most disadvantaged families and to assist their development to the point that they were above national average and nearly comparable to that of the most educated group of families. In effect, the educational intervention nearly closed the cognitive achievement gap at age 3.

Further, the group that was most closely comparable to the original Abecedarian participants, the some-high-school group, showed a 20-point IQ advantage relative to the 17 points in the original Abecedarian experiment. From Figure 13.4 it is also clear that the Abecedarian Approach had neither a positive nor a negative impact on the IQ performance of children from college-educated families. Subsequent inquiry indicated that university-graduate parents of low-birthweight and premature infants used their resources to seek out developmental supports for their children that we were not able to improve upon with our treatment protocol.

HOW LEVELS OF PARTICIPATION ARE ASSOCIATED WITH CHILD OUTCOMES

In the Infant Health and Development Program, linking the process of early educational intervention to outcome provides important insights. The extensive data collected on implementation of the IHDP point to a variety of process factors that are predictive of a child's developmental progress in an early childhood intervention. The factors include, for example:

- Level of children's participation
- Amount of curriculum activities
- Rate of delivery of curriculum activities
- Degree of active experience for parents and children.

A major outcome demonstrated in the IHDP was a 9-point overall difference in IQ between the control and treatment groups at age 3. To explore a possible relationship between this 9-point difference in IQ and the level of children's participation in the intervention, we devised a participation index. This index was the sum of the number of contacts between each family and the intervention program, as measured by number of days a child attended the child development center, the number of home visits completed, and the number of group meetings parents attended.

Figure 13.5 shows the percentage of children who had borderline intellectual performance (IQ < 85) and impaired intellectual performance (IQ < 70) at age 3 according to three levels of program participation (low, medium, and high), compared to children in the control group.

The differences in the percentage of children at borderline or lower IQ at age 3 across the three levels of participation in the early educational intervention were dramatic, with an almost 9-fold reduction in impaired IQ performance associated with high participation relative to controls (Ramey et al., 1992).

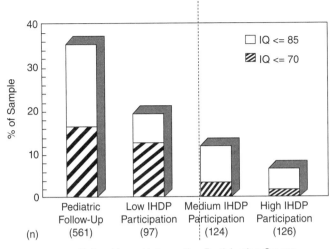

Figure 13.5. Percentage of Borderline (IQ < 85) and Impaired Intellectual Performance (IQ < 70) (IHDP, Infant Health and Development Program)

AMOUNT OF CURRICULUM ACTIVITIES

Another issue to be addressed is how much of the instructional curriculum each child receives when attending the center. This issue, of course, pertains only to the treated condition since the curriculum was not available to control group participants. Table 13.5 shows the mean IQ of children in the treatment group at age 36 months matched to birthweight and level of curriculum activities (low, medium, high) received in the child development center and at home.

The data show a positive relationship between mean IQ and level of curriculum activities for both of the low-birthweight groups. The higher the number of

Table 13.5 Mean IQ at Age 36 Months for Three Levels of Curriculum Activity Received by Children of Two Varying Birthweight Ranges (Infant Health and Development Program)

| | Level of Curriculum Activity/Mean IQ | | |
	Low	Medium	High
Birthweight ≤ 2,000 g	82	95	97
Birthweight 2,001–2,500 g	92	98	100

Source: Sparling et al. (1991).

activities, the higher the child's IQ. Furthermore, among the children who received a low level of activities, those who had a lighter birthweight (< 2,000 g) had a 10-point lower IQ than did those who had a higher birthweight (2,001–2,005 g) (Sparling et al., 1991).

Rate of Curriculum Delivery and Active Experience

In an independent analysis of the year-by-year levels of participation of individual children and families, Blair, Ramey, and Hardin (1995) discovered a clear association between participation levels and cognitive progress at ages 2 and 3. For each year from ages 1 to 3, the days attended by the child in the IHDP Abecedarian Approach Center, the number of home visits, and the number of parent meetings attended predicted cognitive advances or benefits, whereas the child's background characteristics such as maternal education and birthweight did not. That is, these high-risk children's early educational experiences exerted an effect that served to eliminate the usual negative toll of parent education, family's income, and other indicators of very low levels of home stimulation. This represents the strongest evidence to date about a dosage effect: The greater the level of exposure to high-quality learning opportunities, the more the child gained in terms of IQ points each year.

CONCLUSION

In this chapter we have presented the most detailed summary to date of the specific components of the Abecedarian Approach to developmental supports and early childhood education for the first three years of life. The Abecedarian components, in aggregate, have resulted in strong and consistent evidence that developmental delay can be prevented in high-risk children from low-resource families. This conclusion is buttressed by internal evidence that has linked the degree of curriculum implementation to cognitive developmental outcomes at 2 and 3 years of age. Further, the degree of implementation from year to year after the first year of life is directly related to the degree of developmental advance from year to year. We think that these regularities in the data are particularly noteworthy in light of the developmental services that both the control groups and the treated groups received, including nutritional supplements, family services, health care, and referral for developmental problems.

In our opinion, the issue of efficacy of early childhood education for high-risk children is settled. Yes, we can prevent a great deal of developmental delay. For us, the most pressing questions in early childhood education now become: (1) comparative efficacy of different early childhood programs, (2) differential response to treatment, (3) scale-up of effective programs, and (4) standards for programs aimed at preventing developmental delay. It feels good to move beyond the efficacy issue that dominated thinking about early childhood education for half a century.

REFERENCES

Bijou, S. W., & Baer, D. M. (1965). *Child development II: Universal stage of infancy.* New York, NY: Appleton-Century-Crofts.

Blair, C., Ramey, C. T., & Hardin, M. (1995). Early intervention for low birth weight premature infants: Participation and intellectual development. *American Journal on Mental Retardation, 99,* 542–554. PMID 7779349.

Bradley, R. H., Caldwell, B. M., Rock, S. L., Ramey, C. T., Barnard, K. E., Gray, A., . . . Johnson, D. L. (1989). Home environment and cognitive development in the first three years of life: A collaborative study involving six sites and three ethnic groups in North America. *Developmental Psychology, 25,* 217–235.

Burchinal, M. R., Campbell, F. A., Bryant, D. M., Wasik, B. H., & Ramey, C. T. (1997). Early intervention and mediating processes in cognitive performance of children of low-income African American families. *Child Development, 68,* 935–954.

Collier, A. M., & Ramey, C. T. (1976). The health of infants in day care. *Voice for Children, 9,* 7–11.

Dickinson, D. K., & Tabors, P. O. (Eds.). (2001). *Beginning literacy with language: Young children learning at home and school.* Baltimore, MD: Brookes.

Gunnar, M. (1998). Quality of early care and buffering of neuroendocrine stress reactions: Potential effects on the developing human brain. *Preventive Medicine, 27*(2), 208–211.

Harms, T., & Cross, L. (1977). *Environmental provisions in day care.* Unpublished manuscript.

Hart, B., & Risley, T. (1995). *Meaningful differences in the everyday experience of young American children.* Baltimore, MD: Brookes.

Hirsh-Pasek, K., & Burchinal, M. (2006). Mother and caregiver sensitivity over time: Predicting language and academic outcomes with variable- and person-centered approaches. *Merrill-Palmer Quarterly, 52*(3), 449–485.

Huttenlocher, J. (1998). Language input and language growth. *Preventive Medicine, 27,* 195–199.

Martin, S. L., Ramey, C. T., & Ramey, S. L. (1990). The prevention of intellectual impairment in children of impoverished families: Findings of a randomized trial of educational day care. *American Journal of Public Health, 80,* 844–847. PMID 2356909.

McGinness, G., & Ramey, C. T. (1981). Developing sociolinguistic competence in children. *Canadian Journal of Early Childhood Education, 1,* 22–43.

McVicker Hunt, J. (1961). *Intelligence and experience.* New York, NY: Ronald Press.

Piaget, J., & Inhelder, B. (2000). *The psychology of the child* (H. Weaver, Trans.). New York, NY: Basic Books.

Ramey, C. T., Breitmayer, B. J., Goldman, B. D., & Wakeley, A. (1996). Learning and cognition during infancy. In M. Hanson (Ed.), *Atypical infant development* (pp. 311–364). Austin, TX: Pro-Ed.

Ramey, C. T., Bryant, D. M., Sparling, J. J., & Wasik, B. H. (1985). Project CARE: A comparison of two early intervention strategies to prevent retarded development. *Topics in Early Childhood Special Education, 5,* 12–25.

Ramey, C. T., Bryant, D. M., Wasik, B. H., Sparling, J. J., Fendt, K. H., & LaVange, L. M. (1992). Infant Health and Development Program for low birth weight, premature infants: Program elements, family participation, and child intelligence. *Pediatrics, 89,* 454–465. PMID 1371341.

Ramey, C. T., & Campbell, F. A. (1984). Preventive education for high-risk children: Cognitive consequences of the Carolina Abecedarian Project. *American Journal of Mental Deficiency, 88,* 515–523. PMID 6731489.

Ramey, C. T., Collier, A. M., Sparling, J. J., Loda, R. A., Campbell, F. A., Ingram, D. L., & Finkelstein, N. W. (1976). The Carolina Abecedarian Project: A longitudinal and multi-disciplinary approach to the prevention of developmental retardation. In T. D. Tjossem (Ed.), *Intervention strategies for high risk infants and young children* (pp. 629–665). Baltimore, MD: University Park Press.

Ramey, C. T., McGinness, G., Cross, L., Collier, A., & Barrie-Blackley, S. (1981). The Abecedarian approach to social competence: Cognitive and linguistic intervention for disadvantaged preschoolers. In K. Borman (Ed.), *The social life of children in a changing society* (pp. 145–174). Hillsdale, NJ: Erlbaum Associates.

Ramey, C. T., & Ramey, S. L. (1999). *Right from birth: Building your child's foundation for life.* New York, NY: Goddard Press.

Ramey, S. L., & Ramey, C. T. (2005). How to create and sustain a high-quality workforce in childcare, early intervention, and school readiness programs. In M. Zaslow and I. Martinez-Beck (Eds.), *Critical issues in early childhood professional development.* Baltimore, MD: Paul H. Brookes, pp. 355–368.

Ramey, C. T., & Smith, B. (1977). Assessing the intellectual consequences of early intervention with high-risk infants. *American Journal of Mental Deficiency, 81,* 318–324.

Ramey, S. L., Ramey, C. T., & Sonnier-Netto, L. (2008, 2012). *The Four Diamonds Checklist.* Unpublished manuscript.

Ramey, C. T., Sparling, J. J., & Ramey, S. L. (2012). *Abecedarian: The ideas, the approach, and the findings.* Los Altos, CA: Sociometrics.

Ramey, C. T., Yeates, K. O., & Short, E. J. (1984). The plasticity of intellectual development: Insights from preventive intervention. *Child Development, 55,* 1913–1925. PMID 6510061.

Sapolsky, R. M. (1996). Why stress is bad for your brain. *Science, 273*(5726), 749–750.

Siegel, S. (1956). *Nonparametric statistics for the behavioral sciences.* New York, NY: McGraw-Hill.

Snow, C. E., & Dickinson, D. K. (1991). Skills that aren't basic in a new conception of literacy. In A. Purves & E. Jennings (Eds.), *Literate systems and individual lives: Perspectives on literacy and schooling* (pp. 179–192). Albany: State University of New York Press.

Sparling, J., & Lewis, I. (1979). *LearningGames® for the first three years: A guide to parent/child play.* New York, NY: Walker & Co.

Sparling, J., & Lewis, I. (1984). *LearningGames® for threes and fours: A guide to adult/child play.* New York, NY: Walker & Co.

Sparling, J., Lewis, I., Ramey, C. T., Wasik, B. H., Bryant, D. M., & LaVange, L. M. (1991). Partners: A curriculum to help premature, low-birth-weight infants get off to a good start. *Topics in Early Childhood Special Education, 11,* 36–55.

Tout, K., de Haan, M., Kipp-Campbell, E., & Gunnar, M. (1998). Social behavior correlates of adrenocortical activity in daycare: Gender differences and time-of-day effects. *Child Development, 69,* 1247–1262.

Tyler, R. W. (1950). *Basic principles of curriculum and instruction.* Chicago, IL: University of Chicago Press.

Vandell, D. L., Belsky, J., Burchinal, M., Steinberg, L., & Vandergrift, N. (2010). Do effects of early child care extend to age 15 years?: Results from the NICHD study of early child care and youth development. *Child Development, 81*(3), 737–756.

Vygotsky, L. S. (1978). *Mind in society: The development of higher psychological processes.* Cambridge, MA: Harvard University Press.

Vygotsky, L. S. (1986). *Thought and language.* Cambridge, MA: MIT Press.

Whitehurst, G. T., Epstein, J. N., Angell, A. C., Payne, A. C., Crone, D. A., & Fischel, J. E. (1994). Outcomes of an emergent literacy intervention in head start. *Journal of Educational Psychology, 86,* 542–555.

Whitehurst, G. J., Galco, F. L., Lonigan, C. J., Fischel, J. E., DeBarshe, B. D., Valdex-Menchaca, M. C., & Caufield, M. (1988). Accelerating language development through picture book reading, *Developmental Psychology, 24,* 552–559.

🦇 TEST YOURSELF 🦇

1. **How early is a developmental delay and lack of school readiness detectable in children who are at-risk because they are from poor and undereducated families?**

   a. The first year of life

   b. The second year of life

   c. The third year of life

   d. The fourth year of life

2. **In the Abecedarian longitudinal studies, the control groups of children who did not receive the Abecedarian Approach received the same levels of support as the educationally treated children for**

   a. Additional health care

   b. Free and unlimited nutritional supports

   c. Active social work services to the families

   d. Timely referrals when any problems were detected or suspected

   e. All of the above

   f. None of the above

3. **The Abecedarian Approach emphasizes four key educational elements. The key elements include all of the following except**

   a. Learning games

   b. Educational toys

   c. Conversational reading

   d. Language priority

   e. Enriched caregiving

4. **The conceptual rationale for the Abecedarian learning games derives from theoretical insights of**

   a. J. McVicker Hunt

   b. Lev Vygotsky

   c. Jean Piaget

   d. Bijou and Baer

   e. All of the above

   f. None of the above

(continued)

(*continued*)

5. *True or False?*: **Since the time of the Abecedarian studies, careful observational research has documented that high-resource families versus low-resource families show large and significant differences in adult language input to children.**

6. **Dimensions of children's experiences at home and in classrooms during the preschool and kindergarten years that have been found to relate to later literacy success are**

   a. Exposure to varied vocabulary

   b. Opportunities to be a part of conversations that use extended discourse

   c. Home and classroom environments that are cognitively and linguistically stimulating

   d. All of the above

   e. None of the above

7. **The following element of the Abecedarian Approach has the special role of imbuing all of the child's day with educational potential and meaning:**

   a. Learning games

   b. Conversational reading

   c. Language priority

   d. Enriched caregiving

8. *True or False?*: **The National Institute for Child Health and Human Development (NICHD) Study of Early Child Care and Youth Development found no relationship between sensitive and responsive caregiving and better cognitive and language outcomes for children.**

9. **The Abecedarian study of low-birthweight infants found that the Abecedarian Approach provided the greatest relative benefits to the children of families with mothers whose educational level was**

   a. Less than high school graduate

   b. High school graduate

   c. Some university

   d. University graduate

10. **In the Abecedarian studies, which process factor(s) was(were) predictive of children's developmental progress in an early childhood intervention program?**

   a. Level of children's participation

   b. Amount of curriculum activities

   c. Rate of delivery of curriculum activities

   d. Degree of active experience for parents and children

   e. All of the above

Answers: 1. b; 2. e; 3. b; 4. e; 5. True; 6. d; 7. d; 8. False; 9. a; 10. e

ABOUT THE EDITORS

Jennifer Mascolo, PsyD, NCSP, is a full-time lecturer in the Graduate School Psychology program at Teacher's College, Columbia University. Jennifer is also a nationally certified school psychologist and a licensed psychologist in New York and New Jersey who provides assessment and consulting services to individuals, organizations, and districts in her area(s) of expertise. Her research interests include intelligence, the relationship between academic and cognitive functioning, and assessing and intervening with specific learning disabilities. Dr. Mascolo has coauthored three books, including the first and second editions of the *Achievement Test Desk Reference* and *Essentials of the WJ III Tests of Cognitive Abilities* as well as several book chapters and peer-reviewed journal articles focused on using and interpreting specific cognitive and academic measures as well as assessing, diagnosing, and intervening with specific learning disabilities.

Vincent C. Alfonso, PhD, is a former professor in the Graduate School of Education at Fordham University in New York City and current dean of the School of Education at Gonzaga University in Spokane, Washington. He is co-editor with Dawn Flanagan of *Essentials of Specific Learning Disability Identification*; and coauthor of *Essentials of Cross-Battery Assessment, Third Edition* and *The Achievement Test Desk Reference: A Guide to Learning Disability Identification, Second Edition.* He is president of Division 16 (School Psychology) of the American Psychological Association (APA), fellow of Divisions 16 and 5 of the APA, and a certified school psychologist and licensed psychologist in New York State. He has been providing psychoeducational services to individuals across the lifespan for more than 20 years.

Dawn P. Flanagan, PhD, is Professor of Psychology at St. John's University in Queens, New York City, and Clinical Assistant Professor at Yale Child Study Center, Yale University, School of Medicine in New Haven, CT. She is a widely published author and serves as an expert witness, learning disability consultant, and test and measurement consultant and trainer for organizations both nationally and internationally. Her recent books include *Essentials of Cross-Battery Assessment,*

Third Edition, Essentials of Specific Learning Disability Identification, and Contemporary Intellectual Assessment: Theories, Tests and Issues, Third Edition. Dr. Flanagan is primary author of six online professional development programs that may be accessed via www.SLDidentification.com. She is a Fellow of the American Psychological Association and Diplomate of the American Board of Psychological Specialties.

INDEX

ABOUT THE CD-ROM

INTRODUCTION

This appendix provides you with information on the contents of the CD that accompanies this book. For the latest information, please refer to the AbouttheCD.txt file located at the root of the CD.

System Requirements

Make sure that your computer meets the minimum system requirements listed in this section. If your computer doesn't match up to most of these requirements, you may have a problem using the contents of the CD.

- A computer with a Web browser
- A CD-ROM drive

Note: Many popular spreadsheet programs are capable of reading Microsoft Excel files. However, users should be aware that formatting might be lost when using a program other than Microsoft Excel.

Using the CD

To access the content from the CD, follow these steps:

1. Insert the CD into your computer's CD-ROM drive.
2. Select Home.html from the list of files.
3. Read through the license agreement by clicking the License link near the top-right of the interface.
4. The interface appears. Simply select the material you want to view.

WHAT'S ON THE CD

The following sections provide a summary of the material you'll find on the CD.

Content

Not only will you find each contributor's profile, but this CD also contains case studies, worksheets, and handouts corresponding to certain chapters. They are:

- From Chapter 1, the DOTI form and Rapid References 1.14–1.20.
- A case study corresponding to Chapter 2, "Essentials of a Tiered Intervention System to Support Unique Learners: Recommendations from Research and Practice"
- Data on the Phonological Awareness Screening Test (PAST) and *Equipped for Reading Success: A Comprehensive, Step-by-Step Program for Developing Phonemic Awareness and Fluent Word Recognition*, both written by David A. Kilpatrick, contributor of Chapter 4, "Tailoring Interventions in Reading Based on Emerging Research on the Development of Word Recognition Skills"
- Lessons, handouts, and additional material corresponding to Chapter 6, "Selecting and Tailoring Interventions for Students with Mathematics Difficulties"
- An activity, resources, and self-assessment rubric corresponding to Chapter 7, "Selecting and Tailoring Interventions for Students with Written Expression Difficulties"
- A case study corresponding to Chapter 10, "Interventions for Students with Executive Skills and Executive Functions Difficulties"

Applications

Adobe Reader
Included on this CD is a link to download Adobe Acrobat Reader for viewing PDF files. For more information and system requirements, please go to www.adobe .com.

OpenOffice.org
Included on this CD is a link to download OpenOffice.org for viewing spreadsheet files. For more information and system requirements, please go to www .openoffice.org.

OpenOffice.org is a free multiplatform office productivity suite. It is similar to Microsoft Office or Lotus SmartSuite, but OpenOffice.org is absolutely free. It includes word processing, spreadsheet, presentation, and drawing applications that enable you to create professional documents, newsletters, reports, and presentations. It supports most file formats of other office software. You should be able to edit and view any files created with other office solutions.

Shareware programs are fully functional, trial versions of copyrighted programs. If you like particular programs, register with their authors for a nominal fee and receive licenses, enhanced versions, and technical support.

Freeware programs are copyrighted games, applications, and utilities that are free for personal use. Unlike shareware, these programs do not require a fee or provide technical support.

GNU software is governed by its own license, which is included inside the folder of the GNU product. See the GNU license for more details.

Trial, demo, or evaluation versions are usually limited either by time or functionality (such as being unable to save projects). Some trial versions are very sensitive to system date changes. If you alter your computer's date, the programs will time out and no longer be functional.

TROUBLESHOOTING

If you have difficulty installing or using any of the materials on the companion CD, try the following solutions:

- *Turn off any antivirus software* that you may have running. Installers sometimes mimic virus activity and can make your computer incorrectly believe that it is being infected by a virus. (Be sure to turn the antivirus software back on later.)
- *Close all running programs.* The more programs you are running, the less memory is available to other programs. Installers also typically update files and programs; if you keep other programs running, installation may not work properly.
- *Reboot if necessary.* If all else fails, rebooting your machine can often clear any conflicts in the system.

CUSTOMER CARE

If you have trouble with the CD-ROM, please call the Wiley Product Technical Support phone number at (800) 762-2974. Outside the United States, call 1 (317) 572-3994. You can also contact Wiley Product Technical Support at http://support.wiley.com. John Wiley & Sons will provide technical support only for installation and other general quality control items. For technical support on the applications themselves, consult the program's vendor or author.

To place additional orders or to request information about other Wiley products, please call (877) 762-2974.

CUSTOMER NOTE: IF THIS BOOK IS ACCOMPANIED BY SOFTWARE, PLEASE READ THE FOLLOWING BEFORE OPENING THE PACKAGE

This software contains files to help you utilize the models described in the accompanying book. By opening the package, you are agreeing to be bound by the following agreement.

This software product is protected by copyright and all rights are reserved by the author, John Wiley & Sons, Inc., or their licensors. You are licensed to use this software on a single computer. Copying the software to another medium or format for use on a single computer does not violate the U.S. Copyright Law. Copying the software for any other purpose is a violation of the U.S. Copyright Law.

This software product is sold as is without warranty of any kind, either express or implied, including but not limited to the implied warranty of merchantability and fitness for a particular purpose. Neither Wiley nor its dealers or distributors assumes any liability for any alleged or actual damages arising from the use of or the inability to use this software. (Some states do not allow the exclusion of implied warranties, so the exclusion may not apply to you.)